Lecture Notes in Computer Science 14047

Founding Editors

Gerhard Goos
Juris Hartmanis

The series Lecture Notes in Computer Science (LNCS), including its subseries Lecture Notes in Artificial Intelligence (LNAI) and Lecture Notes in Bioinformatics (LNBI), has established itself as a medium for the publication of new developments in computer science and information technology research, teaching, and education.

LNCS enjoys close cooperation with the computer science R & D community, the series counts many renowned academics among its volume editors and paper authors, and collaborates with prestigious societies. Its mission is to serve this international community by providing an invaluable service, mainly focused on the publication of conference and workshop proceedings and postproceedings. LNCS commenced publication in 1973.

Xiaowen Fang

Editor

HCI in Games

5th International Conference, HCI-Games 2023
Held as Part of the 25th HCI International Conference, HCII 2023
Copenhagen, Denmark, July 23–28, 2023
Proceedings, Part II

 Springer

Editor
Xiaowen Fang
DePaul University
Chicago, IL, USA

ISSN 0302-9743 ISSN 1611-3349 (electronic)
Lecture Notes in Computer Science
ISBN 978-3-031-35978-1 ISBN 978-3-031-35979-8 (eBook)
https://doi.org/10.1007/978-3-031-35979-8

This Springer imprint is published by the registered company Springer Nature Switzerland AG
The registered company address is: Gewerbestrasse 11, 6330 Cham, Switzerland

Foreword

Human-computer interaction (HCI) is acquiring an ever-increasing scientific and industrial importance, as well as having more impact on people's everyday lives, as an ever-growing number of human activities are progressively moving from the physical to the digital world. This process, which has been ongoing for some time now, was further accelerated during the acute period of the COVID-19 pandemic. The HCI International (HCII) conference series, held annually, aims to respond to the compelling need to advance the exchange of knowledge and research and development efforts on the human aspects of design and use of computing systems.

The 25th International Conference on Human-Computer Interaction, HCI International 2023 (HCII 2023), was held in the emerging post-pandemic era as a 'hybrid' event at the AC Bella Sky Hotel and Bella Center, Copenhagen, Denmark, during July 23–28, 2023. It incorporated the 21 thematic areas and affiliated conferences listed below.

A total of 7472 individuals from academia, research institutes, industry, and government agencies from 85 countries submitted contributions, and 1578 papers and 396 posters were included in the volumes of the proceedings that were published just before the start of the conference, these are listed below. The contributions thoroughly cover the entire field of human-computer interaction, addressing major advances in knowledge and effective use of computers in a variety of application areas. These papers provide academics, researchers, engineers, scientists, practitioners and students with state-of-the-art information on the most recent advances in HCI.

The HCI International (HCII) conference also offers the option of presenting 'Late Breaking Work', and this applies both for papers and posters, with corresponding volumes of proceedings that will be published after the conference. Full papers will be included in the 'HCII 2023 - Late Breaking Work - Papers' volumes of the proceedings to be published in the Springer LNCS series, while 'Poster Extended Abstracts' will be included as short research papers in the 'HCII 2023 - Late Breaking Work - Posters' volumes to be published in the Springer CCIS series.

I would like to thank the Program Board Chairs and the members of the Program Boards of all thematic areas and affiliated conferences for their contribution towards the high scientific quality and overall success of the HCI International 2023 conference. Their manifold support in terms of paper reviewing (single-blind review process, with a minimum of two reviews per submission), session organization and their willingness to act as goodwill ambassadors for the conference is most highly appreciated.

This conference would not have been possible without the continuous and unwavering support and advice of Gavriel Salvendy, founder, General Chair Emeritus, and Scientific Advisor. For his outstanding efforts, I would like to express my sincere appreciation to Abbas Moallem, Communications Chair and Editor of HCI International News.

July 2023   Constantine Stephanidis

HCI International 2023 Thematic Areas
and Affiliated Conferences

Thematic Areas

- HCI: Human-Computer Interaction
- HIMI: Human Interface and the Management of Information

Affiliated Conferences

- EPCE: 20th International Conference on Engineering Psychology and Cognitive Ergonomics
- AC: 17th International Conference on Augmented Cognition
- UAHCI: 17th International Conference on Universal Access in Human-Computer Interaction
- CCD: 15th International Conference on Cross-Cultural Design
- SCSM: 15th International Conference on Social Computing and Social Media
- VAMR: 15th International Conference on Virtual, Augmented and Mixed Reality
- DHM: 14th International Conference on Digital Human Modeling and Applications in Health, Safety, Ergonomics and Risk Management
- DUXU: 12th International Conference on Design, User Experience and Usability
- C&C: 11th International Conference on Culture and Computing
- DAPI: 11th International Conference on Distributed, Ambient and Pervasive Interactions
- HCIBGO: 10th International Conference on HCI in Business, Government and Organizations
- LCT: 10th International Conference on Learning and Collaboration Technologies
- ITAP: 9th International Conference on Human Aspects of IT for the Aged Population
- AIS: 5th International Conference on Adaptive Instructional Systems
- HCI-CPT: 5th International Conference on HCI for Cybersecurity, Privacy and Trust
- HCI-Games: 5th International Conference on HCI in Games
- MobiTAS: 5th International Conference on HCI in Mobility, Transport and Automotive Systems
- AI-HCI: 4th International Conference on Artificial Intelligence in HCI
- MOBILE: 4th International Conference on Design, Operation and Evaluation of Mobile Communications

List of Conference Proceedings Volumes Appearing Before the Conference

1. LNCS 14011, Human-Computer Interaction: Part I, edited by Masaaki Kurosu and Ayako Hashizume
2. LNCS 14012, Human-Computer Interaction: Part II, edited by Masaaki Kurosu and Ayako Hashizume
3. LNCS 14013, Human-Computer Interaction: Part III, edited by Masaaki Kurosu and Ayako Hashizume
4. LNCS 14014, Human-Computer Interaction: Part IV, edited by Masaaki Kurosu and Ayako Hashizume
5. LNCS 14015, Human Interface and the Management of Information: Part I, edited by Hirohiko Mori and Yumi Asahi
6. LNCS 14016, Human Interface and the Management of Information: Part II, edited by Hirohiko Mori and Yumi Asahi
7. LNAI 14017, Engineering Psychology and Cognitive Ergonomics: Part I, edited by Don Harris and Wen-Chin Li
8. LNAI 14018, Engineering Psychology and Cognitive Ergonomics: Part II, edited by Don Harris and Wen-Chin Li
9. LNAI 14019, Augmented Cognition, edited by Dylan D. Schmorrow and Cali M. Fidopiastis
10. LNCS 14020, Universal Access in Human-Computer Interaction: Part I, edited by Margherita Antona and Constantine Stephanidis
11. LNCS 14021, Universal Access in Human-Computer Interaction: Part II, edited by Margherita Antona and Constantine Stephanidis
12. LNCS 14022, Cross-Cultural Design: Part I, edited by Pei-Luen Patrick Rau
13. LNCS 14023, Cross-Cultural Design: Part II, edited by Pei-Luen Patrick Rau
14. LNCS 14024, Cross-Cultural Design: Part III, edited by Pei-Luen Patrick Rau
15. LNCS 14025, Social Computing and Social Media: Part I, edited by Adela Coman and Simona Vasilache
16. LNCS 14026, Social Computing and Social Media: Part II, edited by Adela Coman and Simona Vasilache
17. LNCS 14027, Virtual, Augmented and Mixed Reality, edited by Jessie Y. C. Chen and Gino Fragomeni
18. LNCS 14028, Digital Human Modeling and Applications in Health, Safety, Ergonomics and Risk Management: Part I, edited by Vincent G. Duffy
19. LNCS 14029, Digital Human Modeling and Applications in Health, Safety, Ergonomics and Risk Management: Part II, edited by Vincent G. Duffy
20. LNCS 14030, Design, User Experience, and Usability: Part I, edited by Aaron Marcus, Elizabeth Rosenzweig and Marcelo Soares
21. LNCS 14031, Design, User Experience, and Usability: Part II, edited by Aaron Marcus, Elizabeth Rosenzweig and Marcelo Soares

22. LNCS 14032, Design, User Experience, and Usability: Part III, edited by Aaron Marcus, Elizabeth Rosenzweig and Marcelo Soares
23. LNCS 14033, Design, User Experience, and Usability: Part IV, edited by Aaron Marcus, Elizabeth Rosenzweig and Marcelo Soares
24. LNCS 14034, Design, User Experience, and Usability: Part V, edited by Aaron Marcus, Elizabeth Rosenzweig and Marcelo Soares
25. LNCS 14035, Culture and Computing, edited by Matthias Rauterberg
26. LNCS 14036, Distributed, Ambient and Pervasive Interactions: Part I, edited by Norbert Streitz and Shin'ichi Konomi
27. LNCS 14037, Distributed, Ambient and Pervasive Interactions: Part II, edited by Norbert Streitz and Shin'ichi Konomi
28. LNCS 14038, HCI in Business, Government and Organizations: Part I, edited by Fiona Fui-Hoon Nah and Keng Siau
29. LNCS 14039, HCI in Business, Government and Organizations: Part II, edited by Fiona Fui-Hoon Nah and Keng Siau
30. LNCS 14040, Learning and Collaboration Technologies: Part I, edited by Panayiotis Zaphiris and Andri Ioannou
31. LNCS 14041, Learning and Collaboration Technologies: Part II, edited by Panayiotis Zaphiris and Andri Ioannou
32. LNCS 14042, Human Aspects of IT for the Aged Population: Part I, edited by Qin Gao and Jia Zhou
33. LNCS 14043, Human Aspects of IT for the Aged Population: Part II, edited by Qin Gao and Jia Zhou
34. LNCS 14044, Adaptive Instructional Systems, edited by Robert A. Sottilare and Jessica Schwarz
35. LNCS 14045, HCI for Cybersecurity, Privacy and Trust, edited by Abbas Moallem
36. LNCS 14046, HCI in Games: Part I, edited by Xiaowen Fang
37. LNCS 14047, HCI in Games: Part II, edited by Xiaowen Fang
38. LNCS 14048, HCI in Mobility, Transport and Automotive Systems: Part I, edited by Heidi Krömker
39. LNCS 14049, HCI in Mobility, Transport and Automotive Systems: Part II, edited by Heidi Krömker
40. LNAI 14050, Artificial Intelligence in HCI: Part I, edited by Helmut Degen and Stavroula Ntoa
41. LNAI 14051, Artificial Intelligence in HCI: Part II, edited by Helmut Degen and Stavroula Ntoa
42. LNCS 14052, Design, Operation and Evaluation of Mobile Communications, edited by Gavriel Salvendy and June Wei
43. CCIS 1832, HCI International 2023 Posters - Part I, edited by Constantine Stephanidis, Margherita Antona, Stavroula Ntoa and Gavriel Salvendy
44. CCIS 1833, HCI International 2023 Posters - Part II, edited by Constantine Stephanidis, Margherita Antona, Stavroula Ntoa and Gavriel Salvendy
45. CCIS 1834, HCI International 2023 Posters - Part III, edited by Constantine Stephanidis, Margherita Antona, Stavroula Ntoa and Gavriel Salvendy
46. CCIS 1835, HCI International 2023 Posters - Part IV, edited by Constantine Stephanidis, Margherita Antona, Stavroula Ntoa and Gavriel Salvendy

47. CCIS 1836, HCI International 2023 Posters - Part V, edited by Constantine Stephanidis, Margherita Antona, Stavroula Ntoa and Gavriel Salvendy

https://2023.hci.international/proceedings

Preface

Computer games have grown beyond simple entertainment activities. Researchers and practitioners have attempted to utilize games in many innovative ways, such as educational games, therapeutic games, simulation games, and gamification of utilitarian applications. Although a lot of attention has been given to investigate the positive impact of games in recent years, prior research has only studied isolated fragments of a game system. More research on games is needed to develop and utilize games for the benefit of society.

At a high level, a game system has three basic elements: system input, process, and system output. System input concerns the external factors impacting the game system. It may include, but is not limited to, player personalities and motivations to play games. The process is about game mechanism and play experience. System output includes the effects of game play. There is no doubt that users are involved in all three elements. Human Computer Interaction (HCI) plays a critical role in the study of games. By examining player characteristics, interactions during game play, and behavioral implications of game play, HCI professionals can help design and develop better games for society.

The 5th International Conference on HCI in Games (HCI-Games 2023), an affiliated conference of the HCI International Conference, intended to help, promote, and encourage research in this field by providing a forum for interaction and exchanges among researchers, academics, and practitioners in the fields of HCI and games. The Conference addressed HCI principles, methods, and tools for better games.

This year, researchers from around the world contributed significant amounts of work in multiple themes. Regarding game design and development, researchers reported their continuous efforts in addressing game design from both system and user/player perspectives. It is noteworthy that a major portion of the papers are related to research work dedicated to improving our society through gamification, serious games, and learning games. The papers included in the proceedings represent the professionalism and commitment to society of the HCI in Games community.

Two volumes of the HCII 2023 proceedings are dedicated to this year's edition of the HCI-Games Conference. The first volume focuses on topics related to game design and development, as well as gamification and serious games. The second volume focuses on topics related to games for learning, as well as understanding players and the player experience.

The papers in these volumes were included for publication after a minimum of two single–blind reviews from the members of the HCI-Games Program Board or, in some cases, from members of the Program Boards of other affiliated conferences. I would like to thank all of them for their invaluable contribution, support, and efforts.

July 2023   Xiaowen Fang

5th International Conference on HCI in Games (HCI-Games 2023)

Program Board Chair: **Xiaowen Fang,** *DePaul University, USA*

Program Board:

- Amir Zaib Abbasi, *King Fahd University of Petroleum and Minerals, Saudi Arabia*
- Dena Al-Thani, *HBKU, Qatar*
- Abdullah Azhari, *King Abdulaziz University, Saudi Arabia*
- Barbara Caci, *University of Palermo, Italy*
- Ben Cowley, *University of Helsinki, Finland*
- Khaldoon Dhou, *Texas A&M University-Central Texas, USA*
- Kevin Keeker, *Sony Interactive Entertainment, USA*
- Daniel Riha, *Charles University, Czech Republic*
- Owen Schaffer, *Bradley University, USA*
- Jason Schklar, *UX is Fine!, USA*
- Fan Zhao, *Florida Gulf Coast University, USA*
- Miaoqi Zhu, *Sony Pictures Entertainment, USA*

The full list with the Program Board Chairs and the members of the Program Boards of all thematic areas and affiliated conferences of HCII2023 is available online at:

http://www.hci.international/board-members-2023.php

HCI International 2024 Conference

The 26th International Conference on Human-Computer Interaction, HCI International 2024, will be held jointly with the affiliated conferences at the Washington Hilton Hotel, Washington, DC, USA, June 29 – July 4, 2024. It will cover a broad spectrum of themes related to Human-Computer Interaction, including theoretical issues, methods, tools, processes, and case studies in HCI design, as well as novel interaction techniques, interfaces, and applications. The proceedings will be published by Springer. More information will be made available on the conference website: http://2024.hci.international/.

General Chair
Prof. Constantine Stephanidis
University of Crete and ICS-FORTH
Heraklion, Crete, Greece
Email: general_chair@hcii2024.org

https://2024.hci.international/

Contents – Part II

Contents – Part I

Game Design and Development

Gamification and Serious Games

Games for Learning

Exploring Virtual Reality (VR) to Foster Attention in Math Practice – Comparing a VR to a Non-VR Game

Meike Belter[1]([✉])[iD], Heide Lukosch[1][iD], Robert W. Lindeman[1][iD], Yuanjie Wu[1][iD], and Frank Steinicke[2][iD]

[1] HIT Lab NZ, University of Canterbury, Christchurch, New Zealand
meikebelter@icloud.com, info@hitlabnz.org
[2] Human-Computer Interaction, Department of Informatics, Universität Hamburg, Hamburg, Germany
frank.steinicke@uni-hamburg.de

Abstract. Virtual reality (VR) and games have become an increasingly feasible combination for learning in formal education. The immersive nature of VR has potential for improving learning motivation, engagement, as well as the overall learning experience. Immersive games may be particularly useful for children struggling with attention when engaging in high-focus cognitive learning tasks such as solving math equations. However, there is a lack of research that directly compares VR and non-VR games. Therefore, in our study, we analyzed the effect of VR on attention in a math practice task. We compared a baseline version of a VR game to both (i) a non-VR 3D desktop version, and (ii) an immersive VR version, which included gamification elements such as rewards and a virtual agent, since both are known to be able to increase attention. We specifically investigate whether these findings can be transferred to VR environments. In a between-groups study design, we tested the three versions of the game with 70 children (aged 12-13) in a diverse German school environment. The results show significant differences in motivation, engagement, focus, and attention across the three conditions. Overall, the game was well received by the children independent of the condition tested, however better rated across VR conditions.

Keywords: Virtual Reality Games · Education · Educative Technology

1 Introduction

As Virtual Reality (VR) technology grows increasingly accessible, VR games for learning are becoming more and more available for various consumer headsets. This development has also attracted research in formal educational environments. In recent years, various studies have examined VR for learning in

Supported by the Applied Immersive Gaming Initiative (AIGI).

school contexts [1–3]. VR in the form of interactive 360-degree videos and tours, VR tutorials, and VR for creative performance, have shown positive effects on engagement, motivation, and learning outcomes [2–4]. At this stage, using VR as a supportive educational tool in schools seems promising from a student acceptance point of view [1,3], though limitations, such as a lack of experience in facilitation, resource availability, mixed results on learning effectiveness, as well as environmental constraints, constrain its usage as a new teaching approach. However, VR technology provides enormous potential due to some specific characteristics. For instance, VR can display fully customizable immersive virtual environments (VEs) in which users might feel a high sense of presence, natural movements and behavior are possible, and the positive effects of VR on motivation and engagement have been shown in previous studies [3,5,6].

This presents a high potential of VR for learning scenarios that require motivation and engagement.It has been shown that 5-10 percent of children in schools struggle with, among other things, hyperactivity, as well as attention deficits [7]. Hyperactivity is a state of constant movement, even to an excessive degree, and when inappropriate. Inattentiveness refers to the cognitive process of concentrating on one task or aspect, while disregarding other information, such as distractions from the environment [8,9]. This makes tasks such as for example focusing on practicing math especially challenging, and often leads to poor academic performance [8].

A traditional classroom environment may be distracting, and a lack of movement may not be accommodating to all learning styles [9,10]. Because of this, a match between VR's natural characteristics and learning needs for children that struggle with focus, attention and hyperactivity seems promising. A first prototype of a math VR practice game that accommodates for those learning needs was already created and tested on 15 participants (aged 10-13) prior to this study [11]. Based on the outcomes, the prototype was improved, and further conditions defined. In the scope of this prior research, it was observed that personal characteristics and familiarity with VR influence usability and user experience (UX), which are both predictors for motivation and engagement, and consequently connected to attention [12–14]. Hence, for a successful implementation of VR in a school context, VR should be designed to be usable by a diverse range of individuals with differing personal characteristics, including inattentive and hyperactive behavior traits. Additionally, it has been identified by scholars such as Akman et al. [15]that measuring the effects of immersive VR in education remains difficult due to its incomparability to non-immersive VR options, such as mobile or desktop learning applications. Moreover, especially for children who struggle with attention deficits and hyperactivity, students often perform better when they are given a purpose, reward, and positive reinforcement by a pedagogical agent [16,17]. Based on that, three conditions of the game were tested, aimed at investigating the potential of VR in a diverse school environment for math practice. The effects on attention were captured through UX, usability, motivation, and engagement measures

2   Related Work

As defined by Norman [18], there are several requirements for effective learning environments. They should be motivational, provide a balanced level of difficulty, cultivate direct engagement, limit distractions, be goal- and procedure-based, and provide feedback as well as interaction at a high intensity. Since educational games can be customized and allow for engagement, motivation, reward, and a great level of interactivity [19], they seem fit as promising learning environments. Moreover, game-based learning can offer great levels of meaningful engagement with a task or content, and provide the space for learning activities that trigger emotions, enable interaction, and increase motivation [20,21]. Moreover, this approach may be able to combat a widespread attitude of young learners, indifference towards learning. Finally, games can cater to a diverse range of different learning styles and needs [21], as they are highly customizable [21]. Certain learner groups, such as children that are affected by Attention Deficit Hyperactivity Disorder (ADHD), often struggle with motivation and engagement when working on a task [7,10]. When these factors are compromised, focus and attention are often low [22]. Hence, they may increase when motivation and engagement are present. Researchers such as Slusarek et al. [23] also state that motivation can significantly impact task performance. Moreover, as argued by Douglas [22], novel or interesting tasks can lead to improved focus and attention when learning.

Games are already used to improve focused attention and on-task behavior. A study by Shaw et al. [24] showed an increase in on-task activity by children with ADHD when executing a game-like Conners's Continuous Performance Test II (CPT II), compared to the same test without the use of game elements. A game has now also been approved for the first time by the US Food and Drug Administration (FDA) for treating children with ADHD, with promising results. This game, EndeavorRx, was created to improve cognitive processes combatting deficits related to ADHD, such as inattention and hyperactivity [25]. VR allows users to enter computer simulated environments that replace the real world and is often described as highly immersive [5]. Literature can also be found in the space of VR for learning. A study by Nobrega et al. [4] explored the usability of VR for language teaching in a Brazilian public school and found a strong effect on motivation and engagement. Further, Newbutt et al. [6] examined VR in schools for children on the autism spectrum and reported that those children preferred a technologically advanced HMD, and found the experience enjoyable, comfortable, and exciting. Additionally, a positive level of willingness and confidence was seen as well. Akman and Cakir [15] conducted a comparative study, whereby an educational VR math game was compared with mobile application games for fractions. A positive effect on achievement and engagement was found, however the comparability of the two conditions was highlighted as subject to many limitations, including the comparison of different games for VR and non-VR. This presents an opportunity for further comparative studies.

2.1 Connecting Prior Work

There are several tools and techniques in education that are commonly used to accommodate attention in focus. In a previous study, we created a VR math practice game for children in schools. We based that game on tools and techniques to address inattention [26]. This included the following requirements:

- No imposition of time limits.
- Creation of a non-arousing, aesthetically pleasing, welcoming, and safe environment.
- Option for movement.
- Production of visual features that are: identifiable, semantically different, and close to the field of vision (the ground).

The game was tested on 15 children (aged 10-13) in a New Zealand based primary school [11]. We observed that the game led to high levels of task-engagement, very good user experience and good usability.

The current study is a continuation of this work and focuses on motivation and engagement and UX as determining factors for attention. In a previous study, [26] we defined more potential requirements for the creation of attention-keeping VR environments. Two of them were the inclusion of a reward system, and the usage of a virtual agent. Children that struggle with attention are shown to have an altered perception of reward, making them more receptible to it [27]. Children with ADHD, for example, have poor self-control and little persistence when engaging in a task. When feedback in the form of a reward is provided, this can lead to [28]. Moreover, children with attention deficits may benefit from more frequent praise, and clear task-instructions, as well as task reminders [29]. To further develop this first game prototype, a reward system and a virtual agent were incorporated into the game for this study. This study was designed to add insights to the field in two regards: the potential benefits of using VR for attention over using a 3D desktop version of the same game. Secondly, the effect of using a reward system and a virtual agent in a VR game, compared to the same VR game without these features. We hypothesize that motivation, engagement, and UX are connected in supporting attention.

3 Method

As the game this study reports on builds on the earlier version of a VR math equation game that was first tested in a prior study [11], the aim of the current study was to further develop the game and include a 3D desktop version. Additionally, another VR version was introduced consisting of a reward system as well as positive affirmation and guidance from a virtual agent. For this, three different conditions were introduced. Condition "BasicVR" refers to an improved version of the game from our previous study [11]. Condition "EnhancedVR" denotes an enriched VR game, with a reward system and virtual agent added. Condition

"Desktop" refers to a 3D desktop version of the game. The mixed-method app-roach explored engagement and motivation through observational indicators and the User Engagement Scale (UES) [13], UX through the lens of learning experi-ence using heuristic observation and the UXKQ questionnaire [30]. Lastly, UX was also looked at from a usability perspective, utilizing elements of the Fun-Toolkit [31]. All measures were taken across all three conditions and consequently compared. In this paper, we analyze focus, attention, and user experience under all three conditions, whereby EnhancedVR and Desktop are compared against BasicVR.

3.1   Game Design

Unity was used for designing the different game conditions. To create the three conditions, we took BasicVR as the starting point for Desktop and EnhancedVR. For Desktop, we converted the experience to run on a desktop computer using a normal monitor (i.e., no HMD). For EnhancedVR, we added the reward system and virtual agent to BasicVR. The basic idea of the game was to solve equations in VR based on a target number provided. First, the participant had to go through either one or three training rooms, depending on the condition (see 1). The training rooms provided the opportunity to become familiar with the game mechanics, such as locomotion and object manipulation in VR, or for Desktop, mouse, and keyboard navigation of the virtual space. Once the training rooms were completed, the participant found themselves in the game environment.

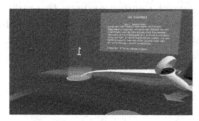   

(a) Training Room   (b) Game Objects

Fig. 1. Training Room Example and Interactable Game Objects

The environment was purposefully kept empty to foster focus and attention on the task, as there were no distractors [11]. Moreover, colors were chosen to be accommodative of individuals who struggle with arousal modulation or sensory related matters [11]. Balls marking mathematics operators and cubes marking numbers could be found on the ground. All objects were interactable and could be picked up and thrown around by using ray-interaction and pressing/releasing the trigger button (for VR versions) and performing a physical throwing motion (see Fig. 1). The throwing motion for Desktop provided a similar mechanism to the one used for the VR versions and functioned on mouse down/up for hold-ing and releasing the objects. A mouse sliding motion simulated the throwing motion. The balls and numbers needed to be thrown into dedicated snap zones, corresponding to the target operator/number. Other than the medium chosen and interaction specific modifications, Desktop was equivalent to BasicVR. However, for EnhancedVR, a reward system as well as a virtual agent were added (see Fig. 2).

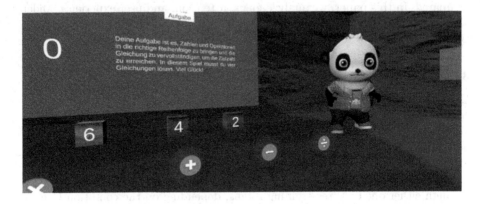

Fig. 2. Virtual Agent.

The reward system amounted to points that could be collected, as this has shown to be motivating and engaging for young people struggling with attention [26]. A virtual agent in the form of a humanoid Panda was used to provide a narrative to the game, as well as positive reinforcement and praise. Further, the virtual agent functioned as a tool to bring attention back to the game task every two minutes by providing positive affirmation. This was shown to increase motivation, focus, and attention [16].

3.2 Experimental Setup

This user study design and protocol was approved by the Human Research Ethics Committee of the University of Canterbury, Christchurch, New Zealand, under the reference number HREC 2022/23. A between-groups study design was implemented. In total 70 grade 7 students (aged 12-13) from a diverse German school were assigned at random to one of the conditions. Due to organizational constraints, 22 joined BasicVR, 22 Desktop, and 26 EnhancedVR. The game test was conducted with a maximum duration of 10 min per participant, independent of condition. We utilized a standardized observation protocol to capture attention through motivational, engagement, as well as usability and UX indicators. Moreover, after the test, each participant received a post-test questionnaire. This questionnaire consisted of different elements from the Fun-Toolkit [31] and the UXKQ [30], that provided a better understanding of learning and user experience. The Fun-Toolkit [31] is often used for usability research with children and provides an easy-to-navigate interface that allows for fast opinion capturing and was thought to be applicable for this research study. The UXKQ is a questionnaire designed for children, measuring several indicators under the constructs of "Learning development" (e.g., Good for learning/Bad for learning), "General Game" (e.g., Exciting/Boring), and "Design" (e.g., Friendly/Unfriendly). Moreover, the UES [13] was part of the post-questionnaire to understand the level of user engagement, including constructs on "Focused Attention", as well as "Perceived Usability", opinions on the "Aesthetics" of the game, and the feeling of "Reward."

The user study was carried out over a period of two weeks within the daily school environment of the participants. The test was set up in a separate, lockable room at the school. The room measured approximately 20m2 allowing for enough space to separate the test area from the questionnaire area and to provide enough empty space for participant safety while in VR. Participants were guided in pairs to the room and briefed before participation was allowed. This briefing included reminders on safety and well-being before, during, and after the test. Verbal consent from the participants was sought. Water as well as chairs were provided and ready to use in case of physical or mental health concerns.

4   Results

The following section lays out the findings. SPSS was used for statistical analysis.

4.1   Questionnaires

The results from the Fun-Toolkit categories of the post-test questionnaire were analyzed. Across all three conditions (BasicVR, EnhancedVR, and Desktop), when asked how the game was liked, participants indicated either "Brilliant", "Really good", or "Good". For BasicVR, 77.3% found the game "Brilliant", while 22.7% found it "Really good". In comparison, 69.2% of participants from EnhancedVR reported "Brilliant", and 26.9% reported "Really Good". However, for Desktop, 40.9% of individuals found the game "Really Good", and 36.4% found it "Good". According to the Fisher-Freeman-Halton Exact Test (expected count less than 5), all findings are statistically significant (p<.001). Regarding the training room(s), a different pattern was apparent. For BasicVR, 50% found the rooms to be "Brilliant", and 36.4% reported "Really good". EnhancedVR found the rooms equally "Brilliant" and "Really Good", both at 38.5%. Participants under the Desktop group experienced the training room as "Really Good" (45.5%), and "Good", also at 45.5%. A Pearson Chi-Square test was performed and reported a statistical significance at p=.030. From the Again-and-Again table element of the questionnaire the following data emerged. This element consisted of four questions:

- Would you recommend your friends to play the training rooms again? (Q1)
- Would you use the game again to train math (Q2)
- Would you use Virtual Reality/a computer again to play the game? (Q3)
- Would you play this game again in your school to train math? (Q4)

The three answer categories were "Yes", "Maybe", and "No". Figure 3 displays a summarized version of answers per condition (n=70, B = BasicVR, C=EnhancedVR, D=Desktop). For Q1, 100% of participants in BasicVR would recommend the game to their friends. This is more than for EnhancedVR at 96.2%, and Desktop with 77.3%. "Maybe" was indicted by 3.8% within group EnhancedVR and 13.6% within Desktop. Only group Desktop reported here "No", at 2.9%. Under Fisher's exact test, the findings are statistically significant (p=.034). For Q2, a similar pattern can be seen. Again, 100% under BasicVR indicated here "Yes", while 96.2% within group EnhancedVR rated "Yes", as well as 68.2% within group Desktop. EnhancedVR reported maybe here at 3.8%, whilst Desktop reported "Maybe" at 22.7%. Only group Desktop indicated "No" under Q2 at 2.9%. The findings were statistically significant at p=.003 under Fisher's exact test. Furthermore and likewise under Fisher's exact test, findings for Q3 were not significant at p=.078. Lastly for Q4, 100% of group BasicVR indicated "Yes", compared to 92.3% under EnhancedVR, and 68.2% under Desktop. EnhancedVR amounts to 7.7% under "Maybe", and Desktop to 22.7%. "No" was only indicated by group Desktop at 9.1%. The findings are statistically significant at p=.011, under Fisher's exact test.

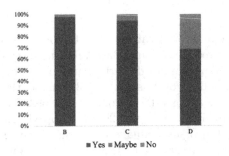

Fig. 3. Strength of Answers per Condition (Q1-4), N=70.

Thirdly, the UX indicative UXKQ data was statistically analyzed. Overall, 11 out of 16 semantic differential items, under three constructs (learning development, game general, design) showed a statistically significant association with the version of the game played. Fisher's Exact Test was performed to examine the relation, as for several items the expected count showed less than 5. The items with a statistically significant difference per condition are discussed in the following and explained per item on a 1-5 scale.

BasicVR was rated by 72.7% of the participants with a "1", as being good for learning (on a 1-5 scale). This was followed by EnhancedVR, where 69.2% indicated "1". Most participants that tested the Desktop version indicated "2" on the

1-5-point scale for learning (40.9%), whilst 36.4% rate this item with "1". For the scale of learning motivation, 92.3% of EnhancedVR participants indicated that the game motivated them to learn with a "1", compared to 86.4% in BasicVR. For EnhancedVR, "2" was most often indicated, amounting to 50%. Looking at progress, 61.5% of participants under EnhancedVR rated their progress with a "1". For BasicVRand Desktop, progress was most often rated with a "2", at 54.5% BasicVR and 45.5% for Desktop. Furthermore, on the scale Exciting-Boring, EnhancedVR participants ranked excitement level with a "1" at 84.6%. This is higher than for BasicVR (68.2%), and Desktop (27.3% for "1", 50% for "2"). EnhancedVR and BasicVR were perceived to work better than Desktop. Under EnhancedVR, 76.9% indicated "1" for works well, whereby 72.7% of BasicVR gave the same rating. Desktop most often received a "2" for this scale (45.5%). Most participants of EnhancedVR experienced the game to work fast, rated with a "1" by 73.1%, followed by BasicVR participants at 54.5%, and Desktop at 40.9%. The semantic differential item Fun-Serious received a "1" (fun) by 90.9% of BasicVR participants, 84.6% of EnhancedVR, and 45.5% of Desktop participants. However, EnhancedVR participants rated the game with 92.3% more often as entertaining (1 out of 5), compared to BasicVR (72.7% rated "1"), and Desktop, where most participants rated entertainment factor with a "2" (50%). Examining design related results, BasicVR found the game to be well assembled most often, with 86.4% giving a "1" rating. This is followed by EnhancedVR, with a "1" rating at 76.9%. Desktop most frequently rated this item with a "2" (50%). Looking at the friendliness level of the game, participants under EnhancedVR most often rated this semantic differential item (Friendly-Unfriendly) with a "1" (92.3%), compared to 81.8% in BasicVR and 50% in EnhancedVR. Lastly, the scale Cheerful-Sad showed most individuals indicating "1" (cheerful) in EnhancedVR, with 65.4%. This is followed by BasicVR at 59.1%, and Desktop where most often a rating of "2" was indicated (63.3%).

Lastly, the UES part of the post-test questionnaire was analyzed, providing an insight into the engagement of the children with the game. We used an already validated UES questionnaire in the context of health apps; therefore, a principal component analysis (PCA) was run for each of the constructs (Focused attention, Perceived usability, Aesthetics, Reward) aiming at explaining the variance in the variables and to understand and confirm the degree of correlation amongst the variables under each construct in our study. The PCA was rotated at varimax. For each construct analysis, coefficients, reproduced, anti-image, and a Kaiser-Meyer-Olkin (KMO) test as well as Barlett's test of sphericity (BTS) was reported. After indicating correlation amongst variables under the components, mean values were taken for each construct and compared across all three versions of the game (see Fig. 4). For the construct of focused attention (FA), in total six variables were measured. In our analysis, the first principal component was moderately correlated with all variables ($>.5$), indicating a relationship between the variables, and explaining 65.3% of the total variance. BTS was significant (p¡.001), and KMO showed very good factorability at 0.807. FA showed the highest average scores under EnhancedVR, second highest under

BasicVR, followed by Desktop. This was statistically significant based on a one-way ANOVA test (p <;001). PCA was less clear for the construct of Perceived Usability (PU). Overall, PU was strongest in EnhancedVR, however the findings were not statistically significant (p=0.66). For the construct of Aesthetics (AE), all PCA indicators showed a correlation amongst the construct variables. Component one was able to explain 57.5% of total variance, with moderate loadings (>.5) across the component for all five variables. In terms of differences amongst groups, the ANOVA test revealed no statistically significant (p=0.96) differences. Reward (RW) was constructed from nine variables, with a moderately strong correlation. All variables loaded strongly into principal component 1, explaining 57.68% of variance. BTS showed significant and the KMO score is very good (0.837). EnhancedVR reported the highest mean scores for this construct, whereby BasicVR reported the second highest, followed by Desktop. This was statistically significant (p>.001). Figure 4 provides an overview of means per construct. Across all UES constructs, BasicVR and EnahncedVR were close in mean scores, whereby Desktop showed a greater difference.

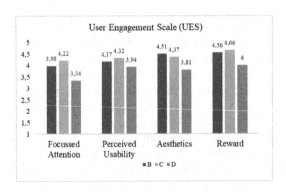

Fig. 4. Means per Construct (UES)

5   Conclusion and Discussion

Overall, it can be concluded that both VR versions seemed to be more engaging, motivating, and better at keeping attention than Desktop. More participants under BasicVR and EnhancedVR liked the game and training room(s) compared to Desktop. Despite these differences, in terms of difficulty level and the suitability of the game for learning, no clear difference was observed between the three groups. Hence, it can be assumed that also the desktop version of the game was considered a suitable learning tool. Further, 45.5% of Desktop participants found the game to be most fun, therefore it seems the desktop version can also provide positive user experience. However, Desktop was perceived to not work as well as the other versions. This may be linked to unfamiliarity with navigating a virtual 3D-desktop space. This is in line with a study by Inal and Wake [32], concluding that game familiarity positively impacts ones feeling of competence, immersion, emotions, and flow. Lastly, the greatest drawback in applying the 3D-desktop version of the game is the significantly lower focused attention. Focused attention refers to attention that is directed rather towards one specific task compared to being generally attentive within a situation [13]. Focused attention seems to have a relationship with motivation, and both are often seen as a predictor for immersion (the sense of presence) in games [33]. In this study, it may be that the lower level of motivation for group D, also stands in relationship to a lower level of focused attention.

Taking a closer look at EnhancedVR, with its reward system and positive reinforcement through a virtual agent, mean scores under the reward construct, as well as for the construct of focused attention and perceived usability were slightly higher compared to BasicVR. This supports literature stating that the use of positive reinforcement and reward may promote overall engagement [26]. Moreover, EnhancedVR was perceived as slightly more entertaining, exciting, and friendly. However, excitement and entertainment can also lead to physical arousal, which can counteract attention especially in children that struggle with arousal modulation [27]. Supporting this, in this study the off-task behavior observed most often stemmed from attempted interaction with the virtual agent, which lead to further distractions. This finding can be supported by literature such as by Schroeder [34], arguing that pedagogical agents may be more distracting than helpful for learning. For BasicVR, the game was found to be "Brilliant" most often, as well as "Fun" more often than EnhancedVR. This may indicate that the enjoyment and fun lie in the interaction with the game mechanics, and the way it is designed. Our BasicVR game shares traits with games under the concept of hypercasual games, which often consist of easy game mechanics, short play sessions, and a minimalistic design [35]. Hypercasual games are often highly engaging and fun. Moreover, in these games, players often want to directly engage in the game task after a tutorial is completed [35]. This may explain why BasicVR rated better on "Fun", due to the simple game mechanics and the minimalistic environment, as well as the option to get playing right after the training rooms were completed (no virtual agent). Also, this may explain why participants under BasicVR indicated more often than under EnhancedVR, that they would recommend playing the training rooms to their friends, despite the fact that the training rooms were the same. Potentially, the rooms were perceived as more fun by BasicVR as it was possible to start the game task directly after completion, with no introduction by the virtual agent. Following that line of reasoning further, the aesthetics of the game were ranked highest by BasicVR and were perceived most often as neat. This also supports the notion of it being the least distracting and most orderly environment for math equation practice in VR, without risking over-arousal states in users [26].

We can conclude from this study that in this case, VR does result in better attention compared to desktop VR, as well as better engagement and motivation. Moreover, VR provides a better overall user experience compared to non-VR.

Regarding the usage of a virtual agent and reward system in VR, we found that adding these does result in a higher level of attention, and overall experience. However, EnhancedVR also resulted in greater off-task behavior and does not perform better under "Fun". Furthermore we conclude, that VR has potential to keep attention as well as motivation and engagement when practicing math in a school environment. For practitioners in education it might be interesting to offer freely available VR education games to children that struggle with attention. It might be best to incorporate VR as additional learning unit for individual children, as the role of the facilitator as point of reference seems to be of significance to the children. For further research, it might be interesting to investigate to what extend and under what conditions the implementation of a virtual agent and reward system can substantially enhance attention, motivation, and engagement, while keeping off-task behaviour low.

Several limitations can be defined for this study. Firstly, due to practicalities, we were not able to recruit an even number of participants per condition, therefore results were analyzed in percentage and attention was paid to comparison levels. Moreover, due to ethical considerations we were not able to collect demographic's, such as the sex, age (besides the general age bracket), or individual ethnicity of the participants (besides general data provided to us by the school). This would have added valuable context to the interpretation of the findings. Lastly, and again due to the nature of working within the school environment, it sometimes was not possible to control the presence of other children, for example during break times. In several cases children other than the participant were present during the game test. For future research it would be beneficial to gather a larger sample size, and to further experiment with VR game elements aiding attention.

References

1. Vishwanath, A., Kam, M., Kumar, N.: Examining low-cost virtual reality for learning in low-resource environments. In: Proceedings of the 2017 Conference on Designing Interactive Systems, pp. 1277–1281 (2017)
2. Guan, J.Q., Wang, L.H., Chen, Q., Jin, K., Hwang, G.J.: Effects of a virtual reality-based pottery making approach on junior high school students' creativity and learning engagement. Interact. Learn. Environ. 1–17 (2021). https://doi.org/10.1080/10494820.2021.1871631
3. Hsu, Y.C.: Exploring the learning motivation and effectiveness of applying virtual reality to high school mathematics. Univers. J. Educ. Res. 8(2), 438–444 (2020)
4. Nobrega, F.A., Rozenfeld, C.C.D.F.: Virtual reality in the teaching of FLE in a Brazilian public school. Languages 4(2), 36 (2019)
5. Virvou, M., Katsionis, G.: On the usability and likeability of virtual reality games for education: the case of VR-ENGAGE. Comput. Educ. 50(1), 154–178 (2008)
6. Newbutt, N., Bradley, R., Conley, I.: Using virtual reality head-mounted displays in schools with autistic children: views, experiences, and future directions. Cyberpsychology Behav. Soc. Networking 23(1), 23–33 (2020)
7. Faraone, Stephen V., et al.: The worldwide prevalence of ADHD: is it an American condition?. World Psychiatry 2(2), 104–113 (2003)

8. Morsanyi, K., van Bers, B.M., McCormack, T., McGourty, J.: The prevalence of specific learning disorder in mathematics and comorbidity with other developmental disorders in primary school-age children. Br. J. Psychol. **109**(4), 917–940 (2018)

9. Mulrine, C.F., Prater, M.A., Jenkins, A.: The active classroom: supporting students with attention deficit hyperactivity disorder through exercise. Teaching Except. Child. **40**(5), 16–22 (2008)

10. Martinussen, R. L., Tannock, R., Chaban, P., McInnes, A., Ferguson, B.: Increasing awareness and understanding of attention deficit hyperactivity disorder (ADHD) in education to promote better academic outcomes for students with ADHD. Exception. Educ. Canada **16**(2-3), 107–128 (2006)

11. Belter, M., Wu, Y., Lukosch, H. Exploring the use of immersive virtual reality games in a formal school environment. In: International Simulation and Gaming Association Conference, Forthcoming

12. Gregory, G., Kaufeldt, M.: Improving student attention, engagement, and perseverance. ASCD, The motivated brain (2015)

13. Holdener, M., Gut, A., Angerer, A.: Applicability of the user engagement scale to mobile health: a survey-based quantitative study. JMIR Mhealth Uhealth **8**(1), e13244 (2020)

14. Silva, M.C.A.P., Maneira, A. and Villachan-Lyra, P.: Digital educational games: inclusive design principles for children with ADHD. Proceed. Play2Learn **2018**, 30 (2018)

15. Akman, E., Çakır, R.: The effect of educational virtual reality game on primary school students' achievement and engagement in mathematics. Interactive Learning Environments, pp. 1–18 (2020)

16. Geng, G.: Investigation of teachers' verbal and non-verbal strategies for managing attention deficit hyperactivity disorder (ADHD) students' behaviors within a classroom environment. Australian J. Teacher Educ. **36**(7), 2 (2011)

17. Jane M. Healy. Your child's growing mind: brain development and learning from birth to adolescence. Broadway (2004)

18. Norman, D.: Things that make us smarter: Defending Human attributes in the age of the machine. Addison -Wesley, New York (1993)

19. Pivec, M., Kearney, P.: Games for learning and learning from games. Informatica **31**(4), 419–423 (2007)

20. Lazzaro, N.: Why we play: affect and the fun of games. Hum. Comput. Interact. Designing Diverse Users Domains **155**, 679–700 (2009)

21. Tang, S., Hanneghan, M., El Rhalibi, A.: Introduction to games-based learning. In: Games-based Learning Advancements for Multi-sensory Human Computer Interfaces: Techniques and Effective Practices, pp. 1–17. IGI Global (2009)

22. Douglas, V.I.: The response of ADD children to reinforcement: theoretical and clinical implications. In: Bloomingdale, L. (ed.) Attention Deficit Disorder: Identification, Course and Rationale, pp. 49–66. Spectrum Jamaica (1985)

23. Slusarek, M., Velling, S., Bunk, D., Eggers, C.: Motivational effects on inhibitory control in children with ADHD. J. Am. Acad. Child Adoles. Psych. **40**(3), 355–363 (2001)

24. Shaw, R., Grayson, A., Lewis, V.: Inhibition, ADHD, and computer games: the inhibitory performance of children with ADHD on computerized tasks and games. J. Atten. Disord. **8**(4), 160–168 (2005)

25. Canady, V.A.: FDA approves first video game Rx treatment for children with ADHD. Ment. Heal. Wkly. **30**(26), 1–7 (2020)

26. Belter, M., Lukosch, H.: Virtual Reality Games for Children with ADHD in Formal Education. In: Int. Simul. Gaming Assoc. Conf. 2022, pp. 211–220. Springer, Cham (2022)
27. Morsink, S., Van der Oord, S., Antrop, I., Danckaerts, M., Scheres, A.: Studying motivation in ADHD: the role of internal motives and the relevance of self determination theory. J. Atten. Disord. **26**(8), 1139–58 (2022)
28. Barkley, R.A.: Impaired delayed responding. In: Routh, D.K. (eds.) Disruptive Behavior Disorders in Childhood. Springer, Boston, MA (1994). https://doi.org/10.1007/978-1-4899-1501-6_2
29. DuPaul, G.J., Weyandt, L.L., Janusis, G.M.: ADHD in the classroom: effective intervention strategies. Theory Pract. **50**(1), 35–42 (2011)
30. Wöbbekind, L., Mandl, T., Womser-Hacker, C.: Construction and first testing of the UX kids questionnaire (UXKQ) a tool for measuring pupil's user experience in interactive learning apps using semantic differentials. Mensch und Comput. **2021**, 444–455 (2021)
31. Read, J.C., MacFarlane, S.: Using the fun toolkit and other survey methods to gather opinions in child computer interaction. In: Proceedings of the 2006 conference on Interaction Design and Children, pp. 81–88 (2006)
32. Inal, Y., Wake, J.: An old game, new experience: exploring the effect of players' personal gameplay history on game experience. Universal Access in the Information Society, pp. 1–13 (2022)
33. Jennett, C.I.: Is game immersion just another form of selective attention? An empirical investigation of real-world dissociation in computer game immersion (Doctoral dissertation, UCL (University College London)) (2010)
34. Schroeder, N.L., Adesope, O.O., Gilbert, R.B.: How effective are pedagogical agents for learning? A meta-analytic review. J. Educ. Comput. Res. **49**(1), 1–39 (2013)
35. Yang, Z., Sun, B.: Hyper-casual endless game based dynamic difficulty adjustment system for players replay ability. In: 2020 IEEE International Conference on Parallel & Distributed Processing with Applications, Big Data & Cloud Computing, Sustainable Computing & Communications, Social Computing & Networking (ISPA/BDCloud/SocialCom/SustainCom), pp. 860–866. IEEE (2020)
36. Özgen, D.S., Afacan, Y., Sürer, E.: Usability of virtual reality for basic design education: a comparative study with paper-based design. Int. J. Technol. Des. Educ. **31**(2), 357–377 (2021)

Students' Learning Outcomes Influenced by Textbook Selection: A Gamification Method Using Eye-Tracking Technology

Ju Chou[1], Bryan Zhao[2(✉)], Gene Hoyt[1], and Sheri Silva[1]

[1] Florida Gulf Coast University, Fort Myers, FL 33965, USA
[2] Northwestern University, Evanston, IL 60208, USA
bryanjxyz@gmail.com

Abstract. In today's society, how humans go about their daily lives is becoming more and more intertwined with digital culture, online networks, and social media. In the contemporary era, students are leaning more towards e-learning and online textbooks compared to physical texts. E-textbooks will be here to stay, and this has raised questions about whether they will replace traditional textbooks indefinitely for the near future. In order for e-textbooks to remain relevant, these digitized textbooks must meet the needs of both students and teachers naturally. This study will utilize eye-tracking technology to present an innovative gamified approach to measure and assess the real-time learning process and learning outcomes from undergraduate students, to compare the effectiveness of three types of textbooks. The results conducted from a pilot study shows positive learning outcomes from the e-textbook reading. Implications for both academic research and practice, as well as suggestions for future studies will be discussed.

Keywords: e-textbook · learning outcomes · eye tracking · gamification

1 Introduction

Textbooks give a great contribution in the teaching-learning process to both teachers and students. Particularly, textbooks have a substantial effect on student achievement. Therefore, textbook selection is one of the critical decisions in education. Currently, faculty members are facing to a dilemma of a textbook selection among hardcopy textbook, e-textbook, and open source materials for textbook selection for their courses. A textbook from a publisher is expensive and may not fit in our curriculum faultlessly. Open source or customized materials are free for students, but reading effectiveness may not be compatible with a publisher's textbook. Several previous studies [1, 2] identified factors affecting textbook selection decisions, such as readability, cost, searchability, etc. However, these studies have been either out-of-date or focused on primary level education. Currently, determining the effectiveness of e-textbooks is complex, as it must take into account a diverse set of factors that may influence their applicability.

X. Fang (Ed.): HCII 2023, LNCS 14047, pp. 17–29, 2023.
https://doi.org/10.1007/978-3-031-35979-8_2

The emergence of e-textbooks is still relatively recent, and certain pre-requisites must be met for their usage, namely an internet connection and electronic device. Unfortunately, despite technological advances, there are still economic difficulties that prevent widespread use of e-textbooks as a work or study tool due to purchase cost. However, physical textbooks are often more expensive than e-textbooks, which has led to a rise in e-textbooks' popularity in the last decade. This study will attempt to answer the question of whether e-textbooks are more effective than physical textbooks, and under what circumstances. Therefore, we will concentrate on students' learning outcomes, which are the core indicator showing the educational effectiveness in higher learning. We will use experimental design to assess the learning outcomes for different types of textbooks and offer useful and efficient suggestions in higher education textbook selection, which will eventually improve students learning outcomes.

2   Literature Review

2.1   Motivators for Students Learning Through E-Textbooks

A prominent issue students are facing is the rise of textbook prices. Textbooks can account for around a quarter of educational expenses when attending a public university. Since 2014, textbooks and supplies for students required classes have increased 82% in the last decade [3]. Tuition and other expenses have also increased. Due to the rise in educational costs, it has led to more students abandoning the use of textbooks needed for their course. Students may even taking less credit hours to avoid textbook costs.

E-textbooks are less expensive than traditional textbooks because they do not require companies to incur printing and shipping costs of digital content. This less expensive approach to textbooks has motivated students to buy digital textbooks over traditional printed textbooks [4]. However, the pricing for e-textbooks falls between new physical textbooks and used physical textbooks. Students were more likely to choose traditional textbooks over e-textbooks if the prices were equivalent to each other [5]. Students often chose the e-textbook option if the price was lower than the price of traditional textbooks, but resorted to physical textbooks if the e-version was more expensive. Research suggests that to achieve at least an 80% adoption rate for e-textbooks, the price of printed textbooks must be 2.5 times more expensive than the online version [3].

Although price seems to be a large factor in students' decision to buy e-textbooks over traditional textbooks, they also consider other factors that can be enhanced using digital textbooks, such as the quality and content that comes with these new textbooks. Thirty-three percent of students in the study agreed that the low-cost affected their decision in buying e-textbooks over traditional textbooks. However, sixty-seven percent of students based their decision to buy digital textbooks on the educational or professional need of the contents within the digital textbook [4]. Students from the study were found to prioritize the categories of price, convenience and mobility, and perceived benefits to be gained. They also paid attention to the reviews and quality of the content.

Another motivator that helps students in adopting e-textbooks is having their learning needs met. Earlier studies heavily focused on the behavior of students towards acceptability of e-textbooks; however, recent studies have been narrowing their research to determine if students' needs are met through digital textbooks. This study presents a student's perspective based on Task-Technology Fit (TTF) and the Consumer Acceptance and Use of Technology (UTAUT) theory. This can better help teachers and software developers design and build the technology around the student's needs.

2.2 Students Experience with E-Textbooks

Aside from the research on economics and quality of digital textbooks, we must consider the experiences and feelings of the students when using these textbooks. This is important for researchers to analyze because the usability of e-textbooks corresponds to the learning outcomes for students.

From the perspective of students, their attitude towards using e-textbooks directly affects their behavioral intentions with the digital textbook. Therefore, if a student is more intrigued or excited to use e-textbooks, the more they will get out of using the digital textbook over the traditional textbook. For older students in college, the interest of using digital e-textbooks comes from the projected usefulness of the software according to their major. A population study was performed on a set of participants in a survey for use of e-textbooks and revealed that engineering students, and students in medicine use e-textbooks more often (see Table 1). This data shows the types of courses that students are studying through e-textbooks.

Table 1. Research population [7].

	College	# of students	Percentage (%)
1	College of Dentistry	697	23%
2	College of Pharmacy & Health Sciences	296	10%
3	College of Engineering	1241	40%
4	College of Information Technology	256	8%
5	College of Business Administration	596	19%
Total		3086	100%

Table 2. Student's choice of printed or electronic textbooks [9].

The students' choice	At the second stage of the experiment, %	At the third stage of the experiment, %
printed and electronic	46.5	48.1
electronic	38.9	42.2
printed	14.6	9.7

Table 3. Teacher's answers to the benefits from e-textbooks [9].

interest of students	79.2%
the amount of illustrative material that provides a practical visual training	67.9%
simplifying of work with the content due to tabs and page lookup capabilities	64.2%
the ability to allocate individual words and phrases for clarity and concentration of attention	35.8 %

Table 4. Demographic of Teachers in study [11].

Participant	Gender	Age Range	Professional Experience (year)	Graduation	Computer Experience	Frequency of using e-textbooks	E-textbook Familiarity Reading Alley	E-textbook Familiarity Speed Up	E-textbook Familiarity Marathon Plus
1	Female	30-39	11-15	Graduate	Moderate	Always	+	-	-
2	Female	30-39	6-10	Undergraduate	Moderate	Always	-	-	-
3*	Male	50-59	>21	Graduate	Low	Seldom	-	-	-
4*	Female	30-39	11-15	Graduate	Moderate	Usually	-	-	-
5	Female	30-39	6-10	Graduate	Moderate	Usually	-	-	-
6	Male	20-29	<5	Undergraduate	High	Always	+	+	-
7	Female	30-39	11-15	Graduate	Moderate	Always	-	-	-

Table 5. The effects on emotion, cognitive load and learning achievement after using e-textbooks with emotional design [17].

Dependent variable	The effects of emotional design on e-textbooks e-textbooks with emotional design (A) vs e-textbooks without emotional design (B)	The effects of digitalization on textbooks e-textbooks (A + B) vs paper textbooks (C)	E-textbooks with emotional design (A) vs paper textbooks (C)	E-textbooks without emotional design (B) vs paper textbooks (C)
Emotion	Yes	No	Yes	No
Cognitive load	Yes	No	No	No
Learning achievement	Yes	Yes	Yes	Yes

Note: "Yes" means a significantly positive effect

An older study suggested that students prefer printed textbooks over digital textbooks by a ratio of 3.6 to 1 [8]. But a more recent study (see Table 2) found that students prefer printed and digital textbooks over reading either a digital textbook or a paper textbook [9]. This could be due to students having a tough time reading text on screens and not being portable. But another reference suggests that less than 5% of students surveyed had reported illnesses such as eyestrains, headaches, etc. caused by reading e-textbooks [3]. The study also mentioned students disliking how distracting e-textbooks can become,

Table 6. Content of each area on one-page document.

C: introduction
D: Enthalpy cycles including the reaction pathway
E: Using Hess's Law example with solutions
F: Summary of the concept

by tempting students to wander to different websites, check instant messages, or do anything non-study related online [10].

Users need time to adapt to innovative technologies, and it makes sense that students would be less likely to want to use digital textbooks over traditional textbooks because they have not had the time to adapt to the technology that e-textbooks use. But when given time to adapt to technology, it was proven that students were adopting e-textbooks more. In just 2 years, 2009 to 2011, their attitudes and behaviors had changed. First students were unaware of the devices that e-textbooks were on and felt that these devices were not suitable to use consistently. The following years it was then reported that students enjoyed using e-textbooks and said that it was their preferred way to read textbooks [8].

Although many students can adapt to this innovative technology, some students are still rooted in learning from a traditional textbook. The argument has also been made that one's ability in technology does not always translate to their formal learning skills. These students that are rooted in textbooks may find e-textbooks more challenging because they must relearn how to absorb information from this new formatting, on top of learning how to navigate and find the materials [6]. Students also view this type of technology as a source of entertainment rather than a learning tool. Because younger students are avoiding mixing work and pleasure, 31–35-year-olds are more likely to buy an e-book over a teenager.

2.3 Teacher's Perception and Experience with E-Textbooks

Research on teachers' viewpoints and adoption behaviors is just as important as studying the students. This is because they are the ones that are assigning the homework, reading etc. with these e-textbooks. As mentioned before, students only value using these e-textbooks when the course learning lines up with the interactive e-textbooks.

Teachers have recognized that e-textbooks give more flexibility for classrooms. During COVID teachers had little notice that their classroom was moving to virtual classes. Thankfully, e-textbooks have been around long enough to be used as a tool during the pandemic. Textbooks are a necessity in the classroom whether the teachings are face-to-face or virtual. One approach could be to screenshare the textbook via PDF or scanned documents, but it can come with its challenges, and even inhibit learning. E-textbooks are the better choice for long distance learning due to the interactive activities such as annotations and other multimedia's that can draw readers in [11]. This also helps teachers be able to work easier and faster during a time of uncertainty, making teaching more effective. Saving time with using e-textbooks is valued to these teachers, along with keeping students engaged (see Table 3). The results also show that teachers see the benefit they most receive from using e-textbooks, is the interest the students have for the content [9]. This makes sense because if the student is more interested in e-textbooks, the more they will be willing to learn from it.

To make learning more effective for their students, teachers are now starting to drop the use of traditional textbooks and become more creative. With the ability to create their own course content, rather than a publisher, it allows for teachers to better instruct their students and prepare them for what the students will need to learn.

Crowd-based and co-author sources are what these teachers are leaning towards more because they can piece together textbooks, something a traditional textbook could not do. This can then maybe even lead to students crafting their own textbook in the future. Teachers like this idea because students are expected to research, collect, organize, and analyze information from various sources [12]. This would then be a textbook tailored to the individual's needs and interests, which allows for the student to add their own personality to their textbook. Which then gives them a sense of gratification, making them more excited to learn. However, this would need to be moderated and controlled in some ways by the instructor of the course. The students will still need some sort of framework to model after.

Technology used in our education system is an innovation and e-textbooks success depend on the acceptance of both students and teachers. Some external factors that influence these teachers to choose e-textbooks over traditional textbooks are the age and gender of the teacher, the support that teachers get from the school, size of the classroom, and the teaching experience they have [13]. Familiarity with the technology being used in the classroom is important for these teachers to have when implementing e-textbooks into their classrooms. A study by EFL teachers discovered this through their participants demographics (see Table 4). It seems the more experienced with technology the teacher is the more likely they are to implement it in their classrooms [11]. There did not seem to be much correlation between teaching experience and their use of e-textbooks, however it seems the teachers who taught over 21 years did not use e-textbooks often. The limitations with this study are the lack of gender representation and not much variation in age ranges. Two participants also had visual defects. The number of participants should have been increased to get a more correct representation of teachers.

2.4 E-Text Designs and Features

The designs that go into e-textbooks are more important than the designs that go into traditional textbooks. E-textbooks need more intentional designs because it is digital. Designs and features can influence students' engagement as well. For example, if a student is not interacting with the e-textbook they will be less likely to understand the text. Thus, publishers of these digital textbooks must be aware of the tools and resources they are adding and keep the students' preferences in mind.

As mentioned before, the market for digital textbooks has become larger over time. This can be both good and bad for students and teachers. In 2015 the NY Department of Education signed a contract with Amazon to provide 1,800 schools, about 1.1 million students, with access to their online database of e-books [9]. This is a benefit to having an open market with e-textbooks because the NY school system did not need to pay for books for each individual school in the state. Saving tons of money and paper. The school pays for the subscription and all teachers and students will have access to the resources free of charge at their level. The downside to having a more open market is the lack of standardization. The helpful tools that come with most e-textbooks are not currently under standardization, although they should be. This study found that the characteristics needed for teachers to feel as though e-textbooks are a better choice were based on quality, availability, and low-no costs (see Fig. 1).

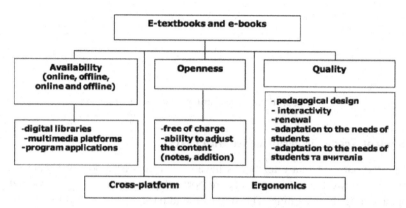

Fig. 1. Characteristics of e-textbooks [9]

The tools that should be standardized for these students are tools such as highlighting, annotating, searching, etc. These tools make students learn more interactively, allowing them to analyze and retain the knowledge read from the e-textbooks better. Mello's study performed a needs assessment to outline these tools and measure how effective they are to students learning. The needs for both students and teachers were the ability to take quizzes, update content providing additional resources, highlighting text, change font and size of text, and functioning hyperlinks [13]. Instructors are also able to gauge where their students are at in the text as well as tracking their progress. Allowing annotations for e-textbooks can make a significant difference to both the cognitive and metacognitive aspects of education. Underlying and highlighting text can also help students recall information as well [14]. In the study students were given an open-ended question to effectively assess their higher learning outcomes. An annotation in the textbook with a link to a video discussing the topic of the opened ended question that would be asked. The software did not track whether or not the student had opened this link though. The group of students who used e-textbooks performed significantly better on the opened end question than those who used a traditional textbook.

In contrast, another study was conducted to gain more understanding of what students are needing to see for features in e-textbooks. This study suggests that students are not using features such as highlighting, notes and links (see Fig. 2). One study supports this idea that extra features that are meant to enhance learning are only distracting to users while also increasing cognitive demand [15].

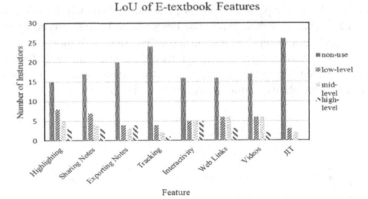

Fig. 2. Frequency distribution by feature [8]

2.5 Student Academic Performance with E-Text

Studying the outcome that e-textbooks have on students is important because it can gauge and measure how well students are both adapting to the e-textbooks and if it is supplementing their learning. The studies found have given a mixed review on how students have performed on tests and other assignments or assessments. This is because many different variables come into play with e-textbooks, especially since all e-textbooks are not the same and have distinctive features to students to help them succeed.

In one study done on students' performance, it was found that students that read digitally showed a lower level of reading comprehension and had trouble recalling information previously read. Furthermore, these students believed that they had understood the material better from reading the content from a digital e-textbook rather than a printed textbook [15]. The study suggested that this is partially due to the distracting aspect that e-textbooks can have. Multitasking was also highlighted as a factor. The findings from the study were that the same students who believed they had experienced a higher level of learning from e-textbooks, showed that these students scored lower on a final unit test. Another study suggests this is due to the high cognitive load that comes with e-textbooks. The limitations to this study would be the use of older resources, as most of the sources ranged anywhere from 1980's to 2008. As of today, technology has become increasingly used in our daily lives, so the cognitive load with navigation would be reduced.

Cognitive load theory is considered a major educational research framework and is commonly used for evaluation learning environments. It is important to consider cognitive load when designing learning tools and content because memory capacity and information processing are related when learning new knowledge [16]. Therefore, if an e-textbook is difficult for a reader to navigate and understand, they will be too busy with the frustration of using the technology to learn the material effectively. Which can cause grades for these students to fall.

In contrast, a study on emotional and cognitive design in relation to e-textbooks mentions that e-textbooks do not cause high cognitive load. It only had positive impacts on cognitive load for students (see Table 5). The results found that the cognitive load is reduced significantly when emotional design is used through e-textbooks. However, the cognitive load is not affected in a positive manner when it is either a digitized text or paper text [17]. Which suggests that the features in e-textbooks have importance in learning achievements through positive effects on student's cognitive load. E-textbooks have no effect on cognitive load, but it positively affects students learning achievements over traditional textbooks.

Learning achievement for students improves through e-textbooks, whether they have the emotional design or not. Which is a good reason for these versions of textbooks to be used more often. In this study emotion had the most significant correlation with learning achievement, and a negative correlation with cognitive load. Cognitive load and learning achievement however have a negative correlation between each other.

3   Research Methodology

Eye tracking is a technique whereby an individual's eye movements are measured so that the researcher knows both where a person is looking at any given time and the sequence in which their eyes are shifting from one location to another. In an attempt to provide reliable measures of cognitive load, along with the eye-tracking data. Therefore, we will know when and where the student is concentrating on which content while he/she is reading. By analyzing the eye-tracking data, we can understand students' reading and learning behaviors and find which type of the textbooks or combinations works the best for the students. Here are our research questions:

- What are the college students' reading and learning behaviors?
- Which could be the best type of textbooks we need to adopt for the best learning outcomes?
- What are the guidelines we can offer to faculty members who are looking for textbooks?

In this study, by adopting gamification, we are trying to fulfill two purposes: 1) Build a reliable method to assess students' learning outcomes using advanced technologies, such as eye tracking; 2) Distinguish the two types of textbooks and identify the advantages of each. We identified three phases as following (success of all deliverables can be measured easily as described in each phase):

Phase One has three milestones: 1) identify one Chemistry topic, such as Hess's Law, prepare two types of reading materials (hardcopy and e-version from a published textbook), and a quiz to evaluate students' learning outcomes;

Phase Two has three milestones: 1) finalize the gamified experimental design; 2) set up the devices and complete necessary gamification programming features; 3) complete the after-test survey design.

Phase Three has two milestones: 1) randomly choose two groups of students (10 students from each class and totally 30 students in each group) from three undergraduate chemistry classes to participate the study (Students in each group will use the same type of textbook. We will ask the students to read the topic-related pages in the textbook while measuring their eye movement using eye tracking. Then, we will give them a short quiz to test what they have learned. At the end, students will fill out an after-test survey to self-report their perceptions about the textbook they have been assigned.); 2) analyze the data from eye tracking device, quiz, and survey results.

4 Pilot Study and Discussion

We randomly picked eight students in an Introductory General Chemistry class and did a pilot study. Right before the students started to learn Hess's Law, we asked these eight students read a one-page textbook document. Four of them read the e-version whereas the other four students read the hardcopy page. Each of the students was given 30 min to complete reading, but some of them finished earlier. They can start the quiz right after they complete their reading. There are 10 multiple choice questions in the quiz. We did not use the survey in the pilot study because we focused on the procedures with eye tracking device in the pilot study. The eye tracking device we used in the pilot study is iMotions EyeTech VT3 Mini Eye Tracker. The software to capture the eye tracking data is iMotions Software Core 7.2.

To analyze the eye tracking data, we divided the one-page document into four areas from top to the bottom, such as C, D, E, and F (see Table 6 for the content). These areas were called Areas of Interest (AOI).

We only concentrated on two eye tracking variables. **Time spent or dwell time** quantifies the total amount of time that students have spent looking at a particular AOI, such as C, D, E, and F. If a student looks at a particular AOI for an extended period of time, it can suggest a strong interest in that area. Conversely, if the duration of the gaze is brief, it could imply that other sections on the screen or in the surroundings might be more captivating. The total amount of fixations counts or gaze points is another variable we collected from the eye tracking. The eye movements between fixations are generally referred to as saccades. When we read, for example, our eyes don't travel smoothly. Therefore, the larger number of fixations counts, the more visual attention has been directed there.

Figure 3 and 4 show the time spent on different AOI with e-text and hardcopy respectively. Averagely, students spent less time when they read the e-text document.

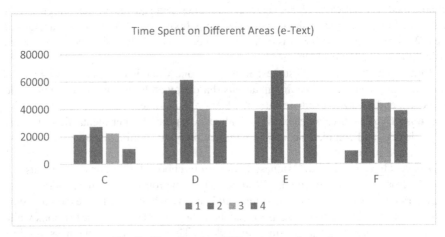

Fig. 3. Time Spent on Different Areas (e-Text)

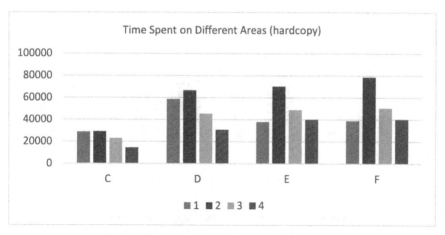

Fig. 4. Time Spent on Different Areas (hardcopy)

Figure 5 and 6 show the Fixations Count on different AOI with e-text and hardcopy respectively. Averagely, students' fixations count with e-text document is less than the count with hardcopy document. The quiz results were shown in the Fig. 7. Students 01 to 04 represents the students who read e-text document whereas students 05 to 08 are the students who read hardcopy documents. Obviously, students with e-text document got higher grade, which could support that, in our pilot study, the learning outcomes from the students who read e-text document is better than that from the students who read hardcopy document. Combined the quiz results with the time spent and the Fixations Count on different AOI, we can demonstrate that, in this pilot study, even though students spent less time reading with less fixations count when they read e-text document, their learning outcomes are better. Thus, from this pilot study, we can summarize that reading e-text document is more efficient for students' learning although this conclusion could not be generalized because of the small sample size.

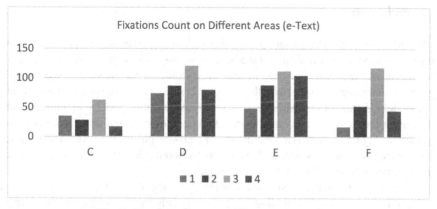

Fig. 5. Fixations Count on Different Areas (e-Text)

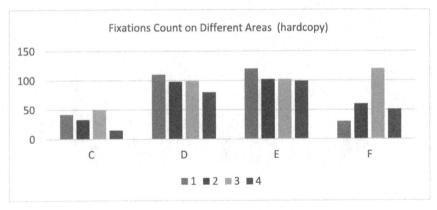

Fig. 6. Fixations Count on Different Areas (e-Text)

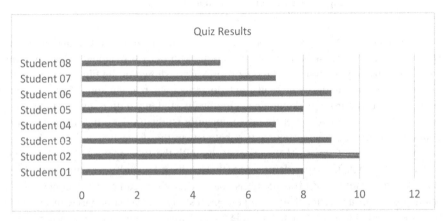

Fig. 7. Quiz Results

5   Conclusions

Student's will be more likely to adopt e-textbooks that meet their needs. These needs are commonly found in several different studies as low-cost, easy to navigate, useful, and if it is required of them. Students must be motivated in such a way that they are constantly engaged with the content, otherwise they lose the benefits of reading e-textbooks. Teachers have helped students transition to this innovative learning tool by getting involved and creating their own curated e-textbooks that meet their curriculum. E-textbooks are projected to stay when there is a combination of well-designed e-textbooks and a teacher to encourage and educate students. This results from out pilot study shows that a better learning outcomes from the e-textbook reading.

This is the first comprehensive study using eye tracking and EEG technology in a learning outcomes study. The findings will not only help faculty members with a better decision in their textbook selection, but also provide useful information/guidelines to textbook publishers. Additionally, this study adopts a new method to assess students' learning behaviors and outcomes in higher education. It helps future in-depth research to expand the current research models in learning outcomes studies.

References

1. Elias, E.C., Phillips, D.C., Luechtefeld, M.E.: E-books in the classroom: a survey of students and faculty at a school of pharmacy. Curr. Pharm. Teach. Learn. **4**(4), 262–266 (2012)
2. Gueval, J., Tarnow, K., Kumm, S.: Implementing e-books: Faculty and student experiences. Teach. Learn. Nurs. **10**(4), 181–185 (2015)
3. Baglione, S. L., Sullivan, K.: *Technology and textbooks: The future*. Taylor & Francis (2016)
4. Trishchuk, O., Figol, N., Faichuk, T., Fiialka, S.: Students' and teachers' perceptions of using electronic textbooks in educational process. Adv. Educ. **7**(15), 116–123 (2020)
5. Masa'deh, R., AlHadid, I., Abu-Taieh, E., Khwaldeh, S., Alrowwad, A., Alkhawaldeh, R. S.: Factors influencing students' intention to use E-textbooks and their impact on academic achievement in bilingual environment: zn empirical study Jordan. Information, **13**(5), 233 (2022)
6. Gerhart, N., Peak, D., Prybutok, V.R.: Encouraging E-textbook adoption: merging two models. Decis. Sci. J. Innov. Educ. **15**(2), 191–218 (2017)
7. Al-Qatawneh, S., Alsalhi, N., Al Rawashdeh, A., Ismail, T., Aljarrah, K.: To e-textbook or not to e-textbook? a quantitative analysis of the extent of the use of E-textbooks at Ajman University from students' perspectives. Educ. Inf. Technol. **24**(5), 2997–3019 (2019)
8. Roberts, K., Benson, A., Mills, J.: E-textbook technology: are instructors using it and what is the impact on student learning? J. Res. Innov. Teach. Learn. **14**(3), 329–344 (2021)
9. Vorotnykova, I.: Organizational, psychological, and pedagogical conditions for the use of e-books and e-textbooks at school. Turk. Online J. Distance Educ. **20**, 89–102 (2019)
10. Hung, W.-H., Hsieh, P.-H., Huang, Y.-D.: Critical factors of the adoption of e-textbooks: a comparison between experienced and inexperienced users. Int. Rev. Res. Open Distrib. Learn. **19**(4) (2018)
11. Soruç, M., Gündüz, Ş: Usability evaluation of E-textbooks by EFL teachers. Shanlax Shanlax Int. J. Educ. **9**(4), 157–162 (2021)
12. Väljataga, T., Fiedler, S.H.D.: Going digital: Literature review on E-textbooks. In: Zaphiris, P., Ioannou, A. (eds.) LCT 2014. LNCS, vol. 8523, pp. 138–148. Springer, Cham (2014). https://doi.org/10.1007/978-3-319-07482-5_14
13. Mello, S., & Matthee, M.: Implementation of electronic textbooks in secondary schools: what teachers need. In: Proceedings of the 15th International Conference on Mobile Learning (2019)
14. Dennis, A.R., Abaci, S., Morrone, A.S., Plaskoff, J., McNamara, K.O.: Effects of e-textbook instructor annotations on learner performance. J. Comput. High. Educ. **28**(2), 221–235 (2016)
15. Slocum-Schaffer, S.A.: Is it really all that? the impact of the digital textbook in Introductory political science classes. J. Polit. Sci. Educ. **17**(sup1), 440–458 (2020)
16. Novak, E., McDaniel, K., Daday, J., Soyturk, I.: Frustration in technology-rich learning environments: a scale for assessing student frustration with e-textbooks. Br. J. Edu. Technol. **53**(2), 408–431 (2021)
17. Chang, C.-C., Chen, T.-C.: Emotion, cognitive load and learning achievement of students using e-textbooks with/without emotional design and paper textbooks. Interact. Learn. Environ. 1–19 (2022)

The Gaming World of Educational Robotics.
A Review Study

Filippo La Paglia[1]([✉]), Daniele La Barbera[1], and Barbara Caci[2]

[1] Department of Biomedicine, Neuroscience, and Advanced Diagnosis, Institute of Psychiatry, University of Palermo, Palermo, Italy
filippo.lapaglia@unipa.it
[2] Department of Psychology, Educational Studies and Human Movement, University of Palermo, Palermo, Italy

Abstract. Educational robotics is considered a powerful tool, not only to learn how to program artificial agents but also to support students in developing *high-order* thinking skills. This paper reports a narrative review of empirical studies performed in the last twenty years, that investigate the effectiveness of using playful robotics as tools for enhancing cognitive abilities such as metacognition, awareness, and problem-solving, also improving planning and executive functions.

The evidence from the scanned literature supports the effective impact of using robotics as an educational metacognitive gaming environment that allows students to monitor themselves and control their learning actions autonomously. Moreover, the data provide scientific support to the hypothesis that educational robotics can improve the ability to plan and control complex tasks, favoring the development of executive functions and math or STEM achievement.

Keywords: Educational Robotics · Learning · Executive Functions · Gaming

1 Introduction

This paper discusses the effectiveness of educational robotics as a mental game. Educational robotics has attracted the high interest of teachers and researchers as a valuable tool to develop cognitive and social skills for students from pre-school to high school and to support learning in STEM (Science, Mathematics, Technology, Informatics), and other interdisciplinary subject activities [1]. Educational robotics is a powerful tool for learning programming skills and enhancing soft skills, such as problem-solving, metacognition, divergent thinking, creativity, and collaboration [2].

Specifically, a narrative review of empirical studies performed in the last twenty years using LEGO® robotics behavior construction kits is reported. Being in the marketplace under the name of LEGO® Ev3, such a game provides users with traditional and computational bricks useful for assembling interactive robots. The user is free to choose the shape of the robot and use the same LEGO® bricks to build small vehicle-shaped robots, *animaloid* or *humanoid* robots. Thus, the robotics behavior construction

X. Fang (Ed.): HCII 2023, LNCS 14047, pp. 30–42, 2023.
https://doi.org/10.1007/978-3-031-35979-8_3

kits are toys subject to inspection because the users could enter both into the mechanisms of construction and those of behavior modification of the toy itself [3]. LEGO® small mobile robots allow psychologists and educators to investigate the development of cognitive, social, metacognitive skills, and executive functions in users involved in educational robotics activities. Indeed, building the robot and then programming its actions to make it achieve a specific goal in the environment demands subjects to mentally anticipate the robot's action, select the appropriate algorithmic procedure, and eventually update it continuously following the feedback provided by robotics actions in the natural environment. The programming of small mobile autonomous robots into the physical environment requires planning, precision in the use of language, the generation and testing of hypotheses, the ability to identify action sequences, and a variety of other mental skills that seem to reflect what thinking is all about. To create a successful program, users must use procedural thinking and understand the logic of the instructions. When creating a program, users think of the NEXT, BEFORE, and UNTIL, all components of logical temporal sequencing.

Given these characteristics, educational robotics activities can enhance mental processes that belong to the cognitive domain of computational thinking, working memory, executive functions, and metacognition, such as problem-solving, planning, inhibition, mental flexibility, initiation, and monitoring/controlling/revising actions. As well, social skills are also enhanced.

In the following sections, we report first the theoretical framework of educational robotics under the constructionism approach [4, 5] (Sect. 2). Then, we discuss a series of empirical studies focusing on the use of LEGO® robots to improve cognitive and social abilities in children of different ages and scholastic levels (Sect. 3). Besides, we focused on empirical studies applying LEGO® robots for assessing or enhancing metacognition (Sect. 4) and executive functions (Sect. 5). Finally, we discuss the practical implications of robotics games for psychologists and educators, under the human-computer interaction perspective (Sect. 6).

2 The Theoretical Framework of Educational Robotics

The development of the first product line of robotics behavior construction kits, named LEGO® Mindstorm Robotic Invention System [6] was due to Seymour Papert, a South African mathematician, having moved to Massachusetts Institute of Technologies (MIT) in Boston after working with Piaget in the 1960s, and founding the epistemological model of constructionism [4, 5]. Observing the typical playful activities of some African children such as, for example, building houses in scale or artifacts in cane, Papert argued that the development of the human mind relies on the process of building concrete materials, called *objects-to-think-with* gamers can show, discuss, examine, and admire. Similarly, by interacting with computers or other robotics instruments, gamers enhance creativity or innovation and concretize their computational thinking [7].

In this theoretical framework, robotics behavior construction kits are real scaffolding that supports the processes of knowledge acquisition [5, 7] since they assign a new value to the physical dimension and the tangible products of human intelligence. Moreover, robotic games contribute to stimulating, at an individual level, the so-called zone of proximal development of each child [8].

The game experience with the robotics behavior construction kits is a *hands-on activity* that appeals to both constructionism and experiential learning [9]. Usually, it consists in assigning the gamers/students, divided into groups of 4–5 subjects, a poorly structured task of building and programming an artificial organism. Next, each group comes with LEGO® building materials and a computer with a programming interface. The subjects are, therefore, left free to create their artificial creature, but have the task of producing a written document called the inventor's document, reporting all the steps taken during the entire process of building and programming the robot [10, 11]. The fundamental elements of this methodology recall the constructionist principles [5, 7], but also those of cooperative learning [12] and experiential or *learning by doing* [13] which can therefore be summarized in the following points:

- Gamers/Students are placed in a learning situation that they control – the entire design and subsequent experimentation of the chosen strategies are managed by the students. The teacher only plays the role of facilitator of the learning process.
- Multiple approaches to learning are offered - the task/game stimulates pupils' creativity and lends itself to multiple solutions. Everyone can best express their learning strategies and cognitive styles.
- The promotion of a sense of community within the group is encouraged - the division of students into working groups that collaborate by sharing ideas and solutions increases the social skills of the subjects.

Playing individually or in a group, users live in a gaming situation where they control, and holly manage the entire design and subsequent testing of the game strategies for adapting the robot's action to the environment. Indeed, the game consists of the initial construction of a robot whose morphology is usually characterized by a central body and peripheral effectors or actuators. An onboard minicomputer represents both the main physical chassis of the robot and its brain. The body/brain is the input and output system processing the robot's behavioral repertory. It is a programmable LEGO® brick, interlocking with holes and buttons that allow the user to connect to it other pieces. It has an internal microprocessor and useful memory to store the processor's firmware or operating system, enabling the robot to operate independently from the computer. The users also assemble in the central body other computational bricks such as motors, light, touch, infrared, or color sensors. Sensors give the robot the possibility to perform specific actions in the real environment (e.g., moving in a dimly lit ambient; avoiding environmental obstacles; following a line). Once the user builds the robot, he/she switches to schedule its behaviors using a software programming application on a computer. Like in a puzzle, the user creates the program-making chains of various types of programming blocks, or commands, such as GO, NEXT, BACK, RIGHT, LEFT, STOP ENGINES, ZIG ZAG, DANCE, AND SHAKE. When the user completes the programming phase, he/she downloads the coding algorithm on the robot and verifies its performance in real surroundings. The robot acts autonomously in the environment, without any cable or another link to the computer. Thus, the game experience offers users a continuous process of construction, programming, and verification of the behavioral repertoires that the robot performs in the real environment.

The playful activities with LEGO® kits create a project-designed gaming environment [14, 15]. Besides, the robot embodies the users' computer thinking – see the concept of embodied cognition [16] – and allows them to adjust it through the continuous feedback received by the autonomous robot [5]. Thus, LEGO® robots represent not only a new playful technological toy but also the origin of a real epistemological revolution based on constructionism [7]. LEGO® robots have a real consistency and, at the same time, provide valuable support for the development of a game based on problem-solving. The robotics game offers multiple approaches to solving the problem of creating a well-structured and efficient robot so that the task stimulates the creativity of gamers. Everyone could express at best their cognitive styles or learning strategies. Gaming activities with robots have a high educational value since they offer gamers the freedom to create objects with subjective meaning, promoting in them a greater motivation to learn [10]. Stimulated by the playful context of learning, students are led to autonomously explore the existing connections between the physical process of the activity they are carrying out and the theoretical concepts underlying it.

For example, during the design of an explorer robot a group of subjects could be able to learn, without using any theoretical support, some technical-scientific concepts such as friction, fraction, and space/time relationship. Furthermore, the drafting of the different inventors' documents pushes the subjects to follow their learning styles. For instance, some groups first may build the robot and only subsequently draft the report; someone else carefully may enucleate the instructions to follow both in the construction and the programming phase, also adding some drawings of the robot; other groups might have further enriched their works by inventing stories with the robot as the protagonist. During the playful activities with the robots, users encounter some key concepts related to engineering, robotics, computer programming, and mechanical design and manage to acquire them autonomously, implementing them directly in the robot [14]. A fundamental role in concept learning acquisition is exercised by the errors made in the attempt to adapt the robot to its environment. During the process of construction and behavioral programming of robots, gamers can understand the particular type of errors they committed and can trace, specifically, 1) hardware errors, concerning the construction of the artifact or the malfunctioning of its elements (e.g. motors, sensors); 2) algorithmic errors, referring to a wrong or unexpected performance of the robot, following the wrong design of the algorithm that carries out the resolution of the mission, according to the environmental inputs; 3) errors connected to the sensors, concerning the malfunctioning of the sensors and/or the incorrect understanding of their functionality, and so on (Martin, 1994b). Engaged in solving specific intellectual challenges and working within a design space (i.e., the design space), where creativity and comparison of multiple solutions were encouraged, gamers experienced a central role within the project, acquiring bottom-up software programming skills without any support. Gamers configure themselves as programmers bricoleurs [17], rather than applying a top/down programming style, based on abstract, hierarchically ordered axioms, and on the implementation of norms and optimal solutions. As well, gamers have continuously built and rearranged their algorithms, according to the concrete feedback provided by the robot [18]. Likewise, the simultaneous possibility of working in peer teams favors the students' acquisition of concepts relating to the management of work groups, leadership, and project management and promotes social skills such as the ability to work in a group, effective communication, etc. Even the final challenge, although experienced by the most competitive gamers as a moment of very strong social judgment, helps to improve the student's motivation to learn and the level of self-efficacy [14].

3 Empirical Studies with LEGO® Robots for Improving Cognitive and Social Skills

Prior work provided empirical evidence that playing with LEGO® robots has a high educational value, especially in the areas of science, technology, mathematics, and engineering (STEM). Scholars introduced these kinds of game activities into schools, performing a comprehensive series of edutainment laboratories (i.e., educational plus entertainment laboratories) with students of different ages and educational grades. Results have shown the effectiveness of playing with robots for the acquisition of technical or scientific high-level concepts [14], and abstract or formal rules that govern the scientific and technological disciplines [2]. Other studies evidenced that robotics behavior construction kits allow children to increase planning and forecasting abilities, logical reasoning skills, perceptual discrimination ability, visuospatial skills, and working memory [19–21].

For instance, Caci and D'Amico [19] involved a group of students attending a middle school in a 12-session LEGO® robotics laboratory and showed that scores at measures of reasoning skills positively related to the ability to program a small LEGO® robot shaped like a vehicle ($r = .608$ $p <. 05$). The authors assigned participants with the robotic task of building/programming a LEGO® robot able to carry out, as quickly as possible, a journey inside a rectangular arena, avoiding an obstacle placed at the center of the trajectory. To evaluate the participants' performance on the robotic task, researchers divided preliminary the whole robotic action into four programming sequences needed for solving the task. Then they assigned scores of $0 =$ no programming sequence, $1 =$ incorrect programming sequence, and 2 points $=$ correct programming sequence, respectively. The results of this study demonstrated that reasoning skills are cognitive precursors of the ability to program a LEGO® robot. Students anticipate and plan the robot's actions to adapt its behavior to the environment. For instance, they program a suitable algorithm for allowing the robot to avoid environmental obstacles and modify its trajectory. As well, they use their reasoning strategies for defining the robots' sensory-motor actions suitable to the task conditions.

Similar results are reported with a sample of middle school students involved in eight four-hour sessions robotic laboratory aimed at building/programming first a LEGO® robot [20]. In this study, participants need to solve a more creative robotic task by defining first a fictional scenario for robot behavior, and then, building the robot arena using pasteboard, colors, and modeling paste. Finally, they could program the algorithms for adapting the robot to the created environment. In the second step of the robotics laboratory, participants also had to recreate the LEGO® scenario using the Kodu Lab virtual game by Microsoft. Results showed that participants' scores in reasoning skills ($r = .72$; $p < .01$) And the speed of visual processing targets ($r = .45$; $p < .05$) were strongly related to the acquisition of LEGO® programming skills.

Other studies showed that LEGO® robots are effective for the improvement of cognitive skills. For instance, [22] involved a group of children, aged between 5–6 years, in a pre-post design based on programming sessions with pre-assembled LEGO® robots.

During the pretesting, they required children to familiarize themselves with LEGO® programming sessions and to anticipate the robot's action in the environment. During the training session, the authors assigned children six programming tasks with an increasing difficulty level. In post-testing, the authors proposed the pretesting programming sessions and measured the increment in the children's ability to anticipate the actions of the robots. Results confirmed that children improved high-order cognitive skills such as planning and prediction abilities. Chioccarello et al. [3] confirmed such results also in an Italian group of 5–6 years aged children. However, they involved children in creating robotics, and microworlds with the assistance of experimenters.

For instance, they built LEGO® robots moving toward sound sources, robotics trees, or robotics birds interacting reciprocally. The authors reported that children made a high frequency of 'if… then' prediction statements during the robotics activities, and followed their cognitive styles. Some children mentally anticipated the actions of the robot and applied systematic and logical planning strategies. Others made hypotheses on robots' actions and tested them empirically in the environment, so applying test-retest heuristics. Recent empirical evidence shows that playful activities with LEGO® robots are also useful tools for the improvement of visual-spatial working memory [20].

Furthermore, playful activities with LEGO® robotics kits are valid for the increasing social skills of people engaged in the game. Players collaborate, share ideas and solutions, and acquire strategies for solving conflicts or disagreements [23]. As well, they improve cooperation and collaboration [24]. Barfurth [23], analyzed the collaborative strategies of fourth and fifth-grade children (8–9 years) by analyzing video transcripts during the activities of construction and programming of small autonomous LEGO® robots. Results showed the emergence of moments of disagreement within the couples, especially during the choice of the robot's behaviors. However, the children were able to overcome the situations of disagreement by activating multiple cognitive actions centered on the discussion/modification of different proposed solutions. To solve the disagreement, the students tried to keep the topic of discussion, created new themes, added new aspects to the topic of initial discussion, tried to integrate their point of view with that of others, or change their position and requested clarifications. In the same perspective, Denis and Hubert [24] highlighted the crucial role of the division of construction and programming tasks among the students. Some children took care of building the LEGO® robot, while others planned it. According to the authors, robotics activities create a learning context that favors the autonomy of children, who focus their interactions on the task, use the materials offered by the kit at will, and act in strategic behaviors of collaboration within the group. Furthermore, they offer companions feedback on the success achieved and give them explanations about the chosen strategies. These encouraging results have subsequently prompted researchers to verify the effectiveness of playing activities with robots in the field of special needs education. Benefits of using playing activities with robots for children with intellectual disabilities. Children with intellectual disabilities might have trouble playing because of their intellectual limitations and cognitive disabilities. They have reduced ability to retain attention and might not understand the meaning of the proposed play, and the meaning of the language used to play. Hence, the author focused on the possibility to customize the playing activity with robots and provided empirical evidence that people with intellectual disabilities can follow their ways of thinking, so giving free rein to their creativity. Other studies have shown that the interaction with robots that express an intentional behavior (e.g., robots that move in a track and sweep away some bricks scattered in it) fosters proactive and finalized attitudes in children with intellectual disabilities [25]. Likewise, Caci and D'Amico [19] demonstrated that playing with robotics kits allows students with intellectual disabilities to increase their academic achievements in all linguistic, mathematical-scientific, and technical subject areas and also promotes the enhancement of perceived self-efficacy, autonomy, and metacognitive control.

Recently, D'Amico and Guastella [26] developed a treatment protocol called RE4BES, which is a collection of guidelines for realizing robotics personalized activities for children with special needs. The results reinforce the idea that the RE4BES protocol can be considered a valuable and innovative tool for the cognitive treatment of children and adolescents with different individual needs. The authors proved the effectiveness of the RE4BES protocol for the empowerment both of cognitive skills (i.e., verbal short-term, working memory) and engagement in the activities. As well, the RE4BES protocol is useful for the reduction of inattentive or hyperactive behaviors.

4   The Effectiveness of LEGO® Robots for Assessing and Enhancing Metacognition

As regards metacognition, a series of papers show that robotics activities may be intended as a new metacognitive environment that allows children to monitor themselves and control their learning actions in an autonomous and self-centered way.

Metacognition is defined as *thinking about thinking* [27] and refers to meta-level knowledge and mental actions used to steer cognitive processes [28]. Researchers widely agree that metacognition can be divided into a knowledge component and a skill component. The knowledge component is the knowledge of cognition, and the skill component is the regulation of cognition. Knowledge of cognition is an individual's awareness of cognition and includes three subcomponents: declarative – i.e., knowing about things, procedural – i.e., understanding about strategies and other procedures, and conditional knowledge – i.e., knowledge of why and when to use a specific strategy. Regulation of cognition indicates an individual's actions or mental activities to control their cognition and includes three types of control: planning, monitoring, and evaluating [29]. Planning refers to goal setting, activating previous knowledge, and determining time. Monitoring comprises the self-testing skills to control learning and can be used to identify problems and modify learning behavior when needed. Evaluation relates to assessing the outcome and procedures of one's learning [30]. Metacognition was recognized as one of the most relevant predictors of accomplishing complex learning tasks [31]. Researchers have shown that students with superior metacognitive abilities are better problem solvers [32], they know when and how they learn best, apply strategies to overcome obstacles [27] and regulate their cognition.

From this perspective, the whole experience of playing with robots may be intended as a metacognitive process that leads users to become more aware and conscious of the way they think, learn, and organize the game itself. Through iterative design and testing, students get immediate feedback on their actions and learn how to deal with challenging situations in a real-world context.

In line with the studies mentioned above, La Paglia et al. [33] provided preliminary results about the association between LEGO® robotics activities and metacognition skills with a group of children attending a primary school. The study analyzed the process of building and programming robots as a metacognitive tool, and it was found that robotics activities may be intended as a new metacognitive environment that allows children to monitor themselves and control their learning actions in an autonomous and self-centered way. Specifically, the authors designed a robotics laboratory for 20 h during a scholastic year, involving twelve children (6 Males and 6 Females; mean age: 9 years; range: 8–10 years), who were randomly selected from all the third, fourth, and fifth forms of the primary school. The whole group was then divided into three subgroups (four children each, 2M; 2F) according to forms and ages.

After the familiarization with the hardware and software elements of the LEGO® robotics kit, all the children were given four construction and programming tasks with an increasing level of difficulty, as measured by the number of LEGO® bricks, which had to be manipulated for constructing the robot body and by the number of programming rules, which had to be linked to create a specific robot behavioral repertory. Specifically, children were assigned four programming tasks:

- Program the motors – Create a robot able to move along a linear route (1 rule);
- Program the motors and the light sensor - *Create a robot able to move and change trajectory if there is a black stain along its route* (4 rules);
- Program the motors and the single bumper: - *Create a robot able to move and change trajectory if there is an obstacle along its route* (5 rules);
- Program the motors and the double bumper - *Create a robot able to move and change trajectory if there is an obstacle along its route* (9 rules).

Each of the tasks provided opportunities for subjects to program and observe the robotic toy and to reflect on the toy's movement. During all the construction and programming sessions the children's metacognitive strategies were registered using two observational grids. The first grid measured the metacognitive abilities employed by students during the construction of the robot, while the second grid measured the metacognitive abilities used by them during the programming phase.

The results show that third-form children made more metacognitive actions based on controlling and retrieving errors than the other two groups during the whole game action. During the programming phase, they made a higher number of self-corrections and they were more focused on their performance than on the robot one, also emphasizing their success. The study was one first attempt to investigate the possibility to use robotics activities as a metacognitive tool. From this perspective, the results allow describing the action of playing with robots as a kind of *thinking with robots* which creates an autonomous and self-centered learning environment and motivates children both at monitoring and at controlling their actions.

In a successive study, La Paglia et al. [1] involved a group of sixty healthy students attending a middle school. The students were randomly selected and assigned to the control and the experimental group, each composed of thirty subjects (15 Males and e 15 Females; mean age: 11 years, range 10–12 years). The study is articulated in assessing the metacognitive skills and beliefs related to the acquisition of the subject's mathematical knowledge evaluated individually, during the pre-test and the post-test, and successively in the educational robot activities only for the experimental group. The metacognitive skills were evaluated individually, during the pre-test and the post-test assessment, using a questionnaire measuring attitudes, beliefs, and control processes influencing math learning. The questionnaire also allows several qualitative observations such as exploring the presence of specific mathematics skills and some aspects of metacognition in mathematics such as the higher-level control processes, forecasting, planning, monitoring, and evaluation. The robotics laboratory was similar to [33] preliminary, the authors defined four LEGO® robotics tasks with increasing difficulty levels measured by the number of LEGO® bricks and LEGO® building and programming sequences needed for solving each of them. During all the educational robotics activities based on the construction and programming of a small mobile LEGO robot, metacognitive strategies were registered using observational grids that provided quantitative and qualitative indicators about the frequency of checks made by subjects to verify if the correct LEGO® bricks were taken and assembled, the frequency of spontaneous self-corrections, the frequency of trough-other corrections made by the experimenters. Results showed that the subjects in the experimental group increased their positive attitudes towards mathematics from pre to post-test and metacognitive control. Indeed, the experimental group showed metacognitive actions based on controlling and retrieving errors, such as enhancing the self-correction index during the programming of the robot and decreasing the help request index more than controls. Likewise, results suggest that using robot LEGO® robotics kits will improve the attitude in mathematics, and it also increases the attitude to reflect on themselves and their learning, and higher-level control components, such as forecasting, planning, monitoring and evaluation exercises, and problems related to implementation.

5   The Effectiveness of LEGO® Robots for Assessing and Enhancing Executive Functions

From a psychological point of view, executive functions refer to a family of adaptive, goal-directed, top-down mental processes needed when people must focus and pay attention to an environmental object or event and when an automatic response would be insufficient. Thanks to executive functions, it is possible mentally play with ideas, take the time to think before acting, meet novel, unanticipated challenges, resist temptations, and stay focused.

La Paglia et al. [34] involved a group of students attending their fifth year at primary school, aged between 9–10 years, to verify the effectiveness of educational robotics on the improvement of executive functions and of the mental process of visuomotor planning, attention skills, planning, and problem-solving. Applying an experimental design, all children were divided into small groups (three or four children for each group), provided with a robot kit, assembled as a small vehicle, equipped with motors, ultrasonic sensors at the front, one pointed straight ahead, and a LED color light mounted on top.

The robotics laboratory followed ten meetings: two hours each, once a week. The task for the participants was to build a robot and, subsequently, plan and program different robotics behavioral repertoires. After explanations of tasks and rules, participants can plan and choose the sequence of actions to complete the tasks. In this way, many different executive functions are stimulated, from the ability to plan a sequence of actions, to problem-solving and cognitive and behavioral flexibility.

The laboratory was intended as a training and each of the tasks provided opportunities for subjects to program and observe the robotic toy and to reflect on the toy's movement. The dynamic actions of the toy created a "shared moment" which was highly visual and in turn provided opportunities for shared attention and group work. Programming robot actions require, for each step, mental anticipation of the action, selection of the appropriate robot command, and continuous updating of the programming to obtain the goal. The cognitive and executive functions of all participants were measured with a neuropsychological assessment before and after the training to obtain an accurate overview of the starting cognitive functioning and to compare the performances of the two groups in terms of improved cognitive abilities.

The results of the study showed an improved performance in the participants' attentional skills, specifically on sustained attention ($p < .001$), divided attention, and visuomotor planning ($p < .01$). Moreover, the performance of the experimental group increased from pre-test to post-tests because of treatment scores on tests measuring mental flexibility, motor planning, and executive control, as well as an increase in planning and problem-solving.

Di Lieto et al. [35] provide an evidence-based approach and quantitative data for evaluating the effects of an intensive educational robotics laboratory on soft high-level cognitive functions in preschool children. They found a significant increase in the executive function domain, working memory, and inhibition skills and these results are coherent with the well-known psychological model of executive function development; working memory and inhibition are the two main early components.

Moreover, the data provide scientific support to the idea that it is possible to quickly improve in 5-year-olds ability to plan and control progressively more complex navigation tasks. For this reason, educational robotics may be suitable for fostering several essential life skills (cognitive and personal development and teamwork) through which children can develop their potential to use their imagination and express themselves in school and social activities.

6 Discussion and Conclusion

This study presents a review of published literature on the use of educational robotics, to identify the potential contribution of robotics as an educational tool, in the context of schools, summarizing relevant empirical findings, and indicating future research perspectives. The review provides empirical evidence on the added value of educational robotics for learning: students develop their metacognitive and problem-solving skills; regulation and self-control components such as planning, and monitoring, are activated. Furthermore, it is very interesting to discover the potential of robots to promote executive functions.

The robotics laboratories create into the school a vibrant, engaging, and fun environment in classrooms. Playing with robot students can evoke and nurture their curiosity and come closer to hands-on experiential learning. Thus, one of the main benefits of educational robotics is that by playing with robots students develop critical thinking and problem-solving skills so they will prepare for the competitive educational and professional society. Educational robotics is perfect for teaching students to think like engineers. They face a full set of tools for building robots that challenge students to create different robotic creations, and with a variety of options, they'll have to use their critical-thinking and problem-solving skills to build them all. As well, the mistakes they make in building and programming robots allow them for learning and exploring different possibilities until they come to a solution. Aside from problem-solving and critical thinking, robotics also stimulates logical and analytical reasoning, higher-order thinking, and computational thinking. By observing the results of their efforts, students can also realize that they wish to turn that satisfying feeling of bringing objects to life into a career. They play in a complex environment that relies on many different capabilities. Through experimenting with robotics, students can discover their strengths, whether they lie in engineering, programming, math, or interest in innovative human-computer-interaction technologies. Programming is the job of the future. According to Forbes, the global number of software developers will increase to 45 million by 2030. So, the demand for programmers is certainly growing worldwide. However, students can find it boring and overwhelming if you teach it in a traditional method that relies on theory and abstract notions. However, by playing at school with physical robots and observing the results of their programming efforts students can change their perception of programming, machine learning, and AI (artificial intelligence). Linking theoretical learning with a practical application can give them a sense of how fascinating programming can be.

As well, educational robotics promotes a culture of teamwork. Playing with robots students realize the importance of relying on others, respecting their ideas, and valuing everyone's contribution. Moreover, they will learn how to listen to others and communicate their ideas. Thus, they develop also *soft skills* that can help them further in life, whether they are interested in programming or not.

In sum, the present paper foreshadows repercussions for the application of robotics in gaming for the short-term strengthening of specific abilities and long-term ones. Robotics is a new frontier for education [21] and could make education more meaningful and relevant to the future needs of society. It supports high-quality and interactive learning in schools and boosts students' skills and knowledge that are necessary for their personal and educational development, reaching their full potential.

The results of the current review study encourage psychologists, pedagogical experts, or game developers to further understand the practical aspects of the utilization of robots in education. Therefore, we believe that robotics toys represent a frontier for computer scientists, engineers, educators, and school psychologists.

References

1. la Paglia, F., la Cascia, C., la Barbera, D.: Educational robotics to improve mathematical and metacognitive skills. Ann. Rev. Cybertherapy Telemedicine **15**, 70–75 (2017)

2. Caci, B.: The effectiveness of using LEGO ® robotics kits as cognitive and social rehabilitative toys. Int. J. Entertainment Technol. Manag. **1**, 34–42 (2020)
3. Chioccariello A, Manca S, Sarti L La fabbrica dei robot. Ital. J. Educ. Technol. **10**, 56–56 (2002). https://doi.org/10.17471/2499-4324/505
4. Piaget, J.: The Psychology of Intelligence and Education. Child. Educ. **42**, 528–528 (1966) https://doi.org/10.1080/00094056.1966.10727991
5. Papert, S.: The Children's Machine. RETHINKING SCHOOL IN THE AGE OF THE COMPUTER, Basic Books, NY (1993)
6. Resnick, M.: Behavior construction kits. Commun. ACM **36**, 64–71 (1993). https://doi.org/10.1145/159544.159593
7. Papert, S., Harel, I.: Constructionism. Ablex Publishing, Norwood, NJ (1991)
8. Vygotsky L.S.: Thought and Language. The MIT Press., Cambridge, Mass
9. Kolb, D.A., Boyatzis, R.E., Mainemelis, C.: Experiential learning theory: Previous research and new directions. In: Perspectives on thinking, learning, and cognitive styles, pp. 227–247. Lawrence Erlbaum Associates Publishers, Mahwah, NJ, US (2001)
10. Resnick, M., Ocko, S., Papert, S.: LEGO/logo--learning through and about design (1990)
11. Resnick, M.: Technologies for lifelong kindergarten. Educ. Tech. Res. Dev. **46**, 43–55 (1998). https://doi.org/10.1007/BF02299672/METRICS
12. Johnson, D.W., Johnson, R.T., Holubec, E.J.: The nuts and bolts of cooperative learning. Interaction Book Company (1994)
13. Kolb, D.A., Boyatzis, R.E., Mainemelis, C.: Experiential learning theory: Previous research and new directions. Perspectives on Thinking, Learning, and Cognitive Styles **227–247** (2014). https://doi.org/10.4324/9781410605986-9
14. Martin FG (1994) A Toolkit for Learning: Technology of the MIT LEGO Robot Design Competition. In: Proceedings for the Workshop on Mechatronics Education. Stanford University
15. Kafai, Y., Resnick, M.: Constructionism in practice Designing, thinking, and learning in a digital world. Lawrence Erlbaum Associates Inc, Mahwah, NJ (1994)
16. Clark, A.: Reasons, Robots and the Extended Mind. Mind. Lang. **16**, 121–145 (2001). https://doi.org/10.1111/1468-0017.00162
17. Claude, L.-S.: The savage mind. University of Chicago Press, Chicago, Illinois (1972)
18. Turkle, S., Papert, S.: Epistemological pluralism and the revaluation of the concrete. In: Harel, I., Papert, S. (eds.) Constructionism, pp. 161–191. Ablex Publishing (1991)
19. Caci, B., D'Amico, A.: Children's cognitive abilities in construction and programming robots. In: Proceedings - IEEE International Workshop on Robot and Human Interactive Communication (2002)
20. Caci, B., D'Amico, A., Chiazzese, G.: Robotics and virtual worlds: An experiential learning lab. In: Chella, A., Pirrone, R., Sorbello, R., Jóhannsdóttir, K.R. (eds.) Biologically Inspired Cognitive Architectures 2012: Proceedings of the Third Annual Meeting of the BICA Society, pp. 83–87. Springer Berlin Heidelberg, Berlin, Heidelberg (2013). https://doi.org/10.1007/978-3-642-34274-5_19
21. Caci, B., D'Amico, A., Cardaci, M.: New frontiers for psychology and education: Robot. Psychol. Rep. **94**, 1372–1374 (2004)
22. Wang, H., Wang, H., Wang, C., Soh, W.Y.C.: Cooperation-based behavior design. Lecture Notes in Computer Science (including subseries Lecture Notes in Artificial Intelligence and Lecture Notes in Bioinformatics) 2377 LNAI:465–470 (2002). https://doi.org/10.1007/3-540-45603-1_61/COVER
23. Barfurth, M.A.: Understanding the collaborative learning process in a technology rich environment. 8–13 (1995). https://doi.org/10.3115/222020.222042
24. Denis, B., Hubert, S.: Collaborative learning in an educational robotics environment. Comput. Human Behav. **17**, 465–480 (2001). https://doi.org/10.1016/S0747-5632(01)00018-8

25. Kolne, K., Bui, S., Lindsay, S.: Assessing the environmental quality of an adapted, play-based LEGO® robotics program to achieve optimal outcomes for children with disabilities. Disabil Rehabil **43**, 3613–3622 (2021). https://doi.org/10.1080/09638288.2020.1743776

26. D'Amico, A., Guastella, D.: The Robotic Construction Kit as a Tool for Cognitive Stimulation in Children and Adolescents: The RE4BES Protocol. Robotics,: Vol 8. Page **8**(8), 8 (2019). https://doi.org/10.3390/ROBOTICS8010008

27. Flavell, J.H.: Metacognition and cognitive monitoring: A new area of cognitive-developmental inquiry. Am. Psychol. **34**, 906–911 (1979). https://doi.org/10.1037/0003-066X.34.10.906

28. Jacobse, A.E., Harskamp, E.G.: Towards efficient measurement of metacognition in mathematical problem solving. Metacogn. Learn. **7**, 133–149 (2012). https://doi.org/10.1007/S11409-012-9088-X

29. Cooper, M.M., Sandi-Urena, S.: Design and validation of an instrument to assess metacognitive skillfulness in chemistry problem solving. J. Chem. Educ. **86**, 240–245 (2009). https://doi.org/10.1021/ED086P240

30. Desoete, A.: Multi-method assessment of metacognitive skills in elementary school children: How you test is what you get. Metacogn. Learn. **3**, 189–206 (2008). https://doi.org/10.1007/S11409-008-9026-0/TABLES/6

31. van der Stel, M., Veenman, M.V.J.: Development of metacognitive skillfulness: A longitudinal study. Learn Individ Differ **20**, 220–224 (2010). https://doi.org/10.1016/J.LINDIF.2009.11.005

32. du Toit, S., Kotze, G.: Metacognitive strategies in the teaching and learning of mathematics. Pythagoras , 57–67 (2009). https://doi.org/10.4102/PYTHAGORAS.V0I70.39

33. la Paglia F, Caci B, la Barbera D, Cardaci M (2010) Using robotics construction kits as metacognitive tools: A research in an Italian primary school. In: Studies in Health Technology and Informatics

34. la Paglia, F., la Barbera, D., Riva, G., Francomano, M.M.: Educational Robotics to develop of executive functions visual spatial abilities, planning and problem solving. Ann. Rev. CyberTherapy Telemedicine **16** 80–86 (2018). https://doi.org/10.2/jquery.min.js

35. di Lieto, M.C., Castro, E., Pecini, C., et al.: Improving executive functions at school in children with special needs by educational robotics. Front. Psychol. **10**, 2813 (2020). https://doi.org/10.3389/FPSYG.2019.02813/BIBTEX

Skull Hunt: An Educational Game for Teaching Biology

Julio Litwin Lima[1] , Carla D. Castanho[1] , Luiz Belmonte[1] ,
Veronica Slobodian[1] , Guilherme Gomes Carvalho[1] , Gabriela Hirata[1] ,
and Julia Klaczko[2(✉)]

[1] University of Brasilia, Campus Universitário Darcy Ribeiro, Asa Norte, DF,
Brasília 70910-900, Brazil
{julio.litwin,luiz.belmonte}@aluno.unb.br,
{carlacastanho,vslobodian}@unb.br
[2] Department of Life Sciences, Natural History Museum, London SW7 5BD, UK
jklaczko@unb.br

Abstract. Difficulties in learning biology (and thus, science) can be associated with abstract concepts, overloaded curricula, and the traditional teaching methodology, which all lead students to learn through memorization, and consequently do not achieve meaningful and enjoyable learning. Given this scenario, our objective was to develop a digital educational game for mobile devices called "Skull Hunt" which aims to be a playful strategy in teaching biology, especially vertebrate anatomy, and zoology, to secondary students. The game has a backend and a front end. The backend uses a Gateway API and a Main API, using C# language (.NET Core) with a monolithic approach and a Client-Server style. The front is managed by a Dashboard, that is responsible for all game activities and allows future insertions, corrections, and analyses. The dashboard uses the ASP.NET framework, with Blazor's cooperation, and the database uses PostgreSQL. Besides, the game uses Augmented Reality via Unity 3D and AR Foundation, allowing it to be played in different operational systems, such as Android and iOS. The basic game concept is a *treasure hunt*, in which students must search for QR codes in the environment that allow the visualization and interaction with vertebrates' skulls using Augmented Reality. From recognizing the skull, students can then answer questions related to the anatomy, biology, and physiology of the observed object. At the end of the game, the person can recover their scores and compare their collectibles with their peers. School teachers can register a class in the dashboard and recover student performance.

Keywords: Augmented Reality · mobile game · zoology

Supported by FAPDF 00193-00001011/2021-93.

X. Fang (Ed.): HCII 2023, LNCS 14047, pp. 43–60, 2023.
https://doi.org/10.1007/978-3-031-35979-8_4

1 Introduction

Biology is a fundamental part of the science curriculum, and several studies have documented that students struggle to learn the concepts and believe that biology is complicated and irrelevant. The difficulties in learning biology (and thus, science) can be associated with abstract concepts, overloaded curricula, and the traditional teaching methodology, which all lead students to learn through memorization, and consequently do not achieve meaningful and enjoyable learning (*e.g.* [1]). This scenario permeates several biology fields, including comparative anatomy and vertebrate zoology [2]. Furthermore, in times of extra exposition to technology, keeping the attention and interest of students in textbooks has been even more difficult. Thus, the inclusion of student-centered teaching strategies and resources can prove to be a solid ally to professors in biology classes.

Gamification is a strategy that can be used in educational contexts when elements typical to games (points, rewards, levels, game stage, etc.) are applied in the classroom or to elaborate educational products. Hence, educational games are part of the gamification strategy that can facilitate the comprehension of biological concepts in a motivating and fun way.

Educational games are produced to provide a ludic strategy for teaching a specific topic [3], therefore uniting the teaching objective with the playful part. They have a clear didactic objective, which can be used to support learning processes in a formal, non-formal, or informal setting by creating immersive learning experiences [4]. Thus, the educational game is a conduit that induces learning, not an end in itself, and can be used to understand concepts and models that are somewhat difficult to learn [4,5]. Educational games can act in knowledge construction, developing cognitive abilities (like logic, memorization, problem-solving, and attention), and resignifying values and behaviors [6,7]).

Despite not being a new strategy, gamification has become increasingly important for teaching in recent years, nurturing problem solving, creative thinking, and filling the gaps of the traditional teaching strategies, centering the students in the learning process [4,8]. Besides, with the progressively widespread access to mobile phones and computers, the market for educational games is also increasing.

The technological advance of the last decades promoted the improvement of graphic resources, resulting in the development of a large digital game industry responsible for producing a myriad of games for numerous platforms [6]. Such games can give an immersive experience to the player, which is motivated to continue in the game. Furthermore, since one of the significant challenges of educators is to arouse interest and motivate students [9], researchers are increasingly interested in how to produce and apply games in an educational framework [10].

There is no unifying theoretical framework for educational games [11,12]. However, a recent revision indicated the use of digital games had positive outcomes in Biology and Natural Sciences education: provided more motivating teaching, addressed theoretical concepts, contributed to the development of essential skills such as problem-solving and the organization of ideas, and increased students' grades [13]. However, one of the major challenges of educational games is allying an attractive gaming experience to the educational purposes of serious games [14]. One tool to make educational games more enticing can be the use of Augmented Reality (AR).

AR is a knowledge processing process that "augments" the individual's understanding by presenting computer-derived virtual data or visuals superimposed with real environment images, enriching the reality perception [15]. Former studies pointed out that AR use in educational games motivates students, enhancing their interest and attention, making it easier to construct knowledge, contributing to the development of students' psychomotor skills, and activating more sense organs [16–19]. In representing the real world and situating the student in it, AR provides opportunities to develop student-centered learning environments [19], can foment positive emotions and sensations, explore the students' inclinations, arouse their interest, and motivate them during the educational process [20–22].

Pokémon Go, a smartphone game that uses AR, was launched in 2016 and was a huge success, being the most downloaded app in the Apple App Store in 2016. The users of the game, while exploring the real world, seek, encounter, catch, and collect virtual species of Pokémon that appear as if they are in the player's real-world location. The caught species are cataloged in the player's collection. The user can "evolve" their Pokémon into more powerful forms and fight with other players [23]. The game has no educational purpose, however, has several positive points that influence our game, the "Skull Hunt". The idea of hunting provides a huge engagement for the players. Additionally, the possibility of collecting species was as well explored by us since, as in Pokémon, our players can collect species information in their field notebook. Finally, the game encourages people to get outside and look for Pokémon species. Our game would encourage the players to look around the explored area while seeking the skulls, which we believe can help engage all exhibitions.

An example of an educational game that deals with zoology concepts is the board game *Mystery on the Zoo*, which simulates a Zoo map and cards with the animals that live there [24]. In the game, the players should discover which animal has disappeared from the Zoo, how the animal runs away, and which is the animal's vertebrate group. The game is cooperative, and the players should use previous knowledge to discover the mystery.

However, up to date, there is no digital educational game that combines AR and permeates concepts related to vertebrate zoology and anatomy. Instead, these biology fields are usually taught through memorization of scientific terms, which are frequently dissociated from the students' reality and soon forgotten, because concepts and terms gain meaning to the student when they can contextualize them with their personal experiences [25]. Furthermore, teaching vertebrates' anatomy and zoology is frequently disconnected from an evolutionary perspective, being mostly descriptive [26]. Thus, the traditional teaching method is unproductive, and students frequently deem these topics as "boring" or "tiresome" [21].

Given this scenario, our objective was to develop a digital educational game for mobile devices called "Skull Hunt", which aims to be a playful strategy in teaching biology, especially vertebrate anatomy, and zoology, to secondary students (11 to 16 years), and promote environmental awareness. The theoretical framework for developing this game is an approach to the Situated Learning Theory called Anchored Instruction [27, 28]. In this approach, the AR allows the inclusion of a problem and the means to solve it in a realistic context, providing the person with a way to solve the aforementioned problem. The game was developed in brazilian Portuguese, being part of the Museum of Biology of University of Brasília, Brazil, permanent exhibition.

2   Skull Hunt: The Game

2.1   Game Design

The development of Skull Hunt, a mobile video game aimed at educating players about the animals of the Brazilian Cerrado biome (savanna region), serves as an excellent example of the potential of combining scientific communication and programming. The project was designed to create an interactive and technologically-enhanced educational tool that could effectively convey scientific knowledge to players. The game's question-and-answer format makes sure that the experience and interface are important. To overcome limitations in animation, different screens and icons were animated, and techniques such as smear frames, follow-through, and particle effects [29] were used to enhance the playful nature of the game, as shown in Fig. 1.

To achieve this, a systematic methodology was adopted that encompassed both the principles of scientific communication and programming. Firstly, a thorough review of the scientific literature was conducted to gain a comprehensive understanding of the subject matter and to identify the key concepts that needed to be communicated through the game (Fig. 2). The design team focused on creating an intuitive and user-friendly interface that provides players with easy access and understanding of the information presented.

A detailed Game Design Document was created that outlined the overall structure and gameplay of the game. This document provided a clear roadmap for the development process, including the visual design and user experience, the game mechanics and features, and the use of AR technology.

The visual communication aspect of the game was crucial in helping players understand and contextualize the knowledge presented [30], and great care was taken to create an immersive and engaging atmosphere [31]. The choice of pixel art, contrasting color palettes, and animations helped to create a visually appealing and cohesive gaming experience [32] (Figs. 4 and 5). The use of QR codes in the real world and a virtual world within the game allowed players to switch between two worlds, with their objective being to answer all of the questions scattered throughout the Museum of Biology (MBio/UnB) while also being able to see vertebrate skulls and take notes. This allows the creation of dynamic gameplay that stimulates curiosity and provides knowledge with each completed stage.

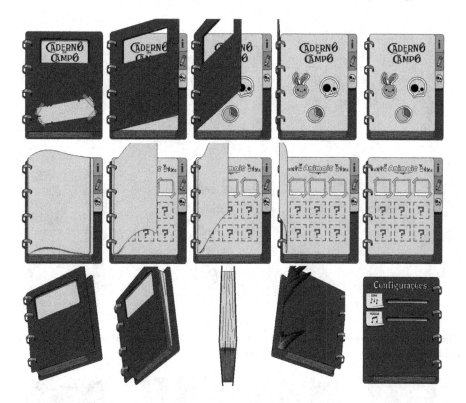

Fig. 1. Moviment of the players "field notebook" in the configuration screen and achievements.

2.2 Gameplay

The Skull Hunt player's objective is to collect information in their *Field notebook* regarding animals from the Brazilian Cerrado biome (Figs. 1 and 3). In order to do so, the player must explore their surroundings (in this case, the Museum of Biology/UnB) and find QR codes scattered throughout the area. Using the mobile camera (Fig. 7) the QR codes allow the visualization and interaction with vertebrates' skulls, revealed in augmented reality (Fig. 6). From recognizing the skull and, therefore, to which vertebrate group the animal belongs, the player can then answer multiple-choice questions related to the anatomy, biology, and physiology of the observed object (Fig. 10). Right answers help the player to acquire *Conservation Footprints*, the in-game currency, which can be used to unlock information regarding different animals in their field notebook. Thus, Skull Hunt has a *treasure hunt* dynamics, where the player begins as a *Nature lover* and, as they answer the questions and acquire the Conservation Footprints, progressively level up until becoming a *Naturalist explorer*.

As the player progresses through the game, the questions become more challenging, requiring a greater understanding of the subject matter. At this point,

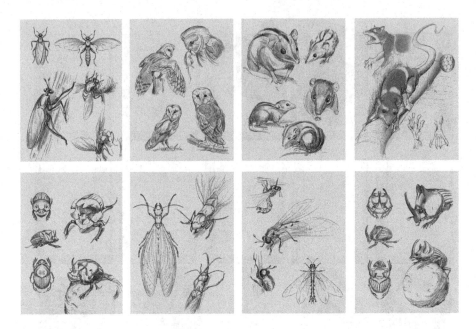

Fig. 2. Study images made from photographs taken in the field or laboratory of selected animals that represent the Cerrado fauna.

Fig. 3. Final representation of the animals for the player's field notebook.

the player can choose to exchange their *Conservation Footprints* for clues (Fig. 8, or they can take a chance and guess, which risks losing those points. This introduces an element of risk and reward, adding to the overall excitement of the game. Nevertheless, if giving a wrong answer on the first try, the player can try again, but the reward will be fewer *Conservation Footprints*. The game statistics, with the player's count of right and wrong answers (Fig. 9) can be accessed on the home screen. If the game is played by a student's class, the professor

Fig. 4. Studies for the user interface.

Fig. 5. Final representation of the user interface and representing the animation button of the AR access.

can get the scores of their students in the *Dashboard* (see next section) to work the syllabus more assertively, according to their performance. The experience is considered complete when the player has acquired all of the animals in their field notebook, thus becoming a successful *Naturalist explorer.*

The gameplay loop of the game is comprised of a series of repeated actions. The player is presented with a challenge, given an empty field notebook, and must complete it by searching for QR codes and answering questions. Correct answers will earn them conservation footprints, which they can exchange for animals' information and pictures to add to their field notebook. This repetitive loop motivates the player to continue exploring the museum and contributes to the game's overarching goal of promoting environmental awareness.

The game is designed to be user-friendly and intuitive, with a tutorial that guides the player through the initial stages. The user interface is playful and engaging, with integrated menus featuring motifs of objects commonly found in a naturalist's kit. The interface is designed to be immersive, featuring colors and shapes that invite exploration, and objects that are similar to those found in the real world.

3 Dashboard

In order to make Skull Hunt not a static game, especially with regard to the game's database, we implemented a dashboard that has two main objectives:

Fig. 6. Augmented Reality using AR Foundation. The bottom right button goes to the Question screen

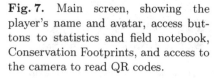

Fig. 7. Main screen, showing the player's name and avatar, access buttons to statistics and field notebook, Conservation Footprints, and access to the camera to read QR codes.

Fig. 8. Hint screen corresponding to a clue to the current question.

(1) to manage data related to visits to the museum, that is, schools, classes, and students who will interact with the game during the visit; (2) and allow the edition of the game questions.

The first contact with the *Dashboard* page is authentication (Fig. 11), where the registered user can access the system. The *Dashboard* is intended to be used by school teachers, where they will be able to record classes and students, and soon after completing the dynamics with the game, they will be able to obtain analysis data. Registering users is no longer a task for the Museum of Biology, and therefore gives autonomy to each school to manage its group of visiting students. However, access permissions to *Dashboard* must be previously authorized by the Museum.

After authentication, the initial screen is displayed, as shown in Fig. 12. It has a navigation menu on the left side of the screen through which you can access the options for managing registered schools, visits, and game questions. It also shows at the top of the screen the sum of data, such as schools, students, visits, and questions, recorded in the database.

Fig. 9. User statistics screen with the player's count of right and wrong answers.

Fig. 10. Question screen. The question is presented at the top, with five possible answers. At the bottom left, there is a *skull* button, where the player can return to the camera. The middle button gives access to a clue to answer the question. The bottom right display shows the *Conservation Footprints* available.

3.1   Schools and Visits

In the first option of the menu, the user will be able to visualize a list of the schools that are in the database (Fig. 13). Still, on this screen, is possible to register new schools and update the list by editing or removing a specific school through the "Actions" button. Registering and editing a school is done through a modal window.

The user can select a school and view its registered data, as well as its added classes. At this point, adding, editing or removing classes is possible, as well as

Fig. 11. Authentication Screen.

Fig. 12. Dashboard home screen.

adding, editing, and removing students. After registering, the school can schedule a visit, including the date, time and the total number of students (Figs. 13 and 14).

3.2 Question Editor

A question editor was developed to make Skull Hunt a dynamic game where we can create, edit, and remove questions. Figure 15 shows a list of questions

Fig. 13. List of registered schools.

Fig. 14. List of scheduled visits.

in the editor, as an example. Each question was categorized by skull type (fish, amphibian, serpent, etc.) and difficulty (easy, medium, and hard). In addition, the editor allows the creation of new types of questions, and even the removal of an entire type, in case it is no longer needed (Fig. 16). The questions can be edited in the modal window (Fig. 17). The user must add the question at the top of the page, the type and difficulty, a clue, and the alternative answers to be shown in the game. Finally, the user must select the expected correct answer on the left.

A QR Code was issued for each skull type. The players will search through the MBio/UnB for those QR codes in the "treasure hunt" dynamic of the game Skull Hunt. The QR code lets the game connect with the questions through a

Fig. 15. List of question registered in the database.

service request. The game will identify the QR code and select a question from the apropriate category (primarly skull type, and secondarly difficulty, as the game advances), that must be answered.

4   Implementation

This section provides implementation details for the Skull Hunt game, addressing aspects related to the software architecture and technologies used.

The development of Skull Hunt was divided into two applications: (1) the first as *Backend*, using two systems, *Gateway API* and *Main API*, as web services, and (2) the second as *Frontend*, responsible for the visualization, game interface, as well as for *Dashboard*.

Backend. The *Backend* is responsible for the entire internal operation of the work, such as data storage, report processing, authentication, and registration, among others. It follows a Client-Server approach and a monolithic structure, which suits the Skull Hunt project.

The programming language C# (.NET Core[1]) was used, as it meets the project requirements and has good performance, and the native ASP.NET *framework*, developed by *Microsoft* that makes it possible to serve millions of requests per second.

Figure 18 presents an overview of the architecture and the relationships between modules with requests made to web services and to the database *PostgreSQL*[2]. All requests are made through the HTTP protocol (Hypertext Transfer Protocol).

---

[1] https://dotnet.microsoft.com.
[2] https://www.postgresql.org.

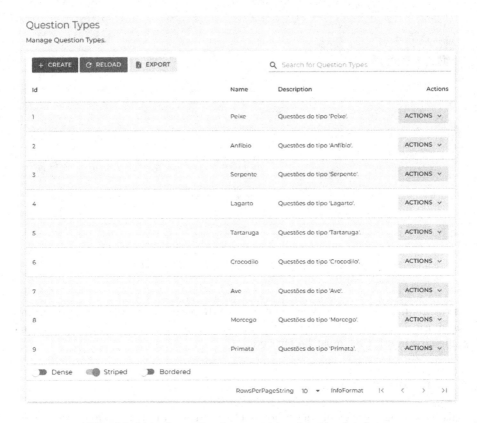

Fig. 16. List of question types registered in the database.

– **Gateway API**: service responsible for exchanging information between the game and the server. The *Gateway API* is responsible for the player's authentication and registration services, thus becoming a protection layer;
– **Main API**: main service responsible for most processing, such as registering, removing or updating questions, generating QR Codes, *uploading* 3D models, and forwarding reports of players' progress. The Main API will also be used by *Dashboard*;

Frontend. *Frontend* is responsible for enabling user interaction with the game and *Dashboard*.

– **Game**: it is responsible for implementing the Skull Hunt interface, such as authentication, registration, access to the camera to read QR Codes, rendering, manipulation of 3D objects in real-time, and all the game logic. For the implementation of this module, the cross-platform game engine *Unity 3D*[3]

---

[3] https://unity3d.com.

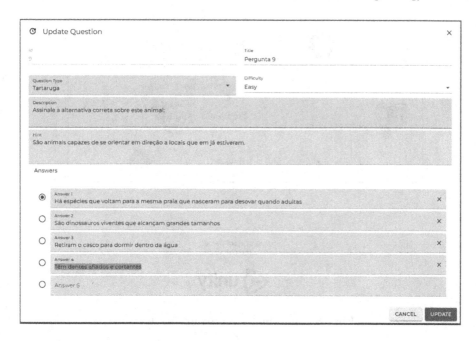

Fig. 17. *Modal* window for editing a selected question.

and *AR Foundation*[4] were used. *AR Foundation* is a specific component for use in *Unity*, and it allowed the implementation of augmented reality functionality in the game, including algorithms for object rendering in physical space and also for reading QR Codes.

– **Dashboard**: it is the system that allows administrative control, with the registration of schools and visitors that will play the game at the museum, and management of the game questions. More precisely, it creates, edits, and removes questions, controls reports, and other questions related to visits. This module rules out any need for museum managers to interact directly with the database. *Dashboard* is built using the ASP.NET *framework* in cooperation with *Blazor*[5].

---

[4] https://docs.unity3d.com/Packages/com.unity.xr.arfoundation@4.1/manual/index.html.

[5] https://dotnet.microsoft.com/apps/aspnet/web-apps/blazor.

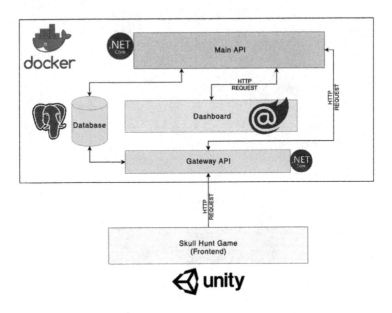

Fig. 18. Skull Hunt software architecture.

5   Conclusion

The development of Skull Hunt represents a systematic and comprehensive app-roach to combining scientific communication and programming, creating a com-pelling and engaging educational tool. The game serves as an excellent example of how technology can be used to make science accessible and fun for students of all ages. The objective of designing and developing an AR educational game was to add more diverse teaching strategies to topics that can be arid and difficult for several students. The Skull Hunt game aims to engage students and teachers in a cooperative and motivated environment.

A pilot test, with three players, was made to test the game application. How-ever, future studies will test the game application in the MBio environment, with students and visitors. For example, it would be interesting to establish whether playing Skull Hunt helps in the meaningful learning of vertebrate zoology and anatomy, and how the backlog information helped the teachers back in school. Also, we intend to assess if the game is a powerful tool to bring environmental awareness and test it in another environment, such as schools or parks, to see if the engagement will be higher or lower.

References

1. Fialho, W.C.G: As dificuldades de aprendizagem encontradas por alunos no ensino de biologia. Praxia, vol. 1, no. 1, pp. 53–70 (2013)
2. Bahar, M.: Students' learning difficulties in biology: reasons and solutions. Gazi Üniversitesi Kastamonu Eğitim Dergisi (2002)

3. Cunha, N.: Brinquedo, desafio e descoberta. FAE, Rio de Janeiro (1988)
4. Aivelo, T,; Uitto, A.: Digital gaming for evolutionary biology learning: the case study of parasite race, an augmented reality location-based game. LUMAT: Int. J. Math Sci. Technol. Educ. **4**(1), 1–26 (2016)
5. Gomes, R.R.; Friedrich, M.: A Contribuição dos jogos didáticos na aprendizagem de conteúdos de Ciências e Biologia. In: EREBIO,1, Rio de Janeiro, Rio de Janeiro, pp. 389–92 (2001)
6. Prensky, M.: Aprendizagem baseada em jogos digitais. Editora Senac São Paulo, São Paulo (2012)
7. Ramos, D.K.: Jogos cognitivos eletrônicos: contribuições á aprendizagem no contexto escolar. Ciências & Cognição **18**(1), 19–32 (2013)
8. Kapp, K.M.: The gamification of learning and instruction: game-based methods and strategies for training and education. John Wiley & Sons (2012)
9. Knüppe, L.: Motivação e desmotivação: desafio para as professoras do Ensino Fundamental. Educar em revista **27**, 277–290 (2006)
10. Kirriemuir, J., McFarlane, A.: Literature Review in Games and Learning. Futurelab, Bristol (2004)
11. Kishimoto, T.M.: Jogo, brinquedo, brincadeira e a educação. Cortez, São Paulo (1996)
12. Starks, K.: Cognitive behavioral game design: a unified model for designing serious games. Front. Psychol. **5**, 28 (2014)
13. Campos, T. R.; Ramos, D.K.: O uso de jogos digitais no ensino de Ciências Naturais e Biologia: uma revisão sistemática de literatura. Revista Electrónica de Enseñanza de las Ciencias, vol. 19, no. 2, pp. 450–473 (2020)
14. Buckingham, D.: Beyond technology - children's learning in the age of digital culture. Polity Press, Cambridge, UK (2007)
15. Abdusselam, M.S., Güntepe, E.T.: Augmented reality: educational resources. In: Reyes Ruiz, G., Hernández, M. (eds.) Augmented Reality for Enhanced Learning Environments, pp. 1–24 (2018)
16. Winn, W.; Windschitl, M.; Fruland, R.; Lee, Y.: When does immersion in a virtual environment help students construct understanding. In: Proceedings of International Conference of the Learning Sciences, pp. 497–503 (2002)
17. Zagoranski S., Divjak S.: Use of augmented reality in education. EUROCON Comput. Tool IEEE Reg. **8**(2), 339–342 (2013). https://doi.org/10.1109/EURCON.2003.1248213
18. Hanson, K., Shelton, B.E.: Design and development of virtual reality: analysis of challenges faced by educators. J. Educ. Technol. Soc. **11**(1), 118–131 (2008)
19. Abdüsselam, M.S.: Teachers' and students' views on using augmented reality environments in physics education: 11th grade magnetism topic example. Pegem J. Educ. Instruct. **4**(1), 59–74 (2014)
20. da Silva, A.R.L., et al.: Gamificação na educação. Pimenta Cultura (2014)
21. Silva, A.S.: Uso de Recurso Educacional com Mídias Interativas e Integradas on-Line em Ensino e Aprendizagem. Dissertação (Mestrado) -Universidade Federal de Itajubá (2013)
22. Studart, N.: A gamificação como design instrucional. Revista Brasileira de Ensino de Física 44 (2021)
23. Dorward, L.J., Mittermeier, J.C., Sandbrook, C., Spooner, F.: Pokémon Go: Benefits, costs, and lessons for the conservation movement. Conserv. Lett. **10**(1), 160–165 (2017)

24. Gomes, C.R.P., Silva, F.A.R.: O "Mistério no Zoo": um jogo para o ensino de zoologia de vertebrados no ensino fundamental II. Revista da SBEnBio **9**, 202–2011 (2016)
25. Krasilchik, M.: Prática de ensino de biologia, 4th edn. Edusp, São Paulo, SP (2004)
26. Oliveira, D.B.G., et al. O Ensino de Zoologia numa perspectiva evolutiva: análise de uma ação educativa desenvolvida com uma turma de Ensino Fundamental. In: Encontro Nacional de Pesquisadores em Educação de Ciência. Campinas (2008)
27. Cognition and Technology Group at Vanderbilt: Anchored instruction and its relationship to situated cognition. Educ. Res. **19**, 2–10 (1990)
28. Cognition and Technology Group at Vanderbilt: looking at technology in context: a framework for understanding technology and educational research. In: Berliner, D.C., Calfee, R.C. (eds.). Handbook of Educational Psychology, pp. 807–840. New York: Macmillan (1996)
29. Williams, R.: The animator's survival kit: a manual of methods, principles and formulas for classical, computer, games, stop motion and internet animators. Macmillan (2012)
30. Lotman, J.M.: Universe of the mind: a semiotic theory of culture. Indiana University Press (2000)
31. Stanchfield, W.: Drawn to Life: 20 Golden Years of Disney Master Classes Volume 1: The Walt Stanchfield Lectures. Taylor & Francis (2013)
32. Gurney, J.: Color and light: a guide for the realist painter. Andrews McMeel Publishing (2010)

Didactical Design Goes Rogue? Children's Playful Explorations While Engaged in Scaffolded Coding Activities Supported by Robots

Jeanette Sjoberg[1]([⊠]) [iD] and Eva Brooks[2] [iD]

[1] Halmstad University, Kristian IV:S Väg 3, 30118 Halmstad, Sweden
Jeanette.sjoberg@hh.se
[2] Aalborg University, Kroghstræde 3, 9220 Aalborg, Denmark
eb@ikl.aau.dk

Abstract. Current society is characterized by rapid development and change, with technology being at the forefront in shaping the future. To accommodate this, it is crucial to equip the next generation with the critical skills and knowledge necessary to navigate in such a world. One way to achieve this is through the introduction and implementation of scaffolded coding activities supported by robots in primary education. In this paper we investigate how coding activities that include educational robots can be used in an educational setting with a class of Danish primary school children, aged 7–8 years old. The study draws from a socio-cultural approach to children's learning and development, elaborating on the concepts of playfulness as a mediated action, the zone of proximal development, and scaffolding. The research questions posed in the study are: (1) How do primary school children adopt didactical instructions in a coding workshop supported by robots? (2) What kind of interactions unfold while children are engaged in coding activities supported by robots? The unit of analysis is children's coding activities during an experimental coding-workshop supported by different robots carried out in a laboratory setting at a Danish university. The robots used in the workshop were Beebot/Bluebot, Dash and Ozobot. The results imply that scaffolding strategies such as task instructions and the design of the learning environment need to be closely connected and carefully considered to engage children in meaningful ways.

Keywords: Coding activities · Didactical design · Educational robots · Exploration · Playfulness · Primary school children · Scaffolding

1 Introduction

The world today is characterized by rapid development and change, with technology being at the forefront in shaping the future. The ongoing digitization of society has also meant a change in the educational sector in various ways. To accommodate this, it is crucial to equip the next generation with the critical skills and knowledge necessary to

X. Fang (Ed.): HCII 2023, LNCS 14047, pp. 61–80, 2023.
https://doi.org/10.1007/978-3-031-35979-8_5

navigate in such a society. Among other things, digital technology and different digital tools have been implemented in schools and subjects such as programming and computational thinking have been inserted into curriculums globally [e.g., 1–3]. Furthermore, programming is often regarded as a procedural skill by those advocating digital inclusion in the curriculum, and that it, as such, possesses the ability to develop children's digital competence and computational thinking [4]. However, even though many primary schools are obliged to work with programming according to the curricula, the knowledge of how to integrate programming and coding activities pedagogically and in a meaningful way in early education is still scarce [5, 6]. An increasingly more common way to integrate programming and coding activities in the early years of primary school is with the support of various robots [5, 7, 8]. Additionally, previous research has pointed out that there are great benefits of using children's creativity [9] and playfulness [10] working with robots in school settings. In such activities children are provided with opportunities to engage in playful explorations while learning a fundamental understanding of coding. Through playful exploration with educational robots, children can develop basic coding skills as well as computational thinking, hence the robots facilitate learning [e.g., 7, 8].

On that note, we aim to contribute to the knowledge in this area by investigating how scaffolded coding activities that include educational robots can be used in an educational setting with primary school children. The present study was conducted through an explorative workshop with primary school children, and the term 'scaffolding' refers here to the didactic design of the activities in the workshop which includes a conscious framework for how the activities can be carried out. The research questions posed in the study are: (1) How do primary school children adopt didactical instructions in a coding workshop supported by robots? (2) What kind of interactions unfold while children are engaged in coding activities supported by robots? In the present paper, we will present the outcomes of the study and discuss them in relation to how primary school children's playful experiences with educational robots in coding activities unfolds by exploration as a result of scaffolded didactical design. In addition, we will elaborate on the results of the study and their implications for the field.

The remainder of this paper is organized as follows: related work is presented in Sect. 2, and an overview of the theoretical starting points is presented in Sect. 3. Research methodology is presented in Sect. 4 and the result of the study is presented in Sect. 5. Discussion and conclusions are in Sect. 6.

2   Related Work

2.1   Educational Robots

One way to achieve knowledge about coding in the early years of education is through the introduction and implementation of coding activities supported by robots in primary education [11]. With the support of robots, children can visualize their code in action and receive instant feedback, making the learning process both engaging and interactive [12]. Several studies have pointed out that robots can help enhance the learning process in educational settings [12, 13], particularly in the sense that the use of educational robots enables students to acquire knowledge in Science, Technology, Engineering, and Mathematics (STEM) subjects, which is becoming increasingly important as technology advances [13, 14]. In a systematic review of empirical studies on teaching and learning robotics content knowledge in K-12 education, a comprehensive analysis of 22 research papers were conducted to, among other things, investigate the instructional implications for teaching. The results indicated that instructional suggestions can be clustered into four themes: open environment, targeted design, appropriate pedagogy and timely support [13]. Furthermore, the results showed that studies using an experimental and/or explorative approach were scarce.

Something that is often highlighted as positive when it comes to the use of robots in early education is that it is usually characterized by so-called hands-on learning: the concrete experience with the robot contributes to developing a deeper understanding of complex concepts and skills [e.g., 11, 12]. This kind of learning is often more engaging and helps to increase students' motivation to develop different skills (especially in relation to STEM subjects), such as critical thinking, collaboration and problem solving [e.g., 14]. Research shows that these components are important prerequisites when it comes to working with coding in school [e.g., 11]. The challenges that usually are lifted when it comes to the use of robots in education often relates to the following aspects: technical difficulties (both in terms of software and hardware); that there is a lack of sufficient pedagogical material (which may mean that teachers sometimes need to develop this themselves); inequality in terms of different schools access to resources and opportunities; and teachers competence: most often teachers may need training on how to use robots in their teaching effectively. Furthermore, they may also need support in developing activities and lessons where robots can be integrated [e.g., 12].

2.2 Coding Activities

The concept of coding can be defined as a process of creating instructions for a machine or computer to carry out specific tasks [11]. Basically, coding connotes that humans leverage the vast processing power and data storage capabilities of computers to perform a wide variety of tasks by providing them with specific instructions in a language understandable to them. These instructions are written in a programming language, which is a syntax for expressing algorithms in a form that can be executed by a computer. The resulting program can be used to automate tasks, solve problems, process data, and much more. Hence, the end result of coding can range from simple scripts that automate repetitive tasks, to complex applications that can transform industries and the way people live and work [e.g., 15]. Coding in primary school can take on various forms and involve several different approaches, depending on the age and ability of the students [e.g., 1, 16]. A few examples of what coding activities in primary school might look like would be block coding, Scratch and robotics. Block coding is a visual method of coding where programs are created by blocks of code being dragged and dropped. Scratch is a block-based programming language developed particularly for the usage of children and young people to create interactive stories, simulations, games and animations.

As previously mentioned, robotics has lately been introduced in primary education to make coding fun and engaging with the support of robots while at the same time teaching fundamental 21st century skills, such as collaboration and problem-solving [e.g., 1, 11, 15, 17]. Research has shown that coding activities in primary school enhances children's ability to stay focused on a task when engaged with challenging yet stimulating problem-solving exploration [15–17]. This approach to teaching and learning not only enhances children's motivation, but also strengthens their creativity and critical thinking abilities [17]. While they are devoted to activities such as designing and building programs, children learn to think logically and systematically which implies that coding helps to develop critical thinking and problem-solving skills [e.g., 1, 18]. In addition, as they work with arising challenges in coding activities, they also learn the importance of perseverance and collaboration in order to solve problems [18, 19]. In summary, through coding activities supported by robots, children can be empowered and equipped with the confidence and competencies required to succeed in a technology-driven society.

3 Theory

The study draws from a socio-cultural approach to children's learning and development, using theoretical grounds from, among others, Wertsch [20], Vygotsky [21], and Bruner [22], elaboration on the concepts of playfulness as a mediated action, the zone of proximal development, and scaffolding.

3.1 Playfulness and Exploration

When children are engaged with coding activities, they explore and discover different strategies and combinations of solutions to create a desired code. This links to the concept of mediated action [20] in the way human actions are mediated through the use of tools within social practices. Wertsch asks the question of "how the introduction of novel cultural tools transforms the action" [20, p. 42]. In this regard, it is relevant to infer that digital technology is a critical tool to take into consideration having cultural as well as social implications. Digital technology thus potentially can transform the ways humans learn, create meaning, communicate, and interact. This also brings attention to the importance of introducing digital technology in schools by including considerations of broader social aspects when it comes to how children use such technology outside of schools [23]. Taking this into account, designing for children's learning and interaction with digital technology in school settings requires didactic designs that are relevant to the children. To fully understand children's actions and operations when interacting with digital technology, there is a need to grasp the wider contextual dimensions of school-based teaching and learning. There exists a danger to narrow the educational use of digital technology to certain skills, in particular related to programming and computational thinking skills [23].

Introducing digital technology in educational settings put emphasis on changing the ethos of only considering a skill-oriented didactic approach but rather contemplate children's exploration, discovery, and playful ways of learning. In this way, the child will be put in the position of leader of her/his own learning. Playfulness has embedded explorative qualities and thus a potential to find new ways of learning and approaching challenges. Playfulness can emerge by enhancing children's opportunities to engage actively in teaching and learning activities [24, 25]. In this way, playfulness goes along with learning, promoting children to think flexible, taking risks with ideas and inter-actions allowing novel thoughts to emerge [26]. Getzels and Jackson [27] underline contextual matters when it comes to designing for playfulness. This is also acknowl-edged in design-based studies, where playfulness is related to creative outcomes [28]. Research has shown a growing interest in intervention to promote playfulness in edu-cational settings, however more research is needed to identify long-term implications [29]. In this paper, our interest is to identify the ways playfulness can be scaffolded to create opportunities for children to learn based on exploration. The issue of scaffolding will be further elaborated in the below section.

3.2 Scaffolding

Vygotsky [30] developed ideas about the impact of social interactions between adults and children to contribute to children's individual learning and development. He also came up with the concept of the Zone of Proximal Development (ZPD) as a way of considering children's progression in learning. Vygotsky's main point of direction was to define children's individual learning and development as taking place in interaction with others and not as a solitary action, for example, "Learning awakens a variety of internal developmental processes that are able to operate only when the child is interacting with people in his environment and in cooperation with his peers" [21, p. 90]. He underscored that qualitative transformation is a "collective form of 'working together'" [31, p. 202]. ZPD can in this way be understood as an active and socially created process rather than a spatio-temporal structure; an activity creating the zone (environment) creating learning-leading development [32]. Here, learning is scaffolded in a way that children can shape and reshape their actions and relationships, as well as the material and tools they have at hand. This calls for sensitive didactic designs and as sensitive teachers.

Bruner's [22] theory of scaffolding was influenced by Vygotsky's theory of ZPD, where he emphasized children's learning as emerging from more knowledgeable others [33]. Researchers such as Wood et al. [33] and Rogoff and Gardner [34] have merely defined ZPD as an instructional tool, where the more knowledgeable others provide just enough support for the less knowledgeable child. Other researchers have moved away from this instrumental application of ZPD, considering it as a creative and improvi-sational activity [35]. This perspective deviates from an understanding of learning as occurring *in* the ZPD towards an active creation *of* the ZPD [36]. Scaffolding in edu-cational settings, then, becomes an action of providing children space where they can actively engage with each other and with the environment. If we can view scaffolding and ZPD as this kind of collaborative activity and process, it is possible to change the view on teaching. The focus, then, is directed towards the relationship between what is to be learned and the creation of an environment fostering active learning and engaging children and teachers in playful endeavours.

4   Methodology

In the present study we investigate a class of first grade Danish primary school children's actions/interactions in an experimental coding-workshop supported by different robots. The present study is an explorative study [37]. The workshop was carried out in a laboratory setting at a Danish university during half a day. The focus was on the children's playful experiences with educational robots in coding activities by exploration as a result of scaffolded didactical design. Here, scaffolding refers to the didactic design of the activities in the workshop which includes a framework for how the activities can be carried out, with a particular focus on collaboration and problem-solving.

An overview of the research methodology is presented in this section: Sect. 4.1 introduces the participants in the study; Sect. 4.2 presents the material which includes the different educational robots used in the study; Sect. 4.3 describes the procedure of the workshop including the different workstations; Sect. 4.4 describes how data have been collected and organized; Sect. 4.5 addresses ethical concerns and issues and Sect. 4.6 presents the analytical approach used in the study.

4.1   Participants

A class of first graders from a Danish primary school, aged 7–8 years old, participated in the study: 8 boys and 9 girls, a total of 17 children. In addition, 3 teachers (1 male, 2 females) accompanied the school children. The children were divided by their teachers into six working groups with 3–4 children per group. During the workshop, the children worked in their groups at the different workstations while their teachers moved between the groups. There was also one researcher or research assistant stationed at each workstation to offer assistance if needed.

4.2   Material

The material used in the coding workshop consisted of different educational robots, scaffolding material (i.e., informative written or visual material about how to operate the robot) and some props (e.g., coloring markers). The educational robots used for coding activities in this workshop were Beebot/Bluebot, Ozobot and Dash. These robots were chosen on the basis of their different ways of approaching coding (coding by pressing buttons with arrows, coding by drawing different color combinations, and coding by using an operating system, e.g., iPad, or Android phone, compatible with apps developed for the specific robot).

Bluebot/Beebot (see Fig. 1) is a simple, user-friendly educational coding robot designed primarily for classroom use (and other educational settings) to introduce children to some of the basic concepts of coding, such as sequencing and directions. The robot has a physical design of a small bug, equipped with sensors and features that allow it to respond to its environment, such as sound, light and color. It can be programmed to move in different directions and distances using a set of buttons or keys on its back that control its movement. This design allows the children to build sequences of actions that the robot will perform and, furthermore, promotes collaboration and problem-solving.

Fig. 1. Bluebot/Beebot

Ozobot (Fig. 2) is an easy-to-use, small, and smart educational robot designed to teach the basics of coding in an interactive and engaging way for young children. Using color combinations, Ozobot can be programmed to follow specific paths and change speeds, among other things. It uses sensors to follow lines and read color codes made by markers, which provides children with an opportunity to be creative while engaged in playful exploration using color combinations to move the robot from one spot to another, making it a versatile tool for exploring a variety of STEM concepts.

Fig. 2. Ozobot

Dash (Fig. 3) is a programmable robot, somewhat bigger than both the Blue-bot/Beebot and the Ozobot and designed to be an interactive tool for teaching coding and computational thinking in a fun and engaging way. Dash is mainly designed for playful engagement and can be controlled using a variety of methods, including block-based coding, text-based coding, and app-based programming. Dash can be connected to a smartphone or a tablet and by the use of an app it can be maneuvered to perform different tasks (such as navigating objects, dancing, responding to voice, singing) while placed on the floor. In addition, Dash can make sounds and is equipped with lighting features.

Fig. 3. Dash

4.3 Procedure

The workshop included six workstations with three different robot assignments: two with Beebots/Bluebots (coding by buttons), two with Ozobots (coding by color markers) and two with the robot Dash (controlled by an iPad). The workshop sessions were outlined as described in Table 1 (below), starting with the introduction of the workshop in which the different workstations were described and explained along with the scaffolding material and the educational robots. This part was led by a research assistant.

In the first step of the workshop, the children were welcomed to the lab with a brief introduction of the lab, participants, the robots in the workshop and some basics about programming and coding. Next, the children were divided by their teachers into six groups with 3–4 children per group, where each group was assigned to a workstation, two groups per workstation. Each workstation had an assignment for the children to solve using the educational robots which involved coding. All groups had approximately 30 min at each workstation and to solve each robot coding assignment, which meant that all children had an opportunity to try all three workstations. There was also scaffolding material (i. e. the written and/or visual instructions) placed at each workstation for the children to look at, and there was one researcher/research assistant at each workstation to guide the children if needed. In the final step of the workshop, there was a joint

Table 1. Overview of workshop sessions and timetable.

Time	Activities undertaken
09:30–09:40	Welcome: presentation of participants
09:40–09:50	Introduction: robots and workstations
09:50–10:20	First workstation (exploratory activity)
10:20–10:35	Short break with refreshments (fruit/water)
10:35–11:05	Second workstation (exploratory activity)
11:05–11:35	Third workstation (exploratory activity)
11:35–12:00	Reflective discussion and evaluation

discussion led by the researchers where the children were asked pre-prepared questions related to the robot assignments and where they got to reflect on their experiences.

The three workstations (times two) were focusing on different coding assignments. The intention was to identify how the children approached the different ways of coding and the instructions given at each of the workstations. In addition, the ambition was to discern how this potentially influenced the kinds of interactions and engagement that developed depending on the different instructions and ways of coding. At Workstation 1, several Bluebots were laid out on a table along with written and visual instructions on how to operate them. In the middle of the table a sheet of cardboard was placed that was divided into a drawn grid of squares, with a drawn school in one corner (see Fig. 4). The task at this station was to code the Bluebot so that it moved from the square it was standing on to the square with the school on in one programmed sequence. This could be made more or less difficult, i.e., depending on if they chose to code the robot to move in a straight line or to take different turns.

At workstation 2, the assignment was to draw a pathway on a paper for the Ozobot to follow. Instructions on how to code with the Ozobot as well as white sheets of paper and different color markers were laid out on the table (see Fig. 5). The children had access to multiple Ozobots. One of the characteristics of this robot is that it changes color depending on the color with which the track was drawn, which means that even this task could be carried out in a more or less challenging way, i.e., how they chose to alter their coloring codes.

Fig. 4. Workstation 1: coding with Bluebot.

Fig. 5. Workstation 2: coding with Ozobot.

Workstation 3 was situated on the floor. Using masking tape, a maze-like path had been created directly on the floor by the researchers (see Fig. 6). The mission at this station consisted of using an iPad and an app to control Dash to move through the path to a final destination (marked with an "x"). At this workstation, the children only had access to two robots, which meant that they had to take turns in using the robot.

Fig. 6. Workstation 3: coding with Dash.

4.4 Data Collection

Each workstation was equipped with a fixed video camera which recorded the group work during the workshop. The ability to review video recordings affords us the opportunity to observe actions and interactions in greater detail, as well as to gather minute details that we might otherwise have missed [37, 38]. Furthermore, the researchers used mobile phones and Ipads to record additional material. Each video recording from the fixed video cameras was approximately 1 h and 40 min long. The additional recordings from the mobile devices consisted of 25 recordings of between 10 s and 2 min long. Overall recorded data consists of approximately 7 h of recordings (since one of the fixed cameras did not work), as well as the researchers field notes from classroom observations.

4.5 Ethical Considerations

Ethical principles for research practice have been applied in the study [39]. Prior to the workshop, teachers as well as parents were informed about the study in writing and the parents had agreed to let their child participate by signing informed consent forms which included information about the study, data collection, anonymity, etc. Three parents were opposed to their children being filmed. The teachers had told the children orally about the study before the workshop, and at the beginning of the workshop, in the welcome part, the research assistant informed the children about the study in more detail. She also informed them that their participation was voluntary and that they could choose to stop participating at any time without questions asked. She then handed out a form for the children to fill out regarding their participation. All children chose to participate, even the children whose parents had opposed their children being filmed. The three children whose parents had not agreed to them being filmed were put together in the same group and this group was not filmed.

4.6 Analysis

All workstations were video recorded during the workshop and afterwards analyzed by means of thematic analysis [40, 41]. The different analytical steps performed in thematic analysis are described in Table 2 below.

Table 2. Overview of steps in thematic analysis.

Steps	Description
Familiarizing	Transcription of data
Initial codes	Arranging data relevant to codes
Searching for themes	Organizing codes into themes
Reviewing themes	Trial of themes and selected excerpts
Defining themes	Generating clear definitions
Finalizing analysis	Finalizing the analysis of selected excerpts

In accordance with the first step of thematic analysis [49], the video recordings were transcribed and then read and reread to get familiar with the data. In the second step, data was systematically arranged into codes out of recurring patterns in the data in relation to the research questions. This step was conducted independently by the researchers. In the next step, the individual open coding conducted by the researchers was compared to get consensus and then organized into potential themes. These were then in turn discussed thoroughly in order to attain the same comprehension and representative excerpts were selected. In the final steps the themes were given clear definitions to reflect the content and the excerpts were finalized. The analysis resulted in two defined themes.

5 Results

The findings illustrate conditions to introduce coding in primary education by support of educational robots as meaningful parts of play and learning. The thematic analysis of the children's participation in the coding workshop resulted in two recurring themes: *Children's engagement/disengagement* and *Children's playful explorations* (see Table 3). The first theme concerning engagement/disengagement were in direct relation to the assignment at hand and to solve it (i.e., the coding with the specific robot at the separate workstations). The second theme concerning playful explorations was connected to the characteristics of the different robots and what they could actually do.

Table 3. Overview of themes and coding categories.

Themes	Coding categories
Children's engagement/disengagement	a. In relation to solving the task b. In relation to task instructions
Children's playful explorations	a. In relation to characteristics of the robot b. In relation to flexible coding strategies

5.1 Theme 1: Children's Engagement/Disengagement

During the workshop, the children showed both engagement and disengagement in relation to the various coding tasks. This was expressed in different ways. In terms of engagement to solving the task, this was shown by the children paying attention to the coding, that they collaborated with each other to solve the coding task, or that they asked an adult (researcher or teacher) for help to solve the task with the coding activity. A clear example of when the children showed engagement to solving the task was at the Ozobot station (see Fig. 7), where the children concentratedly coded for a long time and on several occasions used more sheets of paper to create different coding paths.

Fig. 7. Coding with Ozobot.

The children show interest and commitment to learning the coding features of the Ozobot by trying out different ways when constructing the coding paths, as is shown in excerpt 1.

Excerpt 1

A boy sits at workstation 2 and codes a path for Ozobot on a piece of white paper. He uses different colors of sharpies when coding and then checks how and if Ozobot follows the different colored lines. This procedure is repeated over and over, seemingly tireless.

In this excerpt, the boy is showing engagement to solve the task by continuous coding. He tests his coding periodically to see if it works and when he sees that it does, he continues to code, devoted to the task.

Another example of children's engagement in solving the task is from the Bluebot station. Here, all the children were familiar with the robot and its qualities which meant that they all were more or less confident to use it, which also means that they can use their prior knowledge to make the task more challenging.

Excerpt 2

A girl sits by the table and codes a Bluebot. First, she makes a pretty easy code, making the robot move one square to the side and then the rest of the squares straight to the school. Then she starts over, but this time she counts by pointing her finger at the different squares in a more complex pattern and makes a calculation of how many times she needs to press the buttons on the Bluebot. It nearly makes it but lands on the wrong square. She starts over and tries again until she gets it right.

In excerpt 2 the girl shows commitment to the task as well as expanding the task in order to make the coding more engaging. Just as in the previous example, she repeatedly tests her coding to see if it is correct and then continues to code attentively. Overall, these two examples (excerpt 1 and 2) show how the children's engagement to solving the task was expressed during the workshop.

Disengagement, on the other hand, was shown by the children either not devoting themselves to the task at all or that they first tried to solve the task and then quickly switched to doing something else. This in turn had either to do with them solving the task quickly, i.e., it was too easy, or that they did not manage to solve the task, i.e. it was too difficult. A clear example of this was at the Dash station, where trying to manoeuvre the robot in the narrow track proved to be a challenge for many of the participants. When it turned out to be a difficult task, several of the children quickly switched to doing other things with the robot, such as driving it off the track or spinning it around.

Excerpt 3

Two girls are sitting on the floor. One of the girls controls Dash through an iPad and the other girl is half-lying next to them, focusing on the robot. Initially, they have struggled to get Dash to follow the track, but have given up and are now off track. The girl in control of the iPad tries to make Dash go in a certain direction which doesn't work, the robot goes and spins in the opposite direction. The other girl helps by moving Dash back to the starting point repeatedly. She suggests to the girl with the iPad to keep trying to make different commands to try to get Dash to move in the way they want.

In this excerpt, the children are indeed showing engagement towards coding with the robot (Dash), but disengagement in solving the task due to the task being too difficult. Instead of continuing to solve the task, they engage in another activity.

Furthermore, and in relation to disengagement towards solving the task, some of the children at the Dash station did not engage with the robot at all. This can of course be linked to the fact that at this workstation there were only one robot to use and not one each as there were at the other stations. The task was presented as something that could be solved together and through collaboration and some children were helping each other even if they were not the ones holding the iPad (and thus "controlled" Dash), while others did not get involved at all but did other things, e.g., checked out what was going on at the other workstations or investigated the surroundings and other objects in the lab. Another explanation to why some of the children did not engage with Dash at all can be that the task was perceived as too difficult. The opposite can be related to the

Bluebot station, where some of the children also ignored the task altogether and engaged in other activities instead. In this case an explanation can be that all the children were familiar with the Bluebot from before and perceived the task to be too easy and thus not interesting.

5.2 Theme 2: Children's Playful Explorations

The second theme is connected to playful explorations in relation to exploring the specific characteristics of the different robots, i.e., what else they can do besides the obvious (coding related to the task). One example of how the children's playful exploration was expressed during the workshop is from the Bluebot station (see Fig. 8).

Fig. 8. Coding with Bluebot.

As stated before, all the children were familiar with this educational robot prior to the workshop and they knew how to make the robot move, which meant that they quickly solved the task at the workstation, in much less time than was allotted. This in turn meant that they began to explore the robot's properties and coded it to move in other paths and patterns than the task specified, for example backwards and off the path.

Excerpt 4

Two boys and a girl are sitting at the table at one of the Bluebot stations. One boy repeatedly presses the arrows on the robot's back. The Bluebot moves backwards, outside the cardboard, and almost falls over the edge of the table. The boy laughs. The other boy points out that he is doing it wrong. The first boy takes no notice of him and repeats the same thing again, this time the Bluebot falls off the table but is caught by the boy. Both boys laugh.

This excerpt shows how the boy playfully explores how to use the coding of the Bluebot in an alternative way, not with the goal of solving the task but for the exploration itself. Another example of the playful explorations is expressed below (excerpt 5).

Excerpt 5

Three boys are sitting at the table at one of the Bluebot stations. They have each lined up a Bluebot on a line next to each other and they count down ("one, two, three") before then coding their respective robots by pressing (fast) the different arrows on their backs. The act is reminiscent of a racing competition. As the Bluebots move in different directions, the boys have fun when the robots collide and bump into each other.

Excerpt 5 demonstrates that the children find a completely new area of use for the coding of the Bluebots. Not knowing how the others are supposed to code their robots, they conduct a kind of competition that resembles a mix of rock paper scissors and a race and laugh at the result together. A similar example of playful exploration can be obtained from the Ozobot station (excerpt 6).

Excerpt 6

Three boys are sitting at a table, each color-coding with markers on a sheet of paper for an Ozobot. Two of them have begun to connect their respective paths into a common one. One of the boys leans forward and draws a line in green from the other boy's path to his. After a little while, the third boy also begins to draw his path together with the others', from the other direction. They work together on the transitions from one track to the other so that it not only fits in terms of code but also in terms of form.

In this excerpt, the children have partially deviated from the task by playfully developing it into a joint coding activity. They try out in an exploratory way to see if it is possible to do this way and move on when they notice that it works.

In summary, it is hard to distinguish the difference between disengagement towards the task and playful explorations, since they overlap. To specify, disengagement refers to situations where the children simply give up solving the task. Playful exploration, on the other hand, addresses situations where the children are challenged in solving the task and move away from the instructions to continue exploring opportunities of understanding, e.g., how the robot functions.

6   Discussion

In line with the results from Xia & Zhong [13], the open environment and timely support proved to be of importance in the present study. As for the targeted design, the children were not following the scaffolded material (i.e., the written and/or visual instructions placed at each workstation) in none of the workstations. Instead, they relied on their own ability to explore the functions of the robots or to ask the teachers or the researchers about how to do something. At Workstation 1, coding with Bluebot, all children had previous experience of having tried using Bluebot/Beebot from school. This was clearly shown in the way they approached the mission connected to the station: they used the robots with confidence and did not need to use the information material presented to be able to maneuver them.

The ways the children adopted the coding instructions were influenced by the level of difficulty of the task, which either encouraged or discouraged them to engage with the coding activity. If the task was too difficult or too easy, the children's collaboration became unfocused as the instructions did not adequately function as scaffolding tools [34]. As a consequence, children's creation of ZPD [36] became passively elusive rather than being actively constructed. This is exemplified in Excerpt 3, where two girls gave up the coding task as a result of not managing to control Dash and thus could not find any meaning of the task. The girls were unable to create what Holzman [32] has termed a learning-leading development of coding. On the contrary, when the task was challenging without being too easy or too difficult, the instructions were scaffolding the task and by this created engagement among the children. However, as such not in an instrumental way where the instructions provided just enough support, but they rather invited the children to improvise towards an active creation of the ZPD [36]. Excerpt 2 illustrates this by describing how the girl challenged herself by coding more and more complex patterns and despite failing, she continued until getting it right. In this way, the results revealed that the instructions were both functional and dysfunctional. As such, they highlight the necessary relationship between the instructions of a task and the creation of a learning environment that can engage children in meaningful tasks. When this is adequately considered, learning can be scaffolded in a way that children can create and recreate their actions and relationships, as well as the material and tools they have at hand. Scaffolding in educational settings, then, becomes an action of providing children space where they can actively engage with each other and with the environment.

The kinds of interactions that were unfolding while the children were engaged in coding activities with the robots had to do with the character of the robot. Excerpts 1 and 6 illustrate this by pointing to the ways that Ozobot's coding opportunities opened for persistence and flexibility in approaching the coding. This was evident, for example, in the way the boys explored different ideas and strategies for coding. In Excerpt 1, the boy is highly concentrated and determined in exploring the coding limitations and opportunities offered by Ozobot. He uses different colors and lines to investigate how and if the robot can follow the different colors and lines. This confirms Yousell's [26] study, which states that playfulness can promote children to think flexible, taking risks with ideas and interactions allowing novel thoughts to emerge. In Excerpt 6, three boys have been working on their respective coding tracks and start to connect their paths to one joint coding track. They are concerned about the outcome being aesthetically and functionally working, e.g., that the lines from one track to the next are properly connected so that Ozobot could move in a streamlined way from one coding chart to the next. This emphasizes that introducing coding activities benefit from including space for children's exploration and discovery. This is aligned with Alfieri et al. [24] and Bonawitz et al. [25] putting forward playfulness as embracing explorative qualities and as such offering children opportunities to find new ways of approaching challenges. Based on these outcomes, this study shows that the instructions framing the coding stations also had an open character, which offered the children opportunities to take over the task, i.e., making the task their own. Hence, the tasks became more of a playful experience than a didactic structure.

6.1 Conclusion and Implications

The study aimed to investigate how scaffolded coding activities including educational robots can be used in primary school settings. The outcomes stressed that scaffolding strategies such as task instructions and the design of the learning environment need to be closely connected and carefully considered to engage children in meaningful ways. When this is done, the results indicate that the scaffolding can support children's learning and provide space for children to actively engage with each other and with the environment. Moreover, the results reveal that even though the tasks were framed by instructions about how to perform the coding, they offer an open-endedness which assists children in taking over the task in terms of making it their own. This creates situations where a task becomes a playful experience in contrast to a didactic structure. This has implications for scaffolding strategies when designing for coding activities with educational robots, in particular regarding timely support and to carefully design instructions. On the one hand instructions should clearly frame the task and on the other hand keep them open for children to explore.

Acknowledgments. We gratefully thank all the participating children, teachers and workshop facilitators.

References

1. Papavlasopoulou, S., Giannakos, M.N., Jaccheri, L.: Exploring children's learning experience in constructionism-based coding activities through design-based research. Comput. Hum. Behav. **99**, 415–427 (2019)
2. Chevalier, M., Giang, C., Piatti, A., Mondada, F.: Fostering computational thinking through educational robotics: a model for creative computational problem solving. Int. J. STEM Educ. **7**, 39 (2020). https://doi.org/10.1186/s40594-020-00238-z
3. Brooks, E., Sjöberg, J.: Playfulness and creativity as vital features when school children develop game-based designs. Des. Learn. **14**(1), 137–150 (2022)
4. Wing, J.M.: Computational thinking. Commun. ACM **49**, 33–35 (2006)
5. Brooks, E., Sjöberg, J.: Children's programming of robots by designing Fairytales. In: Brooks, E., Dau, S., Selander, S. (eds.) Digital Learning and Collaborative Practices: Lessons from Inclusive and Empowering Participation with Emerging Technologies, pp. 158–174. Routledge, New York and London (2021)
6. Arfé, B., Vardanega, T., Montuori, C., Lavanga, M.: Coding in primary grades boosts children's executive functions. Front. Psychol. **10**, 2713 (2019)
7. Bascou, N.A., Menekse, M.: Robotics in K-12 formal and informal learning environments: a review of literature. In: ASEE Annual Conference and Exposition, Conference Proceedings (2016)
8. Malinverni, L., Valero, C., Schaper, M.M., de la Cruz, I.G.: Educational robotics as a boundary object: towards a research agenda. Int. J. Child Comput. Interact. **29**, 100305 (2021)
9. Barreto, F., Benitti, V.: Exploring the educational potential of robotics in schools: a systematic review. Comput. Educ. **58**(3), 978–988 (2012)
10. Sjöberg, J., Brooks, E.: Understanding school children's playful experiences through the use of educational robotics - the impact of open-ended designs. In: Fang, X. (ed.) HCI in Games, vol. 13334, pp. 456–468. Springer, Cham (2022). https://doi.org/10.1007/978-3-031-05637-6_29
11. Major, L., Kyriacou, T., Brereton, O.P.: Systematic literature review: teaching novices programming using robots. In: 15th Annual Conference on Evaluation & Assessment in Software Engineering (EASE 2011), Durham, pp. 21–30 (2011)
12. Miller, D.P., Nourbakhsh, I.R., Siegwart, R.: Robots for education. In: Siciliano, B., Khatib, O. (eds.) Springer Handbook of Robotic, pp. 1283–1301. Springer, Heidelberg (2008). https://doi.org/10.1007/978-3-540-30301-5_56

13. Xia, L., Zhong, B.: A systematic review on teaching and learning robotics content knowledge in K-12. Comput. Educ. **127**, 267–282 (2018)
14. Macrides, E., Miliou, O., Angeli, C.: Programming in early childhood education: a systematic review. Int. J. Child-Comput. Interact. **32**, 100396 (2022)
15. Popat, S., Starkey, L.: Learning to code or coding to learn? A systematic review. Comput. Educ. **128**, 365–376 (2019)
16. Pérez-Marín, D., Hijón-Neira, R., Pizarro, C.: Coding in early years education: which factors influence the skills of sequencing and plotting a route, and to what extent? Int. J. Early Years Educ. **30**(4), 969–985 (2022)
17. Bers, M.U., González-González, C., Armas-Torres, M.B.: Coding as a playground: promoting positive learning experiences in childhood classrooms. Comput. Educ. **138**, 130–145 (2019)
18. Moraiti, I., Fotoglou, A., Drigas, A.: Coding with block programming languages in educational robotics and mobiles, improve problem solving, creativity & critical thinking skills. Int. J. Interact. Mob. Technol. (iJIM) **16**(20), 59–78 (2022)
19. Ioannou, A., Makridou, E.: Exploring the potentials of educational robotics in the development of computational thinking: a summary of current research and practical proposal for future work. Educ. Inf. Technol. **23**(6), 2531–2544 (2018). https://doi.org/10.1007/s10639-018-9729-z
20. Wertsch, J.V.: Mind as Action. Oxford University Press, New York (1998)
21. Vygotsky, L.S.: Mind and Society. Harvard University Press, Cambridge (1978)
22. Bruner, J.S.: The act of discovery. Harv. Educ. Rev. **31**, 21–32 (1961)
23. Brooks, E., Sjöberg, J.: A designerly approach as a foundation for school children's computational thinking skills while developing digital games. In: IDC 2020: Proceedings of the Interaction Design and Children Conference, pp. 87–95. Association for Computing Machinery (ACM) (2020)
24. Alfieri, L., Brooks, P.J., Aldrich, N.J., Tenenbaum, H.R.: Does discovery-based instruction enhance learning? J. Educ. Psychol. **103**(1), 1–18 (2011)
25. Bonawitz, E., Shafto, P., Gweon, H., Goodman, N.D., Spelke, E., Schulz, L.: The double-edged sword of pedagogy: instruction limits spontaneous exploration and discovery. Cognition **120**(3), 322–330 (2011)
26. Youell, B.: The importance of play and playfulness. Eur. J. Psychother. Couns. **10**, 121–129 (2008)
27. Getzels, J.W., Jackson, P.W.: Creativity and Intelligence: Explorations with Gifted Students. Wiley, Hoboken (1962)
28. Lucero, A., Arrasvuori, J.: The PLEX Cards and its techniques as sources of inspiration when designing for playfulness. Int. J. Arts Technol. **6**(1), 22–43 (2013)
29. Proyer, R.T., Tandler, N., Brauer, K.: Playfulness and creativity: a selective review. In: Luria, S.R., Baer, J., Kaufman, J.C. (eds.) Creativity and Humor. A Volume in Explorations in Creativity Research, pp. 43–60. Academic Press (2019)
30. Vygotsky, L.S.: Thought and Language. MIT Press, Cambridge (1986)
31. Rieber, R.W., Robinson, D.K.: The collective as a factor in the development of the abnormal child. In: Rieber, R.W., Robinson, D.K. (eds.) The Essential Vygotsky, pp. 201–219. Springer, New York (2004). https://doi.org/10.1007/978-0-387-30600-1_10
32. Holzman, L.: Without creating ZPDs there is no creativity. In: Connery, C.M., John-Steiner, V.P., Marjanovic-Shane, A. (eds.) Vygotsky and Creativity. A Cultural-Historical Approach to Play, Meaning Making, and the Arts, pp. 27–39. Peter Lang, New York (2010)
33. Wood, D.J., Bruner, J., Ross, G.: The role of tutoring in problem solving. J. Child Psychol. Psychiatry **17**(2), 89–100 (1976)
34. Rogoff, B., Gardner, W.P.: Guidance in cognitive development: an examination of mother-child instruction. In: Rogoff, B., Lave, J. (eds.) Everyday Cognition: Its Development in Social Context, pp. 95–116. Harvard University Press, Cambridge (1984)

35. Newman, F., Holzman, L.: Lev Vygotsky: Revolutionary Scientist. Routledge, New York (1993)

36. Lobman, C.: Creating developmental moments: teaching and learning as creative activities. In: Connery, C.M., John-Steiner, V.P., Marjanovic-Shane, A. (eds.) Vygotsky and Creativity. A Cultural-Historical Approach to Play, Meaning Making, and the Arts, pp. 199–214. Peter Lang, New York (2010)

37. Cohen, L., Manion, L., Morrison, K.: Research Methods in Education, 7th edn. Routledge, New York (2011)

38. Knoblauch, H.: Videography: focused ethnography and video analysis. In: Knoblauch, H., Schnettler, B., Raab, J., Soeffner, H.-G. (eds.) Video Analysis: Methodology and Methods, pp. 69–84. PeterLang, Frankfurt am Main (2009)

39. Danish Code of Conduct for Research Integrity: Ministry of Higher Education and Research, Copenhagen, Denmark (2014). https://ufm.dk/en/publications/2014/files-2014-1/the-danish-code-of-conduct-for-research-integrity.pdf. Accessed 7 Mar 2021

40. Braun, V., Clarke, V.: Using thematic analysis in psychology. Qual. Res. Psychol. 3(2), 77–10 (2006)

41. Fereday, J., Muir-Cochrane, E.: Demonstrating rigor using thematic analysis: a hybrid approach of inductive and deductive coding and theme development. Int. J. Qual. Methods 5(1), 80–92 (2010)

Exploring Learners' Flow and Related Design Strategies in Educational Games from a Psychic Entropy Perspective

Shufang Tan[1], Wendan Huang[1], Jialing Zeng[2], and Junjie Shang[1](✉) (iD)

[1] Lab of Learning Sciences, Graduate School of Education, Peking University, Beijing, China
jjshang@pku.edu.cn
[2] Teachers College, Columbia University, New York, NY 10027, USA

Abstract. Flow is a concept derived from positive psychology, which symbolizes a state of profound concentration where one operates at full capacity. Flow experience is one of the evaluation indicators and design objects of educational games. Learning with educational games is a composite process, including playing, learning, reflecting, and other forms of information processing. However, existing flow models and corresponding design principles are generally constructed for entertainment games' pure fun process. Therefore, the flow models need to be adjusted to guide educational game design. Tracing back to the flow theory's original argument, the opposite of flow—"psychic entropy" (chaotic state of information and consciousness in mind)—can provide a lens through which researchers might examine the information-processing mechanism associated with flow in educational games. From this vantage point, this study developed an information processing framework for learners in educational games based on Gagne's information processing theory, explored the factors that may obstruct flow in the learning process, and proposed design strategies to assist learners in experiencing flow.

Keywords: Educational Games · Flow · Psychic Entropy

1 Introduction

Educational games refer to games that are both educational and entertaining, which can help learners develop their knowledge, abilities, intelligence, emotions, attitudes, and values [1]. One value of the educational game is to reshape the way of learning which enables students to acquire as much of their preferred knowledge as possible and experience the joy of learning as well as life [1]. Flow is one of the essential objectives in educational game design [2] as people in flow are deemed "enjoyable" and "effective" in their endeavors [3]. There are evidences that educational games enabling students to achieve flow experiences can enhance learning [4].

In recent years, greater focus has been placed on flow and its applications to educational games. For instance, some researchers adopted flow theory as the design reference of educational game design and developed frameworks of flow design principles and

© The Author(s), under exclusive license to Springer Nature Switzerland AG 2023
X. Fang (Ed.): HCII 2023, LNCS 14047, pp. 81–93, 2023.
https://doi.org/10.1007/978-3-031-35979-8_6

strategies [5–7]. Moreover, there are researchers using flow as an examination of students' subjective experiences in educational games [8–10]. Furthermore, several studies investigated variables influencing flow experience in game-based learning [11–14]. In addition, some researchers took flow as an independent variable, focusing on exploring the influence of flow experience [15, 16].

The limitations of current research primarily stem from two factors. Firstly, as flow is a feeling summarized from individuals' experiences, flow elements are more like the representation of flow characteristics from a subjective perspective rather than a designer's perspective. Thus, the operability of flow elements to guide specific educational game design might be insufficient. Secondly, the flow design strategies, which are currently widely used in the field of educational games, were transferred from the strategies of entertainment games with fun as the primary goal. However, educational games focus more on the learning process rather than pure fun. Learners might engage in more complex cognitive and information processing operations while playing educational games than entertainment games. Besides, most applications of flow theory adopt its "derived" relevant guidance, whereas few researchers returned to the original definition of flow to investigate how to provide learners with the best possible experience in educational games. Therefore, the purpose of this study is to investigate flow from a different perspective, "psychic entropy", which is more closely related to information processing, in order to analyze factors that may impede flow, examine flow theory in the context of educational games, and propose pertinent design strategies.

2 Psychic Entropy: The State Opposite of Flow

Flow was proposed by a positive psychologist Mihaly Csikszentmihalyi. He discovered that the "disorder of consciousness" caused by information overload and overthinking was the source of anxiety, which was referred to as "psychic entropy" [17]. This term is derived from the physical world "entropy", a measure of disorder. Negative entropy (i.e., negentropy) is the tendency to move from disorder to order [18]. Based on this concept, Csikszentmihalyi defined psychic entropy as the information-induced disorder of people's goals and mental structures [17]. Negative effects of psychic entropy may include sadness, loneliness, anger, despair, lack of motivation, withdrawal, disinterest, listlessness, confusion, lack of concentration, distraction, etc.

Csikszentmihalyi suggested that individuals should focus their attention during their activities to prioritize core information and block some information irrelevant to the current activity when confronted with a large amount of information. Therefore, the information processed in the consciousness is consistent with the previously established goal, helping individuals achieve "psychic negentropy" [4]. Since, in this state, a person is completely absorbed in a particular activity, ignoring the existence of other things, every decision and action is perfectly connected to the previous decision or action [19]. Consequently, this state of "psychic negentropy" is known as "flow" [20]. Flow theory is a theory about the allocation of attentional resources, which proposes that achieving a state of flow requires a cohesion of attention, reduction of disorder in information and information processing tasks, and avoidance of falling into a state of psychic entropy. One objective of educational game design is to avoid falling into a state of psychic entropy and achieve and maintain the flow state.

3   Flow in Educational Games

Psychic entropy is concerned with the allocation of attention, analogous to educational game theory's focus on cognitive resources and motivation. It is possible to apply the psychic entropy perspective to the study of flow in educational games which can refine and broaden the flow perspective. Flow theory views the ego as a system that can generate and process information about external conditions and internal states by allocating limited resources such as attention. This viewpoint is consistent with Gagne's information-processing theory [21]. Gagne's information-processing model can represent the information-processing process of learners in educational games, and the "Expectancies" in the model corresponds to the psychic entropy-related elements of attention and goals, making it a suitable framework for analyzing the learning process from a psychic entropy perspective. Based on Gagne's information-processing model, this study views educational games as environments that continually present new information and have an ultimate goal. Learning is viewed as information processing in educational games.

In this study, psychic entropy indicates the degree of disorder in the allocation of learners' attention when confronted with the virtual environment of educational games, which includes resources that occupy the attention and disorganized information processing. An increase in psychic entropy indicates that the information and information processing in the learner's brain tend to be disorderly, whereas a decrease in psychic entropy indicates that the learner has increased the degree of the orderliness of information and information processing.

3.1   Information-Processing Model in Educational Games

The single-player mode is one of the most popular and technically mature educational game modes. In this mode, the information processing of players is more controllable. Thus, this study focuses on the flow of single-player educational games from the perspective of psychic entropy. Based on Gagne's information-processing model [21], this study uses educational games as learning situations and draws a diagram of the information-processing model (as shown in Fig. 1).

To more accurately reflect the information processing in educational games, the framework built in this study is depicted in Fig. 2. The thick black solid line represents information and processes associated with the increase of psychic entropy. The white text box on the black background represents information that may cause internal disorder. The thick gray solid line represents processes associated with decreasing psychic entropy. The dashed line represents the relationship of influence between items. The thin solid line represents the procedure of information processing. The chain line depicts the distribution of attentional resources. According to Gagne's information-processing model, this framework also includes the modules of external information environment provided by the educational game, learner's receptors, sensory register, information processing in the brain, response generator, and effectors. Then, information processing details associated with each module were added to refine them.

The entire process starts with learners' sensory registration of information from the educational game environment, as depicted in Fig. 2. The information derived from educational games is mainly presented through the user interface. Wu suggested the term

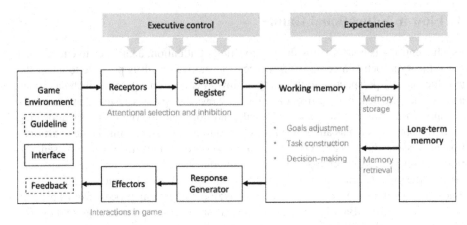

Fig. 1. Information-processing model in educational games

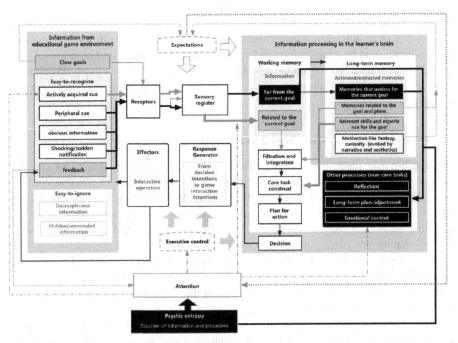

Fig. 2. Information-processing model of learners in educational games from the perspective of psychic entropy

"design entropy" to describe the level of disorder of user interfaces [22]. According to how easily the information can be registered by the senses, in this study, information in the context of educational games is classified as either easily noticed information or easily ignored information. The former category includes information found through active search, information close to task cues, information located in the visual center of the user interface, and information that is shocking or sudden. The latter includes information that is either obscured or difficult to see. At the same time, the information registered by the senses can be further divided into strong correlation information and weak correlation information according to the degree of correlation with the learner's current task goal.

Next, after the external information has been registered, it will be further processed. The information that is strongly or weakly related to the current goal will activate long-term memory. In addition, information is filtered and integrated into working memory to construct the current tasks and make decisions [23]. After a decision is made, the response generator converts the decision intention into game interactions, and then the effector performs the interactive operation in accordance with the educational game, which influences the educational game environment, modifies the environment's state, and receives the environment's feedback.

In summary, psychic entropy in information processing primarily reflects the degree of information and processing disorder in the brain. Attention is used to acquire information related to goal-directed task cues, for executive control throughout information processing, and for unrelated processes.

3.2   Interference Factors in the Flow

As shown in Fig. 2, there are "risk factors" that may disrupt flow (see the thick black solid line and the white text box on a black background). For instance, in the sensory register stage, information that is only marginally relevant to the current goal might be processed. Moreover, during the long-term memory stage, information that is relevant to some of the registered information but not to the goal and not useful for task resolution is also activated, resulting in additional information being processed. In addition, some processes in the active part of the brain will cause distraction, such as reflection, subsequent planning adjustment, and emotional control.

Through the analysis presented above, it is possible to examine the design of educational games from the perspective of psychic entropy and to identify the factors that may impede flow. Following is an analysis of the factors that increase psychic entropy in educational games.

Regarding learning content, factors that influence flow include content, the degree of relevance and structure of these contents, and progress. As for the arrangement and presentation of information, a series of mission challenges will influence the number of parallel tasks and the degree of correlation between these tasks. Furthermore, the information conveyed from educational games will influence the information in working memory and the retrieval from long-term memory. The level of psychic entropy in working memory is influenced by the degree of association between information and goals and the degree of correlation between information. Inappropriate information presentation can bring irrelevant information into the learner's working memory and disrupt the flow of learning.

The interaction interface of educational games serves the function of information presentation, and the design of the interaction interface determines the manner, image, position, and quantity of information that can be perceived. An inappropriate, disorganized, and unappealing interaction interface will have a negative effect on the flow. In addition, the design of the interaction affects the fluidity of translating the decision intent into game interactions, and if the fluency of the interactions is inadequate, it will result in additional resistance to the flow process.

Regarding the design of feedback, the feedback session is an important source of information for assisting learners in determining whether the current action has contributed to the achievement of the goal. If the manner and content of feedback are inappropriate or fail to meet the aforementioned criteria, it will fail to reduce the current psychic entropy and may even interfere with the experience of flow.

The specific gameplay determines the degree of integration between entertainment and education in terms of game design. If the goals of entertainment and learning are fragmented, it may induce the tasks to compete for attention and even interplay, resulting in a decrease in flow. In addition to level design, it must generally correspond to the learning schedule [24]. After dividing a learning goal into smaller stage goals, there should be some correlation between these stage goals. When switching between tasks, if they are poorly correlated, it may disrupt the flow experience.

4   Design Strategies for Educational Games

This study combs the information-processing process in educational games from the perspective of psychic entropy and summarizes the flow interference factors. On the basis of the preceding work and the idea of MDA theory [25], this study summarizes the factors that affect the disorder of information and consciousness and examines where the factors appear in the information-processing process. Then, from the perspective of educational game design researchers, this study proposes design strategies to control the influencing factors and to facilitate the different stages of flow in educational games, to provide a reference for educational game design. "Improving concentration of attention" and "reducing disorder" are the core strategies.

Csikszentmihalyi emphasized that the purpose of distinguishing between psychic entropy and negentropy (flow) was not to eliminate the subtle distinctions between various psychological states but rather to help and reveal the pattern of consciousness from order to chaos. So psychic entropy and flow can be considered as variables with high, medium, and low levels, and there is a transformation relationship between different levels and states. This allows us to divide the flow of educational games into three stages: the beginning stage, the flow stage, and the stage of exiting flow, which clarifies the context of design strategies.

4.1 Beginning of Flow

On the threshold of flow, the information processing system that constitutes consciousness does not focus on a particular range of stimulation, similar to a radar antenna that scans back and forth in the stimulation field and notices actions, objects, feelings, and memories, but without a particular order or pattern. New decisions must be made when confronted with new goals, tasks, and information input; that is, when learners enter the beginning stage of flow, they leave their original baseline state of disordered consciousness, focus on a series of related stimuli, and exclude irrelevant thoughts and emotions

[26]. At this stage, the disorder degree of consciousness increases, and then, as a result of the action, attention can be focused on the goal-related information, the disorder degree decreases, and the flow level increases gradually.

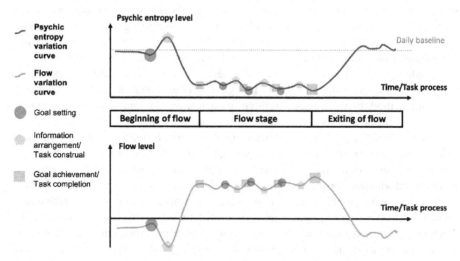

Fig. 3. Psychic entropy and flow variation curves based on Csikszentmihalyi's theoretical assumptions

As depicted in Fig. 3, if there are interference factors in the beginning stage of flow, it may be difficult to decrease psychic entropy when the flow is initiated. Learners may be unable to break away from the baseline state of psychic entropy level in daily life, and there may be an increase in the degree of internal disorder, making it difficult for learners to enter the flow state. In other words, the user interface at the beginning stage of the flow is the first "risk zone" when designing an educational game information environment. This risk factor is reflected in the ease of sensor perception and sensory registration on the one hand and the level of information presentation and organization on the other.

At this stage, it is crucial to provide learners with a clear "current goal," which is a subjective notion of the expected outcome of the activity and a subjective ideology formed in the mind. The goal is directive, which is the expected purpose of the activity and indicates the activity's direction. Only through practice will the activity reach its intended goal. The directional nature of the goal means that it has guiding role of maintaining the relationship between all aspects of the organization and constitutes the core of the system's organizational direction [27].

Educating is a goal-oriented endeavor. Before implementing instructional activities, Gagne requires teachers to articulate the expected learning outcomes in detail. Then, using this outcome as a guide, teachers plan and organize instruction, as well as measure and evaluate students' learning outcomes in accordance with the teaching goals. In educational games, it may not be appropriate to take the teaching goal as a clear goal at the beginning stage of the flow. Goal setting in educational games should be done from the first-person perspective of the learner. The goals set for achieving a state of flow should be specific and focused on the present. The overly ambitious goals make it easy for learners to focus on other factors, such as hope, fear, and anxiety, which decreases their concentration and makes it difficult for them to enter the flow state. What's more, the process of information processing in educational games is not only focused on a single piece of information but a succession of information processing and decision-making operations with subdivided goals and subdivided tasks. When decomposing a task into subtasks and assigning subtasks, it is essential to consider every goal's accessibility.

In addition to the goals that may be inherent to the activity, utilizing skills and overcoming obstacles can also be goals. Designers of educational games can use narrative or reward methods between stages to emphasize to learners the significance of completing current challenges, and boost their sense of accomplishment.

The beginning of the flow will be determined primarily by the user interface's presentation of the current goal. In educational games, the entire process of learning and playing consists of a series of relatively complex tasks that require constant attention to the most pertinent information for the current goal and decision-making. During the process of designing an educational game, it is possible to artificially simplify the information related to the current task, reduce irrelevant information and sort out the information displayed to learners. Moreover, it is necessary to plan the arrangement mode and the visual characteristics of different information, maximize the positive role of the user interface, and reduce the information disorder caused by improper user interface design.

4.2 Flow Stage

A complete flow process of an educational game may include multiple stage tasks and corresponding stage goals, so there are both information-processing processes corresponding to each stage task and the transformation process of different stage goals.

Enhance the Integration of Learning and Playing. In educational games where learning and playing are combined, learners' learning experience and game experience frequently interact. Therefore, it is essential to strengthen the integration of learning and playing. When students achieve the dual flow state from learning and playing, it is the ideal situation. The premise that learners' flow levels of learning are synchronized with their flow levels on play is also an unintentional default idealization assumed by contemporary scholars using the flow model.

However, due to the differences in the design of different educational games and the personalized needs of different players, synchronization of flow levels between learning and play does not always exist. As a result, synchronization of the two should not be applied as a default assumption. It should be the objective of educators and designers. For example, when learners achieve flow during the study, but their skill in games is lower than the challenges required by games, games become obstacles in learning, distracting and depleting learners' energy and lowering their learning efficiency. Moreover, when learners have achieved flow in learning, and their ability in games is far greater than the skills required by the games, they will feel bored in these games, their motivation will decline, and the games will become increasingly tedious as the gap between their existing and required game ability widens. Furthermore, when learners find it difficult to learn, their ability is far below the learning challenges they encounter in educational games, but their game skills far exceed the abilities required by the current games, they will find the games tedious and academic disciplines difficult to learn. In this case, the flaws in game design and the unreasonable placement of learning content will overlap, resulting in more severe negative effects. Additionally, when learners struggle to learn but their ability much lower than the academic challenges they face in educational games, but when they are in the flow zone in the game, educators will be concerned. These learners' frustration with learning content will lead them to pursue a sense of accomplishment in the game, and as a result, they will dislike learning more deeply.

In order to avoid mutual interference between the aforementioned learning process and the game process, it is necessary to improve the integration of learning and play tasks and to merge the process of learning with the process of play while simultaneously focusing on solving the current task to achieve the current goal.

Reduce Irrelevant Parallel Processes. The more significant the correlation between what individuals do and their goals, the more likely they are to be in flow. Processes unrelated to the current task will consume attentional resources, and the results of these processes will not aid learners in approaching the goal of the task. It is necessary to determine whether or not learners are engaged in information processing unrelated to task goals.

In partially linear educational games, determining whether a process is irrelevant is relatively simple, but it will be more challenging in nonlinear or open-world educational games. Regarding how to determine whether learners' information processing and actions are in the right direction in complex nonlinear tasks, an article on flow research published in Nature Communications in 2022 proposes the information theory of flow based on the concept of "means-ends fusion" in social psychology and the concept of "mutual information" in informatics [28]. Although mutual information between means and ends is not the only factor influencing flow, educational game researchers can refer to this flow theory and view actions and desired goals as two distinct sets in flow-producing activities. Effective actions can be linked and matched to desired goals. People must limit their efforts to "actions that are effective for further progress towards the results" if they wish to achieve flow [28]. Otherwise, we risk wasting resources by acquiring knowledge or skills that are unrelated to the goal.

With the above-mentioned method, researchers are better able to determine whether learners are performing actions related to the goal. While processing tasks in educational games, learners may engage in a number of parallel processes that have nothing to do with achieving the current goal. For instance, there might be information activated in long-term memory which is irrelevant to the current task. Therefore, such irrelevant processes must be prevented at the source of information input. Thus, in the specific task execution of educational games, try to avoid presenting information that is not closely related to the current task, and if necessary, try to keep such information in a secondary position that is difficult to notice in visual communication.

In addition, during flow states, according to Dietrich's research, these explicit executive functions, such as self-referential thought, of the frontal cortices are inhibited, thus freeing up more resources dedicated to current goals [29]. Certain processes, such as self-criticism, emotional control, long-term planning, etc., that appear to be essential in educational games are not suitable as parallel processes.

In the design of educational games, the feedback associated with reflection can be separated to form a reflection link distinct from the task link or placed in the same module as the feedback after the completion of the stage task, so that the reflection guidance function can be realized without occupying the attention resources of task processing.

Increase Learners' Focus Through Dynamic Difficulty Adjustment. Dynamic difficulty adjustment is a method for designing game difficulty which is derived from the conventional flow model. It aids in maintaining flow by balancing the relationship between the game's challenge difficulty and the player's current skill level. Its principle can be understood in terms of psychic entropy (the allocation of attention).

When the task is too simple, the learner can complete it with a small amount of attention, and the motivation provided by the goal may be diminished. Then it will be difficult to concentrate on the goal, resulting in an increase in psychic entropy and the risk of exiting flow. In this instance, increasing the difficulty of the current goal will assist learners in refocusing their attention on the core tasks and reducing their psychic entropy by processing information and making decisions in a timely manner [19]. When the task is too difficult, or the goal is unclear, it will lead to a sense of helplessness and confusion even when all the attention is used, which may cause learners to feel inadequate support and self-efficacy, resulting in more emotional processing occupying the initial inadequate attention. The vicious cycle formed by this causes psychic entropy to increase.

Establish New Goals: Restart Flow During Task Switching. The effect of establishing new goals on flow depends on the correlation between the current information represented and the new goals, as well as whether the previous goals were accomplished.

If the previous goal has not been met, it is essential to pay close attention to the compatibility between the new goal and the current environmental information when switching tasks. Because consciousness must maintain its internal order, when a person establishes a previous goal through consciousness, emotion, or thought and new information conflicts with that goal, the order of consciousness will be destroyed. When the direction of a person's task processing is inconsistent with the most recent goal direction, they are unable to control the internal "chaos," which may also result in the exit of the flow state.

If at the end of the previous flow experience, feedback that "the previous goal has been achieved" is received, psychological resources will be released, and people will be able to leave the previous task with a sense of accomplishment and prepare to "restart."

The greater the difference between the new and previous goals, the more information needs to be processed, and the greater the disorder will be. It will increase the level of psychic entropy. People do not return to a higher level of flow until they have completed information processing, task construction for new goals, and re-adaptation to the current tasks.

For a continuous "task group", which is divided into multiple stages with multiple stage goals, when the stage goals are accomplished, the corresponding attention resources can be released. Additionally, if the goal of the follow-up task has a good correlation with the goal of the previous task, it is possible to reduce the risk of psychic entropy increase during internal task switching and accelerate the restart of flow after switching tasks.

Optimize Interactivity to Ensure Implementation. Educational game research concentrates on interaction design. By incorporating an interactive design, educational games become more and more engaging. In addition, from the perspective of psychic entropy, one of the key points is the need to better combine the content, gameplay, adopted software platform, and hardware equipment of educational games so that learners can convert their decisions into operational intentions and then smoothly implement these intentions into the game environment via actions.

4.3 Exiting of Flow

When the goal is finally attained, the challenge concludes, the input ceases, the psychic entropy gradually returns to its initial level, and the flow state gradually fades (see Fig. 3).

If learners will play educational games repeatedly, it is necessary to optimize the ending of each flow. In the learner's task information-processing model depicted in Fig. 2, the area of long-term memory in the upper right corner is related to emotional experience, worldview, or other game-related motivations, which will influence the processing of expected items.

Use Effective Feedback to Produce Positive Emotions. When concluding the use of an educational game, we should provide learners with timely, summative, and accurate feedback on their overall performance so that they receive a response to the game's goal. Although a flow experience itself is a type of reward, helping learners recall "how many great achievements they have made in this flow experience" and giving this flow process a higher meaning will enhance learners' positive emotions and memories about this experience.

Create Task Narrative to Facilitate Subsequent Flow Initiation. Similar background narratives or plot progressions will subjectively increase learners' perception of task relevance. Whether or not the learners have expectations for the next use of the educational game will influence the difficulty of starting the flow the following time. The narrative of a game frequently plays a role in attracting players to develop an emotional connection. Consequently, educational games can also use a preview of the next section of the story to prepare the player for the next flow experience.

5 Conclusion and Reflection

The perspective of psychic entropy can assist educational game researchers in identifying risk areas and interference factors that are difficult to identify from the traditional perspective of flow. This study constructs the information-processing model of educational games from the perspective of psychic entropy, but this model is still in the theoretical derivation stage and requires further experimental validation. Combining the measurement techniques of informatics and neuroscience, we can investigate the use of mathematical methods to improve the model in the future, as well as design research and case study techniques to validate the model.

Currently, the information-processing model and design strategies for educational games proposed in this study have a limited application scope. Due to this study's reliance on Gagne's information-processing model, it is best suited for analyzing educational games with a linear single-player mode. The analysis of educational games with a high degree of freedom, non-task orientation, and creativity, such as sandbox games or multiplayer simulation games, must be explained in greater detail and explored in conjunction with other educational theories.

References

1. Shang, J., Pei, L.: Reshaping the learning style: the core value and future application in education of games. China Educ. Technol. (05), 41–49 (2015). (in Chinese)
2. Annetta, L.A.: The "I's" have it: a framework for serious educational game design. Rev. Gen. Psychol. **14**, 105–113 (2010). https://doi.org/10.1037/a0018985
3. Nakamura, J., Csikszentmihalyi, M.: The concept of flow. In: Csikszentmihalyi, M. (ed.) Flow and the Foundations of Positive Psychology, pp. 239–263. Springer, Dordrecht (2014). https://doi.org/10.1007/978-94-017-9088-8_16
4. Csikszentmihalyi, M.: Learning, "flow", and happiness. In: Csikszentmihalyi, M. (ed.) Applications of Flow in Human Development and Education: The Collected Works of Mihaly Csikszentmihalyi, pp. 153–172. Springer, Dordrecht (2014). https://doi.org/10.1007/978-94-017-9094-9_7
5. Pranantha, D., van der Spek, E., Bellotti, F., Berta, R., DeGloria, A., Rauterberg, M.: Game design and development for learning physics using the flow framework. In: De Gloria, A. (ed.) GALA 2014. LNCS, vol. 9221, pp. 142–151. Springer, Cham (2015). https://doi.org/10.1007/978-3-319-22960-7_14
6. Kiili, K., de Freitas, S., Arnab, S., Lainema, T.: The design principles for flow experience in educational games. Procedia Comput. Sci. **15**, 78–91 (2012). https://doi.org/10.1016/j.procs.2012.10.060
7. Bellotti, F., Berta, R., De Gloria, A., Primavera, L.: Adaptive experience engine for serious games. IEEE Trans. Comput. Intell. AI Games **1**, 264–280 (2009). https://doi.org/10.1109/TCIAIG.2009.2035923
8. Bressler, D.M., Bodzin, A.M.: A mixed methods assessment of students' flow experiences during a mobile augmented reality science game. J. Comput. Assist. Learn. **29**, 505–517 (2013). https://doi.org/10.1111/jcal.12008
9. Yang, Q.-F., Chang, S.-C., Hwang, G.-J., Zou, D.: Balancing cognitive complexity and gaming level: effects of a cognitive complexity-based competition game on EFL students' English vocabulary learning performance, anxiety and behaviors. Comput. Educ. **148**, 103808 (2020). https://doi.org/10.1016/j.compedu.2020.103808
10. Martin-Niedecken, A.L., Rogers, K., Turmo Vidal, L., Mekler, E.D., Márquez Segura, E.: ExerCube vs. personal trainer: evaluating a holistic, immersive, and adaptive fitness game setup. In: Proceedings of the 2019 CHI Conference on Human Factors in Computing Systems, pp. 1–15. Association for Computing Machinery, New York (2019). https://doi.org/10.1145/3290605.3300318
11. Ninaus, M., Moeller, K., McMullen, J., Kiili, K.: Acceptance of game-based learning and intrinsic motivation as predictors for learning success and flow experience. Int. J. Serious Games 4 (2017). https://doi.org/10.17083/ijsg.v4i3.176

12. Hong, J.-C., Tai, K.-H., Hwang, M.-Y., Kuo, Y.-C.: Internet cognitive failure affects learning progress as mediated by cognitive anxiety and flow while playing a Chinese antonym synonym game with interacting verbal–analytical and motor-control. Comput. Educ. **100**, 32–44 (2016). https://doi.org/10.1016/j.compedu.2016.04.009

13. Hong, J.-C., Hwang, M.-Y., Tai, K.-H., Lin, P.-H.: The effects of intrinsic cognitive load and gameplay interest on flow experience reflecting performance progress in a Chinese remote association game. Comput. Assist. Lang. Learn. **34**, 358–378 (2021). https://doi.org/10.1080/09588221.2019.1614068

14. Tsai, M.-J., Huang, L.-J., Hou, H.-T., Hsu, C.-Y., Chiou, G.-L.: Visual behavior, flow and achievement in game-based learning. Comput. Educ. **98**, 115–129 (2016). https://doi.org/10.1016/j.compedu.2016.03.011

15. Hsieh, Y.-H., Lin, Y.-C., Hou, H.-T.: Exploring the role of flow experience, learning performance and potential behavior clusters in elementary students' game-based learning. Interact. Learn. Environ. **24**, 178–193 (2016). https://doi.org/10.1080/10494820.2013.834827

16. Buil, I., Catalán, S., Martínez, E.: The influence of flow on learning outcomes: an empirical study on the use of clickers. Br. J. Edu. Technol. **50**, 428–439 (2019)

17. Csikszentmihalyi, M., Csikszentmihalyi, I.S.: Optimal Experience: Psychological Studies of Flow in Consciousness. Cambridge University Press, Cambridge (1992)

18. Schrödinger, E.: What is Life?: With Mind and Matter and Autobiographical Sketches. Cambridge University Press, Cambridge (1992). https://doi.org/10.1017/CBO9781139644129

19. Kotler, S.: The Art of Impossible: A Peak Performance Primer. Harper Wave (2021)

20. Csikszentmihalyi, M.: Flow. Harper Perennial Modern Classics (2008)

21. Gagne, R.M.: The Conditions of Learning and Theory of Instruction. Wadsworth Pub. Co., New York (1985)

22. Lei, Wu., Li, J., Lei, T.: Design entropy: a new approach for evaluating user experience in user interface design. In: Rebelo, F., Soares, M. (eds.) Advances in Ergonomics in Design, pp. 583–593. Springer, Cham (2016). https://doi.org/10.1007/978-3-319-41983-1_53

23. Ho, M.K., Abel, D., Correa, C.G., Littman, M.L., Cohen, J.D., Griffiths, T.L.: People construct simplified mental representations to plan. Nature **606**, 129–136 (2022). https://doi.org/10.1038/s41586-022-04743-9

24. Ibrahim, R., Jaafar, A.: Educational games (EG) design framework: combination of game design, pedagogy and content modeling. In: 2009 International Conference on Electrical Engineering and Informatics, pp. 293–298 (2009). https://doi.org/10.1109/ICEEI.2009.5254771

25. Hunicke, R., Leblanc, M., Zubek, R.: MDA: a formal approach to game design and game research. In: AAAI Workshop - Technical Report 1 (2004)

26. Csikszentmihalyi, M., Nakamura, J.: The dynamics of intrinsic motivation: a study of adolescents. In: Csikszentmihalyi, M. (ed.) Flow and the Foundations of Positive Psychology: The Collected Works of Mihaly Csikszentmihalyi, pp. 175–197. Springer, Dordrecht (2014). https://doi.org/10.1007/978-94-017-9088-8_12

27. Tao, X.: Dictionary of Education Evaluation. Beijing Normal University Publishing House (1998). (in Chinese)

28. Melnikoff, D.E., Carlson, R.W., Stillman, P.E.: A computational theory of the subjective experience of flow. Nat. Commun. **13**, 2252 (2022). https://doi.org/10.1038/s41467-022-29742-2

29. Dietrich, A.: Neurocognitive mechanisms underlying the experience of flow. Conscious. Cogn. **13**, 746–761 (2004). https://doi.org/10.1016/j.concog.2004.07.002

Mathmages: e-Sports and Mathematics in the Amazon Region

Sylker Teles[1]([⊠]), Isabelly Oliveira[1], Suziane Cundiff[1], Tarcinara Tavares[2], Rodrigo Rosas[3], and Brendo Teles[3]

[1] Federal University of Amazonas, Av. Gen. Rodrigo Octavio 1200, Manaus, Brazil
sylker@gmail.com
[2] State Secretariat for Education of Amazonas, Rua Waldemiro Lustoza 250, Manaus, Brazil
[3] Flying Saci Game Studio, Av. Castelo Branco 504, Manaus, Brazil

Abstract. This article describes the work carried out in the state of Amazonas within the scope of the Mathmages at Schools project. Mathmages is an educational game aimed for teaching mathematics developed from a doctoral thesis with a method called ARCS-REACT. The game was developed by Flying Saci Game Studio with the technical support from Samsung Ocean Center and was implemented in 163 public schools in 34 municipalities in the State of Amazonas. 98 of those schools are located in the capital Manaus and 65 in the countryside of the state. In the final phase of the project, a tournament was held, the Mathmages Arena Tournament (MAT). 105 students from 25 schools in 9 municipalities were classified for the finals. In future research, we intend to test the results of student learnings with the same ARCS-REACT method that originated the game. The project was a pioneering experience in the Amazon, an initiative that promoted digital inclusion in the jungle. The engagement of schools and children during the tournament was inspiring, especially in the communities in the countryside of the state, which showed special dedication. As a result, the schools from the countryside were the best performers in all metrics, except for best overall time per student, which was awarded to the Santo Antônio State School in Manaus, capital city of Amazonas.

Keywords: Educational Games · Mathematics · Amazon

1 Introduction

This paper brings a report of the implementation of the Mathmages game in 163 schools in the state of Amazonas as a part of a joint project between the State Secretariat for Education of Amazonas and Flying Saci Game Studio. Mathmages is an educational game developed in Unity focused on teaching basic mathematics, especially designed for the final years of elementary school. The game is the result of a research carried out at Kyushu University on games and contextual education in 2015. Technical improvements were made after that when Flying Saci Game Studio took part in the Samsung Creative Startups program.

X. Fang (Ed.): HCII 2023, LNCS 14047, pp. 94–104, 2023.
https://doi.org/10.1007/978-3-031-35979-8_7

During the period between 2018 and 2019, 163 schools in 34 municipalities in the Amazon region were included in the project. The project comprised the following phases: development, training, implementation and tourna-ment. The final phase, the tournament, also called MAT (Mathmages Arena Tournament), was an e-sport experience that public schools could participate in, involving students, parents, teachers and administrators in an event that followed the calendar of the Amazonian Mathematics Fair.

The project was a pioneering experience in the Amazon region, an initiative that promoted digital inclusion in the jungle. The engagement of schools and children during the tournament was inspiring, especially in the communities in the countryside of the state, which showed special dedication. As a result, the schools from the countryside were the best performers in all metrics, except for best overall time per student, which was awarded to a school in Manaus, capital city of Amazonas.

2   Contextual Learning: The ARCS-REACT Approach

Mathmages is an educational game for the teaching of basic mathematics (Fig. 1). The game was developed in Unity engine and was born from a doctoral research carried out between 2012 and 2015 at the University of Kyushu with funds from the Japanese Government. During that period a game prototype was developed and tested in a Brazilian school in order to validate a new contextual learning method, named ARCS-REACT [1].

Fig. 1. The Game Mathmages.

ARCS-REACT is a contextual teaching and learning model based on the works of John Keller [2] and Michael Crawford [3]. According to them, it is possible to understand contextual teaching and learning as a social, constructivist and culturally driven educational approach. The learning categories proposed by Teles [1] and used to design the game Mathmages represents a combination of both. Additionally, those categories were given game design objetctives based on Koeffel et al. [4] and Paavilainen [5] as seen in Table 1.

The categories presented in the ARCS-REACT model were used in the prototyping of the game Mathmages. Cooperation and transfer, however, were only incorporated some time later with the game already released. Between 2012 and 2015, the prototype was tested in a school in the city of Manaus, state of Amazonas, Brazil, with students from the 7th grade of a elementary school [1]. The game was completed in 2016 when it received the INOVApps award from the Ministry of Communications of Brazil, allowing the creation of Flying Saci Game Studio which self-published the game in 2016.

Table 1. The ARCS-REACT categories.

Category	Definition	Objectives
Attention	Capturing the interest of learners stimulating the curiosity to learn	• Get the player involved quickly and easily; • Create a great storyline • Should use visual and audio effects to arose interests
Relevance	Meeting the personal needs/goals of the learner to effect a positive attitude	• Provide clear goals, present overriding goal early as well as short-term goals throughout play • Players discover the story as part of gameplay • The game transports the player into a level of personal involvement emotionally
Confidence	Helping the learners believe/feel that they will succeed and control their success	• The Player has a sense of control over their character and is able to use tactics and strategies • A player should always be able to identify their score/status and goal in the game; • Player should be given controls that are basic enough to learn quickly • Players do not need to use a manual to play game

(*continued*)

Table 1. (*continued*)

Category	Definition	Objectives
Satisfaction	Reinforcing accomplishment with rewards (internal and external)	• The game is enjoyable to replay • Make the player feel accomplishment in every play session • The player should receive meaningful rewards
Relating	Build new knowledge with practical experiences	• Provide players with new, evolving content and offer an emergent game world • Players should feel emotionally involved in the game
Experiencing	Build new knowledge with practical experiences	• Players should be able to start playing the game without reading the manual • Provide players with new, evolving content and offer an emergent game world • Players should feel emotionally involved in the game
Applying	Put the created knowledge to use in new problem solving activities	• Challenges in game must match the players' skill levels • The level of challenge should increase as the player progresses
Cooperating	Work in groups to handle complex problems	• Use social contacts as assets in the game and make them part of the game mechanics • The game should support competition and cooperation between players • Provide high-score lists for competing with friends
Transfering	Transfer the acquired knowledge to other students	• Provide means for players to share information and in game resources • The game should support social interaction between players

3   Mathmages at Schools

This article presents the results of a project called Mathmages at Schools, implemented in the state education network in Amazonas, Brazil. This project was carried out alongside the State Secretariat for Education of Amazonas (SEDUC-AM), aiming for the continuous improvement of teaching and learning in the field of Mathematics.

The project arose from the need to invest in tools for the development of logical and mathematical reasoning skills of students in the early and final years of elementary school. The application of game mechanics and aesthetics in an educational context provides opportunities for cognitive development in a ludic way, obtaining a greater engagement from the target audience and promoting significant results in the learning of Mathematics. The edition of Mathmages at School described here began in July 2018 and ended in October 2019.

The project was not only about the game but to introduce technology as a tool for teachers and give them proper data feedback in order to create better learning strategies for the future aiming the weak spots of the students. To achieve those requirements, the project took five steps: Development, Implementation, Training, Tournament and Big Data.

3.1 Early Development

Before dive in the steps of the Mathmages at Schools project, it is worth noting the early stages of the game development. The first prototype of the game, developed at Kyushu University, has earned the INOVApps Award from the Ministry of Communications of Brazil in 2016. That was the spark which started the Flying Saci Game Studio, a small game company focused on educational games. Briefly after that, the studio participated in two major acceleration programs: InovAtiva Brasil and Samsung Creative Startups.

In order to get the game in a stage good enough to take part in such an ambitious project, Flying Saci Game Studio received valuable technical and business support in the Samsung Creative Startups program and the Samsung Ocean Center, a space in the Amazonas State University with many technology tracks, including Games, AR and VR. Thanks to the technical skills learned at Samsung Ocean Center in Manaus, the Flying Saci team could deliver a very polished game, including one of the most technical challenging features: the on-line gameplay.

3.2 Development

The first step consisted in adapting the game to the pedagogical needs of the target schools. First of all, 150 schools were listed using performance in mathematics a the main criteria. A study carried out by Prof. Tarcinara Tavares [6] raised the competencies of the Common National Curriculum Base, BNCC in the Brazilian Portuese acronym [7]. The study was used to assure that the game met those skills so it could be incorporated in Brazilian schools.

Throughout Basic Education, the essential learning defined in the BNCC must contribute to ensure that students develop 10 General Skills, which consubstantiate, in the pedagogical scope, the rights of learning and development. Where competence is defined as the mobilization of knowledge (concepts and procedures), skills (practical, cognitive and socio-emotional), attitudes and values to solve complex demands of everyday life, the full exercise of citizenship and the world of work. The game Mathmages contemplates at least the first 5 of those General Skills, which are:

- Value and use historically constructed knowledge about the physical, social, cultural and digital world to understand and explain reality, continue learning and collaborate in building a just, democratic and inclusive society.

- Exercise intellectual curiosity and resort to the approach proper to science, including investigation, reflection, critical analysis, imagination and creativity, to investigate causes, develop and test hypotheses, formulate and solve problems and create solutions (including technological) based on the knowledge of the different areas.
- Value and enjoy the various artistic and cultural manifestations, from local to global ones, and also participating in diversified practices of artistic-cultural production.
- Use different languages, body, visual, sound and digital - as well as knowledge of artistic, mathematical and scientific languages, to express yourself and share information, experiences, ideas and feelings in different contexts and produce meanings that lead to mutual understanding.
- Understand, use and create digital information and communication technologies in a critical, meaningful, reflective and ethical way in the various social practices (including school ones) to communicate, access and disseminate information, produce knowledge, solve problems and exercise protagonism and authorship in personal and collective life.

Those set of skills were used as a compass to where the game should point out towards a pedagogical goal. There are also Specific Skills in the game based on the BNCC. Those are Mathematic skills from the 1st to 9th grade according to Brazilian Educational System. There are at least 31 Specific Skills present in the game [6].

Another aspect addressed in the development phase was less pedagogical and more technical. It consisted in adapting the project to the technological assets available at each school. A problem encountered was the variety of models of computers, laptops and tablets, as well as different operating systems. This occurs in the public network throughout different administrations due to purchases made in different periods that seek lower prices in bidding processes. As a result, schools have inadequate machines for digital games, in addition to the variety of hardware and software configurations. This variety makes development difficult, as the game needs to have the technical capacity to run in each scenario.

After testing the game on most available computers, the most critical point in performance was the amount of graphic assets or 3D assets present in each scenario. The proposed solution was to use a technique known as pre-rendered backgrounds [8], common in the late 1990s and early 2000s, in the era of 32-bit processors, especially on the Sony's Playstation console. Famous games series like Resident Evil and Final Fantasy have made use of this technique by replacing complex scenarios with still images. The Fig. 2 is a demonstration of how the technique was used in Mathmages.

As a result, the performance was able to meet most of the equipment available in schools. The use of 3D character models with low polygon density combined with textures resolutions between 128 and 512 pixels helped to keep the frame rate within limits that allowed students to play without spoiling the experience and, of course, learning. Additionally, the game was made available in a mobile version for Android devices, ensuring more accessibility.

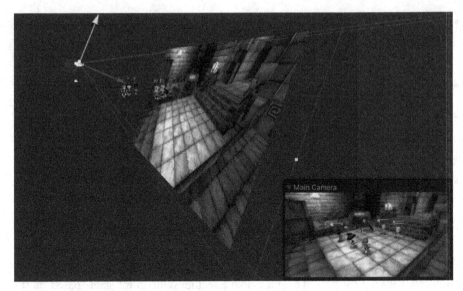

Fig. 2. The pre-render plane and the camera view.

3.3 Training

During the second phase of the project, workshops were held with pedagogical guidelines about the use of the game as a tool for learning Mathematics. During this period, 110 education professionals from 9 municipalities from the State of Amazonas received the training. In addition to the capital, the municipalities of Autazes, Careiro, Careiro da Várzea, Itacoatiara, Iranduba, Manacapuru, Novo Airão and Silves received in-place workshops. Most of the participants in the workshops were teachers. Other professionals were also contemplated such as managers, pedagogues, secretaries and advisors.

In addition to the in-place workshops, a remote workshop was held through a satellite transmission from the SEDUC-AM Media Center on July 2, 2019. The transmission was carried out by the Secretary of State for Education and Sports, SEDUC-AM through the Elementary Education Coordination of DEPPE (Department of Educational Policies and Programs) with the participation of the CEO of Flying Saci, Sylker Teles, and teachers Tarcinara Tavares, Kácia Oliveira, Ana Maria Pinho and Sirlei dos Santos. The transmission reached the places in the Amazon jungle very hard to access. Most of them can be reached only by boat.

3.4 Implementation

From April 29th to July 4th, Flying Saci Game Studio, together with representatives from SEDUC-AM, worked in the field to serve schools in the state education network, installing the Mathmages game and checking the state of computers laboratories visited, since the game has minimum hardware and software requirements.

During the project, 163 schools were served in 34 municipalities in the State of Amazonas, with 98 schools in the capital Manaus and 65 in the interior of the State. The Mathmages game was successfully installed and tested on 538 machines from 105 schools out of the 163 achieved, 50 of which were laptops. However, the 1,111 machines had several problems, most related to hardware or software obsolescence.

3.5   Mathmages Arena Tournament

The fourth stage of the Mathmages Project comprised the inter-school tournament called Mathmages Arena Tournament or M.A.T. At this stage, the best students from schools in the capital and countryside faced each other in elimination rounds and in the grand final held in conjunction with the 2dn Amazon Mathematics Fair on October 22, 2019 at the Federal University of Amazonas, UFAM. The tournament had the participation of 163 schools from 34 municipalities in the state of Amazonas. Of those, 105 students from 25 schools in 9 municipalities were classified for the final stage of the tournament. The first phase of the tournament took place in schools participating in the project, on an itinerant basis (Fig. 3), in the municipalities of Amazonas. The best students of this phase were classified for the final phase.

Fig. 3. First phase of M.A.T. in the city of Itapiranga, Amazonas.

In the last phase of the tournament, the students were separated into groups and faced each other in elimination matches. The finals of the tournament was held at the Federal University of Amazonas (Fig. 4).

The finals were attended by 105 students from 25 schools representing 9 municipalities in the state of Amazonas. At the end, 7 students were champions of the 1st. Edition of the M.A.T.

Fig. 4. Students playing in the M.A.T. finals.

3.6 Big Data

At the end of the project all data collected during the gameplays were converted into reports to SEDUC-AM. No personal data was collected, only players performances based on correct or wrong answers, time taken to answer and skipped questions. Those data were collected with consent and sent to a cloud database in order to be later used as a tool to propose better strategies focusin on students weaknesses and schools and places which were more in need of pedagogic attention.

A technical report was also provided with information about the state of the computer labs in the schools from the public network. The objective of that report was to provide to the State Secretariat a better view of the hardware limitations so a set of actions could be done to update the technological infrastructure of schools.

4 Conclusions

Education in Amazon is very challenging. Most of students that live in the jungle area have to cover great lengths in order to attend classes (Fig. 5), often rowing a canoe. The greatest challenge for this project, however, was the internet conexion, non-existent in some remote regions. Since data collection was very important to fulfill the project's goals, off-line solutions had to be implemented. A Local Network version of the game was developed. That version also had the feature of storing data locally until an internet connection become available. That way, the Mathmages Arena Tournament could happen.

After the tournament, some interesting data could be analyzed. The three best placed municipalities by number of victories were Novo Airão, Iranduba and Itapiranga, respectively. As for the average percentage of correct answers, the three best placed cities were Novo Airão (87.27%), Itacoatiara (87.17%) and Itapiranga (80.89%). The school with the highest average percentage of correct answers was E. E. Nossa Senhora do Carmo de Parintins with 97.8%. In the individual results in percentage of correct answers, the

Fig. 5. Student going to school in Careiro da Várzea area, Amazonas. SEDUC-AM, 2022.

three best schools were E.E. Prof. Fernando Ellis Ribeiro, E.E. Prof. Fernando Ellis Ribeiro and E.E. Prof. Berezith Nascimento da Silva, all from Itacoatiara and all with 100% accuracy. Regarding the average time to answer the questions, the interior was highlighted again, with the three best cities being Parintins (2.016 s), Itacoatiara (2.615 s) and Novo Airão (2.687 s). The best schools in terms of individual results in this regard were E.E. Maria Ivone de Araújo Leite, from Itacoatiara, with 1.437 s, E.E. Quitó Tatikawa, from Itapiranga, with 1.533 s and E.E. Prof. Fernando Ellis Ribeiro with 1.647 s to answer each question. The lowest average time between the schools, however, was with the Santo Antônio State School, in Manaus, with 1.926 s.

An important and necessary final note about this work is that it was not possible to validate the ARCS-REACT method at the end of the project in schools, although it was used for the development of the application in the first place. The reason why it was not possible to carry out tests for this purpose lies in the duration of the program, among other legal obstacles. Although the project lasted a year (a year and a half considering bureaucratic delays), a longer follow-up of the same classes that played Mathmages would be necessary so that the level of learning could be measured compared to a control group, without access to the game. Research of this nature, however, is in future plans. Conducting an extended follow-up of a school with the contribution of teachers and pedagogues to endorse the result.

The Mathmages game is an innovative game that promotes education in a playful way with digital inclusion. The initiative of the Government of the State of Amazonas with this project is in line with the guidelines and foundations of education. Due to the Covid-19 pandemic, the Mathmages nas Escolas project had to be suspended from 2020, but there are plans for it to be resumed in 2022, once again in the state of Amazonas. It is expected that the project can be expanded to other Brazilian states in the future. The game is currently part of DX Gameworks, as well as Flying Saci Game Studio.

Acknowledgements. The authors would like to express their deepest appreciation to the State Secretariat for Education and Sports of Amazonas, for making this project possible; the Kyushu University and professor Kiyoshi Tomimatsu, who guided the theoretical model used to create the game Mathmages; to Samsung Ocean Center Manaus, that offered technical resources to develop and improve the game for mobile devices; to all teachers, pedagogues, parents and students who turn this project into something meaninful.

References

1. Teles, S.T.: Instructional design for contextual learning-based online games. Ph.D. thesis, Kyushu University, Fukuoka (2015)
2. Keller, J.M.: Motivational Design for Learning and Performance: The ARCS Model Approach. Springer, New York (2010). https://doi.org/10.1007/978-1-4419-1250-3
3. Crawford, M.: Contextual teaching and learning: strategies for creating constructivist classrooms. Connections **11**(6), 1–6 (2001)
4. Koeffel, C., Hochleitner, W., Leitner, J., Haller, M., Geven, A., Tscheligi, M.: Using heuristics to evaluate the overall user experience of video games and advanced interaction games. In: Bernhaupt, R. (ed.) Evaluating User Experience in Games: Concepts and Methods, pp. 233–256. Springer, London (2010). https://doi.org/10.1007/978-1-84882-963-3_13
5. Paavilainen, J.: Critical review on video game evaluation heuristics: social games perspective. In: International Academic Conference on the Future of Game Design and Technology, pp. 56–65. ACM, New York (2010)
6. Tavares, T.R.S.: Cultura Digital: O jogo Mathmages como ferramenta no processo de ensino e aprendizagem. Master thesis, Universidad del Sol. San Lorenzo (2022)
7. BNCC Homepage. http://basenacionalcomum.mec.gov.br. Accessed 21 May 2022
8. Meiners, J., Rasmussen, H.: An Adventure in Pre-Rendered Backgrounds. https://www.jmeiners.com/pre-rendered-backgrounds/. Accessed 16 Apr 2022

Enhancing Children's Cultural Empowerment Through Participatory Game Design Based on Hometown Ceramic Culture

Xianhe Zhang🆔 and Baosheng Wang$^{(\boxtimes)}$ 🆔

Hunan University, Changsha, Hunan, China
1286127549@qq.com, walterwang840217@gmail.com

Abstract. Nowadays many local communities lose their voice in the development of local culture and are in a state of disempowerment, children as inheritors and builders of local culture, need to be nurtured in ways that contribute to the future sustainability of their communities. The participatory game design emphasizes the empowerment of children as creative participants. To explore the process and outcome of using participatory game design to empower children in a cultural decline community, participatory workshops were conducted in a primary school with four phases: culture probing & design capacity building, game story creation, game mechanics design, and design reflection. The purpose of our experiment was not only to lead children to design culturally appropriate games but also to use open-ended questions to guide the interviews and to quantitatively and qualitatively analyze the results of children's culturally relevant psychological empowerment during participation, with empowering outcomes including emotional components (learning motivation, place identity), cognitive components (cultural reflection, cultural innovation), behavioral components (cultural sharing, community engagement) and relational components (collaborative ability, community cohesion).

Keywords: Cultural Empowerment · Participatory Game Design · Children Empowerment

1 Introduction

With the development of modernization, the direction of community building has become commercialized and the local community loses its voice in the development of local culture and is in a state of disempowerment, which has led to a reduced awareness of local culture and a lack of motivation in community building. The core of community building lies in people [1], and learning about regional culture can help residents gain a deeper understanding of the historical development process of their local community, enriching their sense of local belonging and identity to the local community. Furthermore, UNESCO believes that the focus of sustainable development of culture is not its cultural expression, but the wealth of knowledge and skills that are passed down from generation to generation. However, today's socio-economic changes and modern lifestyles have

© The Author(s), under exclusive license to Springer Nature Switzerland AG 2023
X. Fang (Ed.): HCII 2023, LNCS 14047, pp. 105–114, 2023.
https://doi.org/10.1007/978-3-031-35979-8_8

raised concerns, including a lack of cultural knowledge among children [2]. The neglect of children as the inheritors and builders of local culture, who have the power to influence the direction of communities, is detrimental to the future sustainability of communities.

Participatory design for children emphasizes regarding children as creative participants in the design process and establishing an equal relationship between the designers and children. Previous research has shown that an important advantage of participatory design is that it gives the opportunity to develop two types of empowering outcomes: a product that meets the needs of the user and the psychological empowerment of the participants. However, most research on children's participatory game design has focused more on the quality of the final products and there is a lack of reliable research on the empowering outcomes of children's participatory game design processes.

This study demonstrates that by conducting workshops to support and guide local primary school children in participatory game design experiments, children could achieve psychological empowerment and enrich their understanding of their home ceramic culture in a community with rich ceramic resources through deep participation. Finally, we summarize this paper with an analytical framework of psychological empowerment regarding emotional, cognitive, behavioral, and relational components of children's participation in design processes in a cultural context [3, 4].

2   Literature Review

2.1   Participatory Game Design with Children

The first of these participatory designs to encourage children as design partners occurred in the Computer Interaction Community classified as collaborative inquiry (CI) [5]. In the trend of children's participation in social research, participatory design methods with children are increasingly being applied in the fields of game design, including the technical [6, 7], social [8], and cultural [9–11] domains. Participatory design should not only develop tangible solutions, but should also produce intangible outcomes that provide psychological empowerment to users and other stakeholders, such as enhancing learning skills [6, 12, 13], design skills [14], and social skills [13, 15]. Serious games have been applied to learning in areas such as health, education, and industry, and by engaging users and increasing their motivation, they have been shown to be particularly useful in education because they promote active participation in the learning process compared to traditional teaching methods. Not only are children keen to spend time playing games, but they also show some interest in enriching their gameplay and even creating their own games. Khaled and Vasalou apply existing PD methods to work with children to design a first-person perspective experience for the Village Voices game, allowing children to learn strategies for organizing conflict resolution [8]. Sim, Cassidy, and Read organized workshops for children to design artifacts - designing interface ideas for museum exhibits in an AR environment to encourage their learning about history and culture and understanding of the concept of augmented reality [11]. Li Worked with children to design a serious game of "Qinhuai lanterns" based on the five elements of user experience, exploring possible pathways and forms of digital transmission of Qinhuai lantern culture [10]. There is relatively little research on the participatory design game with children in the cultural context, instead focusing mainly on the exploration of design products and methods of participation and the low level of children's involvement.

2.2 Psychological Empowerment

The systematic use of the term 'empowerment' emerged in social work in the 1970s [16], defined as the mechanism by which people, organizations, and communities take control of their own lives. It is relevant to the discipline of psychology and has been widely used in a variety of collaborative design contexts, such as social innovation [1], and participatory design [15]. It is a process that refers to how people, organizations, or communities are empowered to take control of their lives and develop critical awareness as well as long-term skills [3]. The first is the help of others through professional support project empowerment, and community empowerment based on the socio-political dimension of group life; the other is self-empowerment, developing the ability to construct and solve problems autonomously and develop critical awareness at the individual level. Zimmerman proposes a nomological network of three components of psychological empowerment, and Christen undertook a new iteration, adding an element of a relational component [3, 4]. The psychological empowerment model consists of (1) emotional (intrapersonal) component, personal self-perceived control of a situation; (2) cognitive (interactive) component, the development of knowledge and skills that can assist in critically understanding a situation; (3) behavioral component, more engagement and participation in action; and (4) relational component, the development of the ability to mobilize interpersonal relationships.

3 Case Study

The experimental site is located in the town of Tongguan in Changsha, Hunan province, which has a unique Changsha kiln culture and was the most popular exporter of kilns during the Tang dynasty, and the large quantity of Changsha kiln porcelain from the Batu Hitam confirms the existence of the ancient maritime Silk Road between China and West Asia. However, the modern cultural path of Tongguan Town has begun to follow the direction of catering to foreign tourists, and apart from the craftsmen who specialize in ceramics, the adults have not devoted much attention to ceramic culture, Most of them choose to work outside the home, except for a small number of adults who are still engaged in selling ceramics in the shopping streets. In contrast, there are still many opportunities for children to learn about culture, and participatory game design workshops can provide a more interesting method for cultural learning. We selected 32 children aged 10–12 and two teachers from Guo Liang Primary School as the study participants and conducted four workshops at the school (see Fig. 1), combining existing participatory design tools [15] and techniques [17] with the children to design a ceramic game design for their hometown based on the serious game design framework [18], investigating the in-depth performance of children's participation in the process. A pre-test and post-test were conducted to understand children's gain and the cultural empowerment 5-point Likert scale (Appendix 1), semi-structured interviews with children and teachers. Quantitative and qualitative methods were used to analyze and identify the framework for psychological empowerment in participatory game design.

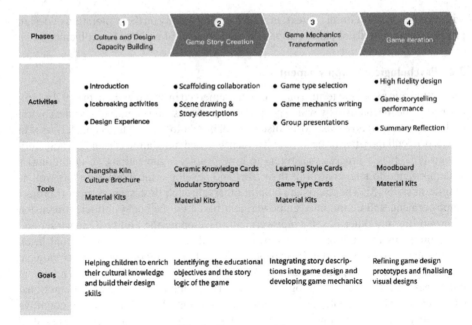

Fig. 1. Process overview.

We conducted 4 workshops in ceramics and art classes every Thursday and Friday. A basic questionnaire was given to the children before the start of the experiment to find out the children's level of cultural awareness, play preferences, and personal interests in advance.

Phase 1&2: Culture and Design Capacity Building & Game Story Creation.

In the first phase, we introduced the children to the culture of Changsha Kiln in three ways by asking them questions about the unique culture of Tongguan Town (see Fig. 2a). In terms of creative capacity building, we conducted design activities including an ice-breaking activity: designing a team logo together to promote teamwork. The main task in phase 2 was to complete the storyboard, and the modular storyboard design tool proposed was used as a scaffold as well as knowledge cards, story description cards, material kits such as scissors, glue, colored pens, and cultural materials as toolkits, Fig. 2b shows the team members working together on the storyboard.

Phase 3&4 Game Mechanics Transformation & Game Iteration.

In phase 3, children were given learning-style cards and game-type cards [19] (see Fig. 2c), to help them quickly match the type of game that corresponds to their learning style and translate the story into an educationally meaningful game. Once the game types were identified, children selected game mechanics to be written on sticky notes and posted on a storyboard to illustrate the game interaction mechanics. Finally, the teams took turns presenting their story prototypes (see Fig. 2d) and all children voted for the best team. In the next phase, all team members refined the game based on their suggestions again, and in the next high-fidelity design phase, relevant mood boards were provided for the children to refer to and complete the visual design of the game interface. Four main scenes were finalized (see Fig. 3) and then we organized a storytelling performance to allow the children to present their game stories more clearly and comprehensively and summarize them.

Fig. 2. Children's participation

Fig. 3. Children's final design and description

4   Cultural Empowerment Framework with Children

Through the questionnaire results as well as interview results using affinity diagram analysis for qualitative analysis, the information collected was mapped to dimensions of psychological empowerment and combined with the pedagogical theories of BLOOM, Gagne [20, 21]. For the definition of subdimensions, it was found that the transfer of the psychological empowerment model to the context of participatory design in cultural communities was reflected as cultural empowerment. Therefore, we proposed the cultural empowerment concept, taking psychological empowerment as the starting point.

Children were chosen as the empowering subject, designers, and teachers amongst others played the role of collaborators, and children's empowerment was achieved through participation from a cultural perspective. The initial cultural empowerment analytical framework for children in the participatory game design process is shown in Table 1.

Table 1. The analytical framework for the cultural empowerment of children's participation

Empowerment categories	Empowerment indicators	Children's performance
Emotion	Learning motivation	Motivation to show a new interest in their local culture
	Place identity	Belonging to a group and having an emotional experience of affection and pride in it
Cognition	Cultural reflection	Critical examination of local cultures and comparisons between cultures
	Cultural innovation	Ability to use cultural resources and personal intelligence to create
Relation	Collaborative ability	Ability to better understand the perspectives of others and build effective relationships with them
	Community cohesion	Emotional sharing between community members
Behavior	Cultural sharing	Building community-based shared cultural experiences using intangible cultural forms such as sharing content
	Community engagement	Active cooperation and participation in locally related industrial construction activities

4.1 Emotion

The emotional empowerment of children is expressed in the recognition of the value of their home culture and the building of identity and attachment to it. The main components include (1) *Learning motivation* - Motivation to show a new interest in their local culture. The workshops activated children's active understanding of their hometown culture. When we reviewed the previous content again in phase 2, more students were willing to share Changsha kilns with us voluntarily. Many students expressed a strong desire to learn about the ceramic culture in the final session by expressing their wish to have more knowledge related to the culture of Changsha kilns explained in their ceramics classes, rather than just learning to make ceramics in the classroom, and the score of Question 5: "I would like to learn more about the ceramic culture of Tongguan Town.", which improved from 3.7 to 4.9, we believe that this proves that children have greatly improved their motivation for active learning. (2) *Place identity* is an integral part of personal identity, which refers to individuals attributing themselves to a group and defining their own identity, and acknowledging their local culture by interacting with the place and having an emotional experience of affinity and pride in it. Among the ratings involving emotional aspects, children rated Question 1: "I am a child of Tongguan Town, where there is a rich ceramic culture." which improved from 4.1 to 4.8. In the final interviews, many students mentioned: "Changsha kilns were very popular with foreigners in the Tang Dynasty, we are the only export-oriented porcelain kiln." This is in stark contrast to the first phase where few students were able to answer after the questions were asked. In addition, place identity was reflected in the performance of the game story, the main characters in the game story were children from Tongguan Town, and the most impressive part of the final performance was a boy who played the role of the village chief and imitated the state of a local old man in Changsha dialect, which was unanimously praised by the teachers and students.

4.2 Cognition

The children's cognitive empowerment is expressed in terms of cultural reflection and cultural innovation. (1) *Cultural reflection* is the understanding and critical examination of the local culture, which develops into the ability to drive the cultural subject's own development and progress. To ensure the accuracy of the knowledge test, we adjusted the order of questions for the post-test questionnaire. The data from the pre-test of the questionnaire and children's responses showed that the children's interpretation of the ceramic culture of their hometown changed from very vague to almost every student being able to describe specifically what they knew about the Changsha kilns. The children's responses were very limited in nature, such as "the need to preserve it" and "to be better known", and did not have any substantive ideas when they were asked about the direction they felt the cultural development of their hometown should go towards. More importantly, in the final test children scored significantly higher on the knowledge questionnaire and appeared more relaxed in answering the questionnaire, indicating that children have gained some understanding and reflective ability in their knowledge of ceramics in their hometown. (2) *Cultural innovation* can be defined as the ability to create using cultural resources and personal intelligence, and when mentioning what he had learned in class during the interview, one student mentioned that he wants to make an aceramic-shaped projection lamp that can show our history on the road by turning on the light and projecting it on the wall, and his desk-mate immediately echoed him saying, "I'll do it with you, I'll make projection lamp for the Batu Hitam." Class teacher Miss Zheng mentioned that some children suggested that they would like to make a ceramic-style notebook and open a ceramic workshop, and one child who loved to sing mentioned that he would like to make an opera stage related to the culture of Changsha kilns to sing on, which proves that the children have a sense of cultural innovation and can turn what they have learned into their own creativity.

4.3 Relation

In the mapping of the relation dimension, we draw on relevant research in community psychology [22]. Relation refers to changes in the ability to collaborate and relate to others resulting from collaborative design processes, including the ability to collaborate and community cohesion. From a micro perspective, children build the capacity to better understand the perspectives of others and to build effective relationships with others – such as (1) *Collaborative ability*, which has been found similarly in other related studies [14]. When first given the task of storyboarding, the children were relatively restrained and many complained to us that their group members were uncooperative and needed help from the designer in assigning activities within the group. However, in the last phase, it was clear that there was less conflict between the children and that they were less likely to complain about each other and more likely to get together to discuss the presentation of the game. In the final Likert scale ratings, the children rated their experience of participating in the workshop very high, and many of them said it was captivating and they would like to participate with their classmates next time. From a macro perspective, this ability to collaborate extends to everyday life as (2) *Community cohesion* - the sharing of emotions between community members. When children were told that the game they had co-designed might be promoted to an online platform for wider use, cohesion was demonstrated by the seriousness with which each child voted and gave design suggestions. We were most pleased that one of the children in the class participating in the experiment was a child with autism, who was in a marginal state in his daily school life. This reflects the inclusive nature of participatory design, where everyone involved in the project is given equal power.

4.4 Behavior

Behavior is defined by the level of participation in the design activity and the continuation of the performance after the design is finished. In the context of cultural empowerment, empowerment in terms of behavior is manifested in (1) *Cultural sharing*, mainly in the use of non-material cultural forms as sharing content to build a community-based shared cultural experience. At the end of the interviews, we noticed that a number of students were still immersed in their previous game designs and sharing and refining the drawn stories with their deskmates. At the end of the workshops, many children came to ask if they could leave their knowledge cards with them. This finding is also reflected in the quantitative analysis, where the scores for the questions related to behavior Question 6: "It was an interesting experience for me to be involved in learning about my home culture." have been improved from 4.0 to 4.9. (2) *Community engagement* refers to children being more proactive in activities related to the cultural industry of their hometowns. The ceramics teacher commented: "The children seemed to have a deeper understanding of ceramic culture and were more active in participating in the ceramic culture public event 'Labor Artisans in School', and some students asked if they could bring games to display as well." This proves that children are more enthusiastic about participating in local cultural activities after participating in the workshop.

5   Conclusion

In this paper, we present an exploration of children's cultural empowerment through participatory game design workshops. Based on the psychological empowerment model, we concluded that the framework of children's cultural empowerment in participatory play design in cultural settings can be categorized into emotional components (learning motivation, place identity), cognitive components (cultural reflection, cultural innovation), behavioral components (cultural sharing, community engagement) and relational components (collaborative ability, community cohesion). The process of empowerment in participatory game design deepens children's understanding of local culture and builds connections with the local community, which facilitates children's future construction and transmission of their local culture and the future sustainable development of local cultural heritage.

Acknowledgments. We are very grateful to the teachers and students who participated in this experiment This research is supported by Hunan Science and Technology Key Research Project (No. 2022GK2070), and Hunan Social Science Foundation (No. 19YBA085).

Appendix 1

Contents of a 5-point Likert scale For each of the five responses, "strongly agree", "agree", "not necessarily", "disagree" and "strongly disagree", they are recorded as 5, 4, 3, 2, and 1 respectively.

1. I am a child of Tongguan town, where there is a rich ceramic culture.
2. I like the characteristic ceramic culture of my hometown and think it has many advantages.
3. I love my hometown, and I am proud of my hometown.
4. I would like to learn more about the ceramic culture of Tongguan Town.
5. In the future, I also want to work on something related to the ceramic culture of my hometown.
6. It was an interesting experience for me to be involved in learning about my home culture.
7. I enjoyed participating in these workshops and found them very interesting.
8. I gained a lot of knowledge through this participatory workshop that I didn't know before.

References

1. Manzini, E.: Design, When Everybody Designs: An Introduction to Design for Social Innovation. MIT Press, Cambridge (2015)
2. Uğraş, T., Rızvanoğlu, K., Gülseçen, S.: New co-design techniques for digital game narrative design with children. Int. J. Child-Comput. Interact. **31**, 100441 (2022)
3. Zimmerman, M.A.: Psychological empowerment: issues and illustrations. Am. J. Community Psychol. **23**, 581–599 (1995). https://doi.org/10.1007/BF02506983

4. Christens, B.D.: Toward relational empowerment. Am. J. Community Psychol. **50**, 114–128 (2012). https://doi.org/10.1007/s10464-011-9483-5
5. Muller, M.J., Kuhn, S.: Participatory design. Commun. ACM **36**(6), 24–28 (1993)
6. Bonsignore, E., et al.: Traversing transmedia together: co-designing an educational alternate reality game for teens, with teens. In: Proceedings of the 15th International Conference on Interaction Design and Children (2016)
7. Iivari, N., Kinnula, M., Molin-Juustila, T.: You have to start somewhere: initial meanings making in a design and making project. In: Proceedings of the 17th ACM Conference on Interaction Design and Children (2018)
8. Khaled, R., Vasalou, A.: Bridging serious games and participatory design. Int. J. Child-Comput. Interact. **2**(2), 93–100 (2014)
9. Hussain, S.: Empowering marginalised children in developing countries through participatory design processes. CoDesign **6**(2), 99–117 (2010)
10. Li: Research on Qinhuai Lantern Digital Inheritance Based on Children's Participation in Game Design (2020)
11. Sim, G., Cassidy, B., Read, J.C.: Crowdsourcing ideas for augmented reality museum experiences with children. In: Vermeeren, A., Calvi, L., Sabiescu, A. (eds.) Museum Experience Design. SSCC, pp. 75–93. Springer, Cham (2018). https://doi.org/10.1007/978-3-319-585 50-5_4
12. Coller, B.D., Scott, M.J.: Effectiveness of using a video game to teach a course in mechanical engineering. Comput. Educ. **53**(3), 900–912 (2009)
13. Nunes, N.J., Nisi, V., Rennert, K.: beEco: co-designing a game with children to promote environmental awareness-a case study. In: Proceedings of the 2016 CHI Conference Extended Abstracts on Human Factors in Computing Systems (2016)
14. McNally, B., et al.: Gains from participatory design team membership as perceived by child alumni and their parents. In: Proceedings of the 2017 CHI Conference on Human Factors in Computing Systems (2017)
15. Simonsen, J., Robertson, T. (eds.): Routledge International Handbook of Participatory Design, vol. 711. Routledge, New York (2013)
16. Bodker, S.: Creating conditions for participation: conflicts and resources in systems development. Hum. Comput. Interact. **11**(3), 215–236 (1996)
17. Winn, B.M.: The design, play, and experience framework. In: Handbook of Research on Effective Electronic Gaming in Education, pp. 1010–1024. IGI Global (2009)
18. Chang, M., et al. (eds.): Learning by Playing. Game-Based Education System Design and Development: 4th International Conference on E-Learning, Edutainment 2009, Banff, Canada, 9–11 August 2009, Proceedings, vol. 5670. Springer, Cham (2009). https://doi.org/10.1007/978-3-642-03364-3
19. Lever-Duffy, J., McDonald, J.B.: Teaching and Learning with Technology, 4th edn. (2011)
20. Adams, N.E.: Bloom's taxonomy of cognitive learning objectives. J. Med. Libr. Assoc. (JMLA) **103**(3), 152 (2015)
21. Gagne, R.: The conditions of learning and theory of instruction Robert Gagné. Holt, Rinehart ja Winston, New York (1985)
22. Christens, B.D., et al.: Adolescents' perceived control in the sociopolitical domain: a latent class analysis. Youth Soc. **47**(4), 443–461 (2015)

Understanding Players and the Player Experience

Comparing Hedonic Consumption Experiences Between MOBA Games and Vrides

Amir Zaib Abbasi[1(✉)], Helmut Hlavacs[2], and Umair Rehman[3]

[1] IRC for Finance and Digital Economy, KFUPM Business School, King Fahd University of Petroleum and Minerals, Dhahran, Saudi Arabia
aamir.zaib.abbasi@gmail.com
[2] Research Group Education, Didactics and Entertainment Computing (EDEN), University of Vienna, Vienna, Austria
helmut.hlavacs@univie.ac.at
[3] User Experience Design, Wilfrid Laurier University, Brantford, Canada
urehman@wlu.ca

Abstract. This study intends to explore the hedonic consumption experience factors comprising imaginal, emotional, and sensory that make statistically difference while comparing multiplayer online battle arena (MOBA) game users with Vride users. We collected two separate data sets including MOBA game users (292) and Vride Users (217). We performed t-test to investigate whether MOBA game users are statistically different in hedonic consumption experiences vs. Vride users. Our findings explicate that MOBA game users are statistically different in imaginal, emotional, and sensory experiences vs. Vride users. This study is distinctive in nature as it explores the hedonic consumption experiences that are statistically different while comparing MOBA game users with Vride users. We also drive theoretical and practical implications from our analyses.

Keywords: Hedonic theory · imaginal · emotional · Sensory · MOBA game · Vride · A casual comparative study

1 Introduction

Information Technology (IT) is one of the essential conditions that facilitate further fulfilment of societal productivity needs. IT, specifically video-gaming has been heavily used for recreational purposes: for fun, to mitigate stress, and to relax [1]. Video-gaming has emerged as a global entertainment sensation that has a wide-ranging economic and cultural impact [2, 3].

Research refers to IT consumption in terms of various classifications that include the computer game consumption [4, 5]. According to Holt [6], envisioning consumption as an '*experience*' addresses the consumer's emotional needs and builds the attachment between the consumer and the focal product being consumed. Similarly, consumption as '*play*' is another dimension through which a connection is created between the consumer and product based on experience, integration and classification. Some examples in this direction include social networking, dating sites, MMORPGs, virtual sports,

X. Fang (Ed.): HCII 2023, LNCS 14047, pp. 117–124, 2023.
https://doi.org/10.1007/978-3-031-35979-8_9

videogames, eSports, and MOBA games [2, 7–11]. This study primarily focus on two kinds of digital technologies comprising MOBA games and virtual rides (Vrides) and both technologies fall under the realm of hedonic products/services [8, 10, 12].

The consumption of hedonic products (e.g. MOBA games and Vrides) refer to an intrinsic and self-motivating consumer behavior that generate playful hedonic experiences comprising imaginal, emotional, and sensory with a product/service [2]. In terms of the consumer experience associated with video games, Abbasi, et al. [2] highlight that consumers stay engaged in the game for long hours as they want to play repeatedly, and they enjoy the euphoric feelings they experience while gaming. In recent times, hedonic consumption experiences have gained more popularity in the scientific world. However, we primarily constrain our discussion pertaining to hedonic consumption experiences that have been investigated on video-gaming and digital technology (i.e. Vrides).

Our systematic review of prior studies on hedonic consumption experiences has emerged into two major streams of researches. The first stream of research only focused few aspects of hedonic factors. For instance, Lowry, et al. [13] and Alzahrani, et al. [14] studied the joy factor within the technology acceptance model (TAM) and theory of planned behavior (TPB) to determine gamers immersion state, behavioral intention to play a video-game, gamers' attitude, and actual use of games. Wu and Holsapple [7] examined imaginal (e.g. escapism, roleprojection, and fantasy) and emotional experiences (e.g. enjoyment, arousal, and emotional involvement) of MMORPGs to assess gamers' behavioral intention to play games and its subsequent effect on usage behavior. Li, et al. [15] estimated the effect of hedonic gratifications (e.g. escapism, fantasy, and enjoyment) on gamers' continuance to play games. Meta-analysis also revealed that enjoyment is one of the hedonic factors that have been studied a lot followed by perceived playfulness, which is quite similar to enjoyment and flow [11, 16]. Sharma, et al. [17] also considered the enjoyment as predictor of continuance intention to play games.

The second stream of research has accounted the whole aspects of hedonic consumption experiences (e.g. imaginal, emotional, and sensory experiences). Abbasi, et al. [2] examined the role of imaginal, emotional, and sensory factors to predict gamers' cognitive, affective, and behavioral engagement in video-gaming. Abbasi, et al. [18] and Abbasi, et al. [10] examined the uni-dimensional factors of hedonic consumption experiences including escapism, roleprojection, enjoyment, fantasy, emotional involvement, arousal, and sensory to predict children's subjective wellbeing pertaining to their smartphone usage and behavioral intention to play MOBA games and its resulting effect on overall gamers' usage behavior. Hollebeek, et al. [8] also followed the uni-dimensional perspective to develop the gamers' attitude towards playing the PUBG game.

Hedonic factors have also been realized in virtual settings but not specifically in the context of Vrides. Vrides is defined as a computer technology that makes use of software-generated realistic sounds, images, videos, and other sensations to replicate a real environment or imaginary settings. Vrides commenced by Virtualistics as technology entertainment service provider in Pakistan that starts up with the VR motion simulator rides termed as Vrides. For instance, Sina and Wu [19] studied consumers' pleasure and arousal as shopping orientation in virtual stores. While Bigne and Maturana [20] assessed the 360 virtual reality video service to trigger store visit and hotel bookings.

Given the thorough review of earlier studies focusing on hedonic consumption factors in video-game and Vrides studies, we witnessed that hedonic factors have been studied in video-games and as well in MOBA games. However, studying the hedonic factors in Vrides remain limited, which require deliberate attention for further investigation. Interestingly, prior studies are scant with reference to studying hedonic consumption experiences between two digital technologies such as MOBA games and Vrides to explore whether users of MOBA games are statistically different from Vrides users in terms of perceived hedonic experiences comprising imaginal, emotional, and sensory. Considering the extracted limitations and research gaps, we intend to investigate the hedonic consumption experiences comprising imaginal, emotional, and sensory between users of MOBA games vs. users of Vrides to explore whether users of MOBA games make statistically difference in hedonic consumption experiences vs. users of Vrides or not.

This study contributes to advancing the literature on hedonic theory in several aspects. First, we apply hedonic consumption experiences including imaginal, emotional, and sensory to assess users' perceived experiences of MOBA games and Vrides. Second, we investigate whether users of MOBA games make statistical difference among hedonic consumption experiences vs. Vrides. Third, uses and gratifications (U&G) is used to explore the factors that act as gratifications for MOBA users vs. Vride users. Fourth, a causal comparative approach is applied to examine the potential differences in hedonic consumption experiences between MOBA users and Vride users.

2   Underpinning Theory

We also introduce Uses and Gratifications (U&G) theory [21] as the theoretical background of this study. The prime focus of this theory is concerned with how people select, use, and engage in their media (which in our case represents the domain of consumer video-game engagement). Rubin [22] presented five assumptions of this theory: media is selected in line with people's goals and objectives, it is used to satisfy needs and wants, selection is affected by social and psychological factors, media competes with other sources to fulfill user wants and needs, and people are at a greater position of influence in their relationship with media.

Based on our study's context, this paper specifically explores the factors that act as gratifications, which make statistical difference in MOBA game users vs. Vride users. Many scholars have utilized the U&G theory in dissimilar environments e.g. social media, internet, games, Vlog viewing, binge-watching movies, and food delivery apps to identify factors that serve as gratifications, which further influence users to use the media or applications [10, 23–26]. However, U&G theory remains unexplored in the context of Vride and comparison study, which make a unique case for this study.

3   Methodology

This study deployed the casual-comparative approach as it is most feasible approach to explore the cause or reason for potential differences between the groups [e.g. MOBA users vs. Vride users; 27]. We utilized this technique as we already had an independent variable including the two recognized groups such as MOBA games users and Vride users. This study's primary objective is to examine the potential differences in hedonic consumption experiences between MOBA games users vs. Vride users.

In this study, we had two groups comprising MOBA game users and Vride users and we assessed both groups on the dependent variables containing imaginal, emotional, and sensory experience. We constructed the study's questionnaire, especially evaluating the hedonic experiences. The items measuring the imaginal, emotional, and sensory experience were adapted from [2] to quantify hedonic experiences pertaining to MOBA game users and Vride users.

Prior to data collection, we calculated the sampling requirement using G*power tool. Using the G*power, we calculated the sampling necessity under t-tests and means: difference between two independent means (two groups) at effect size = 0.5, α err prob = 0.05, power = 0.95, which guided that each group should have 88 respondents and in total 176 responses are minimum required to perform the analyses.

To collect the responses from MOBA game users, we approached the six institutions of Islamabad and Rawalpindi and requested their permission to grant for data collection. Once, we were allowed for data collection, we approached the students at cafeteria and library for data collection. Upon interacting with the students, we asked initial questions (e.g. do you know MOBA games? Which MOBA games do you play), those who knew MOBA games and were actively playing MOBA games. We passed the survey and requested to rate their hedonic consumption experiences driven by MOBA games. In total, 350 questionnaires were distributed and we got 292 valid responses.

Next, we proceeded to collect data from Vride users. To approach Vride users, we targeted entertainment zone (i.e. Funcity, GIGA Mall and Centaurus Mall, Islamabad). Once we reached at the funcity, especially at virtualistic setups, we requested to rate hedonic consumption experiences to users who have already finished the vride. In total, we circulated 230 surveys and received 217 valid responses.

Since our study's main objective is to examine if there is a significant difference in hedonic consumption experiences while comparing MOBA game users vs. vride users. We employed t-test to assess whether the means of two groups are statistically different from each other [28]. In addition to t-test, we also utilized an online tool (https://lbecker.uccs.edu) given by Becker [29] to estimate the effect size. The Cohen's estimation ranges from small (d = 0.2), medium (d = 0.5) or large (d = 0.8) [29, 30]. We also performed the reliability check for both samples using Cronbach's alpha.

4 Data Analysis

Based on the valid responses from both groups, we performed the t-test to explore the significant differences in hedonic consumption experiences between MOBA game users vs. vride users. The findings show that MOBA game users are statistically different from vride users on imaginal, emotional, and sensory experience; hence, three hypotheses are accepted. See Table 1 for descriptive statistics and Table 2 for t-test. We also quantified the effect size of three hypotheses and witnessed small effect. Besides, we checked the reliability using Cronbach's alpha and resulted that hedonic consumption experiences possess values greater than 0.70.

Table 1. Group Statistics

	Group	N	Mean	Std. Deviation	Std. Error Mean	Effect Size
Imaginal-Exp	MOBA users	299	39.66	6.50	0.38	0.24
	VR users	217	38.01	7.30	0.50	
Emotional-Exp	MOBA users	299	42.71	5.55	0.32	0.23
	VR users	217	41.18	7.37	0.50	
Sensory-Exp	MOBA users	299	22.77	4.81	0.28	0.37
	VR users	217	21.02	4.73	0.32	

Table 2. Hypotheses Testing

		Levene's Test for Equality of Variances		t-test for Equality of Means					95% Confidence Interval of the Difference	
		F	Sig.	t	df	Sig. (2-tailed)	Mean Difference	Std. Error Difference	Lower	Upper
Imaginal Exp	Equal variances assumed	4.16	0.04	2.69	514.00	0.01	1.65	0.61	0.45	2.84
	Equal variances not assumed			2.65	432.47	0.01	1.65	0.62	0.42	2.87
Emotion-Exp	Equal variances assumed	3.22	0.07	2.68	514.00	0.01	1.53	0.57	0.41	2.64
	Equal variances not assumed			2.57	383.45	0.01	1.53	0.59	0.36	2.69
Sensory-Exp	Equal variances assumed	0.55	0.46	4.10	514.00	0.00	1.75	0.43	0.91	2.58
	Equal variances not assumed			4.11	469.59	0.00	1.75	0.42	0.91	2.58

5 Discussion

Our study's goal was to determine the potential differences in hedonic consumption experiences while comparing MOBA game users with Vride. This study witnessed that MOBA game users are statistical different in hedonic consumption experiences comprising imaginal, emotional, and sensory than Vride users. In the case of emotional experiences, MOBA game users have greater tendency to generate perceived emotional experiences vs. Vride users. It may be because Vride journey is short in duration and may not provide a longer attachment with simulated rides. More importantly, MOBA games have longer gaming session and provide more opportunities to gamers to emotionally attach with games and can engage for longer period as they have access to those games at their homes as well.

In the context of imaginal and sensory experiences, MOBA game users have more likelihood to elevate imaginal and sensory experiences than Vride users. It may be due to the nature of digital technology. MOBA games are longer in duration and can repetitively play at home and with other fellows. vride is the short duration and expensive ride (e.g. charging 300–500 rupees on average for 2–3 minutes per vride), leaving consumers with insufficient time to appropriately escape naturalistic settings, develop the connection with virtual subject matter within these rides and experience the illusory reality of the virtual environment. Lastly, Vrides cannot intensely embroil human senses of sound, touch, and sight; pleasant sensory experiences due to having low graphics and narratives.

In terms of contributions, this study adds to the existing literature that explores the growing area of human computer interaction, especially in the context of a virtual world. Moreover, framing playful-consumption against the U&G theory allows research to evaluate the role of information technology for entertainment purposes. This allows the focus to shift from productivity-oriented use to gratification-oriented use in IT research. Existing studies have concentrated their focus on productivity-oriented technology. However, our study highlights that video games, although typically considered to be only pleasure-oriented, serve a range of uses related to imaginal, emotional and sensory. The application of the U&G theory may allow future research to explore the uses associated with hedonic consumption in terms of entertainment media. Moreover, we added to the range of hedonic consumption factors that may serve as potential gratifications for MOBA game users vs. Vride users.

In practical terms, our findings can help game developers to better design games in accordance with our findings. For example, instead of emphasizing the correlation between fantasy and gameplay, developers may invest more time and resources into making video games more emotionally engaging. By doing so, game developers can concentrate on the dimensions of playful-consumption experience so that they can meet the required needs of the gamers, which in turn encourages engagement in video game playing, especially for MOBA and eSports games. Moreover, game developers may benefit from incorporating elements that facilitate the hedonic needs that consumers fulfill by playing these games, which in turn influence their subjective wellbeing [31]. This may result in games that allow for greater role projection by personalizing characters, including more emotionally stimulating storylines and elements, as well as emphasizing the audio visual elements that may contribute to favorable sensorial and imaginal experiences. Additionally, game developers may benefit from their attention to factors impacting consumer engagement. The developers of these information systems may benefit from viewing the different "uses" served by pleasure-oriented media and technology. For example, social media developers may choose to incorporate different elements of personalization to facilitate role projection onto online personas. Moreover, other online platforms, such as ecommerce stores, can incorporate aesthetic values to improve the individual's sensory experience. This can extend towards immersive platforms that are used on different devices including websites and applications. Lastly, these findings can extend to practitioners who are developing immersive and virtual reality content. As these findings positively contribute to greater engagement, future renditions of virtual reality platforms may incorporate these elements to facilitate immersion.

Despite study's theoretical and practical implications, our study has a few limitations, which require future investigations. For instance, we only focused on t-test for a comparison study. Future study may apply multigroup analysis to generate more in-depth findings as it allows users to test the structural equation modeling for both groups. This study only examined hedonic consumption experiences comprising imaginal, emotional, and sensory between MOBA game users vs. Vride users. Future study may incorporate lower-order/unidimensional (e.g. escapism, roleprojection, emotional involvement, enjoyment, arousal, fantasy and sensory experience) perspective to examine the potential differences between MOBA game users vs. Vrides [21]. More importantly, future study may investigate the role of engagement factors to explore which digital technology is more engaging and makes significant differences.

References

1. Formosa, J., Johnson, D., Türkay, S., Mandryk, R.L.: Need satisfaction, passion and wellbeing effects of videogame play prior to and during the COVID-19 pandemic. Comput. Hum. Behav. **131**, 107232 (2022)
2. Abbasi, A.Z., Ting, D.H., Hlavacs, H., Costa, L.V., Veloso, A.I.: An empirical validation of consumer video game engagement: a playful-consumption experience approach. Entertain. Comput. **29**, 43–55 (2019)
3. Direction, S.: Gaming the system: how user innovation has transformed the video game industry (2020)
4. Abbasi, A.Z., Ting, D.H., Hlavacs, H., Fayyaz, M.S., Wilson, B.: Playful-consumption experience and consumer videogame engagement in the lens of SR model: an empirical study. In: International Conference on Human-Computer Interaction, pp. 85–104 (2019)
5. Seo, Y., Buchanan-Oliver, M., Fam, K.S.: Advancing research on computer game consumption: a future research agenda. J. Consum. Behav. **14**, 353–356 (2015)
6. Holt, D.B.: How consumers consume: a typology of consumption practices. J. Consum. Res. **22**, 1–16 (1995)
7. Wu, J., Holsapple, C.: Imaginal and emotional experiences in pleasure-oriented IT usage: a hedonic consumption perspective. Inf. Manag. **51**, 80–92 (2014)
8. Hollebeek, L.D., Abbasi, A.Z., Schultz, C.D., Ting, D.H., Sigurdsson, V.: Hedonic consumption experience in videogaming: a multidimensional perspective. J. Retail. Consum. Serv. **65**, 102892 (2022)
9. Abbasi, A.Z., Asif, M., Hollebeek, L.D., Islam, J.U., Ting, D.H., Rehman, U.: The effects of consumer esports videogame engagement on consumption behaviors. J. Prod. Brand Manag. **30**, 1194–1211 (2021)
10. Abbasi, A.Z., Rehman, U., Fayyaz, M.S., Ting, D.H., Shah, M.U., Fatima, R.: Using the playful consumption experience model to uncover behavioral intention to play Multiplayer Online Battle Arena (MOBA) games. Data Technol. Appl. **56**(2), 223–246 (2021)
11. Hew, J.-J., Lee, V.-H., T'ng, S.-T., Tan, G.W.-H., Ooi, K.-B., Dwivedi, Y.K.: Are online mobile gamers really happy? On the suppressor role of online game addiction. Inf. Syst. Front. 1–33 (2023)
12. Holbrook, M.B., Chestnut, R.W., Oliva, T.A., Greenleaf, E.A.: Play as a consumption experience: the roles of emotions, performance, and personality in the enjoyment of games. J. Consum. Res. **11**, 728–739 (1984)

13. Lowry, P.B., Gaskin, J., Twyman, N., Hammer, B., Roberts, T.: Taking 'fun and games' seriously: proposing the hedonic-motivation system adoption model (HMSAM). J. Assoc. Inf. Syst. **14**, 617–671 (2012)
14. Alzahrani, A.I., Mahmud, I., Ramayah, T., Alfarraj, O., Alalwan, N.: Extending the theory of planned behavior (TPB) to explain online game playing among Malaysian undergraduate students. Telematics Inform. **34**, 239–251 (2017)
15. Li, H., Liu, Y., Xu, X., Heikkilä, J., Van Der Heijden, H.: Modeling hedonic is continuance through the uses and gratifications theory: an empirical study in online games. Comput. Hum. Behav. **48**, 261–272 (2015)
16. Hamari, J., Keronen, L.: Why do people play games? A meta-analysis. Int. J. Inf. Manage. **37**, 125–141 (2017)
17. Sharma, T.G., Hamari, J., Kesharwani, A., Tak, P.: Understanding continuance intention to play online games: roles of self-expressiveness, self-congruity, self-efficacy, and perceived risk. Behav. Inf. Technol. **41**, 348–364 (2022)
18. Abbasi, A.Z., Shamim, A., Ting, D.H., Hlavacs, H., Rehman, U.: Playful-consumption experiences and subjective well-being: children's smartphone usage. Entertain. Comput. **36**, 100390 (2021)
19. Sina, A.S., Wu, J.: The effects of retail environmental design elements in virtual reality (VR) fashion stores. In: The International Review of Retail, Distribution and Consumer Research, pp. 1–22 (2022)
20. Bigne, E., Maturana, P.: Does virtual reality trigger visits and booking holiday travel packages? Cornell Hosp. Q. **64**, 226–245 (2022). https://doi.org/10.1177/19389655221102386
21. Abbasi, A.Z., Alqahtani, N., Tsiotsou, R.H., Rehman, U., Ting, D.H.: ESports as playful consumption experiences: examining the antecedents and consequences of game engagement. Telematics Inform. 101937 (2023)
22. Rubin, A.M.: Uses and gratifications. In: The SAGE Handbook of Media Processes and Effects, pp. 147–159 (2009)
23. Bulduklu, Y.: Mobile games on the basis of uses and gratifications approach: a comparison of the mobile game habits of university and high school students. Convergence **25**, 901–917 (2019)
24. Steiner, E., Xu, K.: Binge-watching motivates change: uses and gratifications of streaming video viewers challenge traditional TV research. Convergence **26**, 82–101 (2020)
25. Gregg, P.B.: Social responses to and motivation involving knitting vlog viewing. Convergence **27**, 508–523 (2021)
26. Ray, A., Dhir, A., Bala, P.K., Kaur, P.: Why do people use food delivery apps (FDA)? A uses and gratification theory perspective. J. Retail. Consum. Serv. **51**, 221–230 (2019)
27. Gay, L.R., Mills, G.E., Airasian, P.W.: Educational Research: Competencies for Analysis and Applications. Pearson Higher Ed (2011)
28. Abbasi, A.Z., Ting, D.H., Hlavacs, H., Wilson, B., Rehman, U., Arsalan, A.: Personality differences between videogame vs. non-videogame consumers using the HEXACO model. Curr. Psychol. (2020)
29. Becker, L.A.: Effect size (ES) (2000)
30. Sullivan, G.M., Feinn, R.: Using effect size—or why the p value is not enough. J. Grad. Med. Educ. **4**, 279–282 (2012)
31. Abbasi, A.Z., Khan, M.K., Naeem, F., Albashrawi, M., Ting, D.H., Kumar, S.: Gamers' subjective well-being: the role of peripheral and core elements of eSporst videogame addiction. Curr. Psychol. (2023)

Applicability of Psychophysiological and Perception Data for Mapping Strategies in League of Legends – An Exploratory Study

Ian N. Bandeira[1] , Carla D. Castanho[1] , Tiago B. P. e Silva[2(✉)] ,
Mauricio M. Sarmet[3] , and Ricardo P. Jacobi[1]

[1] Department of Computer Science, University of Brasilia, Brasília, Brazil
[2] Department of Design, University of Brasilia, Brasília, Brazil
tiagobarros@unb.br
[3] Federal Institute of Education, Science and Technology of Paraíba, João Pessoa, Paraíba, Brazil

Abstract. League of Legends is one of the most popular online games today, with a competitive scenario and a solid and constantly growing player base. This work aims to explore a solution that identifies game events and strategies from the convergence of different psychophysiological metrics from seasoned players in order to create tools to reduce the learning curve of these strategies for beginner and intermediate players. To achieve this, experiments with five participants have been conducted that extract, process, and synthesize data from player profiling, Electrodermal Activity (EDA), Interbeat Interval (IBI), facial expressions, and player perception of the match. The EDA and HR data (derived from the IBI metric) proved to be complementary and correspond with game events and strategies, while facial expression data had inconclusive results in all experiments.

Keywords: League of Legends · Psychophysiological Data Analysis · EDA · Heart Rate

1 Introduction

League of Legends (LoL), developed by Riot Games, is a Multiplayer Online Battle Arena (MOBA) game that today has a worldwide community of 180 million active players, with about 32 million players playing simultaneously on daily peaks. MOBA games are a hybrid between the MMO (massively multiplayer online games) and RTS (real-time strategy games) genres, in which, unlike MMOs, games are instantiated. World-building parameters are non-persistent, i.e., each game instance follows the same rules and patterns; however, there is no character and player progression interference between different game instances (matches).

A LoL match consists of two teams of five players each, with the goal of destroying the opposing base to win the game. Each team member controls a character performing a distinct game function. This character, along with its

X. Fang (Ed.): HCII 2023, LNCS 14047, pp. 125–140, 2023.
https://doi.org/10.1007/978-3-031-35979-8_10

team, interacts with the elements and events inserted in the map where the game takes place to acquire advantage of gold and experience over the enemy team – resources used to improve the attributes and skills of the controlled character, respectively.

Besides the game itself, the universe that makes up the narrative of this game expands across several platforms and physical and digital media that dialogue directly with the game, the characters inserted in it, and the interactions between characters inside and outside the game. From animated series ("Arcane", available on Netflix), music production groups composed of characters from the game ("K/DA", "True Damage", "Pentakill") to other Riot Games games ("Legends of Runeterra" – Card Game, "Wild Rift" – Mobile MOBA, "Ruined King: A League of Legends Story" – Turn-based RPG, among others), transmedia content seeks to enrich the story in which the original game is contextualized and offer cosmetics that reference such content, further captivating the game's consumers.

Being a strategy game with a solid competitive community, optimal game strategies are created within the community of high-level competitive players using game mechanics and their characters to affect the overall outcome of matches positively, a phenomenon referred to as *metagaming* [16]. To achieve victory most consistently, both casually and professionally, these sets of strategies address team decision-making and individual player mechanics. Either knowledge of these strategies or the fluid application of them in real-time play are factors that define players with above-average performance.

Many of these strategies are well defined within the game community[1] Many of the events that permeate these strategies or result from them are available in the game analysis data[2] and have been addressed in the literature [8,22]; however, for many of these strategies to be executed, prior preparation is required of the player(s), either psychological or mechanical, to be in the right place at the right time.

Possible tools for analyzing these events and strategies are:

- The game API, which, although highly reliable, has limitations regarding the type of data requested in different types of matches and the number of requests to be made in a match, being used more for gauging statistical information from the variables deemed significant by the game developer [14];
- Adding external code into the game, a method of obtaining any data regarding the game in real-time, including objective data on player positioning and move intent. Both the high development cost, as well as the limited scalability of the program make a trivial implementation of this tool unfeasible for academic analysis. The former is related to the needed knowledge about the inner workings of the game code required both to analyze the desired variables and not to interfere with the game's protection mechanisms, since this method can be used to generate a competitive advantage if misused [24]. The latter occurs since the code injected into the game will be valid only for

---

[1] Available at https://leagueoflegends.fandom.com/wiki/League_of_Legends.
[2] Available at https://developer.riotgames.com/apis#match-v5/GET_getMatch.

the events and strategies of the matches of that specific game. However, it is used in commercial applications known as *in-game companions* or *personal gaming coaches* (e.g. "*Blitz*[3]", "*Mobalytics*[4]").

In this context, the motivation of this exploratory study is given by the following questions: is the player's psychological state aware of such strategies stimulated in the preparation or execution of these strategies? Moreover, if so, would it be possible to converge different physiological responses to identify these events? If the physiological responses correspond to possible in-game events with some reliability, this analysis tool can be used as a methodological basis for creating a taxonomy of possible events in the game, which can be applied not only to the context of League of Legends but also to other games of the MOBA genre.

The possible recognition of events and strategies that can be significant for the course of a match from the behavior of players can generate knowledge that would not only decrease the learning curve of the game, facilitating the recognition of these strategies, but also improve the consistency in the reproduction of these strategies for more experienced players who, even if they have theoretical knowledge about the event itself, may not know how to apply it to an actual match.

Therefore, this work aims to observe whether there is a relationship between changes in the data from different psychophysiological metrics with possible strategies and events within a League of Legends match.

This work is organized as follows: Sect. 2 presents the theoretical framework used to define the methods and tools used in the execution of the study; Sect. 3 contains the documentation on the structure of the experiments performed, with which tools and which methods were used to extract and pre-process the data collected, and what significance each piece of data collected has in the context of this work; Sect. 4 presents the results of these experiments; Sect. 5 deepens the analysis on the validity of the collected data and obtained results to propose future works; and Sect. 6 concludes this work.

2   Theoretical Framework

2.1   Emotion

According to Vallverdú et al. [33], emotions are informational mechanisms used by living entities to provide appropriate sensory-motor responses to external stimuli, as well as a way to attribute meaning to internal stimuli. Among the possible body responses, one can cite changes in body posture, facial expressions, or other physiological changes less apparent to visual observation, such as variation in heart rate or increased sweat production. One of the main challenges to structuring or classifying emotions is the subjectivity with which they can be

---

[3] Available at https://blitz.gg.
[4] Available at https://mobalytics.gg.

analyzed and interpreted since the same emotion can be externalized in different ways, leading to the existence of several taxonomies that seek to encompass and classify emotions [5, 7, 25–27, 34].

According to Nacke [21], early discussions of emotions tended to be evaluated on biphasic spectrums, distinguishing between good and bad, positive and negative, attractive and aversive, or pleasant and unpleasant. Only recently the field is beginning to understand the complexity of affective processes that are often a mixture of positive and negative feelings. Despite this, classical models, such as the circumplex model of affect proposed by Russel [25] or models derived from it [31], are still widely used for analyses in Games User Experience, mainly treating analyses from psychophysiological data [12, 23, 29].

Russell's [25] model of affect consists of a two-dimensional plane containing two axes of independent, biphasic scales, and the author theorizes that emotions can be categorized within this plane. The horizontal axis corresponds to the valence scale, defined as the evaluation of the emotion between positive and negative, i.e., how the individual feels that emotion. In contrast, the vertical axis corresponds to the arousal scale, defined as the evaluation of the emotion relevance, i.e., how strong or weak the emotion is felt by the individual [32].

In the context of this research, the definition of the arousal scale has relevance for its direct and linear correlation with the psychophysiological metric of electrodermal activity (EDA), which was captured in the experiments of this study. However, the recognition and analysis of emotion itself are not significant for what was defined as the objective of this research since it is relevant to analyze a pattern of alternation between psychophysiological data in the execution and preparation of strategies within a match, and not to identify which emotion the player is feeling at a specific moment.

2.2 Psychophysiological Metrics

From the definition by Andreassi et al. [2], "psychophysiology is the study of the relationships between psychological manipulations and the resulting physiological responses, measured in the living organism, to promote understanding of the relationship between mental and bodily processes." Psychophysiology seeks to analyze, from biometric capture instruments [15], the involuntary bodily responses arising from stimuli captured by the body's senses. Cacioppo et al. [6] propose that there are five possible associations between psychological processes and bodily responses:

- **One-to-one relationship**, in which only one psychological process is directly associated with only one bodily response and vice versa;
- **One-to-many relationship**, in which only one psychological process is directly associated with two or more bodily responses;
- **Many-to-one relationship**, in which two or more psychological processes are directly associated with only one bodily response;
- **Many-to-many relationship**, in which two or more psychological processes are directly associated with two or more bodily responses; and

- **Null relationship**, in which there is no association between psychological processes and body responses.

In the analysis of psychological stimuli in bodily responses, more specifically in the relationship between bodily responses and emotions arising from stimuli (the focus of this research), the most common association is that of many-to-one; that is, a bodily response can be associated with several psychological processes [21]. Although it is known that psychological processes can cause several bodily responses, the limitation of biometric capturing instruments makes it only possible to observe punctual physiological stimuli.

Among the psychophysiological metrics that can be gauged, the following will be measured in this study:

Electrodermal Activity (EDA): Linearly correlated to arousal [17] and measured from the change in electrical conductivity of the skin due to sweat production by the eccrine glands, the EDA, also known as Galvanic Skin Response, is a psychophysiological measure that associates with the mentioned physiological stimulus from how excited an individual is when exposed to a punctual or constant psychological stimulus, such as taking a jump scare, watching an advertisement, or playing a game [21].

The EDA signals can be dissected into two main components. A tonic one refers to the measurement of the Skin Conductance Level (SCL), which consists of slow and constant signal changes; and a phasic one represents fast and punctual changes in signal measurements and corresponds to the measurement of the Skin Conductance Response (SCR) [4].

Sensors that measure EDA are largely unobtrusive, low-cost, and generate data that is easy to interpret due to its almost direct relationship with arousal [4]. However, the EDA signals must be captured in a controlled environment since the temperature and humidity of the data capture environment can interfere with eccrine gland activity, generating noise in the output.

Heart Rate (HR): Intrinsically related to heart rate variability (HRV) metrics, the literature shows that HR and HRV are psychophysiological metrics that can be used to capture relationships with both internal and external stimuli when measured in participants in situations of possible stress, such as flight simulators [10], mental stress loads [1], and "tilt" [18], a well-known phenomenon within the esports community and especially LoL, which consists of a constant state of frustration and other negative emotions caused by an event or a player [35], negatively impacting the player's gameplay "tilted" and spreading toxicity to the other players in the match.

Facial Expressions: According to Tan et al. [30], "facial expression analysis consists of the automatic use of recognized facial expressions to infer affective states. Being a video-based approach, it is non-obtrusive compared to current psychophysiological methods. This allows for more authentic play experiences and enables data collection in non-laboratory settings." Although expression analysis is a metric used in research with both constant data and electronic games [18,29,30] and in one-off actions that seek to induce some physiological response [3], there is no consensus on the validity of this psychophysiological metric, as McAllister et al. [20] counterpoint "in playtests it is common for players to remain relatively expressionless, making facial coding very difficult as well as time-consuming" [20], even though they acknowledge that the method is promising for being non-obtrusive.

3 Experimental Setup

Psychophysiological metrics stand out among user experience evaluation techniques as aggregators of quantitative and objective data about an individual influenced by various and different stimuli [19], such as while playing a game. This technique does not replace traditional mechanisms for acquiring and analyzing data about games, even though the data may be more subjective, such as that from a questionnaire, but it seeks to complement these mechanisms. In this study, traditional metrics are used in conjunction with psychophysiological metrics to understand players' attitudes and preferences, aiming to profile both participants under game-related demographics and their gaming sessions under these characteristics.

3.1 Extraction Tools and Procedures

While the analysis of physiological stimuli from biometric capture instruments is compelling for composing studies and playtests due to the unintended (hence unbiased) nature of the captured stimuli adding a robust validity layer, a solid reproducibility layer is equally necessary for the study environments, as a participant is never solely under the influence of the stimuli planned by a given study. In this case, the data extraction process must be executed through a more rigorous procedure than the data analysis and synthesis processes.

The tools for capturing and extracting the psychophysiological data of EDA and IBI (inter-beat interval, later normalized and translated to the analysis metrics HRV and HR) are done by the sensors present in the *Empatica E4 Wristband*, where the EDA and IBI data are captured at frequencies 4 Hz and 64 Hz, respectively.

For the process of obtaining data regarding the player's face (later processed to extract the player's facial expressions) and the screen where the game takes place, two different OBS Studio[5] instances were used, being one responsible for capturing the player's webcam and only a small part of the game screen, which contains a game-time counter (Fig. 1), while the other captures only the screen where the game takes place. Both instances have been configured to have 30 frames per second and to start and stop using the same keyboard shortcut.

Considering that League of Legends is a closed-source game, the correlation analyses between the psychophysiological data and the game events need to be performed later than the experiment if no external code is injected into the game.

---

[5] Available at https://obsproject.com/.

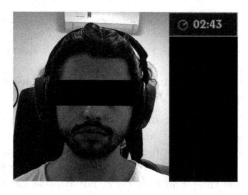

Fig. 1. Instance that captures the webcam along with game-time

Therefore, the synchronization of the data provided by the different capture tools is vital for validating this research.

The experiments were conducted in the same environment to ensure the constancy of elements that could interfere with data collection, such as lighting and temperature. A researcher was present throughout all experiments, and the participants were instructed beforehand to ask questions about their knowledge of jargon and the terms used in the questionnaires applied. Initially, the participants were introduced to an Informed Consent Form, and after signing it, they were instructed to fill out a questionnaire to profile the players participating in the research. The questionnaire presented to the respondents contains 13 closed-ended questions and two short-answer open-ended questions (Q1.7, Q1.8), including demographic questions (Q.1, Q.2), information about in-game patterns (Q1.3–Q1.9), and ratings of Likert-scale statements regarding game engagement, adapted from the questionnaire on online gaming proposed by Dengah et al. [11] (Q1.10–Q1.15). The questions in this questionnaire are available below:

Q1.1 - Which gender do you identify with?

Q1.2 - How old are you?

Q1.3 - Which ranked league do you belong to?

Q1.4 - What was your highest-ranked league?

Q1.5 - How many years have you been playing League of Legends?

Q1.6 - How many games, on average, do you play per week?

Q1.7 - Which champion do you usually play with the most?

Q1.8 - Do you consider yourself a "One Trick Pony"?

Q1.9 - In which positions do you usually play? (Select up to two)

Q1.10 - I feel committed to improving my game, striving to be the best player I can be.

Q1.11 - I try to improve my game even when I'm not actually playing, for example, by visiting online forums and learning from other players.

Q1.12 - I feel mentally and even physically drained after long and intense matches.

Q1.13 - Sou muito influenciado pelas opiniões, perspectivas e exigências de outros jogadores.

Q1.14 - I get annoyed and irritated when players don't take the blame for their words and actions.

Q1.15 - I find it satisfying to run mechanics and rotations over and over until they are almost perfect and automatic.

After filling out the questionnaire, the participants were instructed on how to wear the wristband and what actions they should perform to synchronize the device and the video capture instances. In this case, it was defined that the participants should press the F10 key to start recording the video instances at the 10-s mark of game time, and that they should press the button located on the top of the wristband at the 15-s mark of game time. Since even the simplest events do not occur until the 1:00 min mark of game time, the synchronization steps required do not influence the player's experience.

After the game session, the participant is informed about the concept of "tilt" from Wu et al. [35] definition: "tilt is an emotional reaction to in-game events that cause a deterioration in gameplay. Tilt in e-sports is primarily associated with frustration and anger while playing and arises alongside analyses of toxic or divergent behavior. As in other sports, this phenomenon is followed by repetitive play that can lead to successive losses that negatively impact the player experience and can even disengage players from the game itself."

Then, the participant is introduced to a post-game perception questionnaire to assess how challenging the game was if, at any point, the player "tilted", and if so, what were the reasons that led him to do so. The post-game questionnaire has only closed questions, which are available below:

Q2.1 - Did your match result in victory or defeat?

Q2.2 - On a scale of 0 to 10, how challenging was your game?

Q2.3 - Did you "tilt" at any point in the game?

Q2.4 - If you answered yes to the previous question, which one or ones were the reasons for the "tilt"?

(R1.1) - Your poor performance in the game

(R1.2) - Poor performance of your teammates

(R1.3) - Toxicity of your teammates

(R1.4) - Other (open answer)

Q2.5 - If the toxicity of his teammates were the reason for the "tilt", in which categories of toxicity do what occurred fall?

(R2.1) - Negative attitude (giving up)

(R2.2) - Verbal abuse

(R2.3) - Leaving the game/AFK

(R2.4) - Intentional feeding

(R2.5) - Hate speech

(R2.6) - Cheating

(R2.7) - Inappropriate or offensive user name

(R2.8) - Other (open answer)

The possible answers to question Q2.5 (R2.1–R2.8) were selected from the categories present in the official player reporting system.

3.2   Data Preprocessing

For the files containing the EDA and IBI information, preprocessing was done using **FLIRT** – **F**eature generation too**Lk I**t for wea**R**able da**T**a – proposed by Föll et al. [13], whose function is to translate the files containing the original information coming from the wristband into Dataframes. The EDA preprocessing consists of a modular filtering approach to reduce signal noise and the decomposition of the EDA signal into two signals, referring to the tonic and phasic components mentioned in Sect. 2.2, while for the IBI signal, the tool processes it into signals resulting from HR using NN intervals, a normalized heartbeat interval metric filtered of equipment noise.

The video containing the player's facial expressions is decomposed into frame images that are then evaluated en masse by an edited version of the open source tool *deepface* [28], using already known evaluation models such as *OpenCV* and *RetinaFace* to evaluate and create a percentage graph of emotions, those being Happy, Neutral, Surprise, Sad, Angry, Fear, and Disgust.

4   Results

Data were obtained from 5 participants, four of whom identify as cis men and one as a cis woman (Table 1 - Q1.1), aged between 22 and 25 years (mean = 24.2; stdev = 1.3) (Table 1 - Q1.2). All participants were undergraduate students from the University of Brasilia and were chosen based on availability and ranked rating in League.

Table 1. Pre-experiment Questionnaire (Q1.1–Q1.9)

Player	P1	P2	P3	P4	P5
Q1.1	Cis Man	Cis Man	Cis Woman	Cis Man	Cis Man
Q1.2	25	24	22	25	25
Q1.3	Plat 2	Day 4	Plat 2	Day 4	Day 4
Q1.4	Day 4	Day 2	Plat 1	Day 3	Day 4
Q1.5	≥ 7 *years*	≥ 7 *years*	5 *and* ≤ 7 *years*	≥ 7 *years*	≥ 7 *years*
Q1.6	1 to 3	3 to 5	5 to 7	0 to 1	1 to 3
Q1.7	Ezreal	Lux	Soraka	Sejuani	Lee Sin
Q1.8	No	No	No	No	No
Q1.9	ADC, Sup	Mid, Sup	Sup	Top, JG	JG, Mid

Due to the exploratory nature of this study, strict filtering of possible participants was necessary, considering that they should have technical knowledge of the game mechanics and its events so that these could be gauged. This filtering was done from the league in that the participant was placed and which league was his record (Table 1 - Q1.3, Q1.4). The league a player is in interferes directly with the technical quality of the matches he/she participates in, i.e., the higher the league, the more skilled the players in that league are. The league of the current participants ranges between Platinum 2 and Diamond 4 (statistically speaking, these leagues correspond to the best 4.4% and 1.9% of the world's ranked players, respectively, with a mean = 2.9% and standard deviation = 1.37%), while the record league participants range between Diamond 4 and Diamond 2 (corresponding to the best 1.9% and 0.85% of the world's ranked players, respectively; with mean = 1.80% and standard deviation = 0.86%).

The highest league the player has achieved is of significance to the study because for a player to maintain his/her position in higher leagues, he/she needs to play constantly, and from the frequency of weekly matches of the respondents (Table 1 - Q1.6), one played zero to one match, two played one to three matches, one played three to five matches, and one played five to seven matches weekly.

Regarding the questions asked on the Likert scale (Q1.10–Q1.15), one has stated that most of the participants are committed to their improvement in the game; only one participant stated that he/she tries to improve his game by ways outside the game; most players stated that they feel drained physically and mentally after a long and intense game, are influenced by the possible actions coming from other players, and are irritated by the lack of commitment and self-responsibility of other players. A large part of the respondents feels accomplished when executing previously learned and trained mechanics and rotations (Fig. 2).

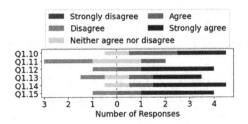

Fig. 2. Answers to the Likert scale questions (Q1.10–Q1.15)

After a thorough analysis of the game sessions, it was established that while each player had one to three games, only the first game of each participant was considered for this study. This decision was made considering that there is no defined time frame for the psychophysiological data to return to a relaxed state without game-related stimuli, which could make the validity of the analysis unfeasible. Another four instances of the analysis generated twenty matches selected for analysis, all of which were from the same five participants over different times.

However, to maintain the validity of the results and to avoid any potential confounding factors that could jeopardize the analysis, only five of these instances were chosen for display. The reason for this was due to the potential for bias, as the participants might have had an idea about the objective of the research after multiple instances. This could have influenced their behavior and impacted the validity of the results. The images generated from the data helped in observing peaks and valleys in the distribution, enabling a manual analysis of the correlation between the psychophysiological data and events during the match.

As an example, in this paper, the data from the matches played by players P3 and P4, represented in Figs. 3 and 4, respectively, will be further arranged and analyzed.

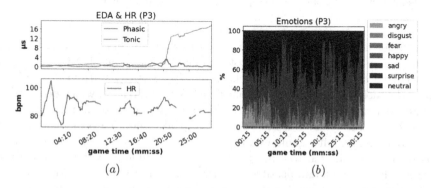

Fig. 3. Figure (a) contains the graphs regarding the EDA and HR metrics for Player 3 (P3), while Figure (b) contains the distribution of emotions from the analysis of facial expressions captured from the same participant during the match.

Observing the data in Fig. 3(a), there are two graphs, the upper one containing the tonic and phasic components of the AGE, measured in micro siemens (μs). In contrast, in the lower figure, we have the data referring to heart rate (HR), measured in beats per minute (bpm). It can be seen that there are comparatively small peaks in amplitude in the EDA phasic component at approximately 10:25 and 14:35, medium peaks in amplitude at approximately 18:45 and 24:00, and a comparatively large peak in amplitude at 21:00.

By observing these cited peaks, it is possible to analyze that at the same time they occur, there is a response within the same minute range of the data referring to HR, a behavior that also occurs in Fig. 4. However, there are peaks and valleys in the HR data in both figures that are not matched by a change in the EDA data but are related to events in the match, whether preparation and execution of neutral objectives, group fights, or ambushes.

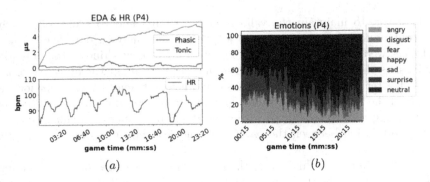

Fig. 4. Figure (a) contains the graphs regarding the EDA and HR metrics for Player 4 (P4), while Figure (b) contains the distribution of emotions from the analysis of facial expressions captured from the same participant during the match.

Another fact that became evident was the individuality of how each player reacts to game stimuli: while the most significant peak in phasic EDA for player P3 occurred as a result of a game-changing play, at the 20:50 min mark of the game: the most significant peak in phasic EDA for player P4, which occurred at the approximately 10:30 min mark of the game, was due to an argument with a member of his team. Despite this, many peaks and valleys of phasic EDA and HR correlate with game events. Unfortunately, due to the population of this study being limited to 5 people, it was not possible to perform an analysis between these stimuli and possible player and match profiles as measured by the post-game questionnaire (Table 2). Nevertheless, the conjunction of the EDA and HR metrics proved consistent and complementary as physiological responses to match events.

The data provided from facial expression analysis, presented in Figs. 3(b) and 4(b), have no apparent pattern of peaks and valleys to analyze. In many participants, the data were erratic and without an apparent pattern, which corroborates McAllister et al. [20] statement paraphrased in Sect. 2.2. Notwithstanding, this erratic pattern of data may have occurred due to the chosen game mode, which despite being the most popular competitive mode of gauging individual game performance, consists of two teams with five players each, paired by their league points, who can communicate only by the game's written chat or by predetermined game signals called *pings*. Therefore, it is possible that if a match takes place with a team of players who know each other and have voice communication, while it could generate more meaningful expressions resulting from events, the analysis process would have to be altered so that the emotions coming from facial expressions are captured while a player is speaking.

Table 2. Post-experiment questionnaire (Q2.1–Q2.5)

Player	P1	P2	P3	P4	P5
Q2.1	Loss	Win	Win	Win	Win
Q2.2	8	4	9	1	5
Q2.3	Yes	No	Yes	No	No
Q2.4	R1.2, R1.3	–	R1.2, R1.3	–	–
Q2.5	R2.1, R2.2	–	R2.2, R2.4, R2.5	R2.2, R2.4	R2.2

5 Discussion

According to Dawson et al. [9], although much of the stimuli that cause SCR response, responsible for EDA's phasic component, include high arousal emotions, it is not evident which SCRs are responses to which specific emotions, such as anger, anxiety, or surprise. The experimental paradigm of this study defines that SCR interpretation does not seek to analyze which specific emotion generated the SCR stimulus but instead whether the timing of the changes in SCR signals correspond to the preparation, execution, and completion of events within a League of Legends match. Thus, this finding does not interfere with the validity of this work.

In the present study, great care was taken to ensure the validity of the results by strictly gathering and processing the game sessions. The decision to analyze only the first game of each participant was made to avoid any potential bias that could have arisen from the participants being aware of the objective of the research. Despite these efforts, our results are still limited by the lack of participants who meet a certain threshold in ranked matches. This limitation could have implications for the generalizability of our findings, as the results may not be representative of the population at large. Nevertheless, the results of this study provide important insights into the correlation between psychophysiological data and events during the match and serve as a foundation for future research in this area.

However, possible future work from this paper could address specific player effects, such as "tilt", and how this affects different player profiles. Even though, analyses that rely on prior player knowledge and performance, such as this one, have the drawback of requiring participants belonging to an extremely niche part of the community within an already niche community.

Another possible threat to this work's validity is the auxiliary equipment in the environment where the experiments were conducted. Although all the tests were done in the same space under the same conditions, the players who agreed to participate in the experiment had their peculiarities regarding the game settings and the peripheral equipment used to play (mouse, keyboard, monitor). For a player to perform, it is important that he/she is comfortable with his playing conditions. If not, this external factor can cause frustration and "tilt" not desired by the study but likely to be detected by the biometric sensors.

To mitigate this threat, participants were recommended to bring their peripheral equipment if they wished. Adjustments were made to the game resolution and custom shortcuts for the greatest comfort and fluidity in the player's actions.

There is also the manual analysis of the game video footage to gauge what qualifies to be an in-game event or not, which can be seen as arbitrary about what is gauged. To mitigate this threat, the analysis of the peak and valley points of the data were mapped and then gauged if they had any relationship to a game event in order to reduce this arbitrariness. The game has numerous events, and for as many of these as possible to be detected, a great understanding of the game is required on the part of both the experiment participants and the leading researcher, who is also part of the league average of the players participating in the experiment.

6   Conclusion

This paper explored psychophysiological data and traditional methods to assess the possibility of mapping League of Legends game events. The findings of this research favor the joint use of EDA and HR data to gauge in-game events while concluding that data from facial expression analysis is not ideal for this search setting. Furthermore, this study contains an analysis that converges several traditional and psychophysiological research methods, where traditional methods seek to profile participants and effectively verify that they are in fact part of the target population.

As this exploratory study obtained satisfactory results, although preliminary due to the limited number of matches analyzed in the experiment, it sets a precedent that there is the possibility of using this analysis to assess events and, in the future, create a taxonomy of these events based on psychophysiological data, aiming to facilitate the use of technical terms of the game within academia and solve possible disagreements about the definition of some minor events. Furthermore, this study also opens opportunities so that this analysis, now done on League of Legends, can be performed for other games of the same genre that follow a similar structure since all the analysis is done using data from sensors and player perception, not requiring changes in parameters and steps of extraction, pre-processing, and data analysis.

References

1. Anderson, A.: Comparison of baroreceptor sensitivity with other psychophysiological measures to classify mental workload. Doctor of Philosophy, Iowa State University (2020). https://doi.org/10.31274/etd-20200624-85
2. Andreassi, J.L.: Psychophysiology: Human Behavior & Physiological Response, vol. 1, 4th edn. Psychology Press (2000)
3. Aslam, S., Zwart, N., Gouweleeuw, K., Verhoeven, G.: Classification of disappointment and frustration elicited by human-computer interaction: towards affective HCI, August 2019

4. Braithwaite, D.J.J.: A guide for analysing electrodermal activity (EDA) & skin conductance responses (SCRs) for psychological experiments, p. 42 (2013)
5. Cacioppo, J., Gardner, W., Berntson, G.: The affect system has parallel and integrative processing components. J. Pers. Soc. Psychol. **76**, 839–855 (1999). https://doi.org/10.1037/0022-3514.76.5.839
6. Cacioppo, J.T., Tassinary, L.G., Berntson, G.: Handbook of Psychophysiology, March 2007. https://doi.org/10.1017/CBO9780511546396
7. Cannon, W.B.: The James-Lange theory of emotions: a critical examination and an alternative theory. Am. J. Psychol. **39**(1/4), 106–124 (1927). https://doi.org/10.2307/1415404
8. Cruz, A.C.S.: League of legends: an application of classification algorithms to verify the prediction importance of main in-game variables, p. 5 (2021)
9. Dawson, M.E., Schell, A.M., Filion, D.L., Berntson, G.G.: The electrodermal system. In: Cacioppo, J.T., Tassinary, L.G., Berntson, G. (eds.) Handbook of Psychophysiology, 3rd edn., pp. 157–181. Cambridge University Press, Cambridge (2007). https://doi.org/10.1017/CBO9780511546396.007
10. De Rivecourt, M., Kuperus, M.N., Post, W.J., Mulder, L.J.M.: Cardiovascular and eye activity measures as indices for momentary changes in mental effort during simulated flight. Ergonomics **51**(9), 1295–1319 (2008). https://doi.org/10.1080/00140130802120267
11. Dengah, H.J.F., Snodgrass, J.G., Else, R.J., Polzer, E.R.: The social networks and distinctive experiences of intensively involved online gamers: a novel mixed methods approach. Comput. Hum. Behav. **80**, 229–242 (2018). https://doi.org/10.1016/j.chb.2017.11.004
12. Fernandes, M.V.: Ajuste dinâmico de dificuldade em jogos digitais : um estudo de caso comparativo entre os modelos afetivo e baseado em desempenho, December 2019. https://bdm.unb.br/handle/10483/29227
13. Föll, S., et al.: FLIRT: a feature generation toolkit for wearable data. Comput. Methods Prog. Biomed. **212**, 106461 (2021). https://doi.org/10.1016/j.cmpb.2021.106461
14. Kica, A., Paolillo, T.J., O'Donnell, L.R., La Manna, A.J.: Analysis of data gathered from league of legends and the Riot games API, March 2016
15. Klarkowski, M., Johnson, D., Wyeth, P., Phillips, C., Smith, S.: Psychophysiology of challenge in play: EDA and self-reported arousal. In: Proceedings of the 2016 CHI Conference Extended Abstracts on Human Factors in Computing Systems, CHI EA 2016, pp. 1930–1936. Association for Computing Machinery, New York, May 2016. https://doi.org/10.1145/2851581.2892485
16. Kokkinakis, A., et al.: Metagaming and metagames in Esports. Int. J. Esports (2021). https://eprints.whiterose.ac.uk/179913/
17. Lang, P.J.: The emotion probe: studies of motivation and attention. Am. Psychol. **50**(5), 372–385 (1995). https://doi.org/10.1037/0003-066X.50.5.372
18. Lee, J.S.: Exploring stress in Esports gaming: physiological and data-driven approach on tilt. Ph.D. thesis, UC Irvine (2021). https://escholarship.org/uc/item/61p8c951
19. Mandryk, R.: Physiological measures for game evaluation. In: Isbister, K., Schaffer, N. (eds.) Game Usability, pp. 207–235. Elsevier, Amsterdam (2008). https://doi.org/10.1016/B978-0-12-374447-0.00014-7
20. McAllister, G., Mirza-Babaei, P., Avent, J.: Improving gameplay with game metrics and player metrics. In: Seif El-Nasr, M., Drachen, A., Canossa, A. (eds.) Game Analytics: Maximizing the Value of Player Data, pp. 621–638. Springer, London (2013). https://doi.org/10.1007/978-1-4471-4769-5_27

21. Nacke, L.E.: An introduction to physiological player metrics for evaluating games. In: Seif El-Nasr, M., Drachen, A., Canossa, A. (eds.) Game Analytics: Maximizing the Value of Player Data, pp. 585–619. Springer, London (2013). https://doi.org/ 10.1007/978-1-4471-4769-5_26

22. do Nascimento Junior, F.F., Melo, A.S.C., da Costa, I.B., Marinho, L.B.: Profiling successful team behaviors in league of legends. In: Proceedings of the 23rd Brazillian Symposium on Multimedia and the Web, WebMedia 2017, pp. 261–268. Association for Computing Machinery, New York, October 2017. https://doi.org/ 10.1145/3126858.3126886

23. Oliveira, R.R.A.: Análise de diferentes algoritmos de ajuste dinâmico de dificuldade que utilizam dados de atividade eletrodérmica em jogos digitais, May 2021. https:// bdm.unb.br/handle/10483/28952

24. Ornelas, P.Y.: Injeção de DLL: um estudo de caso aplicado à jogos, October 2019. https://bdm.unb.br/handle/10483/29228

25. Russell, J.A.: A circumplex model of affect. J. Pers. Soc. Psychol. **39**(6), 1161 (1980)

26. Schachter, S., Singer, J.: Cognitive, social, and physiological determinants of emotional state. Psychol. Rev. **69**(5), 379–399 (1962). https://doi.org/10.1037/ h0046234

27. Scherer, K.R.: Emotion as a multicomponent process: a model and some cross-cultural data. Rev. Pers. Soc. Psychol. **5**, 37–63 (1984)

28. Serengil, S.I., Ozpinar, A.: HyperExtended LightFace: a facial attribute analysis framework. In: 2021 International Conference on Engineering and Emerging Technologies (ICEET), Istanbul, Turkey, pp. 1–4. IEEE, October 2021. https://doi.org/ 10.1109/ICEET53442.2021.9659697

29. Siqueira, E.S., Santos, T.A.A., Castanho, C.D., Jacobi, R.P.: Estimating player experience from arousal and valence using psychophysiological signals. In: 2018 17th Brazilian Symposium on Computer Games and Digital Entertainment (SBGames), Foz do Iguaçu, Brazil, pp. 107–10709. IEEE, October 2018. https:// doi.org/10.1109/SBGAMES.2018.00022

30. Tan, C.T., Bakkes, S., Pisan, Y.: Inferring player experiences using facial expressions analysis. In: Proceedings of the 2014 Conference on Interactive Entertainment, Newcastle, NSW, Australia, pp. 1–8. ACM, December 2014. https://doi. org/10.1145/2677758.2677765

31. Thayer, R.E.: The Biopsychology of Mood and Arousal. Oxford University Press, New York (1989)

32. Valenza, G., Lanata, A., Scilingo, E.P.: The role of nonlinear dynamics in affective valence and arousal recognition. IEEE Trans. Affect. Comput. **3**(2), 237–249 (2012). https://doi.org/10.1109/T-AFFC.2011.30

33. Vallverdú, J., Trovato, G.: Emotional affordances for human–robot interaction. Adapt. Behav. **24**(5), 320–334 (2016). https://doi.org/10.1177/1059712316668238

34. Watson, D., Wiese, D., Vaidya, J., Tellegen, A.: The two general activation systems of affect: structural findings, evolutionary considerations, and psychobiological evidence. J. Pers. Soc. Psychol. **76**(5), 820–838 (1999). https://doi.org/10.1037/0022-3514.76.5.820

35. Wu, M., Lee, J.S., Steinkuehler, C.: Understanding tilt in Esports: a study on young league of legends players. In: Proceedings of the 2021 CHI Conference on Human Factors in Computing Systems, CHI 2021, pp. 1–9. Association for Computing Machinery, New York, May 2021. https://doi.org/10.1145/3411764.3445143

Never Correct: The Novel Analysis of Differing Visual (Facial Expression) and Acoustic (Vocalization) Bimodal Displays of the Affective States "Pain", "Pleasure", and "Neutral"

Silvia Boschetti[1]([⊠]) [ID], Hermann Prossinger[1,2] [ID], Violetta Prossinger-Beck[3],
Tomáš Hladký[1] [ID], Daniel Říha[1] [ID], and Jakub Binter[1]([⊠]) [ID]

[1] Faculty of Humanities, Charles University, Prague, Czech Republic
`silvia.boschetti@natur.cuni.cz, jakub.binter@fhs.cuni.cz`
[2] Department of Evolutionary Anthropology, University of Vienna, Vienna, Austria
[3] Dresden International, TU Dresden, Dresden, Germany

Abstract. In real-world scenarios, humans estimate a large proportion of their perceived world contextually and use previous information to adjust or modify their expectations and responses. A typical example of congruence is when a smile (visual modality) is accompanied by a laugh (acoustic modality). Pain and pleasure are extremely intensive affects, rarely correctly assessed. It rarely happens that affective communication is incongruent in different modalities. Intentional combinations of these two affective expressions may be implemented by using audiovisual media. It is to be expected that presentations involving incongruent combinations during gaming and other interactions with machines will alter perceptions and the impact of ambiguity. To evaluate the impact of sensory crosstalk a novel statistical analysis was developed to estimate the impact of each modality. The results show that the visual modality dominates for the pairing pain/pleasure for. The acoustic modality dominates for pain/pleasure, pain/neutral, and pleasure/neutral. For neutral/pain and neutral/pleasure, neither the visual nor the acoustic modality enables highly correct ratings. The findings are of high value to the psychology of perception on a theoretical level and game/media developers as application fields.

Keywords: Visual Displays · Acoustic Displays · Affective states · Dirichlet Distribution · Confusion Matrix · Heat Maps

1 Introduction

Consider an observer watching a single frame extracted from a video and hearing the simultaneous audio signal. In such a case, the person is observing (seeing and hearing) a bimodal signal.

© The Author(s), under exclusive license to Springer Nature Switzerland AG 2023
X. Fang (Ed.): HCII 2023, LNCS 14047, pp. 141–150, 2023.
https://doi.org/10.1007/978-3-031-35979-8_11

If the observer is asked to rate the observation, and the researcher is interested in whether the observer relies on the visual or the acoustic modality when rating, the researcher can modify the presentation. The observer is presented with a video frame as a visual modality together with an audio signal as the acoustic modality, but these two presented modalities are different. The observer has to rely on one of the two modalities. As the researcher knows the visual modality and the acoustic one, he/she can conclude on which modality the observer relied when rating—never on both, because the presented modalities exclude each other. We call such a set-up an incongruent bimodal presentation.

In this paper, we present many women as well as many men (separately) with incongruent bimodal stimuli, namely the pairings of the affective states pain, pleasure and neutral (speech) in all six combinations. These were presented (separately) by males and females, which we call stimuli. Details are described in the Methods section. Nomenclature: we henceforth call the participating observers raters, and the presenting females and the males from which the presentations of the bimodal affective states were derived as female or male stimuli.

In the set-up presented here, the visual and auditory information does not aggregate correctly. One of the few comparable real-life experiences we could find, which gave the name to the perceived phenomenon, is ventriloquism. This ancient art of making it seem as if the voice originates from a different source than the (visually presented) mouth can be traced back to Greek and Roman antiquity and is still used in puppet theaters (Connor, 2000).

Since the invention of recording devices for visual displays (recordings by video cameras, for instance) and those for acoustic accompaniment (microphones attached to recording devices), the possible experimental situation has dramatically changed. We can separate the two recordings and match them incongruently.

There are three incompatible hypotheses which we can test by comparing incongruent recordings: (1) The more intensive affective display (vocalization or facial expression) dominates over the less intensive one. (2) The unambiguous input (irrespective of the intensity) will dominate over the ambiguous one. (3) The hypothesis predicted by the sensory dominance theory (Hutmacher, 2019), which expects one sensory input to always be dominant over the other one, irrespective of the displayed intensity or the modality.

2 Materials and Methods

Incongruent pairings (such as the visual stimulus pain with the acoustic stimulus neutral speech) were presented to 902 raters (526 women and 376 men, aged 18–50 years). The raters were to rate whether an incongruent pairing was perceived as positive (for pleasure), negative (for pain), or neutral (for neutral speech) using a keyboard or touch-screen. The data were collected in the Czech Republic in 2021 via the agency Czech National Panel (narodnipanel.cz) and a science-oriented online portal pokusnikralici.cz using the online platform for data collection Qualtrics™. Prior to their commencing to rate, the participants supplied their (biological) sex and their age to the nearest year. Criteria for inclusion were: (a) age of raters between 18 and 50 years, and (b) at least a minimal experience with adult media, since the displays and the vocalizations used in this study were extracted from such materials.

From the numerous audio-visual materials, ten were chosen (five with female expressers and five with male expressers). Based on the plot in each of these ten, three frames with faces and three audio tracks were selected (one each of neutrality, pleasure, and pain). The two highly intensive facial expressions (pain and pleasure) were also tested for the difference by using an Artificial Neural Network algorithm (Prossinger et al., 2021).

We used KDE (Kernel Density Estimation) to find the distribution of ages of the female and the male raters, separately. We then determined the estimators, in particular the HDI$_{95\%}$ (the Highest Density Interval at 95% significance (Kruschke, 2015)). A large overlap of this interval documents no significant difference in the age distributions.

We tallied whether the rating was correct because the visual modality was rated correctly, or whether the acoustic modality was rated correctly, or whether neither modality was rated correctly (which we tallied as 'both incorrect').

For every rater sex and for every stimulus sex and for each bimodality, the chosen responses are Dirichlet distributed. There are $2 \times 2 \times 6 = 24$ such distributions. For each, we calculated the mode (a 3D vector). The entries in the columns (i.e. the suite of the six pairings for female raters of the acoustic stimuli, say) male versus female are also Dirichlet distributions. We used Monte Carlo methods for pairwise comparisons.

Lastly, we determined whether female raters of stimulus for one sex for a specific modulus significantly differ from that of another sex. These comparisons are Beta distributions; a detailed description of the method of finding the significance is in the Appendix. We repeated these significance calculations for the other rater sex and then also for the mixing of the sexes of the raters with the sexes of the stimuli.

Table 1. The descriptors and the estimators for the ages of the raters, separated by (biological) sex. ϖ is the expected value (estimated by $\varpi = \int_0^{60} u \times pdf\,(\text{KDE}, u)du$, where KDE is the kernel density estimation), and HDI$_{95\%}$ (highest density interval: the interval with a 95% probability of observing an age; (Kruschke, 2015)). We observe that for both the male and the female raters, the mode is considerably different from the expected age ϖ. The *pdf*s of the KDE distributions and the histograms are in Fig. 1.

Estimator	Male Raters	Female Raters
N	376	526
Range (years)	18–50	18–50
Mode (years)	41.7	27.0
ϖ (years)	33.6	30.9
Mean (years)	33.6	30.9
HDI$_{95\%}$ (years)	16.4–50.3	15.8–49.8

3   Results

Figure 1 and Table 1 show that the distributions of the male and female raters' ages have different modes. We use KDE (kernel density estimation) with a Gaussian kernel because, as Fig. 1 shows, it is not to be expected that raters of either sex have a parametric distribution or even a superposition of one or two such parametric distributions. We also note that modes and expectation values differ between the rater sexes and, furthermore, modes and expectation values differ for the raters of the same sex. The $HDI_{95\%}$ uncertainty interval is very broad, so we can consider the distributions for both rater sexes to be comparable to a uniform distribution of respective ages. The confusion matrix shows that the two distributions are not significantly different.

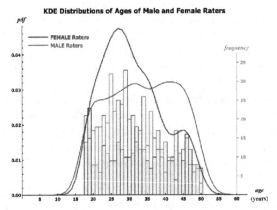

Fig. 1. The distributions of the ages of males and of females estimated using a KDE (kernel density estimation) with a Gaussian kernel. Superimposed of the graphs of the two *pdf*s are the two histograms of the registered ages, separated by sex (scale of frequencies on the right). Modes, expected values, means, and $HDI_{95\%}$ of both distributions are listed in Table 1. The two distributions are not significantly different; the confusion matrix is $\begin{pmatrix} 46.3 & 53.7 \\ 28.3 & 71.7 \end{pmatrix}$% (the method of computing this confusion matrix is described in (Boschetti et al., 2022)).

For the column comparisons for each modality (Fig. 2), no significant difference was observed. Figure 3 shows two examples: the two Dirichlet distributions for two sets of ratings. The extent of overlap between the *pdf*s of these indicates the significance level. In Fig. 3, the overlap is extraordinarily small, so the differences in rating (the off-diagonal entries in the confusion matrix) are highly significant. All the off-diagonal entries in all the confusion matrices were much less than 1×10^{-3} (not shown), therefore, for each comparison for each modality there is a significant difference in rating distributions.

For the visual modality, we observe that one bimodal affect display (pleasure with pain) is markedly different from all other affective displays (Fig. 2). For the acoustic modality, we observe that the pairings pain with pleasure, pain with neutral, and pleasure with neutral are significantly different from all other pairings. For the incorrect ratings (if raters chose neutral, say when the visual display is positive and the acoustic display is negative) only the pairing neutral with pleasure is significant.

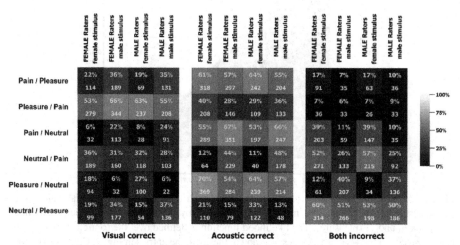

Fig. 2. The heat map of the distributions of incorrect (or possibly guessed) ratings by male and female raters of male and female stimuli. The numbers (light cyan) in the squares are the number of occurrences. Color-coding of the background is of the fraction (in percent) of the occurrences, also displayed as off-white numerical values. We observe that for the pairing pain/pleasure, the visual modality dominates. We also observe that the acoustic modality dominates for pain/pleasure, pain/neutral, and pleasure/neutral. For neutral/pain and neutral/pleasure, on the other hand, neither the visual nor the acoustic modality enables highly correct ratings.

We conclude that for the pleasure/pain pairing, the visual modality is far superior to the acoustic modality (namely, that of pain). For the three pairings pain/pleasure, pain/neutral, and pleasure/neutral, the acoustic modality dominates. To summarize: Fig. 2 shows that the visual modality pleasure dominates when paired with pain as an acoustic modality, whereas for the acoustic modality, pleasure dominates with the visual modality pleasure, and the acoustic modality neutral dominates when paired with pleasure and with pain. Only for the pairing neutral pleasure were the raters (of either sex) incapable of rating the dominant modularity correctly (Fig. 2).

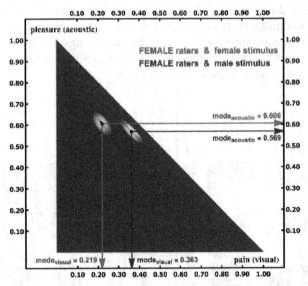

Fig. 3. The likelihood functions of the Dirichlet distributions of the bimodal pairings of pain/pleasure of the female and male stimuli, as rated by the female raters. The probabilities are s_1 (pain) and s_3 (pleasure). The likelihood function is defined over the triangle shown in purple, because $s_1 + s_2 + s_3 = 1$. Modes are shown; these are the entries in Fig. 2. Contours (yellow, are in steps of $\frac{1}{14}\otimes_{max}$. The contours do not overlap, clearly showing that the rating distributions are significantly different. (Color figure online)

For the visual modularity, the comparison of the female ratings of male versus female stimuli was significantly different from that of the male raters rating these two stimuli (Fig. 4). This significant difference (again for the visual modularity) was also observed for pain/neutral, pleasure/neutral and neutral/pleasure.

For the acoustic modularity, the comparisons of female versus male raters showed a significant difference for pain/neutral, neutral/pain, and neutral/pleasure (Fig. 4). Visually, no combinations of raters and stimuli showed a significant difference.

We observe no pattern of significant differences for male versus female raters for a given stimulus (Fig. 4); neither visually nor acoustically. However, there are three exceptions; female versus male raters rate the female stimuli significantly differently for one visual pairing (pleasure/neutral) and two acoustic pairings (pleasure/pain and pleasure/neutral).

4 Discussion

Because of the presented incongruence, no rater could rate both presented modalities correctly, but could rate both incorrectly (because there existed a third choice/option).

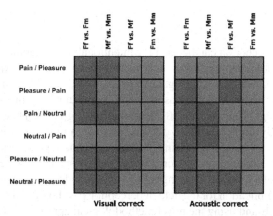

Fig. 4. A heat map of the distributions of significant differences between female (**F**) versus male (**M**) raters rating female (**f**) or male (**m**) stimuli in all eight combinations. The bright red squares display significant differences. Significance has been determined by calculating whether the mode of the Beta distribution of the comparison is significantly different from $s = \frac{1}{2}$, based on the entries displayed in Fig. 2. (The method is explained in the Appendix). For $\frac{20}{48} = \frac{5}{12} = 41.6\%$ of the combinations, there are significant differences. We observe that for neutral/pain the acoustic modality leads to a significantly different rating by female raters rating female stimuli versus male stimuli and, likewise, by male raters rating female stimuli versus male stimuli. For pleasure/pain, the female raters' ratings of female stimuli versus male stimuli are significantly different for both the visual and acoustic modes. For male raters, this is not the case. (Color figure online)

The patterns we found a document that hypothesis (1) is not rejected, but (2) and (3) are rejected. The study of the ability to correctly attribute emotional and affective expressions of others was impacted by recent papers showing counterintuitive evidence that affective states with high intensity are harder to correctly assess from facial expression (Aviezer et al., 2012; Boschetti et al., 2022; Binter et al., 2023). This is confirmed (Fig. 2); the acoustic modality allows for reliable ratings. When extremely intensive facial and vocal displays are rated, the accuracy is usually low, since the stimuli appear inherently ambiguous (Aviezer et al., 2012; Wenzler et al., 2016; Boschetti et al., 2022; Binter et al., 2023). We find that whenever there is a contradictory bimodality involved, then the ambiguity is suppressed—a novel, unexpected finding.

Only in one pairing of incongruent affective states with incongruent modularity do we find evidence of sensory crosstalk: when the visual modularity makes the rating of acoustic modularity impossible. The raters are confused for pairing neutral (visual) with pleasure (acoustic).

Although raters of either sex are consistent in ratings based on the visual modularity (Fig. 2), they rate the affective states displayed by stimuli of different sex significantly differently in $\frac{2}{3}$ of the pairings. For the acoustic modularity, in $\frac{1}{2}$ of the pairings, there are significantly different ratings of the displayed incongruent modularity.

5 Conclusion

The alteration of perception can be used for intentional modifications of scenarios as a 'twist' (i.e. a novel ambiguity) which can, if well placed, cause unexpected effects on players (consumers and users) of the gaming product. On the other hand, we know from previous research, that pain and pleasure were overwhelmingly incorrectly attributed incongruent pairings. The impact of intentional incongruence generating ambiguity may be specifically implemented by the creators of gaming scenarios (for example, characterizing versus mischaracterizing a villain in crime-type games). Our investigations contribute to communicating to creators of gaming scenarios the effectiveness—or ineffectiveness—of incongruent pairings of two effects and a natural expression. Furthermore, there is an implication for the field of perception psychology since this unexpected result can be only found using the novel methodological approach developed by one of the authors (HP) for this very reason.

Funding and Acknowledgement. The research and data collection was supported by Czech Science Foundation (Grant No. 19-12885Y "Behavioral and Psycho-Physiological Response on Ambivalent Visual and Auditory Stimuli Presentation").

Ethics Statement. The project was evaluated and approved by the Ethical Committee of the Faculty of Science, Charles University, as part of broader project (7/2018). GDPR regulations were followed at all times.

Conflicts of Interest. The authors declare no conflicts of interest.

Appendix

We show a method of determining whether two sets of ratings are significantly different with an example (Fig. A-1). The rating entries of the female raters for the male stimuli are n_1 and the entries for the male raters for the male stimuli are n_2; then the Beta distribution is $\mathcal{BM}(n_1 + 1, n_2 + 1)$. The two boundaries $\left[\frac{1}{2}, u_{\text{upper}}\right]$ of the HDI (Highest Density Interval) are determined by $pdf\left(\frac{1}{2}\right) = pdf\left(u_{\text{upper}}\right)$. (Comment: solving for u_{upper} requires computing power.) The probability of HDI is determined by

$$\text{HDI}_{\text{probability}} = \int\limits_{\frac{1}{2}}^{u_{\text{upper}}} pdf(s)ds$$

Comment: this integral can be easily computed using the CDF (Cumulative distribution function) of the Beta distribution: probability $=$ $\mathrm{CDF}\big(\beta\mathcal{M}(n_1 + 1, n_2 + 1), u_{\text{upper}}\big) - \mathrm{CDF}\big(\beta\mathcal{M}(n_1 + 1, n_2 + 1), \frac{1}{2}\big)$.

If the computed probability is less than 95%, then the significance level is greater than 5%. In this case, the deviation of the mode from $\frac{1}{2}$ is insignificant and the differences between the rating distributions are insignificant. In the example, shown in Fig. A-1, the probability is 60%; the significance level is therefore 40% and the observed difference in the rating distributions is insignificant.

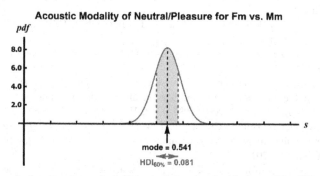

Acoustic Modality of Neutral/Pleasure for Fm vs. Mm

mode = 0.541

$\mathrm{HDI}_{60\%} = 0.081$

Fig. A-1. A graph showing the method of determining the significance of the difference between two ratings of the same modality by raters of different sex (female **F** versus male **M**) of the male stimuli **m**. In this example, the analysis for the acoustic modality is shown, and the rating numbers of female and male stimuli are the concentration parameters of the Beta distribution (each increased by $+ 1$). s is the (Bayesian) probability. The mode of the distribution is shown, flanked by the upper and lower bounds of $\mathrm{HDI}_{60\%}$. The dashed orange lines indicate equal likelihoods. The area shaded in orange is the probability that the mode is significant, in this case, $100\% - 60\% = 40\%$. The mode is not significantly different from $\frac{1}{2}$, and the ratings by the females and the males of the male stimuli is not significantly different at the 5% significance level.

References

Bertelson, P., Aschersleben, G.: Temporal ventriloquism: crossmodal interaction on the time dimension. 1. Evidence from auditory-visual temporal order judgment. Int. J. Psychophysiol. **50**(1–2), 147–155 (2003). https://doi.org/10.1016/S0167-8760(03)00130-2

Boschetti, S., Prossinger, H., Hladký, T., Machová, K., Binter, J.: "Eye can't see the difference": facial expressions of pain, pleasure, and fear are consistently rated due to chance. Hum. Ethol. **37**, 46–72 (2022). https://doi.org/10.22330/he/37/046-072

Binter, J., Boschetti, S., Hladký, T., Prossinger, H.: "Ouch!" or "Aah!": Are Vocalizations of 'Laugh', 'Neutral', 'Fear', 'Pain' or 'Pleasure' Reliably Rated? (2023). https://psyarxiv.com/rf7vw/

Brandner, J.L., Pohlman, J., Brase, G.L.: On hits and being hit on: error management theory, signal detection theory, and the male sexual overperception bias. Evol. Hum. Behav. **42**(4), 331–342 (2021)

Caelen, O.: A Bayesian interpretation of the confusion matrix. Ann. Math. Artif. Intell. **81**(3–4), 429–450 (2017). https://doi.org/10.1007/s10472-017-9564-8

Connor, S.: Dumbstruck: A Cultural History of Ventriloquism. Oxford University Press, Oxford (2000)

de Gelder, B., Pourtois, G., Weiskrantz, L.: Fear recognition in the voice is modulated by unconsciously recognized facial expressions but not by unconsciously recognized affective pictures. Proc. Natl. Acad. Sci. USA **99**(6), 4121–4126 (2002). https://doi.org/10.1073/pnas.062018499

Gregorić, B., et al.: Recognition of facial expressions in men and women. Medicina Fluminensis **50**(4), 454–461 (2014)

Hess, U., Blairy, S., Kleck, R.E.: The intensity of emotional facial expressions and decoding accuracy. J. Nonverbal Behav. **21**, 241–257 (1997)

Hutmacher, F.: Why is there so much more research on vision than on any other sensory modality? Front. Psychol. **10**, 2246 (2019)

Kruschke, J.K.: Doing Bayesian Data Analysis. A Tutorial with R, JAGS, and STAN, 2nd edn. Elsevier/Wiley, Waltham (2015)

Perilloux, C., Easton, J.A., Buss, D.M.: The misperception of sexual interest. Psychol. Sci. **23**(2), 146–151 (2012)

Pourtois, G., de Gelder, B., Vroomen, J., Rossion, B., Crommelinck, M.: The time-course of intermodal binding between seeing and hearing affective information. NeuroReport **11**(6), 1329–1333 (2000). https://doi.org/10.1097/00001756-200004270-00036

Pourtois, G., de Gelder, B., Bol, A., Crommelinck, M.: Perception of facial expressions and voices and of their combination in the human brain. Cortex **41**(1), 49–59 (2005). https://doi.org/10.1016/S0010-9452(08)70177-1

Shimojo, S., Shams, L.: Sensory modalities are not separate modalities: plasticity and interactions. Curr. Opin. Neurobiol. **11**(4), 505–509 (2001). https://doi.org/10.1016/S0959-4388(00)00241-5

Vroomen, J., Driver, J., de Gelder, B.: Is cross-modal integration of emotional expressions independent of attentional resources? Cogn. Affect. Behav. Neurosci. **1**(4), 382–387 (2001). https://doi.org/10.3758/CABN.1.4.382

Wada, Y., Kitagawa, N., Noguchi, K.: Audio-visual integration in temporal perception. Int. J. Psychophysiol. **50**(1–2), 117–124 (2003). https://doi.org/10.1016/S0167-8760(03)00128-4

Are Patterns Game for Our Brain? AI Identifies Individual Differences in Rationality and Intuition Characteristics of Respondents Attempting to Identify Random and Non-random Patterns

Silvia Boschetti[1]([✉]) [ID], Hermann Prossinger[1,2] [ID], Tomáš Hladký[1] [ID], Daniel Říha[3] [ID], Lenka Příplatová[1] [ID], Robin Kopecký[1] [ID], and Jakub Binter[1]([✉]) [ID]

[1] Faculty of Sciences, Charles University, Prague, Czech Republic
`silvia.boschetti@natur.cuni.cz`, `jakub.binter@fhs.cuni.cz`
[2] Department of Evolutionary Anthropology, University of Vienna, Vienna, Austria
[3] Faculty of Humanities, Charles University, Prague, Czech Republic

Abstract. In our everyday life we rely on set of heuristics that involve estimation of meaningful connections between events. In human evolutionary history, it was less costly to overestimate the meaning. The psychological phenomenon of apophenia (overperception of patterns) is then an adaptive response. It may manifest also as overperception of visual patterns (pareidolia). The underperception was rarely studied and researchers mainly used unsuitable stimuli sets for the purpose. After researching this phenomenon using patterns with transparency, geometric shapes, and color (Boschetti et al., 2023), we developed new set of black and white high-contrast stimuli. These were presented to participants four times in different orientations to limit guessing to 6% chance. Using ANN (Artificial Neural Networks), we associated the responses to the Rational Experiential Multimodal Inventory Subscales Rationality and Intuition. We were able to identify two clusters for each subscale and found associations of the participant responses with pattern identification success (or lack thereof). Our discoveries extend previous findings concerning this phenomenon and provides us with a foundation for constructing and designing artificial environments with high attention to cues given to users.

Keywords: Random Patterns · Non-random Patterns · Rationality · Intuition · Clustering Algorithms · Artificial Neural Networks · Apophenia · Apoidolia

1 Introduction

The ability to correctly detect and recognize patterns is fundamental for human while they interact with the environment irrespective of whether it is real or virtual. The ability to distinguish between what is relevant and meaningful and what is not is an essential part of the decision-making process that underlies every behavior: the more accurate the detection of an existing pattern the more effective the decision among behavioral options.

© The Author(s), under exclusive license to Springer Nature Switzerland AG 2023
X. Fang (Ed.): HCII 2023, LNCS 14047, pp. 151–161, 2023.
https://doi.org/10.1007/978-3-031-35979-8_12

However, in terms of cost-benefit, false positive (detection of a pattern in a random distribution) and false negative (failure in detecting a pattern when one is actually present) errors are very different: Error Management Theory (EMT) claims that over-detection of patterns is safer than under-detection (Johnson, 2009). For this reason, the bias for over-detection of pattern (called apophenia) is considered an advantage and is, arguably, an evolved mechanism in humans (Barrett, 2000).

The cognitive and perceptual bias is a tendency that construes how we perceive and interpret the world. The subjective sensitivity to pattern detection can lead to the miss-attribution of agency to non-living objects (Hyperactive Agency Detection Device) and ultimately to supernatural beliefs (Barrett, 2000). Indeed, cognitive and perceptual biases are candidate for explaining the emergence and the perseverance of paranormal beliefs (Willard & Norenzayan, 2013). Previous studies have associated the overperception of patterns with different types of beliefs in the supernatural, beliefs in the paranormal and assigning meaning to coincidence of events that are only due to chance (Zhou & Meng, 2020; Bressan, 2002).

The specific type of apophenia is the perception of a pattern in visual stimuli and is called pareidolia. Most of the work on pareidolia involves the overperception of faces, which are a very specific type of visual stimulus (Tsao & Livingstone, 2008) and the results of such studies may not be generalizable to stimuli different from facial ones. Another problem occurs when the stimuli chosen are naturally occurring (i.e. clouds, stains). Is it possible to control the extent of naturalness present or absent in an imaged pattern? Furthermore, even though such stimuli are suitable for detecting pareidolia (as false positive error in perception), they cannot be used to detect the false negative error (called apoidolia; Boschetti et al., 2023). Both apoidolia and pareidolia have been found to be more strongly related to thinking styles than to religious beliefs or belief in magic. This outcome was found in a previous study that used colored stimuli created by a multidimensional random number generator to produce maps of random colored squares underlined with geometrical figures as patterns (Boschetti et al., 2023).

Specifically, the REIm (Rational/Experiential Multimodal Inventory; Norris & Epstein, 2011) was designed to measure the functionality of the experiential system of reasoning (based on the associative processes heuristic and intuitive) and the analytical system (based on high cognitive and meta-cognitive abilities and rule-based processing).

For this study we used two subscales from the REIm: one measuring *rationality* and the other measuring *intuition*. Furthermore, instead of colored stimuli we used black and white stimuli reminiscent of QR codes (Fig. 1), thereby maximizing the visual contrast in the elements of the stimulus. There is one further (important) limitation of the previous studies, namely, *The Lady Tasting Tea* problem (Fisher, 1956): how to avoid the observer from guessing the correct answer; more specifically, minimizing the probability of supplying a correct answer merely due to chance.

This simple, straightforward perceptual test presented here can be used as a diagnostic tool for users and profile creators when intending to maximize the experience in human-computer interactions. It also allows for addressing complex psychological phenomenon while limiting the number of response options.

2   Materials and Methods

2.1   Participants

A total of 174 participants from Italy and the Czech Republic responded to the queries about Rationality and Intuition. They (henceforth called respondents) also attempted to identify which of the eight presented distributions of black and white squares (henceforth called patterns) were random and which were non-random (henceforth called random and non-random patterns).

Fig. 1. Two of the eight patterns presented to the respondents. For every rectangle presented, they were asked to identify which pattern is random and which is nonrandom. The random patterns were presented four times, once as generated by the (quasi) random number generator, once after mirroring across the horizontal axis, once after mirroring across the vertical axis and once after rotating by 90°. Likewise, for the nonrandom pattern. The eight patterns were presented in randomized order, so as to prevent any possible memory effects. The reason for presenting each random and each non-random pattern four times is to suppress *The Lady Tasting Tea* effect (details in the text).

2.2   Stimuli

Four random patterns were generated, as well as four non-random ones (two are shown in Fig. 1). Respondents were asked to identify which of the patterns were random and which were not. We presented each pattern four times in order to avoid *The Lady Tasting Tea* problem (if a two-option challenge is presented to a respondent, the chance of correct identification is $\frac{1}{2}$; this chance is far too high; if the challenge is presented four times in random order, then chance of correct identification without guessing is $\frac{1}{2^4} = \frac{1}{16} \sim 6\%$; Fisher, 1956). We did not repeat the presentations 5 times, because of possible uncontrollable effects due to the tiring of the participants.

2.3 Questionnaire

We used the Rational/Experiential Multimodal Inventory (REIm; Norris & Epstein, 2011) to measure two aspects of thinking styles, namely analytic/rational and intuitive (specifically an automatic/experiential approach to construction and interpretation of the perceived world). The questionnaire is composed of four independent subscales, one for a rational system and three for different aspects of the experiential system. The subscales used in the present study are: Rationality (12 queries) and Intuition (10 queries); both are listed in the Appendix. We narrowed down our analysis to these two subscales because, from a theoretical prospective and from the results of a previous study (Boschetti et al., 2023), they are the most relevant. The responses were on a 5-point scale ranging from R1 (Completely False) to R5 (Completely True); we note that none are cardinal numbers.

2.4 Statistical Methods

The responses to the queries are ordinal numbers, not cardinal numbers (Blalock, 1960). They may not be directly converted into cardinal numbers, because a change in the choice of the mapping results in a change the statistical signal. (The statistical analysis is then the statistical analysis of the mapping, not of the data). Rather, the responses must be mapped into unit vectors. If a response to a query is 'B', say, then the vector is $\left(0\ 1\ 0\ 0\ 0 \right)^T$. If a respondent identifies a pattern as random, the response is $\left(1\ 0 \right)^T$, and if it is non-random, then the response is $\left(0\ 1 \right)^T$.. The response vectors are then concatenated; the resulting vector is called a feature vector (Murphy, 2012). For Rationality and pattern identification, the dimension of the feature vector is $4 \times 2 + 4 \times 2 + 12 \times 5 = 76.$. This feature vector has interdependencies (perhaps nonlinear ones). In order to avoid the 'curse of dimensionality' (Bellman, 1961), dimension reduction is necessary. We used an artificial neural network (specifically, an autoencoder) to dimension reduce the feature vector. The autoencoder will also detect nonlinear interdependencies among the components of the feature vectors. We then use a clustering algorithm (in our case, DBSCAN; Ester et al., 1996) to identify the clusters in the space of the dimension-reduced feature vectors.

We can 'backtrack' the mapping and identify which points in the dimension-reduced vector space 'belong' to the respondents' feature vectors. We use these identifications for further analyses. AC (Correspondence Analysis; Benzécri, 1973; Greenacre, 2007; Beh & Lombardo, 2014) of the contingency table (pattern identification versus thinking style) allows us to determine whether there exist associations and, if so, how many.

We repeat the above procedure for the combination of responses to the queries of the Intuition questionnaire and the *same* identification of random and non-random patterns by the participants.

3 Results

3.1 Pattern Identification

We observe that only 3 (1,7%) of the 174 participants succeeded in correctly identifying all 4 nonrandom and all 4 random patterns. Some respondents succeeded in correctly identifying all random patterns, but they did not correctly identify all non-random patterns. Others succeeded in correctly identifying all non-random patterns, but did not succeed in identifying all random patterns. Many respondents succeeded only partially. Most respondents (140; 65% or close to $\frac{2}{3}$) did not succeed in correctly identifying any non-random patterns and any random patterns. We discovered that the relations between the extent of correctly identifying patterns are not independent of the responses to queries; this is valid for both Rationality and Intuition. In fact, cluster analysis shows that in both cases of thinking style (Rationality and Intuition), there are two distinct clusters (Fig. 2 and Fig. 3).

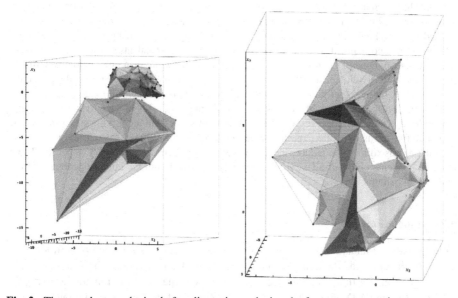

Fig. 2. The two clusters obtained after dimension-reducing the feature vectors using an autoencoder for Rationality (left) and Intuition (right). In both, the points are the coordinates of the dimension-reduced feature vector of each participant's responses to the Rationality or Intuition queries together with the identification of a random or nonrandom distribution of squares. The concave hull connects the points in each of the clusters. For Rationality, Cluster #2 has 39 points and Cluster #1 has 174 points and for Intuition, Cluster #1 has 38 points and Cluster #2 has 175 points. The dimension reduction to 2D did not separate clusters, but dimension reduction to 3D did. The axes are numerical only; they are not directly interpretable.

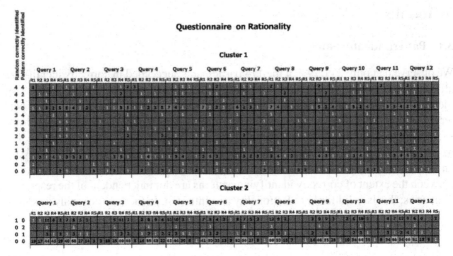

Fig. 3. The distribution of the nonzero entries of nonrandom and random pattern identification versus responses to the rationality queries. Those rows that have no nonzero entries have been deleted. The brightness of the colors identifies the percentages of occurring entries for a response (this fraction is normalized according to the total number of respondents in a cluster). In Cluster #2, for instance, none of the respondents correctly identified more than one random pattern and the greatest majority did not succeed in distinguishing between random and nonrandom patterns. In Cluster #1, on the other hand, many respondents were able to identify random patterns and many (other) respondents could identify nonrandom patterns, without successfully identifying nonrandom patterns. The few respondents who did not succeed in identifying either random or nonrandom patterns (who are expected to be in Cluster #2) are part of this cluster because the autoencoder also dimension reduces the feature vector, which contains the query responses. There are 3 respondents (1.7% of all 174) who correctly identified both the random patterns and the nonrandom patterns.

3.2 Associations

Correspondence analysis is used to find possible associations between pattern identification proficiency and the query response spectrum: the associations for Rationality and the associations for Intuition. We discovered that the signal (the fraction not due to noise) obtained by the SVD (singular value decomposition) of the contingency table is much weaker for Rationality than it is for Intuition. For Rationality, we find two associations (Fig. 5), and for Intuition we find three (Fig. 6 and Fig. 4).

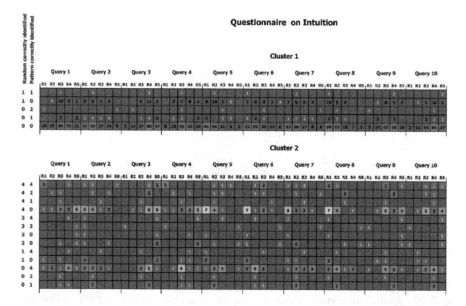

Fig. 4. The distribution of the nonzero entries of nonrandom and random pattern identification versus responses to the Intuition queries. Those rows that have no nonzero entries have been deleted. The brightness of the colors identifies the percentages of occurring entries for a response (this fraction is normalized according to the total number of respondents in a cluster). There are 3 respondents (1.7% of all 174) who correctly identified both the random patterns and the nonrandom patterns; they are distributed almost uniformly across all responses for all queries.

4 Discussion and Conclusion

The orientation in the world is based on heuristics that help the individuals navigate complex situations. Intuition and irrational beliefs can be products of perceptual and cognitive biases, as illusionary perception of patterns and becoming overly reliant on assigning meanings to these perceived patterns.

There have been explanations proposed by cognitive scientists who infer the proliferation of supernatural beliefs to be the results of this and other cognitive biases (Johnson, 2009; Willard & Norenzayan, 2013). Furthermore, EMT also explains the existence of such biases as a compensation for potentially costly mistakes.

We decided to pursue the study of pattern perceptions by introducing two novel elements, namely the use of black and white patterns (rather than colored ones), and multiple (in our case: four) presentations by rotating and mirroring so as to assure that the chance of guessing the correct answer is minimized.

We emphasize that the study presented here is an example of a multidisciplinary approach. Here, psychological investigation techniques were combined with approaches based on novel technology and modern statistical techniques (including, but not limited to, dimension reduction and the use of clustering algorithms) in order to provide novel insights.

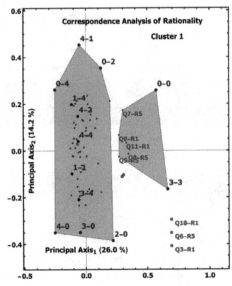

Fig. 5. The result of the correspondence analysis for pattern identification and Rationality: associations. The scree plot of squares of the singular values versus indices of the singular values identified only two singular values as non-noise. The reconstructed matrix has been graphed and the clusters identified via the clustering algorithm DBSCAN identified the categorical variables of nonzero query responses (red) that are associated with the pattern identification responses (purple). The fraction of the square of the Frobenius norm explained by the first two singular values is 40.2%. The magenta dots are query response choices that do not associate with any pattern identification pairs. The unlabeled query responses of one association have not been labelled, as the labels would have rendered that part of this graph unreadable. We point out that a strong association does not infer a high score on the response axes. (Color figure online)

The dimensions for Rationality (60) and Intuition (50), combined with the those for pattern identification outcomes (26), make the multivariate analysis not only nontrivial, but require very large data sets for satisfactory noise minimization. Nonetheless, perhaps surprisingly, we found fascinating signals even in our relatively small data set. We are also aware of how difficult the test is for the participants because the presented patterns tested their skills quite severely. We were surprised that two clusters of the dimension-reduced feature vectors existed in both cases of thinking styles.

By using Artificial Neural Networks to cluster the participants based on their responses to the subscales of REIm (for Intuition and for Rationality, separately) and the results of the pattern identification task we identify two clusters for *each* subscale. In both cases we obtain one cluster in which the participants were more accurate in identifying the patters (or lack of) and another in which the participant exhibited a higher tendency for pareidolia and apoidolia. Each cluster showed associations with specific responses to specific queries, allowing us to estimate their similar psychological profile in the heuristic use in their daily life.

We also succeeded in demonstrating that these associations are the statistically justified descriptors (rather than correlations would be) and we found that there were

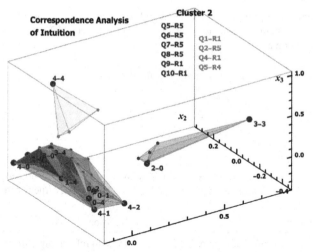

Fig. 6. The result of the correspondence analysis for pattern identification and Intuition: associations. The scree plot of squares of the singular values versus indices of the singular values identified three singular values as non-noise. The coordinates obtained by the reconstructed matrix have been graphed and the clusters were identified via the clustering algorithm DBSCAN. The identified categorical variables of nonzero query responses (green/blue/red) that are associated with the pattern identification responses (purple) show the associations: there are three associations. The fraction of the square of the Frobenius norm explained by the first two singular values is 58.1%. Most remarkable is the observation that the 'perfect' pattern identifiers (participants) associate with the query responses R1 for query Q1, R3 for query Q2, R1 for query Q4, and R4 for query Q5. (Color figure online)

more than one association (two for Rationality and three for Intuition) for those clusters of participants who were more successful in identifying patterns and distinguishing randomness and non-randomness (and therefore not experiencing pareidolia or apoidolia).

We note that the number of associations depended on the thinking styles and their statistical signal strength varied with thinking style. The results are promising; they mark an introduction of a novel approach to research of the phenomenon of apoidolia and extension of the existing research on pareidolia in a healthy population. The knowledge of how individuals orient themselves in the world based on their *believed* pattern presence can improve the design of future real world and virtual world (user) experiences. In the second case, this should be of utmost importance since the creator has almost absolute control over the environment presented to the user.

Funding and Acknowledgement. The research and data collection was supported by Charles University Grant Agency (GAUK "Cognitive Bias, Agency Detection and Pattern Recognition: An Intercultural Quantitative and Experimental Study of Supernatural Belief", project No. 1404120).

We thank to Ladislav Cupa for help with sample collection.

Ethics Statement. The project was evaluated and approved by the Ethical Committee of the Faculty of Science, Charles University, as part of broader project (7/2018). GDPR regulations were followed at all times.

Conflicts of Interest. The authors declare no conflict of interest.

Appendix

Table A-1. The queries for assessment of the two thinking styles. The responses are choices on a five-point scale from "Completely false for me" (R1) to "Completely true for me" (R5).

Query	Rationality	Intuition
Q1	I enjoy problems that require hard thinking	I like to rely on my intuitive impressions
Q2	I am not very good in solving problems that require careful logical analysis	I often go by my instincts when deciding on a course of action
Q3	I enjoy intellectual challenges	I don't think it is a good idea to rely on one's intuition for important decisions
Q4	I prefer complex to simple problems	I trust my initial feelings about people
Q5	I don't like to have to do a lot of thinking	I tend to use my heart as a guide for my actions
Q6	Reasoning things out carefully is not one of my strong points	I enjoy learning by doing something, instead of figuring it out first
Q7	I am not a very analytical thinker	I can often tell how people feel without them having to say anything
Q8	I try to avoid situations that require thinking in depth about something	I generally don't depend on my feelings to help me make decisions
Q9	I am much better at figuring things out logically than most people	For me, descriptions of actual people's experiences are more convincing than discussions about "facts"
Q10	I have a logical mind	I'm not a very spontaneous person
Q11	Using logic usually works well for me in figuring out problems in my life	
Q12	Knowing the answer without understanding the reasoning behind it is good enough for me	

References

Barrett, J.L.: Exploring the natural foundations of religion. Trends Cogn. Sci. **4**(1), 29–34 (2000)

Beh, E., Lombardo, R.: Correspondence Analysis. Theory, Practice and New Strategies. Wiley, Chichester (2014). ISBN 978-1-119-95324-1

Bellman, R.E.: Adaptive Control Processes: A Guided Tour. Princeton University Press, Princeton (1961). ISBN 9780691079011

Benzécri, J.-P.: L'Analyse des Données. Volume II. L'Analyse des Correspondances. Dunod, Paris (1973)

Blalock, H.M., Jr.: Social Statistics. McGraw Hill, New York (1960)

Boschetti, S., Binter, J., Prossinger, H.: Apoidolia: a new psychological phenomenon detected by pattern creation with image processing software together with dirichlet distributions and confusion matrices. In: Proceedings in Adaptation, Learning and Optimization (2023, in press)

Bressan, P.: The connection between random sequences, everyday coincidences, and belief in the paranormal. Appl. Cogn. Psychol. Official J. Soc. Appl. Res. Mem. Cogn. **16**(1), 17–34 (2002)

Ester, M., Kriegel, H.-P., Sander, J., Xu, X.: A density-based algorithm for discovering clusters in large spatial databases with noise. In: Simoudis, E., Han, J., Fayyad, U.M. (eds.)Proceedings of the Second International Conference on Knowledge Discovery and Data Mining (KDD 1996), pp. 226–231. AAAI Press (1996). CiteSeerX 10.1.1.121.9220. ISBN 1-57735-004-9

Fisher, R.A.: Mathematics of a lady tasting tea. The world of mathematics III (part 8), pp. 1514–1521. Simon & Schuster, USA (1956)

Greenacre, M.: Correspondence Analysis in Practice. CRC Press, Boca Raton (2007). ISBN 9781584886167

Johnson, D.D.: The error of god: error management theory, religion, and the evolution of cooperation. In: Levin, S. (eds.) Games, Groups, and the Global Good, pp. 169–180. Springer, Heidelberg (2009). https://doi.org/10.1007/978-3-540-85436-4_10

Murphy, K.P.: Machine Learning. A Probabilistic Perspective. The MIT Press, Cambridge (2012)

Norris, P., Epstein, S.: An experiential thinking style: Its facets and relations with objective and subjective criterion measures. J. Pers. **79**(5), 1043–1080 (2011)

Tsao, D.Y., Livingstone, M.S.: Mechanisms of face perception. Annual Rev. Neurosci. **31**, 411–437 (2008)

Wada, Y., Kitagawa, N., Noguchi, K.: Audio-visual integration in temporal perception. Int. J. Psychophysiol. **50**(1–2), 117–124 (2003). https://doi.org/10.1016/S0167-8760(03)00128-4

Willard, A.K., Norenzayan, A.: Cognitive biases explain religious belief, paranormal belief, and belief in life's purpose. Cognition **129**(2), 379–391 (2013)

Zhou, L.F., Meng, M.: Do you see the "face"? Individual differences in face pareidolia. J. Pac. Rim Psychol. **14**, e2 (2020)

Understanding Individual Differences in Mental Health and Video Games

Matthew Copeman[1,2(✉)] and Jonathan Freeman[2]

[1] Arden University, Middlemarch Park, Coventry CV3 4FJ, UK
mcopeman@arden.ac.uk
[2] Goldsmiths, University of London, New Cross, London SE14 6NW, UK

Abstract. With mental health diagnoses ever increasing in today's world and the services set out to provide help and care for them coming under ever increasing pressure from overuse, it is clear that a new approach is needed to help the numerous amounts of patients waiting for care. This research was setup to investigate the potential of video games and their benefits on mental health. This correlational design took survey responses from 200 participants and their responses to common mental health inventories and personality factors when asked in conjunction with their favourite video game. The data was used to build an understanding of what types of games might be associated with high or low scores across a variety of mental health, including anxiety and depression. Results showed that there were significant findings for games categorised as adventure and role playing, and that these showed associations with lower levels of anxiety, depression, and neuroticism scores, suggesting some ability to control for individual differences with more study. Future studies could aim to understand causal influences in the relationship between games and mental health, to allow for more access to care for patients.

Keywords: Video Games · Mental Health · Individual Differences

1 Understanding Individual Differences in Mental Health and Video Games

Mental health is as under-resourced as it has ever been, with costs also continuing to rise [1]. Although care and provisions exist for patients, they are often overstretched or underfunded. As such, new and innovative approaches are needed to support current health systems. Previous research suggests that video games could offer ways to offer more care to at risks patients by offering a short-term intervention for those with ongoing mental health issues [2]. This would allow patients to take ownership and autonomy of their mental health bridging the gap between symptoms and clinical help. However, this also raises question about the nature of diagnosing mental health symptoms and suggests that the area should not follow strict diagnoses, but a hierarchy of symptomatology to address [3, 4]. The process by which video games might provide help would be very different to the traditional therapeutic route such as Cognitive Behavioural Therapy (CBT) [5]. Instead, video games have the potential to address symptoms directly,

X. Fang (Ed.): HCII 2023, LNCS 14047, pp. 162–175, 2023.
https://doi.org/10.1007/978-3-031-35979-8_13

rather than treat undiagnosed conditions, as suggested by the Hierarchical Taxonomy of Psychopathology (HiTOP) [6–8].

1.1 Hierarchical Taxonomy of Psychopathology

Traditionally, mental health is diagnosed by a healthcare professional, according to a diagnostic manual and after meeting a set of criteria outlined for each diagnosis [9]. The HiTOP model of mental health suggests that rather than looking at specific categorical diagnoses, practitioners should instead look to focus on common symptomology across multiple diagnoses [10, 11]. This is known as the transdiagnostic approach to mental health, as the focus is on dealing with multiple symptoms that are common across diagnoses. When considering the number of mental health diagnoses that are often co-morbid with each other, this approach makes sense as they often struggle with similar underlying symptoms [11]. While no two patients are ever identical, with mental health being more accepted as symptoms with spectrums of severity, this approach could tackle the gap in preliminary care patients need before having access to overworked, understaffed healthcare professionals [5, 6, 12].

To consider options for pre-clinical care, looking at mental health as a hierarchical structure makes sense. For example, the most common diagnoses in today's world and anxiety and depression [13]. For anxiety alone, there are many different subcategories, with their own set of diagnostic criteria [14–18]. Likewise, depression is not a simple descriptor that fits all sufferers equally [14, 19]. However, both diagnoses, and their symptoms, share common facets that can be seen in a vast majority of patients. To help understand this transdiagnostically, the HiTOP model classifies these two sets of conditions as part of the internalising spectra of mental health, with subfactors of fear and distress [10, 11]. By looking at these diagnoses from their symptoms, we can use a pre-clinical intervention to help a larger number of people tackle a broad set of common symptoms, without the need or a specific diagnosis, and still be confident that there will be some benefit for the sufferer [20, 21]. For example, if a patient was to present with symptoms of nervousness, fear of new places or people, and concern over change, there might well be a diagnosis in their future of anxiety disorders, or potentially even obsessive-compulsive disorders. Importantly, those symptoms also occur in generalised anxiety disorder, social anxiety disorders, and any number of other anxieties that one can be diagnosed for [22–24]. In this light, a pre-clinical intervention that can help people with symptom management for their own quality of life makes sense and could act as a lifeline for those waiting for overprescribed clinical time.

Depression is another example of a commonly diagnosed mental health conditions, with striking overlap in its symptoms with other disorders [25]. The HiTOP model suggests that there is overlap to the extent that depression itself does not have a simple trait to the model, but is made up of several spectrums, such as agitation, anhedonia, dysphoria, insomnia, and low well-being [10]. By using the HiTOP in this manner, interventions would be able to reach a wider range of people suffering before their clinical diagnosis. This would bring much needed scope and openness to mental health in general and would allow people to be treated beyond just their label they are assigned through manuals such as the diagnostic and statistical manual of mental disorders (DSM-5) [10, 20, 26]. If we look to understand how mental health can be treated in a much broader spectrum, addressing symptoms rather than diagnoses would be a crucial step forward in streamlining the approach to mental health.

The strength of this approach is that by not necessarily treating any specific diagnosed condition but offering the patient support for a wide range of spectrum-based symptoms, the possibility exists for them to firstly reach clinical care, and secondly be more receptive to it [5, 27–29]. CBT uptake is traditionally quite low, especially among younger adults, and if future patients have experience of an evidence-based practice that is effective in symptom management, then they will be more accepting of an evidence based clinical practice that is designed to actively treat their condition [30–33]. This is how video games can be promoted to the younger generation, as they are much more likely have access to, and play video games.

1.2 Video Games and Mental Health

Video game research has already suggested they can be used to support mental health and well-being [2, 34, 35]. Studies have shown that time spent playing video games can be beneficial for cognitive, social, and metal well-being and growth [34, 36, 37]. This has been furthered recently, showing that an hour a day playing video games can be beneficial and should be considered for most [38]. Recent research from the authors supports this as well, where a mixed methods study showed that not only can games be useful for those with mental health symptoms and diagnoses, but they are actively looked towards and used for symptom and emotional management [39]. While this paper focused on social anxiety, the research helped highlight how mental health does crossover in symptoms. The work suggested that there are types of games that can be useful to those with mental health, highlighting common themes that were found in people who felt like games had helped with their mental health. These included features such as being able to play for roughly 30–60 min. Furthermore, games that were fundamentally built on the idea of escapism from real life and being immersed in another world and feeling a new sense of self. Games that had good characters that could related to were also deemed important by participants. Role playing games or simulation games were highlighted throughout, encapsulating experiences that typically embody solo gameplay time. These types of games were shown as being able to help with mental health for the select number of participants that were invited back to interview, and as such should provide a good basis to start selection criteria for an early intervention model. In the context of why these types of video games should work, based on previous research, this does make sense as this fits within the theoretical scope of Self-Determination Theory (SDT) [40].

1.3 Self Determination Theory

This is where SDT can help to shed light on how to tackle these symptoms through a non-clinical based approach. Conceived originally by work from Deci and Ryan [40], this theory suggests that everyone wants to better themselves. To do this, there are three main innate and universal psychological needs that can be used in self-determination which are, autonomy, relatedness, and competency. Autonomy is the want of a person to feel as though they are in control of their future and direction [41]. This can be applied to mental health, by helping and enabling suffers to feel like they are taking control of their own circumstances, which often arises as a complaint by those suffering, that their mental health is all encompassing, and they are not able to act on it by themselves. Secondly, relatedness is where people desire to feel like they belong to other people, through attachment and understanding of others [42]. With the advancement in storytelling and gameplay mechanics in modern games, the opportunity to help sufferers here is apparent. Mental health sufferers often report that they feel inadvertently disconnected or have specifically shied away from real social engagement and relation because of their own situation. In these instances, video games can give them the ability to engage in basic social interaction again and relate to both human and player characters [43, 44]. Lastly, competency is the understanding that people want to gain mastery in a skill that they are doing, and this speaks to the very heart of video games [45]. Most video games offer progression system, either through character development, story progression, or in a lot of cases, a combination of these two and more besides. Importantly, players often need a good understanding, and competency in the games systems to be able to progress and see through the story of the game, and this is where video games can help mental health. By understanding and gaining competency in a video game, the sense of accomplishment and achievement can potentially bleed in a sufferers real life, and give them confidence in their own ability to succeed where once they might have thought they could not [34, 43]. By applying the principles of SDT to video games, and approaching mental health through this lens, there exists a clear opportunity to further the work originally started by Copeman and Freeman [39] to develop a pre-clinical intervention for mental health using video games. Games that enable this type of learning through play to tackle common symptoms of mental health should then allow players to tackle their own mental health, and act in a way that will enable to get clinical treatment, eventually, through the overworked national health service.

1.4 Personality Traits and Game Choice

Another key factor of mental health is individual differences and understanding that no to patients is the same [46]. To this end, there have been several studies that have looked at personality as a top-level individual difference that could affect people's mental health and their outcomes from treatment [21, 47, 48]. This is important, as from video games sales and research, we know that not everyone wants to play the same type of game [46, 49, 50]. Showing that some games are useful for some types of people, is at the heart of the individual approach, and this is another important factor for this research to consider. In the past, studies have shown that more neurotic individuals tender to suffer more with mental health problems, and this could be as these types of people are typically classified as neurotic because they show emotional instability, anger, and irritability, all of which are common symptoms of anxiety and depression [47, 48]. Contrary to this, people who are high in openness to experience tend to not display such a level of mental ill health, and are typically classified as imaginative, and potentially creative people. As we have highlighted, mental health is not the same for any two individuals, so understanding that certain games might be better suited to different types of people is key, and this is where the approach on personality can help to shed light on this. If people who display higher scores on neuroticism were to show an affinity with a certain type of game, it would be reasonable to suggest that those with high openness to experience scores might not.

As such, this is something to be considered for the application of game choice and is something that will be of interest in the current study.

1.5 Aims of the Current Study

As such, the aims of the current study are to build on work from Copeman and Freeman [39] to understand what type of game might be related to each of the most common diagnoses. By understanding this, and working through common traits that each share, the research will add further evidence to suggest a video game to be used as an early-stage intervention. As such, we hypothesise that games such as adventure and role-playing, with a strong story and character focus that allows players to escape their world and be immersed somewhere else, will show better relationships with mental health symptoms. We also hypothesise that games with a simulation element to them, such as colony managers or sports games, that put the player in the heart of the action and immerse them in the world they are engaged in, will also have a positive relationship with mental health. Lastly, we also hypothesise that openness will be positively associated with mental health outcomes, and neuroticism will be negatively associated with mental health outcomes.

2 Method

2.1 Participants

In total, 197 participants were recruited. Participants ranged in age from 18 to 73 years ($M = 30.83, SD = 8.67$) of these, 88(54%) were female, 71 (43%) male, four others, and one who preferred not to say. Participants were recruited randomly and opportunistically through social media advertisements, and various university campuses. Of these, 62% of participants had completed a bachelor's degree or higher.

2.2 Design

A cross-sectional correlational design was employed for this study. Participants were asked to complete a variety of questionnaires about their favourite game, which the questionnaire then referred to at all points when specific games were required. Ethical approval was achieved prior to commencement of data collection.

2.3 Materials

Participants were asked about their gameplay habits via a slider tabbed from 0–60 min and had an opportunity to state their favourite game and will be highlighted as < game > where this was inserted into questionnaires, which allowed participants to think about specific situations in specific games.

The Ubisoft Perceived Experience Questionnaire (UPEQ) was used [51] to measure competence, relatedness, and autonomy within games, consisting of 21 questions scored on a Likert scale from strongly disagree (1) to strongly agree (5), with the choice of choosing not applicable (0). Questions included were "I was free to decide how I wanted to play" and "I could approach < game > in my own way".

The Patient Health Questionnaire Nine (PHQ-9) was used [52] to measure anxiety and depression symptoms. This consisted of nine questions scored on a Likert scale of Not at all (0) to Nearly Every Day (3). Questions asked about feelings over the last two weeks and included items such as "Little interest or pleasure in doing things" and "Poor appetite or eating".

The Generalized Anxiety Disorder Seven (GAD-7) was also used to measure anxiety ratings [17]. This was structured with seven questions on a Likert scale from Not at all (0) to Nearly Every Day (3). Questions were asked about the participants last two weeks and included items such as "Feeling anxious, nervous or on edge" and "trouble relaxing".

The Improving Access to Psychological Therapies (IAPT, National Collaborating Centre for Mental Health, 2018) phobia scale was used to measure social phobias in participants and was scored on a Likert scale of Would not avoid at all (1) to Always avoid it (5) and asked about three situations that a participant might be in, for example "social situations due to a fear of being embarrassed or making a fool myself".

The IAPT Obsessive-Compulsive Inventory (OCI, National Collaborating Centre for Mental Health, 2018) was used to measure severity of obsessive-compulsive disorder. This 42-item inventory used Likert scale scoring of distress in various situations scoring from Not at all (0) to Extremely (4). Participants were asked to state their own distress when faced with experiences such as "I was and clean obsessively" and "I feel that there are good and bad numbers".

The IAPT Panic Disorder Severity Scale [53] was used to measure participants tendency for, and extent of, panic attacks in a variety of situations. Participants were told the symptoms for panic attacks and asked to rate on a Likert scale from zero to five, a variety of situations in which they felt any of the symptoms listed. The scale was not always the same for each question, but it included an increasing scale of severity for symptom onset and severity, with situations for participants to consider such as "felt anxious about when your panic attack would occur...".

Participants were lastly asked to fill out the Big-Five Personality inventory 44-item (BFI-44) [54]. This inventory measures the five constructs of personality which are openness, conscientiousness, extraversion, agreeableness, and neuroticism, using a Likert scale of Strongly Disagree (1) to Strongly Agree (5). It includes questions such as "I am someone who is talkative" and "I am someone who worries a lot."

2.4 Procedure

Participants were recruited and data obtained through random distributions of an online survey via Qualtrics. After reading an information sheet and consenting to participate, participants filled in their average weekly playtime of video games in minutes and gave the name of their favourite video game. Following this, they completed each of the listed questionnaires: UPEQ, PHQ-9, GAD-7, IAPT Phobia, IAPT OCI, IAPT Panic and the BFI-44. Participants were thanked and debriefed about the aims of the study.

3 Results

To understand what types of games were being played, games were categorised into genres based off the most popular assigned genre on the site igdb.com. This was due to its popularity and exhaustive list of games through the years, that met the demand of the high number of different games reported by participants. In total, 96 different games were reported, so grouping by genre was necessary to understand any potential relationships. Based on information from igdb.com, games were grouped as either Adventure, Role-Playing Game (RPG), Sport, Strategy or Shooter. After incomplete data had been filtered out, 133 responses showed that Adventure was the most played game from our sample with 65 game entries and sport with the least common played with nine entries.

To further understand how each genre might be useful for mental health, we ran a series of correlations with the mental health scales collected from each participant. While there is no way to discern cause and effect, this information can be useful for informing decision making about what types of games are related to lower or higher scores in certain areas of mental health. To do this, we split the sample by genre and ran a series of correlations with each of the main scales we were interested in: UPEQ, PHQ-9, GAD-7, OCI, Panic Disorder Severity and the BFI-44. Since the groups were so vastly different in size, and did not always meet parametric assumptions, a series of Spearman's Rho correlations were carried out across the different genres. To understand the potential relationship, we looked at how different genres of games reported correlations between SDT elements and mental health elements.

For Adventure games, there were some interesting insights gleaned. Some of the main findings were that competence was significantly correlated with openness, $r(38) = .43, p = .005$. Neuroticism and conscientiousness were inversely correlated with the PHQ-9, suggesting that those who are higher in neuroticism playing adventure games, showed higher levels of anxiety and depression, $r(38) = .47, p = .002$. This extended to our obsessive-compulsions measure and neuroticism suggesting similar findings, $r(37) = .50, p = .001$.

For RPGs, there were similarly interesting stories. Competence was negatively related to anxiety and depression through the PHQ-9, $r(21) = -.47, p = .025$. Conscientiousness ($r(14) = -.44, p = .002$) and openness ($r(15) = -.52, p = .034$) also showed negative relationships with anxiety and depression through the PHQ-9. Interestingly for this type of game, Neuroticism showed a positive relationship with both GAD-7 scores, $r(14) = .59, p = .016$, and OCD scores $r(12) = .57, p = .033$.

For sport, even though there less respondents who played sports games, there were still some interesting findings. Autonomy showed relationships with both anxiety through the GAD-9, $r(7) = .70, p = .035$, and agreeableness, $r(5) = -.77, p = .041$.

For games classified as strategy, there were no important significant correlations that concerned this study. The only interesting finding for shooter games was that openness was significantly correlated with competence, $r(6) = .72, p = .043$. These last ones are tenuous at best, as they were the smallest samples, but it is interesting that personality types were still matched with factors of SDT.

The reason for this splitting is to understand the potential for each game to have on specific types of people, as if we look across the whole data set, we can see that certain aspects of SDT have relationships with mental health symptoms, and these could be the basis for use in an intervention. For example, across the whole sample, competence was negatively associated with anxiety and depression from the PHQ-9, $r(105) = -.22$, $p = .024$. This could suggest that finding games that allow people to gain and grow competency could be an important factor in interventions around anxiety. Since in the overall sample, competence and autonomy were correlated, $r(112) = .2$, $p = .031$, and autonomy and relatedness were correlated, $r(113) = .34$, $p < .001$, there is strong evidence that finding a game that people can relate to, gain competency in and feel autonomous in their actions could have beneficial effects on anxiety and depression symptoms, as measured by the PHQ-9. Lastly, to understand what type of game might be useful for such an intervention, we ran a series of correlations with game time and genre assigned, and found that there was a significant, positive correlation between the two, $r(130) = .22$, $p = .010$. The full list of correlations that were significant can be seen in Table 1, ranked by importance of factor and correlations across game genre. As the table shows, there is a lot to unpack with regards to how different games could impact mental health.

4 Discussion

Overall, the purpose of this study was to investigate how video games, using the principles of SDT, could impact and intervene into mental health problems, by tackling their symptoms. This exploratory study had two main hypotheses: games with a strong story focus will show better relationships with mental health symptoms, specifically that story lead, character focused featuring escapism and immersion will be strongly related to mental health symptoms. Secondly, that games such as management or simulation games would also show positive relationships with mental health symptoms. The second hypotheses here was shown to not be true, as there were no significant results from any of the various spectrums measured in relation to strategy or simulation games. This is somewhat founded in evidence, especially when considering the effects that have been looked for in mental health, the ability to escape, and be immersed in a game [55]. While previous research did suggest that this type of game could be something to look at, traditionally strategy games are not best known for their ability to make a player feel immersed in another world, as one of the key features of these games is usually grand management of an entire culture or civilization. This would somewhat indicate lower levels of relatedness and connectedness on an individual level as there would be no key player character to interact as, but a large group of people that the player is trying to channel their identity through [42, 43].

The first hypothesis was somewhat supported, given the data and the relationships that we can claim. There was a strong relationship shown between the key traits of SDT, and importantly this linked in with our findings from adventure games. Competence showed to have a positive correlation with openness, and typically we think of this personality trait as being less anxious in general terms. This also further linked into our findings that suggested people who were higher in neuroticism would tend to score higher in anxiety symptoms and would thus potentially play this type of game more [21, 47, 48]. This was extended to RPGs where we saw a negative relationship between competence

Table 1. Table of significant correlations for game types with factors of self-determination, personality and mental health

Correlation Pair	Adventure	RPG	Sport	Strategy	All Genres
Neuroticism / OCD	0.5	0.57			0.49
Conscientiousness / PHQ	-0.47	-0.7			-0.22
Neuroticism / PHQ	0.47				0.39
Neuroticism / GAD		0.59			0.46
Relatedness / Autonomy	0.42				-0.45
Openness / Competency	0.43				0.36
Competency / PHQ		-0.47			
Extraversion / PHQ			-0.81		-0.29
Agreeableness / OCD				-0.71	-0.28
Openness / PHQ		-0.52		0.62	
Conscientiousness / OCD			-0.86		-0.32
Conscientiousness / GAD			-0.79		-0.27
Autonomy / GAD			0.7		
Agreeableness / Autonomy			-0.77		
Openness / Autonomy					0.24

Note: All figures are Spearman Correlations coefficients significant at p < .05 or lower. Importance of correlation based on colour.

and anxiety symptoms, a strong suggestion that those who play this game might be less anxious because they feel more competent at the game. As we saw from our final round of tests, competence, relatedness, and autonomy were all significantly correlated with each other, and this could be evidence that type of game could be useful for mental health interventions. Further to this, we looked to investigate the play time of games, and from our previous research we understand that shorter sessions of play seem to be beneficial [38], and from the current research, this would suggest that adventure games are typically played for less time throughout the week, but based on all the analyses we have conducted here, there suggests the chance that adventure and RPG games could be best suited to offer these shorter chances at gameplay opportunities, with overall more significant important correlations, but overall less hours played in a week.

Lastly, we saw somewhat expected results across all game genres regarding personality. Neuroticism was highly positively associated with mental health scores, with both tending to rise together. Openness was also shown to be negatively associated with mental health scores, in line with our prediction, and this makes sense when understanding how the two traits are classified in the personality inventory. It could be indicative that games can show us what type of people they might affect best, but it could also speak to a problematic case where those high in neuroticism might not be as approachable or open to a solution around their mental health that involves either directly tackling their mental health themselves, or not having support from a clinical professional [21]. This area is still in need of further research, but the inclusion of an individual difference factor does help to understand the impact that games could potentially have as a pre-clinical intervention.

However, this is not to say that this research is complete or proves that video games can be used in this way. And this research itself is limited by what it can conclude by not setting up and showing any casual relationships between these variables [56]. It does set the scene to understand what type of video game can be used for this type of intervention, however, the lack of any experimental study here speaks to how much can be implied with cause and effect. The study itself was flawed simply because the type of question used to understand the game that participants choose is not an easy question to ask. We understood from the start that asking participants to choose a single game, at a current time point would firstly have many issues around a game that is present to them now, or one from the past that might not have been played before. Also, the time that we asked them to think about, their favourite game could be implied to understand that this is their favourite game right now, but it is possible that participants chose a game that was many ears old, that they had not played in a long time, and might not have remembered all the effects that would come with such a choice. This is, at its heart, a problem with this type of research in general, and something that quantitative research will struggle to understand or grasp, and the next research project in this line should look to focus on understanding the choices behind games chosen, and the reason why these types of games might speak so well to an individual's mental health [57, 58].

Future research in this area could look to further understand the effect that specific games had on individuals. Qualitative interviews, utilising a deeper level of analyses into participants feelings and thought processes into how the games they played affected them could look to bridge the gap that the current research cannot [58]. This should help tie the research together and provide the basis for an experimental study to understand how these various effects work together to hopefully act as intervention. Research suggests that games that can elicit escapism, immersion, and feelings of control autonomy and relatedness should be at the forefront of the research [55]. This would suggest games with a narrative element to them, such as adventure or RPG games, as suggested by this study and the previous work of the authors. However, individual differences must still be accounted for, and it is not reasonable to expect one solution to work for everyone, so there will surely be some other options that present themselves, which can be explored in later steps of the research. However, the outcomes of these research pieces do look promising, and with the potential to suggest a strong model of video games helping mental health symptoms through user directed action.

Overall, the research project was beneficial in highlighting how games could potentially be useful as an early intervention tool for mental health symptoms. By utilising the framework of SDT, we have shown how games can potentially be used to address symptomology of common anxiety and depression diagnoses, by addressing them through the framework of transdiagnostic mental health and the HiTOP model. While the research itself is only correlational in nature, it does provide insight into what type of games are being played by those with common symptomology and provides groundwork for the research to move on and assess individual games, through more in-depth qualitative pieces and through the eventual setup of an experimental piece of research to monitor and assess impacts on mental health. Though this research is still in its early fledgling stage, with experience and more research, there is the distinct possibility that video games could be used in some form of early intervention, as another weapon against mental health and the lack of resources we face as a species.

References

1. Bannister, R.: Underfunded mental healthcare in the NHS: the cycle of preventable distress continues. BMJ **375** (2021). https://doi.org/10.1136/BMJ.N2706
2. Johannes, N., Vuorre, M., Przybylski, A.K.: Video game play is positively correlated with well-being. R Soc Open Sci **8**(2), 202049 (2021). https://doi.org/10.1098/rsos.202049
3. Krueger, R.F., Eaton, N.R.: Transdiagnostic factors of mental disorders. World Psychiatry **14**(1), 27–29 (2015). https://doi.org/10.1002/WPS.20175
4. Hirsch, C.R., et al.: Effects of modifying interpretation bias on transdiagnostic repetitive negative thinking. J. Consult. Clin. Psychol. **88**(3), 226–239 (2020). https://doi.org/10.1037/CCP0000455
5. Schaeuffele, C., Schulz, A., Knaevelsrud, C., Renneberg, B., Boettcher, J.: CBT at the crossroads: the rise of transdiagnostic treatments. Int. J. Cogn. Ther. **14**(1), 86–113 (2020). https://doi.org/10.1007/s41811-020-00095-2
6. Norton, P.J., Paulus, D.J.: Transdiagnostic models of anxiety disorder: theoretical and empirical underpinnings. Clin. Psychol. Rev. **56**, 122–137 (2017). https://doi.org/10.1016/j.cpr.2017.03.004
7. Dalgleish, T., Black, M., Johnston, D., Bevan, A.: Transdiagnostic approaches to mental health problems: current status and future directions. J. Consult. Clin. Psychol. **88**(3), 179–195 (2020). https://doi.org/10.1037/CCP0000482
8. Shah, J.L., et al.: Transdiagnostic clinical staging in youth mental health: a first international consensus statement. World Psychiatry **19**(2), 233–242 (2020). https://doi.org/10.1002/wps.20745
9. American Psychiatric Association, Diagnostic and Statistical Manual for Mental Disorders, Third Revision, Revised (DSM-III-R)., 5th ed. American Psychiatric Publishing, Arlington, VA (1987)
10. Ruggero, C.J., et al.: Integrating the hierarchical taxonomy of psychopathology (HiTOP) into clinical practice. J. Consult. Clin. Psychol. **87**(12), 1069 (2019). https://doi.org/10.1037/CCP0000452
11. DeYoung, C.G., et al.: The distinction between symptoms and traits in the Hierarchical taxonomy of psychopathology (HiTOP). J. Pers. **90**(1), 20–33 (2022). https://doi.org/10.1111/JOPY.12593
12. Gillan, C.M., Seow, T.X.F.: carving out new transdiagnostic dimensions for research in mental health. Biol. Psychiatry Cogn. Neurosci. Neuroimaging **5**(10), 932–934 (2020). https://doi.org/10.1016/j.bpsc.2020.04.013
13. Mental Health Foundation, Mental health statistics: the most common mental health problems, Mental Health Foundation (2020). https://www.mentalhealth.org.uk/statistics/mental-health-statistics-most-common-mental-health-problems. Accessed 14 May 2021

14. Henningsen, P., Zimmermann, T., Sattel, H.: Medically unexplained physical symptoms, anxiety, and depression: a meta-analytic review. Psychosom Med **65**(4), 528–533 (2003). https://doi.org/10.1097/01.PSY.0000075977.90337.E7

15. Beesdo, K., Knappe, S., Pine, D.S.: Anxiety and anxiety disorders in children and adolescents: developmental issues and implications for DSM-V. Psychiatr. Clin. North Am. **32**(3), 483–524 (2009). https://doi.org/10.1016/j.psc.2009.06.002

16. Lewandowski, K.E., Barrantes-Vidal, N., Nelson-Gray, R.O., Clancy, C., Kepley, H.O., Kwapil, T.R.: Anxiety and depression symptoms in psychometrically identified schizotypy. Schizophr Res. **83**(2–3), 225–235 (2006). https://doi.org/10.1016/j.schres.2005.11.024

17. Spitzer, R.L., Kroenke, K., Williams, J.B.W., Löwe, B.: A brief measure for assessing generalized anxiety disorder: the GAD-7. Arch. Intern. Med. **166**(10), 1092–1097 (2006). https://doi.org/10.1001/ARCHINTE.166.10.1092

18. Slee, A., Nazareth, I., Freemantle, N., Background, L.H.: Trends in generalised anxiety disorders and symptoms in primary care: UK population-based cohort study. Br. J. Psychiatry 1–7 (2020). https://doi.org/10.1192/bjp.2020.159

19. Finan, P.H., Smith, M.T.: The comorbidity of insomnia, chronic pain, and depression: dopamine as a putative mechanism. Sleep Med. Rev. **17**(3), 173–83 (2013). https://doi.org/10.1016/j.smrv.2012.03.003

20. Arnold, T., et al.: A brief transdiagnostic pandemic mental health maintenance intervention. Couns. Psychol. Q. **34**(3–4), 331–351 (2021). https://doi.org/10.1080/09515070.2020.1769026

21. Rodriguez-Seijas, C., Eaton, N.R., Krueger, R.F.: How transdiagnostic factors of personality and psychopathology can inform clinical assessment and intervention. J. Pers. Assess. **97**(5), 425–435 (2015). https://doi.org/10.1080/00223891.2015.1055752

22. Demyttenaere, K., Heirman, E.: The blurred line between anxiety and depression: hesitations on comorbidity, thresholds and hierarchy. Int. Rev. Psychiatry **32**(5–6), 455–465 (2020). https://doi.org/10.1080/09540261.2020.1764509

23. Mineka, S., Watson, D., Clark, L.A.: Comorbidity of anxiety and unipolar mood disorders. Annu. Rev. Psychol. **49**, 377–412 (1998). https://doi.org/10.1146/annurev.psych.49.1.377

24. Aina, Y., Susman, J.L.: 'Understanding comorbidity with depression and anxiety disorders. J. Am. Osteopathic Assoc. 106(5 SUPPL), S9–14 (2006). Accessed 10 Jul 2021. https://eur opepmc.org/article/med/16738013

25. Jacobson, N.C., Newman, M.G.: Anxiety and depression as bidirectional risk factors for one another: a meta-analysis of longitudinal studies. Psychol. Bull. **143**(11), 1155–1200 (2017). https://doi.org/10.1037/bul0000111

26. Allan, N.P., Albanese, B.J., Judah, M.R., Gooch, C.V., Schmidt, N.B.: A multimethod investigation of the impact of attentional control on a brief intervention for anxiety and depression. J. Consult. Clin. Psychol. **88**(3), 212–225 (2020). https://doi.org/10.1037/CCP0000484

27. Merry, S.N., Stasiak, K., Shepherd, M., Frampton, C., Fleming, T., Lucassen, M.F.G.: The effectiveness of SPARX, a computerised self help intervention for adolescents seeking help for depression: randomised controlled non-inferiority trial. BMJ **344**(7857) (2012). https://doi.org/10.1136/BMJ.E2598

28. Johnson, D., Deterding, S., Kuhn, K.A., Staneva, A., Stoyanov, S., Hides, L.: Gamification for health and wellbeing: a systematic review of the literature. Internet Interventions **6**, 89–106 (2016). https://doi.org/10.1016/j.invent.2016.10.002

29. Garber, J., Weersing, V.R.: Comorbidity of anxiety and depression in youth: implications for treatment and prevention. Clin. Psychol. Sci. Pract. **17**(4), 293–306 (2010). https://doi.org/10.1111/j.1468-2850.2010.01221.x

30. Spence, S.H., Rapee, R.M.: The etiology of social anxiety disorder: an evidence-based model. Behav. Res. Ther. **86**, 50–67 (2016). https://doi.org/10.1016/j.brat.2016.06.007

31. Karyotaki, E., et al.: Efficacy of self-guided internet-based cognitive behavioral therapy in the treatment of depressive symptoms : a meta-analysis of individual participant data. JAMA Psychiatry 351–359 (2017). https://doi.org/10.1001/jamapsychiatry.2017.0044

32. Sawyer, S.M., Azzopardi, P.S., Wickremarathne, D., Patton, G.C.: The age of adolescence. Lancet Child Adolesc Health 2(3), 223–228 (2018). https://doi.org/10.1016/S2352-4642(18)30022-1

33. Hudson, J.L., Rapee, R.M., Lyneham, H.J., McLellan, L.F., Wuthrich, V.M., Schniering, C.A.: Comparing outcomes for children with different anxiety disorders following cognitive behavioural therapy. Behav. Res. Ther. 72, 30–37 (2015). https://doi.org/10.1016/j.brat.2015.06.007

34. Russoniello, C.V., Fish, M., O'Brien, K.: The efficacy of casual videogame play in reducing clinical depression: a randomized controlled study. Games Health J. 2(6), 341–346 (2013). https://doi.org/10.1089/g4h.2013.0010

35. Halbrook, Y.J., O'Donnell, A.T., Msetfi, R.M.: When and how video games can be good: a review of the positive effects of video games on well-being. Perspect. Psychol. Sci. 14(6), 1096–1104 (2019). https://doi.org/10.1177/1745691619863807

36. Fish, M.T., Russoniello, C.V., O'Brien, K.: The efficacy of prescribed casual videogame play in reducing symptoms of anxiety: a randomized controlled study. Games Health J. 3(5), 291–295 (2014). https://doi.org/10.1089/g4h.2013.0092

37. Pallavicini, F., Pepe, A., Mantovani, F.: Commercial off-the-shelf video games for reducing stress and anxiety: systematic review. JMIR Ment. Health 8(8) (2021). https://doi.org/10.2196/28150

38. Bavelier, D., Davidson, R.J.: Games to do you good. Nature 2013 494:7438 494(7438), 425–426 (2013). https://doi.org/10.1038/494425a

39. Copeman, M., Freeman, J.: Social anxiety strategies through gaming. In: Fang, X. (eds.) HCI in Games. HCII 2022. LNCS, vol. 13334, pp. 309–326 Springer, Cham (2022). https://doi.org/10.1007/978-3-031-05637-6_19

40. Deci, E.L., Ryan, R.M.: Self-determination Theory. In: Handbook of Theories of Social Psychology: vol. 1, SAGE Publications Inc., pp. 416–437 (2012). https://doi.org/10.4135/9781446249215.n21

41. Stone, D.N., Deci, E.L., Ryan, R.M.: Beyond talk: creating autonomous motivation through self-determination theory. 34(3), 75–91 (2009). https://doi.org/10.1177/030630700903400305

42. Ryan, R.M., Deci, E.L.: Intrinsic and extrinsic motivation from a self-determination theory perspective: definitions, theory, practices, and future directions. Contemp. Educ. Psychol. 61, 101860 (2020). https://doi.org/10.1016/J.CEDPSYCH.2020.101860

43. Ryan, R.M., Rigby, C.S., Przybylski, A.: The motivational pull of video games: a self-determination theory approach. Motiv. Emot. 30(4), 347–363 (2006). https://doi.org/10.1007/s11031-006-9051-8

44. Shoshani, A., Braverman, S., Meirow, G.: Video games and close relations: attachment and empathy as predictors of children's and adolescents' video game social play and socio-emotional functioning. Comput. Hum. Behav. 114, 106578 (2021). https://doi.org/10.1016/J.CHB.2020.106578

45. Przybylski, A.K., Rigby, C.S., Deci, E.L., Ryan, R.M.: Competence-impeding electronic games and players' aggressive feelings, thoughts, and behaviors. J. Pers. Soc. Psychol. 106(3), 441–457 (2014). https://doi.org/10.1037/a0034820

46. Hilgard, J., Engelhardt, C.R., Bartholow, B.D.: 'Individual differences in motives, preferences, and pathology in video games: the gaming attitudes, motives, and experiences scales (GAMES). Front. Psychol. 4, 608 (2013). https://doi.org/10.3389/fpsyg.2013.00608

47. Johnson, D., Gardner, J.: Personality, motivation and video games. In: ACM International Conference Proceeding Series, pp. 276–279 (2010). https://doi.org/10.1145/1952222.195 2281

48. Markey, P.M., Markey, C.N.: Vulnerability to violent video games: a review and integration of personality research. (2010). https://doi.org/10.1037/a0019000

49. ISFE, Key Facts 2020 Europe's video games industry (2020). Accessed 18 Jul 2021. https://www.isfe.eu/wp-content/uploads/2020/08/ISFE-final-1.pdf

50. Salmon, J.P., Dolan, S.M., Drake, R.S., Wilson, G.C., Klein, R.M., Eskes, G.A.: A survey of video game preferences in adults: building better games for older adults. Entertain Comput. **21**, 45–64 (2017). https://doi.org/10.1016/j.entcom.2017.04.006

51. Azadvar, A.; UPEQ: Ubisoft perceived experience questionnaire (2018). https://doi.org/10.1145/3235765.3235780

52. Kroenke, K., Spitzer, R.L., Williams, J.B.W.: The PHQ-9: validity of a brief depression severity measure. J. Gen. Intern. Med. **16**(9), 606 (2001). https://doi.org/10.1046/J.1525-1497.2001.016009606.X

53. National collaborating centre for mental health, The improving access to psychological therapies manual, pp. 1–15, 2018, Accessed 28 Oct 2022. https://www.england.nhs.uk/wp-content/uploads/2018/06/the-iapt-manual.pdf

54. John, O.P., Srivastava, S.: The big-five trait taxonomy: history, measurement, and theoretical perspectives (1999)

55. Li, D., Liau, A., Khoo, A.: Examining the influence of actual-ideal self-discrepancies, depression, and escapism, on pathological gaming among massively multiplayer online adolescent gamers. Cyberpsychol. Behav. Soc. Netw. **14**(9), 535–539 (2011). https://doi.org/10.1089/cyber.2010.0463

56. Kirk, R.E., Kirk, R.E., Experimental Design. In: Handbook of Psychology, Wiley, Hoboken (2003). https://doi.org/10.1002/0471264385.wei0201

57. Deegan, P.E.: The importance of personal medicine: a qualitative study of resilience in people with psychiatric disabilities. Scand. J. Public Health Suppl. **33**(66), 29–35 (2005). https://doi.org/10.1080/14034950510033345

58. Colder Carras, M., et al.: Connection, meaning, and distraction: a qualitative study of video game play and mental health recovery in veterans treated for mental and/or behavioral health problems. Soc. Sci. Med. **216**, 124–132 (2018). https://doi.org/10.1016/j.socscimed.2018.08.044

An Exploration of Feared Versus Fearless Attack Attitudes Using the Chess Personalities of Virtual Chess Players

Khaldoon Dhou[✉]

College of Business Administration, Texas A&M University -Central Texas,
Killeen, TX, USA
kdhou@tamuct.edu

Abstract. Chess has emerged as a promising domain for psychologists, marketers, computer scientists, and experts from many other domains. In this paper, the author explores attack behavior in chess via the employment of virtual chess players. In other words, he investigates two virtual grandmasters: Chigorin and Waitzkin. Although the two grandmasters have the same level of strength, they have two different chess personalities that determine their attitudes during chess games. While Waitzkin is an attacker grandmaster, Chigorin tends to be a feared attacker, and he leans more toward the defensive side. The investigation is conducted by collecting data from the two grandmasters while competing against three other class-A virtual players. The results were consistent with the previous research that shows the importance of chess strategy in the outcomes of the game. Generally, a chess grandmaster with an attacking strategy performed better than a grandmaster with a defensive strategy. Likewise, the less skilled players (i.e., class-A virtual players) performed differently although their ratings are almost the same. These findings can be valuable to chess software designers and for training chess players of different skills and personalities.

Keywords: chess personality · attack · defense · virtual human · grandmaster

1 Introduction

Chess has long been a question of great interest in a wide range of fields, including psychology, computing, business, and medicine [5,12,18,25,28]. Among the most highly notable achievements in the domain of chess is the development of virtual humans that have the capability to behave as real humans and defeat top grandmasters. A virtual chess player can be defined as a computer simulation that mimics a real chess player. Virtual chess players have different strengths ranging from beginners to top-rank grandmasters such as Kasparov and Anand. Additionally, like real players, each chess player is characterized by a chess personality defined as his attitude to react to game scenarios and describes his playing style [7–9,27]. The personalities of chess players come in different variations, such as attacking and defensive styles. For example, the chess personality of Kasparov is characterized by his rapid calculations and the ability to choose creative opening styles. It is essential to mention that the personality of a chess player does not necessarily provide an indication of his chess strength. For example, two players might play at the same strength while having different personalities.

The reason behind choosing virtual over real chess players in this experiment is threefold. First, virtual players offer much flexibility in terms of designing the experiments and choosing the opponents. In other words, the utilization of virtual players is a practical approach that allows conducting experiments on various parameters that can be very hard to be managed using real chess players. Second, virtual humans allow exploring personalities of players who exist in different eras. For example, a previous study [7] investigated the chess personalities of Anderssen (1818–1879) and Leko (1979-now) via conducting chess games that match each of them with other less skilled players of various styles. Third, virtual chess players made it easier to explore the competition between world champions and examine their performance while playing against less skilled players of various classes.

In this research article, the author investigates the personalities of two virtual grandmasters: Waitzkin and Chigorin. While Waitzkin is known for his fearless attacking style and deep understanding of the endgame, Chigorin has a feared attacking personality. The games used in the current study are obtained from the Chessmaster Grandmaster Edition, a highly reputable software in the chess community. The two virtual grandmasters are estimated to play as strong as real world-class grandmasters. For the purpose of this research, the author conducts experiments that match each of the virtual grandmasters with three other class-A virtual players: a player who has almost complete ignorance of the center of the board, a player who chooses openings to trap his opponents, and a player with solid opening knowledge and strong control over the board. The three players have almost the same rating, which is a measurement of a player's strength while competing against other players in the chess community. The main research questions addressed in this article are as follows:

- Is there a difference between the performance of two virtual grandmasters that have the same strength but vary in their fear-of-attack personalities while competing against class-A players?
- How do class-A players that differ in personalities perform against two grandmasters that vary in terms of fearing attack?

2   Related Work

Research into chess psychology has a long history. Early works began with de Groot experiments that targeted chess masters and beginners [6]. In his experiment, he allowed chess players of different levels to have a look at meaningful chess positions over a period of time and to build them from memory after that. He noticed that chess masters did a better job than beginners. Later, the same work was repeated, but with meaningless positions over the board, and the performance of all players dropped [4]. Existing research in chess psychology found that advanced chess players are able to identify certain chess positions and encode them in chunks that consist of certain patterns along with connections between them [5]. That is to say, the main component of a chess player's skill lies in his ability to recognize chess patterns based on his previous experience. Although searching for the best move is another component, research shows that the search algorithms of grandmasters are no different than those of class-A players [16].

A chess player is generally classified into a specific category according to his rating, which is a numerical value that is given to a chess player based on his performance while competing against other players in the chess community [14]. The world of chess is generally governed by two organizations: the World Chess Federation (FIDE) and the United States Chess Federation (USCF). Both two organizations assign ratings to chess players based on their performances. Although the rating of chess players is a significant factor that determines the strength of a chess player, chess personality is another factor that seems to be generally neglected. The chess personality is defined as the attitude of chess players while competing against others. For example, a chess player can be an attacker, defensive, or a mixture of both. Research shows that chess players can perform differently depending on their chess personalities and those of their opponents [7,8]. It is essential to mention that chess personality is a term that differs from the actual personality of a chess player.

The extensive search shows that the topic of chess personality began with the paper of Kerpman [20], who explored the personalities of many chess players that set them aside from others in the community. Recent developments in the field of AI have led to a renewed interest in chess personalities by designing studies that explore players of various personalities. The author employed virtual humans to investigate chess personalities and explore how they behave in different circumstances. The exploration includes grandmasters and less skilled players such as Kasparov, Waitzkin, and many others. The first study that explored chess personalities was designed to investigate the performance of two grandmasters against other less skilled players [7]. That is to say; the author explored how an attacker and defensive grandmasters of the same rating perform when they play against less skilled players. Additionally, he investigated the performance of the other competitors in the experiment. They found that the performance of a chess player can differ depending on the personality of his opponent. In addition to the study in [7], the author followed up with many studies that explore various personalities of many other grandmasters and less skilled players [2,8–11]. The outcomes from all these studies reveal that chess players can perform differently depending on their personalities and the personalities of their opponents.

Much of the current literature on chess players pays more attention to their actual personalities than their chess personalities. One study by Vollstädt-Klein et al. [28] explored the personalities of strong chess players and how they can affect their chess skills. Their findings reveal that female chess players were happier and more successful than other females, which was not the case for males. Similarly, Stafford [26] explored chess games that exist in large databases and found that female chess players perform better than expected when they compete against other male players. Additionally, Iqbal and Nagappan [19] evaluated a group of winning chess movement series captured from games played by males and females. They found that there are factors that are unlikely to be affected by gender, such as perception and appreciation. In similar, but a different vein, Bilalić et al. [1] investigated the personalities of two groups of kids: one who plays chess and another who does not play. They found that, in general, kids who were attached to chess did better in specific tests than their peers.

While there is a plethora of studies that explore the personalities of real chess players, the extensive search revealed that there are very few studies that employ virtual humans to explore chess personalities. The author believes that there is a demand for more studies that investigate virtual players and their applications in many domains. The current research article augments the chess literature that explores how virtual chess players and their applications to further understand chess personalities and how they are compared during competitions.

3   Method

3.1   Participants

All the participants in this study are virtual chess players from the Chessmaster Grandmaster Edition, a highly esteemed software in the chess community. The author chooses five virtual chess players: two grandmasters and three class-B players, as follows:

- Waitzkin: a top-rank grandmaster who is a fearless attacker and is characterized by his deep understanding of the endgame.
- Chigorin: a top-rank grandmaster who tends to fear attack and employs a positional playing style
- Buck: a class-A player who is rated at 2355 USCF. While his openings tend to have more captured pieces, his weakness lies in his ignorance to the center of the game.
- J.T.: a class-A player who is rated at 2330 USCF. He prefers to play certain openings that attract his opponents to fall into traps he has already prepared
- Lili: a class-A player who is rated at 2394 USCF. She has a solid opening knowledge, but she prefers certain disadvantageous directions of play. Additionally, she knows how to control the center well.

The descriptions of all the virtual players are provided by the Chessmaster Grandmaster Edition. The virtual players utilized in the experiment simulate players that exist in real life.

3.2   Materials

The current design involves the employment of two independent variables:

– The chess personality of the grandmasters was manipulated. For half of the games, Waitzkin was chosen, and the other half was played by Chigorin.
– The chess personality of the class-A players varied between the personalities of Buck, J.T., and Lili. The descriptions of the three personalities are provided in the participants' subsection.

The current design has two dependent variables: the Chessmaster agreement percentage with the moves made by a grandmaster and the Chessmaster agreement percentage with the moves made by a class-A player. The color of the grandmaster was employed as a between-subjects factor. The design resulted in two grandmaster personalities (Waitzkin vs. Chigorin) by three class-A player personalities (Buck, J.T., and Lili) repeated measures ANOVA. The virtual players in the experiment were selected according to the following criteria:

– The class-A players have different chess personalities; however, they have almost the same USCF rating.
– The grandmasters have the same strength; however, one of them is a fearless attacker, and the other is defensive.

4   Results

Each of the dependent variables was recorded for each of the games conducted in the experiment. All the effects were considered significant at $p < 0.05$.

4.1   The Chessmaster Agreement Percentage with the Moves Made by a Grandmaster

The main effect of the grandmaster personality had a significant influence on the Chessmaster agreement percentage with the moves made by a grandmaster, $F(1, 84) = 9.448$, $p = 0.003$. The Chessmaster significantly agrees more with the moves made by Waitzkin ($M = 97.857$) as compared to the moves made by Chigorin $M = 97.171$.

The color of the grandmaster interacted significantly with the personality of a grandmaster to affect the Chessmaster agreement percentage with the moves made by a grandmaster, $F(1, 84) = 12.183$, $p = 0.001$. In other words, the color of a grandmaster had a different effect depending on the personality of the grandmaster involved. To further investigate the interaction, the author conducted paired samples t-tests. A paired samples t-test reveals that with the Black color, Waitzkin ($M = 98.186$, $SD = 2.007$) outperforms Chigorin (96.721, $SD = 3.115$), $t(128) = 4.445$, $p < 0.001$.

The main effect of the class-B player has a significant influence on the Chessmaster agreement percentage with the moves made by a grandmaster, $F(2, 168) = 9.639$, $p < 0.001$. Paired samples t-tests reveal that there is a significant difference between the Chessmaster agreement percentage with the moves made by grandmasters when they compete against Lili ($M = 98.070$, $SD = 2.042$) compared to J.T. ($M = 96.977$, $SD = 2.851$), $t(171) = 4.126$, $p < 0.001$; and when they compete against Lili ($M = 98.070$, $SD = 2.042$) as opposed to Buck($M = 97.494$, $SD = 2.599$), $t(171) = 2.483$, $p = 0.014$.

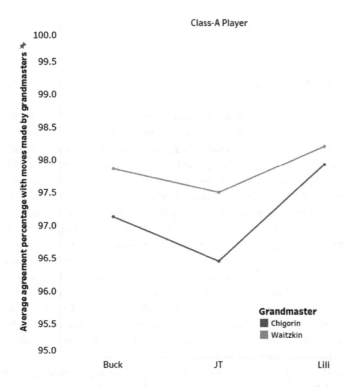

Fig. 1. The Chessmaster agreement percentage with the moves made by the virtual grandmasters: Chigorin and Waitzkin

4.2 The Chessmaster Agreement Percentage with the Moves Made by a Class-A Player

The main effect of the class-A player personality is significant on the Chessmaster agreement percentage with the moves made by class-A players, $F(2, 168) = 7.125$, $p = 0.001$. Paired samples t-tests reveal significant mean differences between the Chessmaster agreement percentages with the moves made by Lili ($M = 94.651$, $SD = 4.057$) as opposed to the moves made by Buck ($M = 93.180$, $SD = 4.167$), $t(171) = 3.584$, $p < 0.001$; and the moves made by Lili ($M = 94.651$, $SD = 4.057$) as opposed to the moves made by J.T. ($M = 93.163$, $SD = 4.834$), $t(171) = 3.002$, $p = 0.003$.

Additionally, there is a statistically significant interaction between the effects of a grandmaster color and the personality of a grandmaster, $F(1, 84) = 9.483$, $p = 0.003$. With a grandmaster playing with White pieces, class-A players did better when they played against Chigorin ($M = 94.000$, $SD = 4.252$) as opposed to Waitzkin ($M = 92.636$, $SD = 4.786$). With a grandmaster playing with Black pieces, the Chessmaster agrees significantly more with the moves made by class-A players competing against Waitzkin ($M = 94.512$, $SD = 4.006$) as opposed to them competing against Chigorin ($M = 93.512$, $SD = 4.406$), $t(128) = 2.057$, $p = 0.042$.

5 General Discussion

The present experiment was designed to explore how moves made by an attacker grandmaster are compared to those made by another grandmaster who fears attack. Additionally, the experiment explored the movements made by three class-A players while competing against the two grandmasters. All the players employed in the experiment are virtual; however, they simulate players that exist in real life. Consistent with the author's previous study [7], this research found that although virtual chess players can have the same strength level (i.e., ratings), they can perform differently according to their chess personalities.

One interesting finding is that a virtual grandmaster with an attacking strategy performs better than a grandmaster who leans more towards fearing attack (See Fig. 1). This finding is consistent with that of the author in [7,10], which shows the competition against two virtual grandmaster: a defensive and an attacker. In [7,10], the author explored the personalities of an attacking grandmaster (i.e., Anderssen) and a defensive grandmaster (i.e., Leko). The findings show that the Chessmaster agrees more with the moves made by Anderssen as opposed to the ones made by Leko.

Previous studies conducted by the author in the same domain reveal that the personality of a virtual chess player can affect how he performs against players of other personalities. That does not only apply to less skilled players, but it also applies to top-rank grandmasters. For instance, in one study [8], the author explored the personality of Kasparov while competing against other less skilled players of class-A. The study found that the performance of Kasparov varies based on his opponent. Interestingly, the findings in [8] are consistent with the findings in the current study. In [8], Kasparov did better when he competed against a player who prefers to gain chess material as opposed to one who leans more towards drawing games.

Another key finding of this study is that Lili could significantly perform the other two virtual players in the experiment. One possible explanation is that Lili knows how to well control the center of the board. The existing literature shows that controlling the center is one of the most significant strategies, and sometimes a chess player can sacrifice one of his pieces to control the chessboard [3,15,23]. Additionally, controlling the center of the board has attracted the attention of chess software designers, and it was a feature to be included in chess applications [13]. In a previous study [8], the findings revealed that Kasparov committed more errors when he competed with a player who was strong at controlling the center as opposed to another who preferred gaining chess material. These findings are evidenced by the existing research that shows that controlling the center of the chessboard is more advantageous than maintaining a successful pawn structure [21]. Controlling the center of the chessboard is a significant part of the chess opening phase. Research in computer chess shows that during the actual games between Kasparov and Deep Blue, Kasparov had an excellent performance during the opening and that Deep Blue could not defeat him while in the opening phase [24].

One of the issues that emerge from these findings is the emphasis on exploring chess openings and their importance in chess research and introducing chess to players. Many chess grandmasters emphasized the significance of chess opening as an essential game part. For example, Michael Adams believes that opening is a crucial component of a chess game, and working on an opening is more important than working on any other parts. All these findings broadly support the author's work of other studies in this area linking the game outcomes and the personalities of virtual chess players employed in the experiments [2,7–11]. That is to say, although the rating (e.g., USCF, FIDE) is the criteria that are mainly used to compare the performance against chess players, existing research shows that the personality of a chess player plays an important rule. A player tends to perform differently, and his performance can vary according to his personality and that of his opponent.

6   Conclusion

In this investigation, the aim was to assess how two virtual grandmasters of contrasting personalities perform while competing against three class-A players. Additionally, the study also evaluates how the class-A players perform while competing against the two grandmasters. The data from the present study was collected from virtual chess players that simulate real players. This study has shown that in general, a grandmaster who is an aggressive attacker performed better than a grandmaster who has a defensive personality. The findings of this investigation complement those of earlier studies.

The findings from the current study shed new light on how critical some chess aspects are, such as chess personalities and game phases. Chess personalities can be further explored to design chess applications to train players of different levels and personalities. Additionally, chess personalities can be investigated to explore how they can be employed in other domains that require developing continuous strategies, such as marketing. For example, some marketers consider a defensive marketing strategy [17], while others are geared towards aggressive strategies [22]. This would be a fruitful area for further work that explores a relationship between marketing and chess strategies. In general, the author believes that the findings of this study might be of interest to researchers from different domains that explore strategies. Although these findings are interesting from an academic perspective, more research is needed to determine their practicality in real-life scenarios.

References

1. Bilalić, M., McLeod, P., Gobet, F.: Personality profiles of young chess players. Personality Individ. Differ. **42**(6), 901–910 (2007)
2. Caci, B., Dhou, K.: The interplay between artificial intelligence and users' personalities: a new scenario for human-computer interaction in gaming. In: Stephanidis, C., et al. (eds.) HCII 2020. LNCS, vol. 12425, pp. 619–630. Springer, Cham (2020). https://doi.org/10.1007/978-3-030-60128-7_45
3. Cannice, M.V.: The right moves: Creating experiential management learning with chess. Int. J. Manag. Educ. **11**(1), 25–33 (2013). https://www.sciencedirect.com/science/article/pii/S1472811712000535
4. Chase, W.G., Simon, H.A.: The mind's eye in chess. In: Visual Information Processing, pp. 215–281. Elsevier (1973)
5. Chase, W.G., Simon, H.A.: Perception in chess. Cogn. Psychol. **4**(1), 55–81 (1973)
6. De Groot, A.D.: Thought and choice in chess, vol. 4. Walter de Gruyter GmbH & Co KG (1978)
7. Dhou, K.: Towards a better understanding of chess players' personalities: a study using virtual chess players. In: Kurosu, M. (ed.) HCI 2018. LNCS, vol. 10903, pp. 435–446. Springer, Cham (2018). https://doi.org/10.1007/978-3-319-91250-9_34
8. Dhou, K.: An innovative employment of virtual humans to explore the chess personalities of Garry Kasparov and other class-a players. In: Stephanidis, C. (ed.) HCII 2019. LNCS, vol. 11786, pp. 306–319. Springer, Cham (2019). https://doi.org/10.1007/978-3-030-30033-3_24
9. Dhou, K.: A novel investigation of attack strategies via the involvement of virtual humans: a user study of josh Waitzkin, a virtual chess grandmaster. In: Stephanidis, C., Harris, D., Li, W.-C., Schmorrow, D.D., Fidopiastis, C.M., Zaphiris, P., Ioannou, A., Fang, X., Sottilare, R.A., Schwarz, J. (eds.) HCII 2020. LNCS, vol. 12425, pp. 658–668. Springer, Cham (2020). https://doi.org/10.1007/978-3-030-60128-7_48
10. Dhou, K.: An exploration of chess personalities in grandmasters and class-a players using virtual humans. Int. J. Entertainment Technol. Manag. **1**(2), 126–145 (2021)
11. Dhou, K.: An exploration of the fear of attack strategy in chess and its influence on class-a players of different chess personalities: an exploration using virtual humans. In: Fang, X. (ed.) HCII 2021. LNCS, vol. 12789, pp. 185–195. Springer, Cham (2021). https://doi.org/10.1007/978-3-030-77277-2_15
12. Dilmaghani, M.: Gender differences in performance under time constraint: evidence from chess tournaments. J. Behav. Exp. Econ. 101505 (2019). https://www.sciencedirect.com/science/article/pii/S2214804319303052
13. Donninger, C., Kure, A., Lorenz, U.: Parallel brutus: the first distributed, FPGA accelerated chess program. In: 18th International Parallel and Distributed Processing Symposium, 2004. Proceedings, p. 44. IEEE (2004)
14. Elo, A.E.: The rating of chessplayers, past and present. Arco Pub. (1978)
15. Fischer, R.: A bust to the king's gambit. Am. Chess Q. 3–9 (2015)
16. Gobet, F., Jansen, P.J.: Training in Chess: A Scientific Approach. Education and Chess (2006)
17. Hauser, J.R., Shugan, S.M.: Defensive marketing strategies. Market. Sci. **2**(4), 319–360 (1983)
18. Iqbal, A.: A computational method of optimizing chess compositions to enhance aesthetic appeal. In: 2021 2nd International Conference on Artificial Intelligence and Data Sciences (AiDAS), pp. 1–6 (2021)

19. Iqbal, A., Nagappan, S.: A computational aesthetics assessment of chess playing quality between the genders. In: Proceedings of 2018 the 8th International Workshop on Computer Science and Engineering, WCSE. vol. 2018, pp. 313–317 (2018)
20. Karpman, B.: The psychology of chess: (richard reti). Psychoanal. Rev. (1913–1957). **24**, 54 (1937)
21. Kotok, A.: A Chess Playing Program for the IBM 7090 Computer, pp. 48–55. Springer, New York, New York, NY (1988). https://doi.org/10.1007/978-1-4757-1968-0_6
22. Kurt, D., Hulland, J.: Aggressive marketing strategy following equity offerings and firm value: the role of relative strategic flexibility. J. Mark. **77**(5), 57–74 (2013). https://doi.org/10.1509/jm.12.0078
23. Montero, B., Evans, C.: Intuitions without concepts lose the game: mindedness in the art of chess. Phenomenology Cogn. Sci. **10**(2), 175–194 (2011)
24. Newborn, M.: Deep blue and garry kasparov in philadelphia. In: Kasparov versus Deep Blue: Computer Chess Comes of Age, pp. 235–278. Springer, New York (1997). https://doi.org/10.1007/978-1-4612-2260-6_9
25. Schlickum, M.K., Hedman, L., Enochsson, L., Kjellin, A., Felländer-Tsai, L.: Systematic video game training in surgical novices improves performance in virtual reality endoscopic surgical simulators: a prospective randomized study. World J. Surgery **33**(11), 2360–2367 (2009)
26. Stafford, T.: Female chess players outperform expectations when playing men. Psychol. Sci. **29**(3), 429–436 (2018)
27. Ubisoft: Chessmaster grandmaster edition. https://chessmaster.uk.ubi.com/xi/index.php
28. Vollstädt-Klein, S., Grimm, O., Kirsch, P., Bilalić, M.: Personality of elite male and female chess players and its relation to chess skill. Learn. Ind. Differ. **20**(5), 517–521 (2010). https://www.sciencedirect.com/science/article/pii/S1041608010000403

Biofeedback-Controlled Video Games for Emotional Regulation

Alexis Espinoza, Joaquín Larraín, and Francisco J. Gutierrez(⊠)

Department of Computer Science, University of Chile, Beauchef 851, West Building, Third Floor, Santiago, Chile
{alexis.espinoza,joaquin.larrain}@ug.uchile.cl, frgutier@dcc.uchile.cl

Abstract. Stress and psychological distress in the workplace are behind a large number of physiological and mental concerns. As a way to face this, modern businesses have increasingly embraced active pauses and short breaks to favor relaxation and distraction for reducing emotional burden and increasing productivity. To that respect, mindfulness and quick-bite video games are among the go-to options for taking a rest. In this paper we explore how to introduce biofeedback in casual—short—video games as a way to assist the player in regulating their emotional state. Biofeedback, i.e., the use of biological signals (such as heart rate) as a way to inform and/or control an interactive application, has been increasingly attracting the attention of HCI researchers and practitioners, particularly in the design and development of health applications in wearable devices, such as smartwatches. However, its use in entertainment and video games is still in the making. To bridge this gap, we report the design and development of a biofeedback-controlled microgame for emotional regulation, based on the pleasure/arousal model. This game, which dynamically self-affects its difficulty based on the player's heart rate variation, allows the player to navigate through different emotional states, such as stress, excitement, calm, and languishment. We evaluated the prototype application through a proof of concept, showing that the underlying game mechanics indeed altered the player's pleasure and arousal. The obtained results are a first step toward exploring how biofeedback in video games can be exploited as a mechanic to regulate emotional valence in players.

Keywords: Biofeedback · Video Game · Emotional Valence · Regulation · Player Experience · Design

1 Introduction

In current times, psychological stress is widespread in society. High levels of stress may trigger psychological disorders and physiological concerns, such as social anxiety and a progressive deterioration of the immune system [19]. As a way to address this problem, work organizations and management have been steadily shifting toward providing active breaks and dedicated time-blocking for relaxation, mindfulness, and overall distress. In fact, several studies have shown

X. Fang (Ed.): HCII 2023, LNCS 14047, pp. 186–197, 2023.
https://doi.org/10.1007/978-3-031-35979-8_15

that these techniques are useful for reducing emotional burden, hence boosting productivity [8,15].

In that respect, computing technology is everyday more affordable. This has triggered the design of novel interaction mechanisms and empirical studies on the potential impact that technological development has on human behavior. In particular, application domains such as gaming, have gained increased attention from the human-computer interaction research community [2]. In particular, video game design has embraced novel interactive hardware (e.g., virtual reality headsets and wearable devices), which push the limits of new interaction mechanics and user interfaces (e.g., natural, gestural, and organic interaction).

Following this line of reasoning, biofeedback, i.e., the capture, processing, and interpretation of biological signals as an input control in a software application, is increasingly being used in the design of interactive computing systems, such as video games [22]. For instance, Bin et al. [23] conducted a systematic literature review on biofeedback strategies for managing stress, where they conclude that new technologies and design insights can further advance immersion, involvement, and presence in interactive applications (such as video games). In that respect, Zelada and Gutierrez [24] explored how biofeedback, and particularly dynamic difficulty adjustment in video games, positively impacts player experience ad flow. Likewise, Russoniello et al. [17] and Villani et al. [20] show that video games can have a positive impact in mental health and emotional regulation. Building upon the detected opportunity, in this paper we explore how to design gaming experiences—grounded in biofeedback—to support player emotional regulation.

To do so, we designed and developed a prototype video game of the score attack genre (i.e., a game where the player must achieve the highest score they can). The video game is controlled by the means of a wearable activity tracker to continuously measure the player's heart rate that connects to a computer via bluetooth, as well as their emotional feedback using an affective slider [1], i.e., a digital self-assessment scale for the measurement of human emotions. Therefore, when the video game detects a variation in the emotional state of the player, it automatically adapts its difficulty (e.g., pace and number of obstacles on screen), as a way to motivate the player to be aware of their emotional valence, hence assisting them to achieve a particular emotional state. Such a goal is achieved by mapping the player's heart rate variation to the emotional state provided by them with the affective slider.

The emotional regulation process is based in the *Pleasure/Arousal* model (Fig. 1) for representing emotions, first introduced by Graziotin et al. [9]. This model consists on assessing the emotional state of an individual in terms of their valence (i.e., pleasure) and arousal. That is, valence measures the positivity or negativity of a particular emotion, whereas arousal stands for the intensity of such emotion.

In order to assess the effectiveness of the proposed video games for regulating emotions, we conducted a controlled user study following a between-subjects empirical design. In order to control for the effect of the initial emotional state,

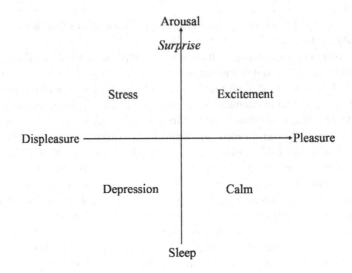

Fig. 1. Pleasure/Arousal model [9]

we exposed participants to either a stimulation or relaxing source, aiming to increase or decrease the initial heart rate measure, which would then be used as a groundtruth for comparing the variation of heart rate and affective state throughout the gaming session. Furthermore, we asked participants to complete the *Self-Assessment Manikin* [4] (SAM, from now on), which is a psychometrically valid and reliable tool for assessing emotional states. Such an instrument was applied at the beginning and the end of the intervention. The empirical procedure was approved on ethical grounds by an Institutional Review Board, where participants had to provide explicit, free, and informed consent. On the one hand, we observed that all SAM dimensions increased after the gaming session when aiming to increase arousal. On the other, arousal is reduced for the game aiming to relax the player. These results show that users, overall, tend to display the emotional states that were hypothesized during design.

The rest of this paper is structured as follows. Section 2 reviews and discusses related work. Section 3 presents the biofeedback-controlled video game prototype that was designed, in order to map and traverse the different emotional states built in the Pleasure/Arousal model. Section 4 is devoted to present the empirical setup and results of a user study aiming to effectiveness of the proposed method for assisting players to regulate their emotional states with the biofeedback-controlled game. Finally, Sect. 5 concludes and provides perspectives on future work.

2   Related Work

Detecting and measuring human emotions is a complex task, which does not have clear standards and scientific definitions [3]. Over the years, researchers in affective computing [7,13,14] have progressively conceived sophisticated algorithms and proposed models to accurately detect and measure sentiment and emotion. In particular, in this work we adhere to the Pleasure/Arousal representation of emotions, as conceived by Graziotin et al. [9]. This model consists on assessing the emotional state of an individual, based on their valence (i.e., the positivity or negativity of the emotion) and their arousal (i.e., the intensity of said emotion). For instance, by using this model it is possible to characterize the *relaxed* state as an emotion with high valence and low arousal, whereas *excited* is an emotion with low valence and high arousal.

Biofeedback, i.e., measuring and processing human signals [11], is increasingly being used the design of interactive computing systems, such as video games [22, 24]. This implies computing a baseline measure for the player, when they are not subject to external influences, and constantly monitor the differences with regard to this value as a way to detect any abrupt change. In particular, the use of biofeedback in the design of gaming experiences is still relatively novel in the industry [24].

In that respect, Siqueira et al. [18] defined a process to assess player experience according to emotional valence and arousal. To assist this task, the authors used facial recognition software as well as sophisticated biofeedback measures, such as electrodermal activity. Their approach was evaluated in a lab setting, without explicitly studying the validity of this approach in player experience and video games. As such, biofeedback has been extensively used to assess emotional states [10,12]. In particular, both heart rate [6] and the self report of subjective experiences [16] are sensitive to the measures of emotional arousal and valence, respectively.

According to Robinson and Clore [16], the self assessment of the emotional state of an individual is significantly more accurate and effective when it is performed alongside the task that interacts with such a state. Therefore, in the case of a video game, we should devise a mechanism that does not interrupt the game flow. Following that line of reasoning, Bradley y Lang [5] proposed the Self-Assessment Manikin (SAM), which is a visual assessment tool for measuring an individual's affective reaction to a specific stimulus. Likewise, Watson et al. [21] proposed the Positive and Negative Affect Schedule (PANAS), which is a valid and reliable questionnaire aiming to objective measure the current emotional state of an individual.

Furthermore, Betella and Verschure [1] conceived the Affective Slider, i.e., a visual representation of a scale ranging from positive to negative emotional states, as an interactive alternative to SAM. Its effectiveness was empirically assessed in a controlled experiment by evaluating emotional states with a standard set of images that represent semantic categories in psychology. The main advantage of the Affective Slider is that it does not require written instructions for easily understanding how to gauge emotional states, as well that it is easy to reproduce in digital applications.

3   Video Game Design

We designed a video game structured around three main components: (1) a connection interface with an activity tracker for continuously measuring the player's heart rate; (2) a video game mode for reaching the *excited* emotional state; and (3) a video game mode for reaching the *relaxed* emotional state. Both video game modes can be selected from an interactive menu at the beginning of the play session, and each one also considers an affective slider for capturing the emotional state of the player. The video game was developed using the Godot engine, given its ease of implementation for 2D video games. Figure 2 depicts the overall structure of the developed prototype.

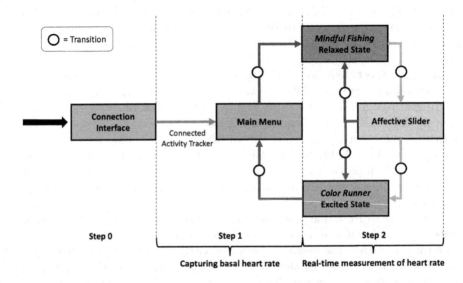

Fig. 2. Video Game Components

The following subsections provide more details on the design rationale behind each video game component.

3.1   Capturing Heart Rate

In order to ease user appropriation of the prototype video game, we opted to use a widely available mass-market device. Among the possible options, we selected the Xiaomi MiBand family of activity trackers, mainly due to their reduced cost and acceptable accuracy. Building on our own previous work [24], we implemented a connector to link the activity tracker with the video game. This connection was developed as a socket in C++, over a server-client architecture allowing TCP connections running over Bluetooth LE.

In the context of the video game, as depicted in Fig. 2, there are two stages where we collect the player's heart rate. On the one hand, we obtain the of the resting heart rate variation (measured as the average of measures obtained during game setup), which will be used as a base measure for inferring whether the player is changing their emotional state. This stage is necessary because basal heart rate varies substantially from individual to individual (e.g., due to their gender, age, physical activity level, among others). On the other hand, once the player is actively engaged in the video game, we obtain real-time measures of their heart rate every 4 s (which is the sampling rate of a typical off-the-shelf activity tracker, such as the Xiaomi MiBand 3, which was the device used during user tests).

3.2   Video Game Mode 1: Color Runner – State: Excited

This video game mode allows players to shift from a calmer emotional state to one of excitement (cf. Fig. 3). The current player heart rate is displayed at the top of the screen and the color palette reflects the desired emotional state to be reached. In this case, warmer hues map an emotional state of excitement.

The challenge in this video game mode consists of an infinite horizontal scroll, following the principles of the runner genre. In order to trigger emotional arousal, the game scenario is designed with a warmer color palette as well as an upbeat music tempo. We also added visual effects, such as explosions and tremors for providing a more intense interaction. The game controls are simple, limiting the navigation to the space bar for performing jumps. If the player's heart rate increases over the basal measure (as computed in stage 1), then the player gets a bonus score, hence inviting them to engage more with the video game. Once the player gets 70 points, they are invited to fill in the affective slider (cf. Fig. 4).

3.3   Video Game Mode 2: Mindful Fishing – State: Relaxed

This video game mode allows players to shift from a stressed emotional state to one of calm and relaxation (cf. Fig. 5). The current player heart rate is displayed at the top of the screen and the color palette reflects the desired emotional state to be reached. In this case, colder hues map an emotional state of relaxation.

The challenge in this video game mode consists of a fishing game, following the principles of casual simulation games. In order to reduce emotional arousal, the game scenario is designed with a colder color palette as well as a more relaxing music tempo, inviting the player to breathe in periodically following mindfulness principles (e.g., calm rain, wind blows, bird tweets, beach ambiance). The game controls are simple, limiting the navigation to the space bar for controlling the fishing rod. If the player's heart rate decreases beyond the basal measure (as computed in stage 1), then the difficulty of the video game decreases, hence inviting the player to engage more with the interactive challenge. Once the player gets 70 points, they are invited to fill in the affective slider (cf. Fig. 6).

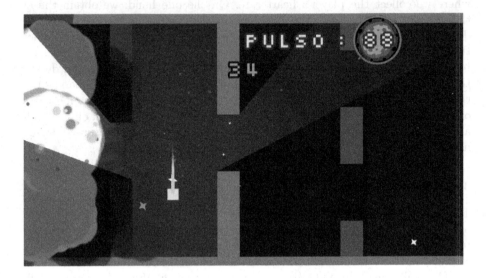

Fig. 3. Video game mode: *Color Runner*

Fig. 4. Affective slider for the *Color Runner* game mode. Note the warmer color tones.

Fig. 5. Video game mode: *Mindful Fishing*

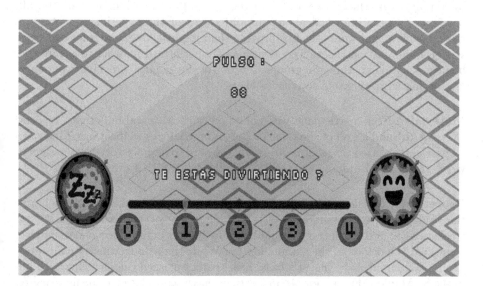

Fig. 6. Affective slider for the *Mindful Fishing* game mode. Note the colder color tones.

4 Proof of Concept

As a way to explore the effectiveness and potential acceptance of the proposed emotional regulation effect, we conducted a comparative user study (proof of concept) with both prototype microgames. In this section we describe the followed empirical setup and discuss the obtained results with regard to the use of biofeedback as a design strategy for emotional regulation in video games.

4.1 Methodology

We ran a within-subjects experiment, in which we randomly assigned the study participants in two independent groups: (1) playing the *Color Runner* video game and (2) playing the *Mindful Fishing* video game. In order to control the empirical conditions, all participants: (1) wore the same kind of wearable activity tracker (i.e., a Xiaomi MiBand 3, which was provided to the participants at the beginning of the experiment); (2) followed the same empirical procedure; and (3) were not told of the existence of emotional regulation nor difficulty adjustment in any of the versions of the video game they played.

Participants. For simplicity reasons, we followed a convenience sampling strategy, recruiting a total of 47 participants (14 female, 33 male, all aged between 19 and 24 years old). All of these were, at the time of the experiment, college students in engineering. 24 of such participants were assigned to the *Color Runner* group, whereas 23 were assigned to the *Mindful Fishing* group. In order to comply with ethical standards in experimentation with human subjects, all participants were informed about the objectives of the experiment, potential risks, benefits, and were asked to provide their explicit, free, and informed consent. Randomization checks were continuously performed in order to ensure the homogeneity of experimental groups in terms of age, gender, previous experience interacting with wearable activity trackers.

Materials. Each participant was equipped with a wearable activity tracker (Xiaomi MiBand 3), all of the same model and technical specifications. Likewise, all participants used the same mouse and keyboard to interact with their assigned video game, which ran on a MSI GE63 Raider RGB 8RE gaming laptop.

Procedure. At the beginning of the session, we explained every participant the study goals, what kind of data was going to be collected with the activity tracker (without disclosing if it would have any impact in the video game), and we connected the device to the gaming laptop. While the activity tracker calibrates itself and computes the player's basal heart rate, we asked the participant to fill in the SAM questionnaire for obtaining their entry scores for emotional pleasure, arousal, and dominance. Then, the participant is asked to play their assigned video game for a time span of 10 min. Once finished, they had to fill in once again the SAM questionnaire, this time for obtaining their exit scores for emotional pleasure, arousal, and dominance.

Data Collection and Analysis. During each session, we collected SAM scores to explore whether the game had an impact on the player's emotion states. We ran statistical analyses in order to study whether there existed differences in the mean—or median—scores for all dimensions of emotional expression (i.e., valence, arousal, and dominance as measured by the SAM questionnaire), i.e., repeated-measures T test (if the assumptions for running a parametric test are met), or a Wilcoxon ranked-sign test (if the normality and homoscedasticity assumptions are not met). The tests were all conducted at a significance level of $\alpha = 0.05$ using the base installation of R.

4.2   Results

Given that the collected measures do not follow a normal distribution (as analyzed after applying Shapiro-Wilk tests), we opt to run Wilcoxon signed-rank (V) over the differences of median values along each dimension. Consequently, we compute Cliff's delta (δ) as a measure of effect size in this case, instead of Cohen's d. Table 1 summarizes the obtained results, as reported by the study participants before and after their assigned gaming session. Scores in the SAM scale range from 1 to 9, as follows: valence (ranging from 1, i.e., *unpleasant* to 9, i.e., *pleasant*); arousal (ranging from 1, i.e., *calm* to 9, i.e., *aroused*); and dominance (ranging from 1, i.e., *controlled* to 9, i.e., *in control*).

Table 1. SAM scores before and after the game session

	Color Runner					Mindful Fishing				
	Mdn Bef	*Mdn* Aft	*V*	*p*	δ	*Mdn* Bef	*Mdn* Aft	*V*	*p*	δ
Valence	6	7	0	<.001	−0.659	6	7	11	<.001	−0.644
Arousal	5	6	7	<.001	−0.573	5	4	205.5	<.001	0.858
Dominance	5	6	0	<.001	−0.829	5	5	36.5	.535	−0.104

Regarding the Color Runner game, results of the analysis indicated that there was a significant difference in the perception of all valence, arousal, and dominance, all positive toward the end of the session. This means that players indeed felt more activated—or excited—after the game session. In particular, this proves that the design hypothesis carried during the conception of the video game (i.e., shifting the player from a calm state to a more excited one) was proved as valid.

In the case of the Mindful Fishing game, we observe that there was a significant difference in the perception of valence and arousal after the end of the session, but no difference was observed for dominance. More in particular, players tended to feel less aroused by the end of the game session, which proves that the design hypothesis carried during the conception of this video game (i.e., shifting the player from a stressed state to a more calm one) was proved as valid.

5   Conclusion and Future Work

In this paper we explored the feasibility of developing biofeedback-controlled video games for emotional regultation. In particular, we conceived two microgames, which extensively use the player's heart rate as input measure for attempting to shift a player from one emotional state to another.

By adhering to the Pleasure/Arousal model, we conceived several mechanics for achieving the goal of shifting a player from a calm state to an excited one (Color Runnner), and conversely, from a stressed emotional state to a more relaxed one (Mindful Fishing). In order to study the effectiveness of the proposed approaches, we ran a proof of concept using the Self-Assessment Manikin questionnaire as a valid and reliable instrument for gauging the player's emotional state before and after each gaming session. The obtained results show that players indeed shifted their emotional states, in line with the design hypothesis that informed the development of each prototype video game.

In future lines of research, we will seek to build up on the Pleasure/Arousal model to conceive new mini games for assisting players in regulating their emotional states, as desired. This includes not only designing new game mechanics, but also study positive psychology principles that would sustain the desired effect. Likewise, from a technical point of view, we will explore how to port the developed experience to be used with a larger variety of hardware. Today, the variety of affordable smartwatches and activity trackers in the market is thriving, so it would be interesting to conduct larger user studies to verify the ecological validity and external validity of the approach followed in this paper.

References

1. Betella, A., Verschure, P.F.M.J.: The affective slider: a digital self-assessment scale for the measurement of human emotions. PLOS ONE **11**(2), 1–11 (2016)
2. Birk, M.V., Wadley, G., Abeele, V.V., Mandryk, R., Torous, J.: Video games for mental health. Interactions **26**(4), 32–36 (2019)
3. Bradley, M.M., Lang, P.J., Lane, R., Nadel, L.: Cognitive neuroscience of emotion. In: Lane, R.D.R., Nadel, L., Ahern, G.L., Allen, J., Kaszniak, A.W. (eds.) Cognitive Neuroscience of Emotion, pp. 242–276. Oxford University Press (2000)
4. Bradley, M.M., Lang, P.J.: Measuring emotion: the self-assessment manikin and the semantic differential. J. Behav. Ther. Exp. Psychiatry **25**(1), 49–59 (1994)
5. Bradley, M.M., Lang, P.J.: Measuring emotion: the self-assessment manikin and the semantic differential. J. Behav. Ther. Exp. Psychiatry **25**(1), 49–59 (1994)
6. Cacioppo, J., et al.: Handbook of emotions (2000)
7. Calvo, R.A., D'Mello, S., Gratch, J., Kappas, A. (eds.): The Oxford Handbook of Affective Computing. Oxford University Press, Oxford, New York, December 2014
8. Fritz, C., Ellis, A.M., Demsky, C.A., Lin, B.C., Guros, F.: Embracing work breaks: recovering from work stress. Organ. Dyn. **42**(4), 274–280 (2013)
9. Graziotin, D., Wang, X., Abrahamsson, P.: Understanding the affect of developers: theoretical background and guidelines for psychoempirical software engineering. In: Proceedings of the 7th International Workshop on Social Software Engineering, SSE 2015, pp. 25–32. ACM, New York, NY, USA (2015)

10. Hazlett, R.L., Benedek, J.: Measuring emotional valence to understand the user's experience of software. Int. J. Hum.-Comput. Stud. **65**(4), 306–314 (2007). evaluating affective interactions

11. Huang, Y.-C., Luk, C.-H.: Heartbeat Jenga: a biofeedback board game to improve coordination and emotional control. In: Marcus, A. (ed.) DUXU 2015. LNCS, vol. 9188, pp. 263–270. Springer, Cham (2015). https://doi.org/10.1007/978-3-319-20889-3_25

12. Mauss, I.B., Robinson, M.D.: Measures of emotion: a review. Cogn. Emotion **23**(2), 209–237 (2009)

13. Picard, R.W.: Affective computing for HCI. In: Proceedings of HCI International (the 8th International Conference on Human-Computer Interaction) on Human-Computer Interaction: Ergonomics and User Interfaces-Volume I - Volume I, p. 829–833. L. Erlbaum Associates Inc., USA (1999)

14. Picard, R.W.: Affective computing: challenges. Int. J. Hum.-Comput. Stud. **59**(1–2), 55–64 (2003)

15. Rhee, H., Kim, S.: Effects of breaks on regaining vitality at work: an empirical comparison of 'conventional' and 'smart phone' breaks. Comput. Hum. Behav. **57**, 160–167 (2016)

16. Robinson, M.D., Clore, G.L.: Episodic and semantic knowledge in emotional self-report: evidence for two judgment processes. J. Personality Soc. Psychol. **83**(1), 198–215 (2002)

17. Russoniello, C., O'Brien, K., Parks, J.: The effectiveness of casual video games in improving mood and decreasing stress. J. Cyber Ther. Rehabil. **2**, 53–66 (2009)

18. Siqueira, E.S., Santos, T.A.A., Castanho, C.D., Jacobi, R.P.: Estimating player experience from arousal and valence using psychophysiological signals. In: 2018 17th Brazilian Symposium on Computer Games and Digital Entertainment (SBGames), pp. 107–10709, October 2018

19. Taylor, A.H.: Physical activity, anxiety, and stress. Physical activity and psychological well-being, pp. 22–52 (2003)

20. Villani, D., Carissoli, C., Triberti, S., Marchetti, A., Gilli, G., Riva, G.: Videogames for emotion regulation: a systematic review. Games Health J. **7**(2), 85–99 (2018). pMID: 29424555

21. Watson, D., Clark, L.A., Tellegen, A.: Development and validation of brief measures of positive and negative affect: the panas scales. J. Pers. Soc. Psychol. **54**(6), 1063 (1988)

22. Yu, B.: Adaptive biofeedback for mind-body practices. In: Extended Abstracts of the ACM SIGCHI Conference on Human Factors in Computing Systems, CHI 2016, pp. 260–264. ACM, New York, NY, USA (2016)

23. Yu, B., Funk, M., Hu, J., Wang, Q., Feijs, L.: Biofeedback for everyday stress management: a systematic review. Front. ICT **5**, 23 (2018)

24. Zelada, E., Gutierrez, F.J.: Dynamic difficulty adjustment of video games using biofeedback. In: Bravo, J., Ochoa, S., Favela, J. (eds.) Proceedings of the International Conference on Ubiquitous Computing & Ambient Intelligence (UCAm I 2022), Springer, Cham, pp. 925–936 (2023). https://doi.org/10.1007/978-3-031-21333-5_91

"Should My Best Prove Insufficient, We Will Find Another Way": Time Loop Mechanics as Expressions of Hope in Digital Games

Monica Evans[✉]

School of Arts Humanities and Technology, The University of Texas at Dallas, Richardson, TX 75080, USA
mevans@utdallas.edu

Abstract. Many digital games use mechanics, user interface design, and inter-action design to explore themes of science fiction and technology, including the ramifications of time travel and time manipulation. Time loop games, in which a character repeats the same time period or sequence of experiences indefinitely, are surprisingly optimistic, even when the game world, content, or scenario is emo-tionally challenging. While all digital games allow players to manipulate time at a basic level, time loop games emphasize mastery-through-repetition in both gameplay and narrative. Unlike time travel narratives in other media, time loop games cannot help but express optimism, as the game's mechanics and interface encourage players to continually manipulate the game world until the best of all possible outcomes is achieved. It follows that time loop games are a clear example of narrative expressed through mechanics and interface, as well as a way to express hope in difficult times. This paper uses a humanities-based critical methodology to explore how the structure of time loop games reinforces feelings of optimism and hope through iterative improvement and eventual mastery of game systems, and examines both seminal and recent time loop games including *The Legend of Zelda: Majora's Mask, Returnal, Deathloop*, and *Outer Wilds*.

Keywords: Digital games · game mechanics · game design · time travel · time loops

1 Introduction – Digital Games as Science Fictional Medium

Digital games are an ideal medium for expressions of science fiction narratives, which center thematically on humanity's changing relationship with science and technology [1]. While a substantial proportion of digital games are speculative or science fictional in content, fewer address the core themes of science fiction as a medium. Those that do often take advantage of games as technological artifacts and explore science fiction themes through direction applications of interface design, often by encouraging or requiring used to interact directly with the game's actual systems, simulations, and interfaces for narrative purposes. *Thomas Was Alone, The Swapper, NieR:Automata, TACOMA*, and *In Other Waters*, are particularly successful examples of games that take full advantage

X. Fang (Ed.): HCII 2023, LNCS 14047, pp. 198–209, 2023.
https://doi.org/10.1007/978-3-031-35979-8_16

of digital interfaces to explore science fiction themes, such as positioning the player as an artificial intelligence that experiences the world through a graphical user interface in *In Other Waters*, or the narrative implications of saving or deleting actual game data in *NieR:Automata*.

One sub-genre of science fiction, the time-loop story, has proved surprisingly popular in recent speculative digital games. While most if not all digital games allow users to experiment with time – at least by virtue of the near-ubiquitous save function, which allows players to replay sections of games at will – games that center on narrative time travel are often positive or uplifting, including influential titles like *Chrono Trigger*, *The Legend of Zelda: Ocarina of Time*, and *Prince of Persia: The Sands of Time*. This stands in stark contrast to time travel stories in literature and cinema, which tend toward the metaphysical implications of time travel and often center on cautionary tales, end-of-the-world scenarios, and the oppressions of determinism [2]. Digital games, on the other hand, are designed to be won, and structured such that players make multiple attempts at challenges until ultimately succeeding, often by getting gradually more skilled at the game [3, 4]. Time loop narratives, which are similarly repetitive in design, are poised to take full advantage of this mechanical structure, particularly in the ways that players directly interface with the mechanics of time during play, which allows for visceral narrative expressions.

Time loop games encourage players to believe they are improving a flawed or broken game world by mechanically interacting with time itself through the game's user interface. This pattern holds true even when a game's content is challenging or emotionally charged, as with the civilization-destroying supernova that occurs every twenty-two minutes in *Outer Wilds*. or the echoes of guilt and trauma that pervade the punishingly difficult loops of *Returnal*. Ultimately, time loop stories in digital games can be read as expressions of hope, in that a given game's mechanics, systems, and interface allow players to manipulate time until the best of all possible outcomes is achieved. These games are clear examples of narrative expressed through mechanics and are worth examining both as exemplars of an interactive medium and as case studies for how digital games may naturally tend toward constructive optimism, as a direct result of their focus on improving player skill.

2 Time Loops as Narrative and Mechanical Devices

2.1 Time Loops in Fiction

As a narrative device, time travel is older than the genre of science fiction: stories that include time traveling and time manipulation include Dickens' *A Christmas Carol* in 1845, Irving's *Rip Van Winkle* in 1819, and Malory's *Mort D'Arthur* in 1485. In science fiction, the earliest seminal work is H.G. Wells' *The Time Machine*, which introduces both the concept of a vehicle and "the idea of conscious control and scientific direction implied in the machine's function" [5]: in other words, that time can be manipulated and controlled by an individual human operator. In the following decades, writers explored various literary structures and themes centered on time travel: adventure stories, commonly taking place in the Age of the Dinosaurs; timeslip romances; people or devices wreaking anachronistic havoc; time paradoxes; time tourists, especially to and from apocalyptic futures; time police or protectors; explorations of the temporal beginnings and ends of the universe; and the metaphysics of time travel [2]. Fictional time travel is both popular and enduring, as it allows writers to reflect on the nature of time, humanity's relationship to time, and how technology influences history [2]. It also allows for a certain amount of self-referential writing: as expressed by many authors but most notably Robert Silverberg, "the only workable time machine ever invented is the science fiction story" [6]. Lastly, time travel is notable for being one of the few science fiction devices to be considered entirely out of reach [7]: unlike cloning, terraforming, genetic modification, artificial intelligence, or any other number of popular topics in science fiction, time travel as expressed in everything from the film *Back to the Future* to Ted Chiang's "Story Of Your Life" is functionally impossible, and will remain so for the near future.

In time travel fiction, the time loop story is considered a sub-genre that centers on the use of a time loop, a plot device in which periods of time "are repeated and re-experienced by a character's consciousness" and in which there is "some hope of breaking out of the cycle of repetition" [8]. This is functionally different than a causal loop, in which time travel causes a series of events to have no logical starting point, often referred to as the bootstrap paradox after Robert Heinlein's "By His Bootstraps." [8]. Causal loops by definition cannot be changed; the time loop, in opposition, is marked by minor to significant changes in each loop, often the product of a character or characters attempting to break free of the loop and return to the progression of time. Often, characters escape a time loop by perfecting the best possible sequence of events, growing as a person, or both. The quintessential time loop film is the 1983 comedy *Groundhog Day*, but recent entries to the genre include *Edge of Tomorrow*, *Timecrimes/Los Cronocrimines*, and *Palm Springs*. In television, time loops can serve as the series' central conceit as with *Russian Doll*, or function as stand-alone or bottle episodes in long-running shows from *Star Trek* to *Dr. Who*. One well-loved example of the time loop episode is "Window of Opportunity" in *Stargate SG-1*, which subverts the expected structure by having its main characters take every tenth loop off to pursue increasingly ridiculous, consequence-free shenanigans, including hitting golf balls through the titular Stargate [9].

As compared to time travel stories as a whole, time loop stories can be surprisingly uplifting. When structured such that characters can remember previous loops, the time loop can transform "the imprisoning circularity into an upward spiral, a learning curve" [8], which is markedly different than dystopian, nihilistic, or otherwise negative explorations of the ramifications of time travel.

2.2 Time and Mechanics in Digital Games

Digital games have always had an unusual relationship with time. Firstly, most if not all modern digital games include a save function, a key feature for developing complexity and nuance in design, as modern games are generally too long to be completed in a single session [10, 11]. Save functions generally fall into two categories: games which allow players to save at any time, or which automatically save every few minutes; and games that allow saving only at designated points, a design constraint held over from early, less technologically powerful games [12], but both structures are valid and allow for game time to be manipulated by the player. Secondly, digital games consider game time, sometimes called fictional time, or "the time of the events in the game world," to be separate from play time or "the time span taken to play a game" [10]. While play time progresses naturally, taking into account times when players pause or step away from a game, game time can be squashed and stretched through various mechanics and systems, including but not limited to day/night cycles; timed sections or scenarios; functions that allow players to speed up, slow down, suspend, or rewind the flow of time; and various explicit time travel mechanics [11]. Players also experience time differently during play, and this "transformation of time" often causes the player's sense of time to "stretch or shrink" during periods of intense involvement [4].

Given this complex relationship with time, it follows that digital games are not only an ideal medium for science fiction narratives, but for time travel narratives as well. As a plot mechanism, time travel has been prevalent since the earliest days of the medium and is a central feature of some of gaming's most influential titles, from *Chrono Trigger Day of the Tentacle*, and *The Legend of Zelda: Ocarina of Time* in the nineties to *Braid*, *Bioshock Infinite*, and *Life is Strange* in more recent years. Time loops in particular share structural similarities with many digital games in which failure, sometimes represented by the main playable character's "death," often results in resetting the game a few seconds or minutes back to a previous save point. While time travel is a near-constant feature in game development, time loops have been particularly prevalent in the last five years, featuring heavily in recent games including *Deathloop, Outer Wilds, Returnal, The Sexy Brutale, Minit, Twelve Minutes, The Forgotten City, Loop Hero*, and *Elsinore*, to the point that one gaming journalist declared 2021 "the year of the time loop" [13], and another claimed time loops as the plot device that most speaks to our increasingly anxious times [14]. The naturally positive bent of the time loop, as well as its similarity to the structural foundations of digital games, may explain its increased popularity in game development in recent years.

3 Defining the Time Loop Game

3.1 The Structure of Time Loop Games

To write a time travel story, the author must first decide how time travel works, which requires defining the nature and rules of time itself. H.G Well's *The Time Machine*, one of the earliest significant time travel narratives, is influential both for the invention of the time machine as scientific device and for how closely Wells' description of time matches the revolutionary view of spacetime that Einstein would present a decade later [15]. That said, authors are not restricted to realistic descriptions of time, and can design coherent, internally functional rules for time travel that have next-to-no basis in physics. This holds true for narrative descriptions of time travel in digital games, but more specificity is needed when discussing mechanical time travel: a system in which players have some control over how game characters or objects travel through time in the game world. As noted earlier, any digital game with a save function arguably contains a mechanical time loop, but a "time loop game" requires a stricter definition. For the purposes of this article, a time loop game is one in which the time loop is diegetic, explicitly real, and central to the game's narrative and mechanical experience. Players may or may not be afforded some control over the loop, both at the game's start and over the course of play; and breaking or otherwise mastering the loop is a central concern of the game's protagonist, whether or not that mastery is ultimately possible.

First, the time loop is diegetic: both the player and the game's major characters know they are in a time loop, and characters in the game directly address the time loop's existence. This excludes digital games in which a mechanical time loop is present but a narrative one is not: for example, Link's numerous potential deaths in *The Legend of Zelda: Breath of the Wild* are not considered part of the game's canonical story. If Link dies, the game resets to the player's last save point and the experience continues as if the death had never happened, with the exception that the player retains foreknowledge of upcoming challenges. In other words, the existence of a save function does not qualify a given title as a time loop game.

Second, the time loop is explicitly real: in the context of the game, the time loop exists due to science, technology, magic, or another in-game mechanism. The loop's explicit realness is more important than its functionality. Players of *Outer Wilds* spend a significant amount of time exploring how the twenty-two-minute time loop functions, including a visit to a high-energy physics lab with interactable black and white holes; players of *Deathloop* only need to know that the loop is caused by "The Anomaly" and can be broken by assassinating eight Visionaries. Regardless of how much game time is spent on exploring the loop's functionality and causes, both *Deathloop* and *Outer Wilds* acknowledge that their respective loops exist. In contrast, *Twelve Minutes* positions its central time loop as the product of the main character's imagination, a "psychosexual mind palace" that expresses a "failed attempt to envision a world in which you happily get to continue your relationship" with your wife, without processing a significant amount of past trauma [16]. *Returnal* is arguably an edge case in that the game's ambiguous ending allows for multiple interpretations, one of which is that the entire experience takes place in the moments before main character Selene's death in a car crash [17]. Generally, however, *Returnal*'s time loop is treated as a real-world consequence of crash-landing on Atropos, and Selene's experiences are accepted as explicitly real by most interpretations.

Third, the time loop is central to the game experience and persists throughout the entire game, rather than being restricted to one level or minigame. *Minit* is minimalistic in narrative and mechanics, but the player's entire experience is focused on fixing the cursed sword that is causing time to loop in sixty-second increments. Likewise, *Outer Wilds*, *Deathloop*, and *Returnal* are all mechanically and narratively focused on their respective time loops. *Braid*, on the other hand, is structured such that the player can manipulate time differently in each level: time can be rewound indefinitely in World 2, desynchronized from game objects in World Three, and slowed with a placeable ring in World Six. While the fourth area arguably contains a manipulable casual loop, *Braid* is better defined as a time manipulation game rather than a time loop game.

3.2 Time Loops and Player Control

Time loop games offer players differing levels of control over the central loop. This control can be delineated with the following parameters: whether time progresses naturally, whether the player has any direct control over the loop during play, whether the loop can be broken or otherwise fundamentally changed, and whether breaking the loop constitutes "winning" or otherwise completing the game.

First, does time progress naturally during play: does the game make use of game time, play time, or both? Time progresses naturally in *Outer Wilds* for the majority of play: the central loop takes exactly twenty-two minutes of real time, whether the player spends that time exploring the game's star system or standing still. If the player dies or chooses to meditate through the remainder of the loop, *Outer Wilds* switches briefly to game time and resets the loop immediately, while implying that the remaining minutes of the loop play out normally even though the player does not experience them. Likewise, *Returnal* tracks how many minutes and hours the player has spent on Atropos in real time, which progresses forward no matter how long the player spends in each biome. There are two exceptions in which *Returnal* uses game time: it is unclear whether significant time passes between each of Selene's deaths, and game time is applied during the major narrative break between Act 1 and Act 2, in which approximately sixty-three years pass, expressed by a cinematic montage. This is not the case with *Deathloop*, in which a loop takes one full day but the player explores each of Blackreef's areas in four time periods: morning, noon, afternoon, and evening. A morning session can take anywhere from a few minutes to as long as the player wants: time will not progress to noon until they leave the area and select the next time of day. Additionally, some in-game events are triggered by the player's arrival: for example, visionary Harriet's ritual killing of the mask-maker Amador always takes place in Karl's Bay in the morning, but the killing itself only begins when the player enters Hanger 2, as it is intended to be interrupted.

Next, does the player have direct control over the time loop during play? In most cases the answer is no, often because breaking or otherwise gaining control over the time loop is the player's ultimate goal and will only be achieved at the game's end. In *Returnal*, *Deathloop*, and *Outer Wilds*, the primary way players interact with the loop is to die: in all three games, the main character's death will reset the loop. Some games allow players to skip forward in time, such as by choosing to meditate in *Outer Wilds* or skipping an earlier time period to advance to a later one in *Deathloop*, but these are quality of life design decisions rather than explicit control: the time loop is implied to progress naturally even though the player is choosing to skip ahead. Generally, players have more control in games where the loop is linked to the main character than in those where it resets due to an external force. In *Returnal*, the loop only resets when Selene dies, so players can prevent time from looping by staying alive as long as possible. This design structure is fully exploited at the shocking end of Act 1, in which Selene escapes the planet, returns to Earth, and lives another sixty-three years before dying of old age – at which point she wakes up on Atropos as her younger self, still stuck in the game's central loop.

Lastly, can the time loop be broken or otherwise manipulated by the game's end, and is gaining control over the loop considered "winning" or completing the game? For many time loop games, the answer is yes: from *Minit* to *The Forgotten City* to *The Legend of Zelda: Majora's Mask*, the end of the game involves breaking the loop and allowing time to progress naturally, whether that means returning to Hyrule proper as in *Majora's Mask* or accepting the natural end of the universe as in *Outer Wilds*. *Deathloop* ends with a choice: players can break the loop and allow main character Colt Vahn to leave Blackreef and return to whatever remains of his normal life; or they can choose to protect the loop, allowing Colt to pursue a meaningful relationship with his daughter Julianna. Unusually, *Returnal* implies that the central time loop cannot be broken, and that main character Selene will remain trapped indefinitely, which complements the game's roguelike design structure.

In time loop games, the amount of control afforded over the loops affect the game experience significantly, in that players are directly working toward narrative or mechanical mastery of the loop. This mastery lends a sheen of optimism to even the bleakest game worlds, scenarios, and content, and must be addressed when examining the emotional impact of time loop games.

4 Time Loops as Expressions of Hope

Time loop games involve failure, futility, frustration, and repetition, but often end in positive ways. *The Legend of Zelda: Majora's Mask* is both a seminal time loop game and the darkest game by far in the Legend of Zelda series, described as the saddest, strangest, and bleakest story in the series' thirty-five-year history [18, 19]. Many of the game's themes and side quests are distinctly negative, but the ending is uplifting: Termina is saved from the falling moon, Skull Kid and his friends are reunited, and Link returns to Hyrule with a clearer, more empathetic understanding of loneliness. Other time loop games end in a similarly positive way: *The Sexy Brutale* ends with main character Lafcadio Boone forgiving himself for a series of past transgressions. *The Forgotten City*'s multiple endings range from saving one worthy person to saving the entire city by winning a philosophical debate with the God of the Underworld. Even *Minit*, minimalistic in both mechanics and story, ends with the player fixing the cursed sword and returning the world to normal. But other time loop games take place in much bleaker worlds, ones in which a positive or optimistic ending may seem unattainable. Three of these games, *Returnal, Deathloop,* and *Outer Wilds*, present unusually hopeful endings, primarily due to the ways that players interact with the mechanics of the central time loop both during play and at each game's conclusion.

4.1 *Returnal*: Time Loops and Acceptance

Even for a horror-themed roguelike, *Returnal* is bleak. The game begins when Selene, a pilot and ASTRA Corporation scout, crash lands on the restricted planet Atropos in search of a mysterious signal she calls "White Shadow." Immediately, she finds multiple corpses of herself, most of which play recordings of Selene failing to escape the planet, before being brutally killed by a tentacled monster and reawakening at the crash site to try and escape again. Mechanically, *Returnal* is punishingly difficult, ensuring that the player will die early and often to Atropos' various hostile life forms; and the terrain and layout of Atropos' biomes change after every death, meaning that players must chart a new escape route every time. From an aesthetic standpoint, *Returnal* takes inspiration from cosmic horror, Lovecraft, and the films of David Lynch, and per game director Harry Krueger is intended to make the player feel "like a rat trapped in an everlasting maze" while gradually losing their sanity [20].

Once Selene manages to escape the planet, things get even bleaker. After three unforgiving biomes, Selene finally returns to Earth where a cinematic montage shows her living out the remaining sixty-three years of her life and dying peacefully of old age, at which point she wakes up back on Atropos as her younger self, still trapped in the planet's loop. This begins Act II of the game, in which Selene's focus shifts from escape to understanding how and why she became trapped. Both acts of *Returnal* include an incongruous "twentieth century house," which leads Selene to repressed memories: she is the victim of child abuse at the hands of her mother Theia, her own child Helios likely died in a car crash, and the "White Shadow" may be Selene herself. Much of *Returnal*'s narrative is open to interpretation – for example, the child that drowns may be Helios or Selene herself, nearly drowned by her mother – but it is abundantly clear that Selene believes she needs to atone and suffers intense guilt over her mother, her child, and her decision to leave Earth for a career in space.

As noted earlier, *Returnal*'s time loop cannot be broken: Selene remains trapped on the planet at the game's conclusion, doomed to struggle indefinitely in a hostile, unforgiving environment. Surprisingly, the game ends on an unusually positive note, in that Selene not only reckons with her past trauma but comes to a place of acceptance. In her final log, she says "I cannot atone, so I accept.... This is my home. The sense of belonging I was searching for is here. This is my place in the stars" [21]. Additionally, Atropos is far less of a threat than at the game's beginning, in that players that reach the end have managed to pass through at least three difficult biomes multiple times without a single death. The planet's horrors have been routinized and no longer pose a threat to the player. For a game centered on child abuse, visceral alien horror, and an unbreakable time loop, *Returnal*'s end is remarkably positive, due to both its narrative themes of acceptance and grace and the player's mastery of the game mechanics and environment.

4.2 *Deathloop*: Time Loops and Familial Bonds

Like *Returnal*, *Deathloop* centers on a traumatic parent-child relationship. The game's opening scene features main playable character Colt Vahn being brutally murdered by a woman named Julianna before waking up in perfect health on an empty beach. Quickly, it becomes clear that Colt and Julianna are two of nine Visionaries who live on Blackreef, a hedonistic, sixties-inspired island that has been caught in a time loop for an undisclosed period of time. As the only two inhabitants of the island that retain their memories of prior loops, Colt and Julianna are at odds: Colt has decided to break free by killing all nine Visionaries in a single loop, including Julianna and himself; and Julianna is determined to protect the loop by killing Colt in each successive loop before he succeeds. Stylistically, *Deathloop* takes its cues from a wide range of action and science fiction films, particularly the French anthology *The Fourth Dimension*, James Bond films, and the films of Guy Ritchie, John Carpenter, and Quentin Tarantino [22]. In other words, Blackreef is fun, and only later is it clear how hollow, unfulfilling, and ultimately nihilistic the island and its inhabitants have become.

Deathloop is designed such that there is only one correct sequence of major events that allows Colt to assassinate nine Visionaries in one day, leaving himself and Julianna for last. Their final confrontation focuses on three facts: Julianna is Colt's daughter, he has murdered her hundreds of times, and her protection of the loop has less to do with Blackreef's eternalist philosophy than with her desire to have a real father-daughter relationship with Colt. At game's end, the player can choose to kill Julianna, which breaks the loop and returns Blackreef's inhabitants to an apparently apocalyptic world; or they can spare Julianna, which resets the game as normal but with Julianna and Colt together on the beach, now working towards a stronger, more emotionally stable relationship [23]. Interestingly, there is disagreement about which choice leads to the canonically "good" ending, but general agreement that the ending in which Colt spares Julianna is the "happy" one, regardless of whether that choice is considered fair, ethical, or right [24].

The choice to break or protect *Deathloop*'s central loop is framed as a choice between values: returning to the real world, free will, and actions with consequences; or pursuing a good relationship with your only remaining family. In either case, the ending each player chooses will uphold those values, reading as the positive result of multiple, gradually perfected attempts to shape the events of one day in Blackreef. Additionally, progressing through the game requires both combat skill and attention to detail, and much of Colt's daily experience in Blackreef involves searching for clues, learning about the Visionaries, researching the island's history, and ultimately deciding whether it too is worth preserving. *Deathloop* ends as a meditation on time itself, offering the player "an opportunity to rethink the present as... a juncture in time that is as bound to the troubles of the past as it is to the fleeting possibility of a redemptive, and even emancipatory, future" [25]. Whether the result of that meditation is improved familial bonds or the pursuit of free will, *Deathloop* ends on a positive note, both because of the player's choices and their hard-earned understanding of the game world.

4.3   *Outer Wilds:* Time Loops, Curiosity, and Hope

On its surface, *Outer Wilds* is nowhere near as dark as many other time loop games, sharing more stylistic commonalities with exploratory, science-positive games like *Myst* and *Kerbal Space Program.* The player controls an unnamed Hearthian, part of a research team exploring a small solar system to learn about the Nomai, an extinct civilization that was searching for the Eye of the Universe. It quickly becomes apparent that the solar system is trapped in a twenty-two-minute time loop that ends with the explosion of the system's sun. The Hearthians have been trapped in this loop for an undisclosed amount of time, and the main character has only recently gained the ability to remember previous loops. After significant exploration and research, logged between loops in the player's ship, two things become clear: the time loop is caused by a Nomai device that uses the power of a supernova to indefinitely search for the Eye of the Universe; and the Nomai never successfully deployed the device. Instead, the sun has reached the end of its life cycle – along with every other star in the visible sky – because the universe is coming to a natural end, and the time loop has been triggered by accident.

In any number of heroic games, the player's achievable task would be to save the universe. Instead, *Outer Wilds* challenges players to come to terms with the end of everything: the time loop can be broken but the universe cannot be saved, and the only available task at the game's end is to travel to the Eye of the Universe and observe the universe's last moments. Remarkably, the canonical ending of *Outer Wilds* is positive and uplifting. While the existing universe and everything in it will die, including the main character, the Eye can be convinced to set a new universe in motion, which the player encourages by gathering their friends around a quantum campfire and making music. Characters present in the game's final scenes have come to a place of quiet acceptance and curiosity about what may come next, with dialogue like "I got to help make something pretty cool, so I've got no complaints" and "This song is new to me, but I am honored to be a part of it" [26]. *Outer Wilds* includes multiple easter-egg-like endings, mostly centered around the potential shenanigans available when the loop has been broken but the player has not yet reached the Eye, including one where the player "dies" in a dream and another in which the High Energy lab can be used to break the fabric of reality. Canonically, the true ending is the result of thorough exploration, intelligent connections, and peaceful acceptance that the player has discovered, experienced, and enjoyed everything the game world has to offer, as well as a cheerful interest in the universe that will come next.

The ending of *Outer Wilds* encourages reflection, but the game mechanics are focused on curiosity, particularly scientific and technological discovery. Both the Nomai and Hearthians are driven by a desire to understand how their world works: in particular, players familiarize themselves with Nomai philosophy through reading messages and research notes, most of which are fervent and often humorous discussions about the joys of scientific progress (notably, "Be Curious on Your Journey!" and "Science compels us to explode the sun!") [26]. This familiarization both with the Nomai and the quirks of each individual planet is key to progressing through the game: "There are no upgrade trees or unlockables here. Instead… *knowledge* is progress" [27]. Additionally, the time loop is gradually exposed not as a prison or trap, but a mechanism by which further exploration becomes possible: players can traverse the game world at will secure in the knowledge that they will never run out of twenty-two-minute increments of time, can never irreparably break or damage the things they are studying, and will always be encouraged to try again. At its end, *Outer Wilds* is a hopeful, curious, and optimistic game about the bleak end of the universe, made possible through the use of time loop mechanics as both a central narrative mystery and a structure for enthusiastic exploration and discovery.

5 Conclusion

Time loop stories in digital games can be read as an expression of hope, in that the game's mechanics and interface encourage and allow players to manipulate time until the best of all possible outcomes is achieved. It follows that time loop games express narrative experiences through interface and mechanics, in many cases focused on optimism and hope in increasingly difficult times. From a game development standpoint, it is worth considering whether digital games may tend toward optimism as a whole, intentionally or otherwise, given that their interactive structures often focus on skill improvement, knowledge acquisition, and the eventual mastery of the game space: In other words, no matter how bleak or terrifying the game content, players will eventually overcome it, which is itself a positive and uplifting outcome. Ultimately, time loop games are a worthwhile example of how game developers and interactive creators can create works of art that speak to the difficult times we currently inhabit, and the hope that will be necessary to survive and ultimately thrive in them.

References

1. Evans, M.: The needle and the wedge: digital games as a medium for science fiction. Vector: The Critical Journal of the British Science Fiction Association 291, 15–23 (2020)
2. Time travel: The Science Fiction Encyclopedia, https://sf-encyclopedia.com/entry/time_t ravel. Accessed 10 Feb 2023
3. Schell, J.: The Art of Game Design: A Book of Lenses, 3rd edn. CRC Press, New York (2020)
4. Salen, K., Zimmerman, E.: Rules of Play: Game Design Fundamentals. The MIT Press, Cambridge (2003)
5. Lawler, D.: Approaches to Science Fiction. Houghton Mifflin, Boston (1978)
6. Silverberg, R., (ed.) Trips in Time: Nine Stories of Science Fiction. Dutton Juvenile (1977)
7. Bly, R.: The Science in Science Fiction. BenBella Books, Dallas (2005)
8. Time loop, The Science Fiction Encyclopedia. https://sf-encyclopedia.com/entry/time_loop. Accessed 10 Feb 2023
9. Storm, J.: Approaching the Possible: The World of Stargate SG-1. ECW Press, Toronto (2005)
10. Juul, J.: Half-Real: Video Games Between Real Rules and Fictional Worlds. The MIT Press, Cambridge (2011)
11. Ryan, M-L.: Avatars of Story. University of Minnesota Press (2006)
12. Adams, E., Rollings, A.: Andrew Rollings and Ernest Adams on Game Design. 1st edn. New Riders Publishing (2003)
13. Bailes, J.: Loops, I did it again – why 2021 was the year of the time loop story, NME. https://www.nme.com/features/gaming-features/loops-i-did-it-again-why-2021-was-the-year-of-the-time-loop-story-3123836. Accessed 10 Feb 2023
14. Stoeber, J.: Time loops are a weird genre for an anxious time, Polygon,
15. https://www.polygon.com/videos/22907078/time-loops-12-minutes-deathloop-elsinore. Accessed 10 Feb 2023
16. Gleick, J.: Time Travel: A History. Vintage Books, New York (2016)
17. Price R.: Twelve Minutes might have the worst video game ending of the year, Kotaku. https://kotaku.com/twelve-minutes-might-have-the-worst-video-game-ending-o-1847540262. Accessed 10 Feb 2023
18. Tyrer, B.: Returnal ending explained: how Housemarque's devastating story hides in plain sight, GamesRadar. https://www.gamesradar.com/returnal-ending-explained-how-hou semarques-devastating-story-hides-in-plain-sight. Accessed 10 Feb 2023
19. MacDonald, K.: Why The Legend of Zelda: Majora's Mask still matters, Kotaku. https://kotaku.com/why-the-legend-of-zelda-majoras-mask-still-matters-1655550826. Accessed 10 Feb 2023
20. Skott, S., Bengtson, K.S.: 'You've met with a terrible fate, haven't you?' A hauntological analysis of carceral violence in Majora's Mask. Games Cult. 17(4), 593–615 (2022)
21. Green, H.: A third-person, action, roguelike, bullet-hell arcade thriller: The making of Returnal, Game Developer. https://www.gamedeveloper.com/gdc2022/a-third-person-action-rog uelike-bullet-hell-arcade-thriller-the-making-of-returnal. Accessed 10 Feb 2023
22. Returnal, Housemarque Games, Sony Interactive Entertainment (2021)
23. Egan, T.: Arkane Studios' Studios' Sébastien Mitton explains the 13 movies that inspired Deathloop, Polygon. https://www.polygon.com/22700733/deathloop-movies-inspir ation. Accessed 10 Feb 2023
24. Deathloop, Arkane Lyon, Bethesda Softworks (2021)
25. Lindner, N.: Why Deathloop's ending is so disappointing, ScreenRant.com. https://screen rant.com/deathloop-endings-disappointing-bad-colt-julianna-arkane/. Accessed 10 Feb 2023
26. Solis, G.: Deathloop is a unique reflection on time and history, Wired. https://www.wired.com/review/deathloop-game/. Accessed 10 Feb 2023

27. Outer Wilds. Mobius Digital, Annapurna Interactive (2019)
28. Walker, A.: 'Outer Wilds' is a captivating sci-fi mystery about the end of the world, Vice. https://www.vice.com/en/article/mb8p7y/outer-wilds-is-a-captivating-sci-fi-mystery-about-the-end-of-the-world. Accessed 10 Feb 2021

Your Favorite Gameplay Speaks Volumes About You: Predicting User Behavior and Hexad Type

Reza Hadi Mogavi[1]([✉]), Chao Deng[2], Jennifer Hoffman[2], Ehsan-Ul Haq[1], Sujit Gujar[3], Antonio Bucchiarone[4], and Pan Hui[1,5,6]

[1] Hong Kong University of Science and Technology, Hong Kong Sar, China
{rhadimogavi,euhaq}@connect.ust.hk
[2] Accessible Meta Research and Development, Michigan, USA
{cdeng,jhoffman}@accessiblemeta.org
[3] International Institute of Information Technology, Hyderabad, India
sujit.gujar@iiit.ac.in
[4] Fondazione Bruno Kessler, Trento, Italy
bucchiarone@fbk.eu
[5] Hong Kong University of Science and Technology, Guangzhou, China
panhui@ust.hk
[6] University of Helsinki, Helsinki, Finland
pan.hui@helsinki.fi

Abstract. In recent years, the gamification research community has widely and frequently questioned the effectiveness of one-size-fits-all gamification schemes. In consequence, personalization seems to be an important part of any successful gamification design. Personalization can be improved by understanding user behavior and Hexad player/user type. This paper comes with an original research idea: It investigates whether users' game-related data (collected via various gamer-archetype surveys) can be used to predict their *behavioral characteristics* and *Hexad user types* in non-game (but gamified) contexts. The affinity that exists between the concepts of *gamification* and *gaming* provided us with the impetus for running this exploratory research.

We conducted an initial survey study with 67 Stack Exchange users (as a case study). We discovered that users' gameplay information could reveal valuable and helpful information about their behavioral characteristics and Hexad user types in a non-gaming (but gamified) environment.

The results of testing three gamer archetypes (i.e., *Bartle, Big Five,* and *BrainHex*) show that they can all help predict users' most dominant Stack Exchange behavioral characteristics and Hexad user type better than a random labeler's baseline. That said, of all the gamer archetypes analyzed in this paper, *BrainHex* performs the best. In the end, we introduce a research agenda for future work.

Keywords: Game · Gamification · archetypes · Bartle · Big Five · BrainHex · Prediction · User behavior · CQA · Hexad

© The Author(s), under exclusive license to Springer Nature Switzerland AG 2023
X. Fang (Ed.): HCII 2023, LNCS 14047, pp. 210–228, 2023.
https://doi.org/10.1007/978-3-031-35979-8_17

1   Introduction

Over the years, games have found an integral place in the daily lives of many people around the globe [4,16,42,48]. They can be found everywhere, from people's homes to their phones and, more recently, even in the metaverse [18,30,40]. They offer endless opportunities for personal development [11,14], creativity [50], and fun [10]. According to the Entertainment Software Association's most recent survey, conducted in February 2022, more than 200 million Americans (nearly two thirds) regularly play at least one type of video game to bring joy and happiness into their lives [13].

However, not all gamers enjoy the same types of games (or gameplays) [37,38,46]. In fact, player preferences can vary widely based on various individual and contextual factors such as *personality, age, gender, occupation, daily life schedule, cultural background, expenses,* and *accessibility* [7–9,45,46]. Fortunately, however, there are now several applicable gamer models (or archetypes) in the literature that have proven helpful in describing *parts of* these various complexities using simple (and reasonably easy-to-conceptualize) player attributes.

Three of the **most frequently cited archetypes** of gamers in the human-computer interaction (HCI) and gameplay research communities (e.g., *CHI Play* [28]) are *Bartle* [5], *Big Five* [26], and *BrainHex* [35].

Bartle's taxonomy of player types, for example, states that players can be divided into four groups based on how they like to play games: *achievers, socializers, explorers,* and *killers*. In brief, *achievers* like to rack up achievements and badges; *socializers* favor interacting with other players; *explorers* favor gaining knowledge about the game world and its mechanics; and finally, *killers* favor lurking and competing against other players.[1]

While such gamer archetypes may strike some scholars (and readers) as oversimplifications, they do a good job of providing a *holistic overview* of some of the most common gamer interests that developers and game designers should be aware of [23,25]. Consequently, it is witnessed that many giant game companies (e.g., *Nintendo, Ubisoft,* and *Blizzard*), research institutes, and interest groups worldwide spend hundreds to thousands of dollars annually to collect such data from gamers through a variety of survey methods.

▷ **Our research here presents an exploratory study that seeks to understand what else can be inferred from such survey data on people's game (or gameplay) interests. More specifically, we want to investigate whether gamer archetypes (such as Bartle) can tell us anything helpful about user behavior in *non-game contexts* and *Hexad user types*.**

1.1   Background

Gamification has recently become an independent field of study in the HCI communities, and it historically has strong ties to the *gaming industry*. The term

---

[1] More information can be found in the Section of Literature Review.

gamification is *often* defined as the use of game design elements (such as badges, points, and leaderboards) in non-game contexts (such as education, business, health, and crowdsourcing) [12,24,43]. According to the extant literature, gamification has the ability to change user behavior [3,29] and can have both positive (e.g., [19,31]) and negative effects (e.g., [19,20,22]) on user activities. This relevant prior knowledge motivates us to explore the possibility of using players' game-related data to predict their most dominant user behavior in gamified (but non-game) environments.

Beyond User Behavior. Aside from user behavior, another vital topic worth discussing in any gamified environment is determining users' gamification preferences. Here, we are curious to find out whether game-related data can also be used to predict users' gamification preferences. To investigate users' gamification preferences more systematically (and practically), we employ *Hexad*, which is a well-established empirical framework often used to identify and understand users' gamification preferences (or *Hexad type*) [23,32,39].

Hexad Framework. According to the Hexad framework, different Hexad types include (1) *Philanthropists* (provoked by: purpose), (2) *Socializers* (provoked by: relatedness), (3) *Free Spirits* (provoked by: autonomy), (4) *Achievers* (provoked by: competence), (5) *Players* (provoked by: extrinsic rewards), and (6) *Disruptors* (provoked by: their urge to change).

In recent years, an increasing number of HCI researchers have explored many inventive methods for predicting Hexad types other than the typical surveying approach that is developed by Tondello et al. [47]. Each method has its own unique benefits and drawbacks and, when necessary, can be used in a variety of situations and contexts. For example, a research conducted by Altmeyer et al. showed that user-generated smartphone data can help predict Hexad types and potentially tailor gamification without requiring direct user interaction [1]. Nevertheless, as is evident, some people may have privacy and security concerns about sharing their smartphone data with gamification designers and developers. In another study, Kimpen et al. conducted an expert consensus study with a group of 11 experts and argued that banking data could as well be helpful in predicting Hexad types [27]. **With this background in mind, our research presents a new way to predict gamers' Hexad types based on the information about their game and gameplay preferences when such information is available.**

1.2   Research Context

The non-game context chosen for investigation in this article is **Stack Exchange**, which is a popular example of *Community Question Answering Websites (CQAs)*. CQAs such as Stack Exchange, Quora, and Zhihu are among the most important Computer Supported Cooperative Work (CSCW) applications that have been in the interest scope of the HCI and gamification research communities for a long time [20,22,44]. These platforms help millions of people worldwide ask and answer questions online and serve as helpful knowledge repositories on different topics [44]. As shown in Fig. 1, CQAs typically use various

(a) Reputation Points and Badges   (b) Leaderboard

Fig. 1. Anonymized snapshots of Stack Exchange's gamification mechanisms: reputation points, badges, and the leaderboard

gamification elements such as badges, points, and leaderboards to incentivize user participation and prevent churn (i.e., user dropouts) [34].

1.3   Key Contributions

In summary, our **main contributions** to the existing body of knowledge in this area are as follows:

- According to our findings, there is a notable correlation between people's preferences for specific types of gameplay and their behavioral characteristics in non-game (but gamified) contexts, as well as their preferences for specific types of gamification.
- According to our results, all player archetypes can (to some extent) help predict user behavior in Stack Exchange (a non-game gamified context) and their Hexad type better than the baseline of a random labeler. However, of all the gamer archetypes studied in this paper, *BrainHex* is the one that has the best performance.
- Our research can help eliminate (or mitigate) the need for parallel surveys of people's preferences about games and gamification. This study shows that game-related data can be used to make reasonable inferences about people's dominant behavioral attributes and preferences for gamification. Thus, our research findings could help game/gamification researchers and survey respondents save time, money, and energy.
- Last but not least, our findings encourage HCI researchers and practitioners to think outside the box and apply their existing knowledge resources/tools (such as player archetypes) to solve broader and different types of problems (e.g., predicting Hexad user type). In the ever-expanding HCI community of today, finding creative and novel solutions to domain-related issues appears to be quite essential.

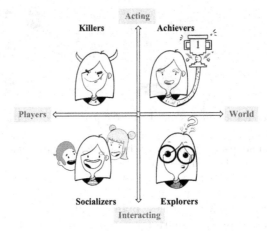

Fig. 2. Bartle's taxonomy of gamer types: Achievers, Socializers, Explorers, and Killers

2 Literature Review

This section reviews the literature in the areas of gamer archetypes, gamification, and Hexad user/player types.

2.1 Gamer Archetypes

Personalization and customization of the gaming experience are essential to ensure that gamers have the most fun and enjoy their time. Three of the most commonly cited gamer archetypes used for this purpose in the HCI and gameplay research communities are *Bartle* [5], *Big Five* [26], and *BrainHex* [35]. A great deal can be gleaned about gamers from each of these archetypes.[2]

□ **Bartle's Taxonomy of Player Types.** According to the gamer taxonomy developed by Bartle in 1996, gamers who play in multiplayer virtual worlds can be divided into four types: *achievers*, *socializers*, *explorers*, and *killers*. As shown in Fig. 2, these categories are determined by classifying gamer preferences along two dimensions, i.e., players-world spectrum (*horizontal axis*) and acting-interacting spectrum (*vertical axis*). Each gamer type is defined as follows [41]:

Achievers are defined as those who like to *act in the world*. They are gamers who want to feel that they have achieved something significant (often scarce) in the game; they place great value on the element of *competence* described in the *Self-Determination Theory (SDT)*. According to this theory, people need a sense of *competence* (being skilled and effective), *relatedness* (being connected to others), and *autonomy* (being master of their behavior) in order to be satisfied enough to perform certain actions [22,49].

---

[2] In this text, the terms *typology*, *archetype*, *model*, and *behavioral traits* are sometimes used interchangeably.

Explorers, on the other hand, like to *interact with the world*. They are gamers who want to engage with the full scope of the system and explore its boundaries and hidden secrets; they naturally value the element of *autonomy* in self-determination theory the most.

Socializers enjoy *interacting with other players*. They are gamers who want to use the system to meet new people and make new friends; socializers, according to the self-determination theory, are interested in the element of *relatedness*. Finally, **killers** are gamers who take pleasure in doing things to other people or *acting on other players*. They enjoy competing with others, and the *competence* element of the self-determination theory appeals to them the most.

Currently, the most common empirical method for determining an individual's Bartle type is Dr. Matthew Barr's survey method, known as Bartle test.[3]

□ **Big Five Personality Traits.**[4] In psychology, personality traits go beyond the game/gamification world [23] and are understood as patterns of *thought, feeling*, and *behavior* that are relatively **persistent** throughout a person's life [17]. Developed and disseminated primarily in the 1980 s and 1990 s, the model of Big Five personality traits include *conscientiousness, agreeableness, neuroticism, openness*, and *extraversion* [23]. Below, we summarize the main characteristics of each personality trait:

- **Conscientiousness** shows the proclivity for self-control, discipline, tenacity, organization, and responsibility toward others.
- **Agreeableness** indicates the emotional feelings such as empathy and concern for the needs of others, altruism, trust, and cooperation.
- **Neuroticism** describes a person's proclivity to be under psychological pressure (instability) and to experience negative emotions such as depression, anxiety, and anger.
- **Openness**[5] describes a person's imaginative, creative, curious, risk-taking, and adventurous tendencies.
- **Extraversion (or extroversion)** describes a person's tendency to be gregarious, friendly, warm, and enthusiastic about activities that involve interaction with others, such as making new friends or participating in group projects.

TIPI (Ten Item Personality Measure) is currently the most widely used method for measuring a person's Big Five personality traits [15].

□ **BrainHex Player Typology.** The BrainHex typology was developed in the early 2010 s.s. It was inspired by several sources and references, including *earlier typology approaches, discussions of play patterns*, the *literature on gameplay emotions*, and most importantly, the relevant *neurobiological studies* [6,35]. This typology divides gamers' playing motivations into seven categories [35]: *Seeker* (motivated by exploration), *Survivor* (driven by fear), *Daredevil* (motivated by excitement), *Mastermind* (motivated by strategy), *Conqueror* (motivated by challenge), *Socializer* (motivated by social relationships), and *Achiever*

---

[3] http://matthewbarr.co.uk/bartle/.
[4] Also called *Five-Factor Model of Personality*.
[5] Also called *Openness to Experience*.

(motivated by goal achievement). In the following, we summarize and explain each of these categories based on the explanations provided by Lennart Nacke et al. [35]:

- **The Seeker** loves to explore the environment and have adventures. Endormorphin is released when a seeker's brain is exposed to rich patterns of interpretable information (often sensory), activating the pleasure center in their brain.
- **The Survivor** takes pleasure when exposed to a high level of suspense induced by fear or anticipation of frightening situations, at least in the context of fictional activities (e.g., horror movies and video games). Among survivors, the arousal neurotransmitter epinephrine amplifies the impact of dopamine triggered by the receipt of rewards. However, it still needs to be determined whether the pleasure of fear should be evaluated by the intensity of the fright itself or by the relief felt afterward.
- **The Daredevil** revels in the thrill and peril of playing on the edge and taking risks (e.g., playing at extreme heights or participating in a car race at extreme speeds). Similar to Survivors, epinephrine is a reward enhancer in daredevils.
- **The Mastermind** takes pleasure in solving complex puzzles, developing clever strategies, and making the most efficient decisions. The pleasure and decision centers of a mastermind's brain are closely connected, and good decisions are inherently rewarded. The mastermind archetype is very similar to Bartle's explorer type.
- **The Conqueror** describes a challenge-seeking gamer who is not content with easy victories. Difficult situations stimulate the release of epinephrine (adrenalin), associated with arousal and excitement, and norepinephrine, associated with anger. Regardless of gender, testosterone is also thought to play a role in this archetype. According to the literature, the conqueror archetype is weakly related to Bartle's killer type.
- **The Socializer** enjoys interacting with others, hanging out with trusted people, talking with them, and assisting them. This archetype is linked to the social center of the brain, which is the primary neural source of oxytocin, a neurotransmitter associated with trust. The name of this archetype alludes to Bartle's socializer archetype.
- **The Achiever** describes a goal-oriented gamer motivated by long-term achievements. In this archetype, the release of dopamine and stimulation of the brain's pleasure center contribute to a sense of personal fulfillment. The name of this archetype alludes to Bartle's achiever archetype.

Currently, most HCI and gameplay researchers and practitioners use the official *International Hobo Questionnaire* [33] to determine the BrainHex types of their research participants.

2.2   Gamification and Hexad

In recent years, gamification has emerged as an essential research topic in the fields of HCI, CSCW, and Learning at Scale. Simply put, gamification is the application of game design elements such as *badges*, *points*, and *leaderboards* in non-game contexts [12]. However, the mere addition of badges, points, and leaderboards to a system/service does not guarantee user engagement or lead users toward a desired behavior [19,20,22]. According to Nicholson, a good gamification design should support its target users in making *meaningful* connections between their personal goals and the use of gamification [36]. This is important because it can help improve users' behavioral outcomes and experiences. The literature suggests that a tailored gamification design can help promote the formation of such perceptual connections [22,23,36].

☐ **Hexad** [47] is a framework widely used by the gamification research community to adapt gamification in various systems and applications. It is based on the *self-determination theory (SDT)* [49]. Hexad framework helps gamification researchers and designers understand users' *motivations* for interacting with different types of gamification elements in different environments. Below, we review the main characteristics of each Hexad type (according to [47]):

- **Philanthropists** seek *purpose* and *meaning*. They are altruistic and willing to help or give without expecting anything in return.
- **Socializers** are motivated by *relatedness* (as described in SDT). They want to interact with others and form social bonds.
- **Free Spirits** are motivated by *autonomy* (as described in SDT). They enjoy creation and exploration without any controls or restrictions.
- **Achievers** seek *competence* (as described in SDT). They want to prove their worth by taking on challenging tasks and moving up in a system.
- **Players** are after the *extrinsic rewards*. They are willing to engage in any activity (regardless of the type) in order to receive a reward within a system.
- **Disruptors** are driven by their will to initiate a *change* (either positive or negative) in the system. They enjoy challenging the system.

The survey approach developed by Tondello et al. [47] is the most common method for determining a user's Hexad type. However, as the Hexad framework becomes more popular, new approaches to predicting the Hexad types are being developed that can be useful in a variety of situations based on the availability of different types of data [1,2,27]. Our research here contributes to this field of study by introducing a novel method for predicting Hexad types based on people's gamer archetypes.

3 Method

This section describes the details of our participant recruitment, the survey collection, Stack Exchange data, correlation analysis, and the final ablation study.

3.1 Participant Recruitment

To increase the diversity of our research participants, we used a variety of sources to recruit them, including Stack Exchange chat rooms and social media platforms such as Facebook and Twitter.[6] Inclusion criteria were 1) age over 18 years; 2) more than *six months* of active participation in at least one Stack Exchange forum;[7] and 3) having at least some *occasional* engagement with games and different gamification schemes (self-reported via seven-point Likert scales).[8]

In this way, we recruited 67 Stack Exchange users (23 female) with different demographics and varying levels of exposure to games and gamification. The age range of the participants is between 18 and 45 years (mean = 28.21, SD = 9.36). The ethnic distribution of our research participants is as follows: Asian (n = 27), White (n = 14), Hispanic and Latino/a (n = 10), Black or African American (n = 7), Native American (n = 2), mixed race (n = 2), and other races (n = 5). According to our initial screenings, on the seven-point Likert scale, the average user engagements of our participants with games and various gamification schemes (prior to our research) are 4.82 (SD = 1.12) and 4.30 (SD = 0.93), respectively.[9]

3.2   Survey Collection

All of our research procedures have been approved by the IRB at the Hong Kong University of Science and Technology. After obtaining informed consent from all research participants, we asked them (via email) to complete four online surveys (three for gamer archetypes and one for Hexad) within one to two days of receiving the email. The HKUST Qualtrics website was used to collect all responses, allowing participants to take breaks between (and during) surveys and to measure the time it took them to complete each survey. Upon successfully receiving the answers, each participant was given HK$ 40 as a token of appreciation. All survey responses for each participant were stored under their unique Stack Exchange IDs for further analysis. The average completion times (in minutes) for the Bartle, Big Five, and BrainHex are 22.83 (SD = 7.38), 15.25 (SD = 6.94), and 29.50 (SD = 5.66). The average time to complete the Hexad survey is 20.25 min (SD = 4.18).

3.3   Stack Exchange Data

Stack Exchange Data Explorer[10] was used to collect each participant's CQA data using their Stack Exchange IDs. This data includes information about each participant's posting behavior, i.e., their posts' exact timestamps and peer-evaluated posting quality scores.[11] Different types of posts in the CQA of Stack Exchange include *questions*, *answers*, and *comments*. In this context, user posts *closed* and

---

[6] Two moderators from Stack Exchange assisted us throughout the recruitment process.

[7] This measure allows us to avoid studying the behavior of churned users [20].

[8] i.e., 3/7 on the Likert scale, where 7/7 points out the maximum engagement.

[9] Again, 7/7 shows the maximum engagement.

[10] https://data.stackexchange.com/.

[11] The difference between the number of *up-votes* and *down-votes*.

removed by community moderators are regarded as *spam*. *Closed* posts with *negative scores* are also considered *spam*.

In addition to users' posting data, we also collected their metadata on other types of activities, i.e., their voting behavior and edit services.

The oldest post in our dataset was made on July 10th, 2015, and the most recent post was made on September 18th, 2022. The average reputation of research participants in this work is 9,656.04 (SD = 10,067.18). And the number of users in the categories of novice users, low reputation users, established users, and trusted users are n = 8, n = 17, n = 23, and n = 19 respectively. The average number of questions, answers, comments, and spam posts per individual is 43.76 (SD = 26.12), 52.10 (SD = 29.18), 68.11 (SD = 35.92), and 4.08 (SD = 2.23), respectively. Furthermore, the average number of votes and edits per person is 496.92 (SD = 311.55) and 30.74 (SD = 26.62), respectively. The most dominant behavior (action) of each participant in our study is determined by counting the frequency with which user behaviors are repeated.

3.4   Correlation Analysis and Ablation Study

In keeping with the exploratory spirit of our study, we first conduct and present the results from a thorough Pearson correlation analysis on data from collected *game* and *gamification* surveys and data from the participants' *CQA activities*.

Following that, we train the computational models for our prediction tasks (i.e., predicting the dominant user behavior and Hexad type). To this end, we employ a high-performance machine learning model known as Extreme Gradient Boosting (which is also called XGBoost). The reason for using XGBoost is its simplicity and strength in reducing the training bias [21]. We build and compare our models based on various input features derived from our participants' previous survey responses (i.e., Bartle, Big Five, and BrainHex characters). We compare our models (also) against the baseline of a random labeler. The reason for using a random labeler here is because, to the best of our knowledge, there are currently no other (suitable/better) baselines that can be used for comparison with our work. Due to the limited amount of our sample data (for training purposes), we use the metric of five-fold cross-validation error to evaluate and report the performance of all models in this paper. After dividing our data into different folds (for the purpose of cross-validation), we use an up-sampling technique (based on *Bootstrapping*) to address the issue of imbalanced data labels. All models in our study are created and tested on a local PC equipped with an Intel i7-5820k CPU (6 cores @3.3 GHz) and 32 GB RAM using the popular Python library *scikit-learn*.

Table 1. The average cross-validation (CV) error performance of the various prediction models

Prediction Model	Average CV Error Per Category (%)						
	Question	Answer	Comment	Spam	Edit	Vote	Total
XGBoost + Bartle Types	37.01	38.57	68.30	41.39	54.61	62.55	50.40
XGBoost + BiG Five Types	22.13	24.82	35.42	28.75	30.09	48.73	31.65
XGBoost + BrainHex Types	16.10	7.14	21.27	18.32	31.55	51.27	24.27
Random Labeler	84.96	83.50	82.93	85.77	91.32	85.46	85.65

4   Findings

This section presents the findings of our study in three parts: 1) a report of interesting correlations, 2) a report of dominant user behavior prediction, and 3) a report of Hexad user type prediction.

4.1   Interesting Correlations

We conducted n = 192 Pearson correlation tests to uncover the interesting relationships between participants' game-based characters and behavioral profiles in the CQA and between participants' game-based characters and gamification-based characters in general (i.e., Hexad type). For the purpose of illustration, Fig. 3 depicts the correlation plots (tested with a statistical confidence of 99.95) between seeker participants' BrainHex measures (intensities) and the frequencies of seeker users' posting behaviors, i.e., questions (Pearson's r value = +0.24), answers (Pearson's r value = +0.61), comments (Pearson's r value = −0.08), and spam posts (Pearson's r value = −0.02). We observe a statistically significant positive correlation between the seekers' BrainHex measures and their tendencies to post (more) questions and answers inside the CQA community. However, the statistical significance of the negative correlation between seekers' BrainHex measures and their frequencies of commenting and spamming still needs to be proved.

Likewise, Fig. 4 shows the correlation plots (tested with a statistical confidence of 99.95) between seeker participants' BrainHex and Hexad type measures (intensities). The Pearson r values resolved for the Hexad type correlations are as follows: Philanthropist (r = +0.01), Socializer (r = −0.03), Free Spirit (r = +0.25), Achiever (r = +0.19), Player (r = +0.31), and Disruptor (r = +0.18). In the case of the seeker archetype (from BrainHex), only the positive correlations reported for *free spirit* and *player* Hexad measures are statistically significant.

It is worth noting here that different surveys often yield different scales for indicating user characteristics and that there is often a considerable discrepancy between the frequency with which users engage in various activities. With this point in mind, we have therefore normalized all numbers in all figures (and analyses) to lie within the range [0,1] for greater clarity and better comparability. The following are the most important statistically significant findings and conclusions from our correlation analysis:

Bartle. The frequency of questions and answers in the CQA correlates positively with Bartle's *achiever* and *Socializer* measures. We found that the amount of comments and spam posted in the CQA is positively correlated with Bartle's *explorer* and *killer* measures. Bartle's *achiever* measure correlates positively with Hexad's *free spirit*, *achiever*, and *player* intensities. There is also a positive correlation between Bartle's *killer* measure and Hexad's *achiever*, *player*, and *disruptor* metrics (indicators).

Big Five. The number of questions asked, answers given, comments written, and edits made in the CQA correlate positively with the Big Five measures of *openness* and *extraversion*. One of the Big Five dimensions, *conscientiousness*, correlates positively with the frequencies of voting and editing, whereas *neuroticism* correlates negatively with both. Furthermore, the Hexad measures *socializer* and *philanthropist* correlate positively with the Big Five levels of *extraversion* and *agreeableness*. Also, there appears to be a positive relationship between *openness* and Hexad's *free spirit* measure.

BrainHex. The frequency of CQA posts (of any type) correlates positively with the BrainHex *mastermind* and *conqueror* measures. The frequency of questions and answers is proportional to the BainHex *seeker* measure. The BrainHex *daredevil* metric is positively correlated with the frequency of votes and spam. The *socializer* measure, on the other hand, is positively correlated with the frequency of comments and answers. The number of questions a participant asks correlates positively with their BrainHex *survival* measure, while the number of answers correlates negatively with it. Nonetheless, the BrainHex *achiever* measurement is positively correlated with the number of answers provided by the participants identified with that character. In addition, the BrainHex *achiever* metric is positively correlated with Hexad's *philanthropist*, *achiever*, and *player* intensities. The seeker archetype in BrainHex, as noted before, is positively correlated to the measurements of *free spirit* and *player* archetypes in Hexad. In BrainHex, the *daredevil* metric is positively correlated with the *player* and *disruptor* measurements in Hexad. The *socializer* measure in the BrainHex is positively related to the *philanthropist* and *socializer* measures in Hexad.

4.2 Predicting the Dominant User Behavior

Table 1 summarizes the performances of the different prediction models based on their average cross-validation error. Overall, the **combination of XGBoost and the BrainHex user type measures** outperforms all other competing models in predicting the most dominant user behavior. This combination outperforms the Big Five and Bartle models by 26.13% and 7.38%, respectively. In addition, BrainHex consistently outperforms all other models at the categorical level, with the exception of the *editing* and *voting* tasks (where the BrainHex model falls slightly behind the Big Five model). Furthermore, we can see that all gamer archetypes can significantly outperform the prediction of a random labeler. Hence, even in the absence of BrainHex data, the Big Five and then the Bartle model could be used as helpful alternatives. However, the accuracy issue should be considered for more sensitive tasks and decisions.

Table 2. The performance of various models in predicting the Hexad type of the participants

Prediction Model	Average CV Error Per Category (%)						
	Philanthropists	Socializers	Free Spirits	Achievers	Players	Disruptors	Total
XGBoost + Bartle Types	58.60	33.78	43.90	32.38	30.10	52.99	41.95
XGBoost + BiG Five Types	27.32	31.01	32.53	27.58	19.23	43.06	30.12
XGBoost + BrainHex Types	29.17	24.63	28.74	23.10	11.36	41.12	26.35
Random Labeler	83.81	88.78	86.48	84.13	83.90	84.37	85.24

4.3 Predicting the Hexad Type

Similarly, Table 2 summarizes the performances of the various prediction models when predicting the (most dominant) Hexad type. Again, the **combination of XGBoost and the BrainHex user type measures** outperforms all other competing models in accurately predicting the Hexad types. According to the *total* performance results, this model (XGBoost + BrainHex) reduces error by 15.60% compared to the Bartle archetype and 3.77% compared to the Big Five model. Furthermore, with the exception of the *philanthropist* user type (where BrainHex falls 1.85% short of the Big Five model), the BrainHex model (also) outperforms all other competing models at all categorical levels. We should mention here that all gamer archetypes (i.e., Bartle, Big Five, and BrainHex) can significantly outperform the prediction of a random labeler. Hence, in the absence of BrainHex data, the Big Five and then the Bartle model could still be used as viable (helpful) substitutes.

5 Discussion

In this section, we will discuss some of the major limitations of our research and set an agenda for future work.

5.1 Limitations

There are several critical limitations to our research in this paper that should be mentioned. The first and most obvious limitation is the small number of participants in the study. Unfortunately, it is becoming increasingly difficult to recruit participants for research studies such as ours that require lengthy and time-consuming surveys to be completed. Also, due to the limited number of data samples, we decided not to use Deep Learning or other advanced neural network models for our prediction tasks. Future work could focus on collecting more data (on a larger scale) and improving the machine-learning component of the models. In addition to these caveats, the context of our research study itself is a major limitation. Obviously, Stack Exchange is not the best representative for all kinds of online gamified platforms on the Internet. Hence, it is necessary that future studies cross-check the findings of our work also on other (and more diverse) platforms.

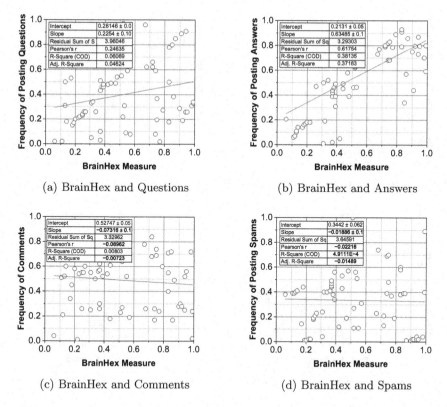

Fig. 3. The correlation plots between seeker participants' BrainHex measures (intensities) and the frequencies of their (a) questions, (b) answers, (c) comments, and (d) spam posts.

5.2   Agenda for Future Research

In the end, we present four interesting research directions for future work. 1) Future player surveys and gamification archetypes (or data collection methods) will need to be less intrusive and collect as little personal information as possible. In addition, the advent of platforms such as the metaverse has necessitated the development of newer and more secure techniques for collecting and disseminating human data. As an idea for future research, we would like to see if it is possible to use people's metaverse-based peripheral data to infer aspects of their personality in order to provide them with better and more tailored gaming/gamification services. 2) Understanding how users and gamification experts perceive and reason about the relationships between different gamer archetypes, CQA behaviors, and Hexad is another interesting research direction for future work that merits being thoroughly explored. Comprehensive qualitative research methods, such as inductive and deductive content analysis, are likely to yield better results in this type of investigation. 3) People's interest in the playful aspects of a gamified platform may be a good indicator of their willingness to stay on

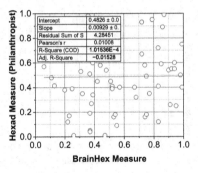

(a) BrainHex and Philanthropist Measures

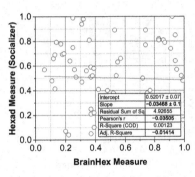

(b) BrainHex and Socializer Measures

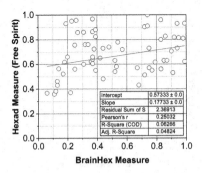

(c) BrainHex and Free Spirit Measures

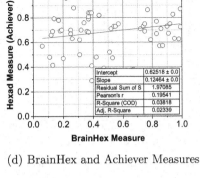

(d) BrainHex and Achiever Measures

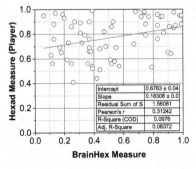

(e) BrainHex and Player Measures

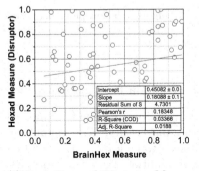

(f) BrainHex and Disruptor Measures

Fig. 4. The correlation plots between seeker participants' BrainHex and Hexad type measures (intensities).

that site for a more extended period of time. Future research could examine and explore this idea further to determine if information about users' gamer and gamification archetypes could help gamified platforms and services detect when a user will churn their websites/services (or become less active/loyal), perhaps in a more timely and accurate manner. 4) Although we found some interesting correlations between gamer archetypes, user behaviors, and Hexad types, our study does not demonstrate or assert any causal relationships. Future research could use controlled experimental designs to determine the presence (or absence) of any causal relationships.

6   Conclusion

In this paper, we investigated whether information about users' game-related data (collected through a series of gamer-archetype surveys) could be used to predict their most dominant behaviors and Hexad user types in a non-gaming (but still gamified) environment. We found some promising results: users' game-related data (i.e., Bartle, Big Five, and BrainHex) could all provide valuable information about their behavioral characteristics and Hexad user types. However, *BrainHex* outperforms the other gaming archetypes studied in this work on the prediction tasks. Finally, we presented our research agenda for future work.

Acknowledgement. The authors would like to thank Mr. Rahman Hadi Mogavi for proofreading and contributing beautiful images to this paper. This research has been supported in part by the MetaHKUST project from the Hong Kong University of Science and Technology (Guangzhou), and 5GEAR and FIT projects from the Academy of Finland.

References

1. Altmeyer, M., Lessel, P., Schubhan, M., Krüger, A.: Towards predicting hexad user types from smartphone data. In: Extended Abstracts of the Annual Symposium on Computer-Human Interaction in Play Companion Extended Abstracts, pp. 315–322. CHI PLAY 2019 Extended Abstracts, Association for Computing Machinery, New York, NY, USA (2019). https://doi.org/10.1145/3341215.3356266
2. Altmeyer, M., Tondello, G.F., Krüger, A., Nacke, L.E.: Hexarcade: predicting hexad user types by using gameful applications. In: Proceedings of the Annual Symposium on Computer-Human Interaction in Play, pp. 219–230. CHI PLAY 2020, Association for Computing Machinery, New York, NY, USA (2020). https://doi.org/10.1145/3410404.3414232
3. Anderson, A., Huttenlocher, D., Kleinberg, J., Leskovec, J.: Steering user behavior with badges. In: Proceedings of the 22nd International Conference on World Wide Web, pp. 95–106. WWW 2013, Association for Computing Machinery, New York, NY, USA (2013). https://doi.org/10.1145/2488388.2488398
4. Barr, M., Copeland-Stewart, A.: Playing video games during the COVID-19 pandemic and effects on players' well-being. Games Culture **17**(1), 122–139 (2021). https://doi.org/10.1177/15554120211017036
5. Bartle, R.: Hearts, clubs, diamonds, spades: players who suit muds. J. MUD Res. **1**(1), 19 (1996)
6. Bateman, C., Lowenhaupt, R., Nacke, L.E., et al.: Player typology in theory and practice. In: DiGRA Conference, pp. 1–24. Citeseer (2011)
7. Boggio, C., Moscarola, F.C., Gallice, A.: What is good for the goose is good for the gander? Econ. Educ. Rev. **75**, 101952 (2020) https://doi.org/10.1016/j.econedurev.2019.101952

8. Cairns, P., Power, C., Barlet, M., Haynes, G.: Future design of accessibility in games: a design vocabulary. Int. J. Hum.-Comput. Stud. **131**, 64–71 (2019). https://doi.org/10.1016/j.ijhcs.2019.06.010
9. Chesham, A., Wyss, P., Müri, R.M., Mosimann, U.P., Nef, T.: What older people like to play: Genre preferences and acceptance of casual games. JMIR Serious Games **5**(2), e8 (2017). https://doi.org/10.2196/games.7025
10. Cole, H., Griffiths, M.D.: Social interactions in massively multiplayer online role-playing gamers. CyberPsychology Behav. **10**(4), 575–583 (2007). https://doi.org/10.1089/cpb.2007.9988
11. Connolly, T.M., Boyle, E.A., MacArthur, E., Hainey, T., Boyle, J.M.: A systematic literature review of empirical evidence on computer games and serious games. Comput. Educ. **59**(2), 661–686 (2012). https://doi.org/10.1016/j.compedu.2012.03.004
12. Deterding, S., Dixon, D., Khaled, R., Nacke, L.: From game design elements to gamefulness: defining "gamification". In: Proceedings of the 15th International Academic MindTrek Conference: Envisioning Future Media Environments, pp. 9–15. MindTrek 2011, Association for Computing Machinery, New York, NY, USA (2011). https://doi.org/10.1145/2181037.2181040
13. (ESA), T.E.S.A.: Essential facts about the video game industry, November 2022. https://www.theesa.com/resource/2022-essential-facts-about-the-video-game-industry/
14. Galleguillos, L., Santelices, I., Bustos, R.: Designing a board game for industrial engineering students. a collaborative work experience of freshmen. In: INTED2019 Proceedings. IATED, March 2019. https://doi.org/10.21125/inted.2019.0075
15. Gosling, S.D., Rentfrow, P.J., Swann, W.B.: A very brief measure of the big-five personality domains. J. Res. Pers. **37**(6), 504–528 (2003). https://doi.org/10.1016/s0092-6566(03)00046-1
16. Granic, I., Lobel, A., Engels, R.C.M.E.: The benefits of playing video games. Am. Psychol. **69**(1), 66–78 (2014). https://doi.org/10.1037/a0034857
17. Grice, J.W., Doorey, M., Lotha, G.: Five-factor model of personality, January 2019. https://www.britannica.com/science/five-factor-model-of-personality
18. Haberlin, K.A., Atkin, D.J.: Mobile gaming and internet addiction: when is playing no longer just fun and games? Comput. Hum. Behav. **126**, 106989 (2022). https://doi.org/10.1016/j.chb.2021.106989
19. Hadi Mogavi, R., Guo, B., Zhang, Y., Haq, E.U., Hui, P., Ma, X.: When gamification spoils your learning: a qualitative case study of gamification misuse in a language-learning app. In: Proceedings of the Ninth ACM Conference on Learning @ Scale, L@S 2022, pp. 175–188. Association for Computing Machinery, New York, NY, USA (2022). https://doi.org/10.1145/3491140.3528274
20. Hadi Mogavi, R., Haq, E.U., Gujar, S., Hui, P., Ma, X.: More gamification is not always better: a case study of promotional gamification in a question answering website. Proc. ACM Hum.-Comput. Interact. **6**(CSCW2) (2022). https://doi.org/10.1145/3555553
21. Hadi Mogavi, R., Ma, X., Hui, P.: Characterizing student engagement moods for dropout prediction in question pool websites. Proc. ACM Hum.-Comput. Interact. **5**(CSCW1) (2021). https://doi.org/10.1145/3449086
22. Hadi Mogavi, R., Zhang, Y., Haq, E.U., Wu, Y., Hui, P., Ma, X.: What do users think of promotional gamification schemes? a qualitative case study in a question answering website. Proc. ACM Hum.-Comput. Interact. **6**(CSCW2) (2022). https://doi.org/10.1145/3555124

23. Hallifax, S., Serna, A., Marty, J.C., Lavoué, G., Lavoué, E.: Factors to consider for tailored gamification. In: Proceedings of the Annual Symposium on Computer-Human Interaction in Play. p. 559–572. CHI PLAY '19, Association for Computing Machinery, New York, NY, USA (2019). https://doi.org/10.1145/3311350.3347167,https://doi.org/10.1145/3311350.3347167

24. Hamari, J., Koivisto, J., Sarsa, H.: Does gamification work? - a literature review of empirical studies on gamification. In: 2014 47th Hawaii International Conference on System Sciences. IEEE (2014). https://doi.org/10.1109/hicss.2014.377

25. Hamari, J., Tuunanen, J.: Player types: A meta-synthesis (2014)

26. de Hesselle, L.C., Rozgonjuk, D., Sindermann, C., Pontes, H.M., Montag, C.: The associations between big five personality traits, gaming motives, and self-reported time spent gaming. Personality Individ. Differ. **171**, 110483 (2021). https://doi.org/10.1016/j.paid.2020.110483

27. Kimpen, R., De Croon, R., Vanden Abeele, V., Verbert, K.: Towards predicting hexad user types from mobile banking data: an expert consensus study. In: Extended Abstracts of the 2021 Annual Symposium on Computer-Human Interaction in Play, CHI PLAY 2021, pp. 30–36. Association for Computing Machinery, New York, NY, USA (2021). https://doi.org/10.1145/3450337.3483486

28. Kumar, N., et al.: A chronology of sigchi conferences: 1983 to 2022. Interact. **29**(6), 34–41 (2022). https://doi.org/10.1145/3568732

29. Kusmierczyk, T., Gomez-Rodriguez, M.: On the causal effect of badges. In: Proceedings of the 2018 World Wide Web Conference, pp. 659–668. WWW 2018, International World Wide Web Conferences Steering Committee, Republic and Canton of Geneva, CHE (2018). https://doi.org/10.1145/3178876.3186147

30. Lee, L.H., et al.: All one needs to know about metaverse: a complete survey on technological singularity, virtual ecosystem, and research agenda (2021). https://arxiv.org/abs/2110.05352

31. Legaki, N.Z., Xi, N., Hamari, J., Karpouzis, K., Assimakopoulos, V.: The effect of challenge-based gamification on learning: an experiment in the context of statistics education. Int. J. Hum.-Comput. Stud. **144**, 102496 (2020) https://doi.org/10.1016/j.ijhcs.2020.102496

32. Lopez, C.E., Tucker, C.S.: The effects of player type on performance: a gamification case study. Comput. Hum. Behav. **91**, 333–345 (2019). https://doi.org/10.1016/j.chb.2018.10.005

33. Ltd, I.H.: Brainhex questionnaire, May 2010. https://survey.ihobo.com/BrainHex/

34. Mogavi, R.H., Gujar, S., Ma, X., Hui, P.: Hrcr: hidden markov-based reinforcement to reduce churn in question answering forums. In: Pacific Rim International Conference on Artificial Intelligence, pp. 364–376 (2019)

35. Nacke, L.E., Bateman, C., Mandryk, R.L.: BrainHex: a neurobiological gamer typology survey. Entertainment Comput. **5**(1), 55–62 (2014). https://doi.org/10.1016/j.entcom.2013.06.002

36. Nicholson, S.: A recipe for meaningful gamification. Gamification in education and business, pp. 1–20 (2015)

37. Orji, R., Mandryk, R.L., Vassileva, J., Gerling, K.M.: Tailoring persuasive health games to gamer type. In: Proceedings of the SIGCHI Conference on Human Factors in Computing Systems, CHI 2013, pp. 2467–2476. Association for Computing Machinery, New York, NY, USA (2013). https://doi.org/10.1145/2470654.2481341

38. Orji, R., Nacke, L.E., Marco, C.D.: Towards personality-driven persuasive health games and gamified systems. In: Proceedings of the 2017 CHI Conference on Human Factors in Computing Systems, ACM, May 2017. https://doi.org/10.1145/3025453.3025577

39. Orji, R., Tondello, G.F., Nacke, L.E.: Personalizing persuasive strategies in gameful systems to gamification user types. In: Proceedings of the 2018 CHI Conference on Human Factors in Computing Systems, CHI 2018, pp. 1–14. Association for Computing Machinery, New York, NY, USA (2018). https://doi.org/10.1145/3173574.3174009

40. Parry, I., Carbullido, C., Kawada, J., Bagley, A., Sen, S., Greenhalgh, D., Palmieri, T.: Keeping up with video game technology: objective analysis of xbox kinect^{TM} and PlayStation 3 move^{TM} for use in burn rehabilitation. Burns **40**(5), 852–859 (2014). https://doi.org/10.1016/j.burns.2013.11.005

41. Reiners, T., Wood, L.C. (eds.): Gamification in Education and Business. Springer, Cham (2015). https://doi.org/10.1007/978-3-319-10208-5

42. Ryan, R.M., Rigby, C.S., Przybylski, A.: The motivational pull of video games: a self-determination theory approach. Motiv. Emot. **30**(4), 344–360 (2006). https://doi.org/10.1007/s11031-006-9051-8

43. Seaborn, K., Fels, D.I.: Gamification in theory and action: a survey. Int. J. Hum.-Comput. Stud. **74**, 14–31 (2015). https://doi.org/10.1016/j.ijhcs.2014.09.006

44. Srba, I., Bielikova, M.: A comprehensive survey and classification of approaches for community question answering. ACM Trans. Web **10**(3) (2016). https://doi.org/10.1145/2934687

45. Thayer, A., Kolko, B.E.: Localization of digital games: the process of blending for the global games market. Tech. Commun. **51**(4), 477–488 (2004)

46. Tondello, G.F., Arrambide, K., Ribeiro, G., Cen, A.J., Nacke, L.E.: "I don't fit into a single type: a trait model and scale of game playing preferences. In: Lamas, D., Loizides, F., Nacke, L., Petrie, H., Winckler, M., Zaphiris, P. (eds.) INTERACT 2019. LNCS, vol. 11747, pp. 375–395. Springer, Cham (2019). https://doi.org/10.1007/978-3-030-29384-0_23

47. Tondello, G.F., Wehbe, R.R., Diamond, L., Busch, M., Marczewski, A., Nacke, L.E.: The gamification user types hexad scale. In: Proceedings of the 2016 Annual Symposium on Computer-Human Interaction in Play, CHI PLAY 2016, pp. 229–243. Association for Computing Machinery, New York, NY, USA (2016). https://doi.org/10.1145/2967934.2968082

48. Troiano, G.M., et al.: Exploring how game genre in student-designed games influences computational thinking development. In: Proceedings of the 2020 CHI Conference on Human Factors in Computing Systems, CHI 2020, pp. 1–17. Association for Computing Machinery, New York, NY, USA (2020). https://doi.org/10.1145/3313831.3376755

49. Tyack, A., Mekler, E.D.: Self-determination theory in HCI games research: current uses and open questions. In: Proceedings of the 2020 CHI Conference on Human Factors in Computing Systems, CHI 2020, pp. 1–22. Association for Computing Machinery, New York, NY, USA (2020). https://doi.org/10.1145/3313831.3376723

50. Urbanek, M., Güldenpfennig, F.: Unpacking the audio game experience: lessons learned from game veterans. In: Proceedings of the Annual Symposium on Computer-Human Interaction in Play, CHI PLAY 2019, pp. 253–264. Association for Computing Machinery, New York, NY, USA (2019). https://doi.org/10.1145/3311350.3347182

Does the Voice Reveal More Emotion than the Face? a Study with Animated Agents

Joshua E. Heller, Nicoletta Adamo$^{(\boxtimes)}$ [iD], Nandhini Giri [iD], and Derek Larson [iD]

Purdue University, West Lafayette, IN 47907, USA
{amehrez,nadamovi,girin,dglarson}@purdue.edu

Abstract. In general, people tend to identify the emotions of others from their facial expressions, however recent findings suggest that we may be more accurate when we hear someone's voice than when we look only at their facial expression. The study reported in the paper examined whether these findings hold true for animated agents. A total of 37 subjects participated in the study: 19 males, 14 females, and 4 of non-specified gender. Subjects were asked to view 18 video stimuli; 9 clips featured a male agent and 9 clips a female agent. Each agent showed 3 different facial expressions (happy, angry, neutral), each one paired with 3 different voice lines spoken in three different tones (happy, angry, neutral). Hence, in some clips the agent's tone of voice and facial expression were congruent, while in some videos they were not. Subjects answered questions regarding the emotion they believed the agent was feeling and rated the emotion intensity, typicality, and sincerity. Findings showed that emotion recognition rate and ratings of emotion intensity, typicality and sincerity were highest when the agent's face and voice were congruent. However, when the channels were incongruent, subjects identified the emotion more accurately from the agent's facial expression than the tone of voice.

Keywords: Facial Expressions · Animated Agents · Perception · Emotions

1 Introduction

Research has shown that animated pedagogical agents (APA) can effectively pro- mote learning (Schroeder et al. 2013; Adamo et al. 2021). However, many questions remain unanswered, particularly concerning their emotional design. With a growing understanding of the complex interplay between emotions and cognition, there is a need to develop life-like agents that provide both effective expert guidance and convincing emotional interactions with the learner (Kim and Baylor 2007). One goal of our research is to develop APAs that can convey clearly perceivable emotions through speech, facial expressions, and body gestures. The study conducted for this paper was a step in this direction, as it focused on how emotions are expressed through voice and face.

Human emotions can be expressed using several modalities: vocal and facial expressions, arm and hand gestures, trunk rotation, head rotation, and leg movements. The face is cited as being the most used resource in identification of emotions (Noroozi et al. 2018).

X. Fang (Ed.): HCII 2023, LNCS 14047, pp. 229–242, 2023.
https://doi.org/10.1007/978-3-031-35979-8_18

However, research by Kraus (2017), suggests that people may be more accurate when hearing another's voice than when solely considering their facial expression. The study reported in the paper examined whether Kraus' findings hold true for animated agents. More specifically, it investigated whether animated agents' facial expressions are a more effective channel for conveying emotions that the tone of voice. The study examined perception of animated agents' emotions in the context of multi-sense communication, e.g., voice + facial expression.

2 Related Work

In animated agents, emotions can be expressed through facial expressions, body movements, and speech. Facial expressions and speech are the modalities that have been studied the most in HCI, computer science and psychology.

The face is cited as being the most used resource in identification of emotional states (Noroozi et al. 2018). The ability of the face to convey emotions and the facial deformations associated with different emotions have been documented in Ekman and Friesen's Facial Action Coding System (FACS) (Ekman and Friesen 1978). The FACS allows animators to draw upon methods outside their own practice to create facial expressions that communicate emotions effectively to the audience (Buchanan 2009). For example, the use of the FACS in the creation of the character Gollum in Lord of the Rings – The Two Towers (2002), resulted in a character which was widely regarded by critics as emotionally believable (Kerlow 2014).

Several approaches for representing facial expressions in animated agents exist. Some computational frameworks are based on discrete representation of emotion; others on dimensional models; and others on appraisal theories (Pelachaud 2009). Approaches that are based on the expression of standard emotions (Ekman and Friesen 1975; Ekman 2003) compute new expressions as a mathematical combination of the parameters of predefined facial expressions (Becker and Wachsmuth 2006; Pandzic and Forcheimer 2002). Approaches based on dimensional models use a 2 dimensional--valence and arousal (Garcia-Rojas et al. 2006) or 3 dimensional--valence, arousal, and power (Albrecht et al., 2005) representation of facial emotions. A new expression is created by mixing the facial parameters of the expressions of the closest standard facial emotions in the representation space. A few approaches use fuzzy logic to compute the combination of expressions of the six standard emotions (Duy Bui et al. 2004), or the combination of facial regions of several emotions (Pelachaud, 2009). Some approaches are based on Scherer's appraisal theory (Scherer, 2001) and model a facial expression as a sequence of the facial articulations that are displayed consecutively as a result of cognitive estimates (Paleari & Lisetti, 2006).

Body movements are particularly important for expressing emotions when the agent is framed in a medium to long shot (Anasingaraju and Adamo-Villani 2020; Meyer et al. 2021), or to convey emotions that are less susceptible to social editing (Ekman and Friesen, 1974). Bodily cues have been shown to be very effective for discriminating between intense positive and intense negative affective states (Avezier et al. 2012). Emotional states can be conveyed through body movement modulation (e.g., the manipulation of motion parameters such as speed or amplitude) or movement type (e.g., a specific body gesture) (Cheng et al. 2020) or a blend of both (Karg et al. 2013). A combination of modalities that include both facial and bodily gestures improve recognition rate of emotion compared to facial cues alone by 35%. The best rate of recognition uses a combination of facial and body gestures with the inclusion of voice (Gunes et al. 2015).

Studies in marketing and psychology, suggest that voice, including both speech content and the linguistic and paralinguistic vocal cues (e.g., pitch, cadence, speed, and volume), is a particularly powerful channel for perceiving the emotions of other people (Kraus 2017). Simon-Thomas et al. (2009) examined how well brief vocal bursts could communicate 22 different emotions. Results showed that vocal bursts can communicate emotions like anger, fear, and sadness, and also less-studied states and highlighted the voice as a rich modality for emotion expression/perception. Kraus (2017) conducted five experiments to test the hypothesis that voice-only communication elicits higher rates of emotion recognition accuracy than vison-only and multi-sense communication in the context of social interactions. Findings support the hypothesis and challenge the primary role of facial expressions in emotion recognition. In a study by Zaki et al. (2009) social targets were filmed while discussing emotional autobiographical events. A group of subjects watched the videos and inferred the targets' emotional states while having access to only visual or auditory information, or both. Findings suggest that auditory, and especially verbal information, is critical to accurate detection of emotion. In a study by Gesn and Ickes (1999) participants viewed video segments of simulated psychotherapy sessions and attempted to identify each client's emotional state. Results showed that, in this particular context, emotion recognition accuracy was primarily dependent upon verbal, rather than nonverbal, cues.

In conclusion, several studies have investigated the role of voice for recognizing people's emotions, however, to our knowledge, no studies have attempted to examine the role of voice versus facial cues for identifying the affective states of animated agents. The work reported in the paper aims to fill this gap.

3 Methodology

The study aimed to answer the following research question: do facial expressions override tone of voice when perceiving the emotion of an animated agent? Drawing from prior research on animated agents and best practices in character animation (Williams 2012), the first hypothesis was that participants' recognition of the emotions displayed by the animated agents would be more accurate when discerned from the agents' facial expressions than from their tones of voice. The second hypothesis was that when comparing the ratings of typicality, sincerity, and intensity of emotions, stimuli with congruent voice/facial expression channels would be rated higher than stimuli with incongruent channels. The third hypothesis was that participants' gender, age and animation experience would have a significant effect on emotion recognition and on typicality, sincerity, and intensity ratings.

The study used a within subject design and collected both quantitative and qualitative data. The independent variables included facial expression-tone of voice congruence (yes/no), participants' gender (male, female, other), age, and animation experience, and emotion type (happy, angry, neutral). The dependent variables were the participants' emotion recognition rate and the participants' ratings of the emotion's intensity, typicality, and sincerity on a 5-point Likert scale (1 = low; 5 = high).

3.1 Subjects

37 people participated in the study. 19 were males, 14 females, and 4 of non-disclosed gender. The age range was 18–56 years old; the animation experience of the subjects ranged from no experience to high experience.

3.2 Materials

Stimuli. The stimuli were 18 animation clips: 9 featured a male agent and the remaining 9 a female agent. The agents exhibited three different facial emotions (happy, angry, neutral), each one paired with three different voice lines spoken in three separate tones (happy, angry, neutral). For example, for the happy emotion, one animation featured an agent with a happy face/happy voice, another an agent with a happy face/angry voice, and a third an agent with a happy face/neutral voice. The facial emotions were based on Ekman and Friesen Facial Action Coding System (Ekman and Friesen 1978). The different facial expressions and tones of the voice lines were validated through a pilot study with eight subjects. Figure 1 illustrates four frames extracted from the animation clips (two per agent).

The agents' models and rigs were downloaded from the internet and the facial expressions were animated by an experienced character animator using keyframe animation in Autodesk Maya software; the characters were manually lip synced to the voice lines. The two characters were rigged with identical facial skeletal deformation systems and the animations were created based on the Facial Action Coding System (FACS) (Ekman and Friesen 1978). Action Units (AU) 6 + 12 were used for the happy expressions, and Action Units 4 + 5 + 7 + 23 for the angry expressions; the neutral facial expressions did not feature any facial deformations. Characters occasionally blinked and slightly changed their gaze direction. The characters were framed from the neck up at a three-quarters angle; no background elements were included in the videos to keep the viewers focused on the characters' faces. The animation frame rate was 24 fps; the length of the videos ranged between 11 and 16 s and varied depending on the voice line being spoken, but each expression and voice line had equal duration.

Evaluation Instrument. The evaluation instrument was an online questionnaire consisting of 54 questions. The first set of questions gathered demographic data, namely participant gender, age range, and animation experience. Then, the 18 stimuli videos were presented to the participants in random order and 4 questions were provided after each video. One question was a multiple-choice question that asked the subjects to identify the emotion they believed the character in the video was conveying (e.g., happy, angry, or other). If a subject selected the "other" option, they were asked to specify what emotion specifically came to mind when viewing the video. The other three questions asked the participants to rate the typicality (how usual the emotion was), sincerity (how convincing/genuine the emotion was) and intensity (how strong the emotion was) of the

Fig. 1. Frames showing the animated agents used in the study. Happy male agent (top left), angry male agent (top right), happy female agent (bottom left), angry female agent (bottom right)

emotion displayed by the character on a 5-point Likert scale (1 = low; 5 = high). Finally, subjects could offer additional comments about the emotion displayed by the character.

3.3 Procedure

The online questionnaire was sent to the participants using several methods including email, online chat threads, and text messages. The questionnaire could be taken at any time and at any location and subjects were only permitted one attempt at the survey. The researcher did not assist respondents in answering the questions beyond providing the instructions included in the survey.

4 Data Analysis

4.1 Cross-Modal Identification of Emotion

Rstudio was used to run a power analysis to determine the needed sample size. The results of the power analysis, which used data from a pilot study with 7 subjects, showed that at least 32 samples were needed for a power of 0.8 at a significance level of 0.05. The analysis of cross-modal identification of emotion was conducted in Python; the subjects' responses were analyzed using a mixed-effect ordinal regression and compared to the fixed responses provided by the experiment. Figures 2–4 show bar graphs that summarize the data. The x-axis represents the facial emotions expressed by the character, and the y-axis represents the number of participants who selected that emotion; each figure relates to a different tone of voice (happy in Fig. 2; neutral in Fig. 3, angry in Fig. 4). The data presented in Figs. 2–4 show a high recognition rate of the correct emotion when the channels were congruent with one another. However, even when the channels were incongruent, subjects identified the emotion based more heavily on the facial expression than the tone of voice. An angry expression was the easiest to identify given any condition, while a happy expression was the most difficult to identify, being perceived more as a neutral expression. Despite this confusion, the facial expression prevailed more often in identifying an emotion than the tone of voice. To analyze the data related to specific emotions, each emotion was given a value that was inputted into an equation to identify its probability. The equation below was employed to calculate the probability of an event as a function of the predictor values for the model and Table 1. The random effect is denoted as τid for each participant:

$$logit(P(Y \leq j)) = \log \frac{P(Y \leq j)}{P(Y > j)} = intercept_j + \beta_{j2}x_{j2} + \ldots + \tau_{id}; j = 1,$$

The j value is the representation of the emotional value, 1 is for angry, 2 is for happy, and 3 is for neutral. For example, the equation measures the probability of an angry expression when j equals 1. Since Y has to be less than or equal to 1, the only option that can be placed within that field is 1 (angry). This was compared to the estimates of the other remaining emotions of happy or neutral, as the second parameter calls for Y to be greater than 1, meaning only 2 (happy) or 3 (neutral) can fit in that field. This is further summarized when compared to the alternative formula meant to calculate probabilities:

$$logit(P(Y \leq 2)) = \log \frac{P(Y \leq 2)}{P(Y > 2)} = intercept_2 + \beta_{2i}x_{2i} + \ldots + \tau_{id},$$

This functions exactly as the previous one did. However, it is meant to iden- tify the probability changes of both happy and angry compared to the baseline neutral expression. Inversely, the function can be written in the form below to identify the probability of a happy value:

$$P(Y = 2) = P(Y \leq 2) - P(Y \leq 1) = \frac{e^{a_2+\beta x}}{1 + e^{a_2+\beta x}} - \frac{e^{a_1+\beta x}}{1 + e^{a_1+\beta x}}$$

After discovering the meaning behind the exploratory studies presented in Figs. 2–4, the meaning behind the patterns was analyzed further utilizing a GLIMMIX procedure in SAS. This enabled the analysis of random variables to be accounted for when inferring relationships between fixed effect predictors and the outcome. Table 1 further elaborates the analysis; a Type III test was conducted to assess whether the significant values offer sufficient statistical data for each factor. Table 1 indicates that the facial variable, tone variable, and their interactions are significant in this model.

To further confirm the validity of the mixed-effect ordinal regression, we cre- ated a confusion matrix to summarize the model performance, as shown in Fig. 5. The confusion matrix shows the software's selections of emotions based on estimates gathered from the data on the x-axis in comparison to the true selections of emotions from participants on the y-axis. The color of the regions is in relation to the frequency of the selections based on these comparisons. For example, the middle square represents a total of 246 participant responses that match the predicted label of happy while the bottom middle square represents 96 responses interpreting the predicted happy emotion as other, as well as the top middle square representing 74 responses interpreting the predicted happy emotion as angry. Refer to Table 2 for the response frequency from the GLIMMIX procedure.

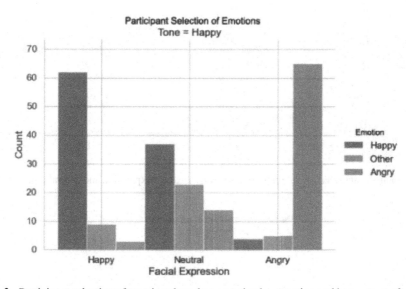

Fig. 2. Participant selection of emotions based on perceived expression and happy tone of voice.

Table 3 presents a series of estimates provided from fixed effects based around the participant's input and the computer's predictions of accuracy values. Estimates were pulled from the data using a cumulative logit parameter to illustrate how the subject responses change from one set of expressions to another. These estimates also showed how significant the contrast of factors was between both expressions and tones of voice. Neutral emotions were the baseline measurement for the estimates, so they always remained 0. The p-value in the last column on the right indicates the significance of each effect. From the results, we can see that the "angry" and "happy" levels of the facial factor both play statistically significant roles in the model. Moreover, combined with previous probability calculations, we can infer that changing the facial level from neutral to angry is estimated to increase the probability of an angry emotion.

4.2   Analysis of Ratings of Emotion Typicality, Sincerity and Intensity

Descriptive statistics show that for the happy emotion, the ratings of typicality, sincerity and intensity were highest when the emotional channels, e.g., facial expression and voice, were congruent (Table 4). These findings support our hypothesis. Surprisingly, for the

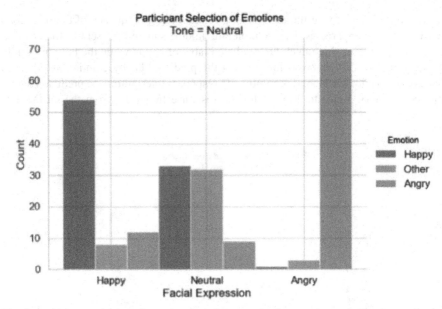

Fig. 3. Participant selection of emotions based on perceived expression and neutral tone of voice.

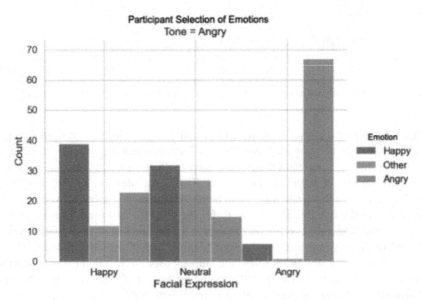

Fig. 4. Participant selection of emotions based on perceived expression and angry tone of voice.

angry emotion, the ratings of typicality, sincerity and intensity were highest when the agent showed an angry face and spoke using a neutral tone of voice rather than an angry tone of voice (Table 5). For the neutral emotion, the congruent condition had the highest ratings, however the differences in ratings between conditions were small (Table 6).

Table 1. Tests of the statistical significance of a variable's ability to reject the null hypothesis based on the factors' two-way interactions.

Type III Tests of Fixed Effects				
Effect	Num DF	Den DF	F Value	Pr > F
Facial	2	650	105.00	<.0001
Tone	2	650	5.30	0.0052
Facial*Tone	4	650	4.25	0.0021
gender	2	26.11	0.09	0.9185
age	2	26.95	0.43	0.6549
experience	2	26.72	0.09	0.9110

Table 2. Respective values for each emotion for formulaic input alongside the sum of each selection from the survey.

Response Profile		
Ordered Value	value	Total Frequency
1	Angry	193
2	Happy	210
3	Neutral	263

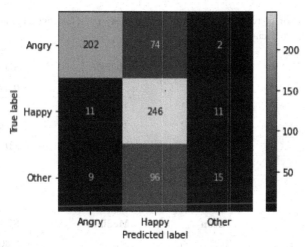

Fig. 5. Confusion Matrix of participant selections compared to computer-predicted selections. The accuracy of these two data sets is represented by the scale to the left of the matrix.

Differences Based on Participants' Age, Animation Experience and Gender. The data was analyzed using a Type III regression method placed on a 5-point Likert scale on

Table 3. Fixed-effect estimates and their significance levels.

Effect	value	Facial	Tone	gender	age	experience	Estimate	Standard Error	DF	t Value	Pr > |t|
Intercept	Angry						-2.1967	1.1624	29.13	-1.89	0.0688
Intercept	Happy						-0.1258	1.1581	29.13	-0.11	0.9142
Facial		Angry					4.0679	0.4126	650	9.86	<.0001
Facial		Happy					0.7457	0.3356	650	2.22	0.0266
Facial		Neutral					0	.	.	.	.
Tone			Angry				0.09007	0.3422	650	0.26	0.7925
Tone			Happy				-0.3969	0.3529	650	-1.12	0.2611
Tone			Neutral				0	.	.	.	.
Facial*Tone		Angry	Angry				-1.8287	0.5176	650	-3.53	0.0004
Facial*Tone		Angry	Happy				-0.4315	0.5349	650	-0.81	0.4202
Facial*Tone		Angry	Neutral				0	.	.	.	.
Facial*Tone		Happy	Angry				-0.4359	0.4746	650	-0.92	0.3588
Facial*Tone		Happy	Happy				0.5450	0.4792	650	1.14	0.2558
Facial*Tone		Happy	Neutral				0	.	.	.	.
Facial*Tone		Neutral	Angry				0	.	.	.	.
Facial*Tone		Neutral	Happy				0	.	.	.	.
Facial*Tone		Neutral	Neutral				0	.	.	.	.
gender				1			-0.2927	0.7343	25.92	-0.40	0.6934
gender				2			-0.2973	0.7877	25.86	-0.38	0.7089
gender				3			0	.	.	.	.
age					2		0.07560	0.8832	26.82	0.09	0.9324
age					4		-0.5555	1.0488	26.92	-0.53	0.6007
age					5		0	.	.	.	.

Table 4. Comparison of typicality, sincerity, and intensity rates for congruent and incongruent happy stimuli - happy facial expression

Happy/Happy	Mean	Median	SD
Typicality	3.57	3	0.89
Sincerity	3.62	3	1.13
Intensity	3.7	3	1.15
Happy/Angry	**Mean**	**Median**	**SD**
Typicality	3.2	3	0.86
Sincerity	3.3	3	1.13
Intensity	3.01	3	0.93
Happy/Neutral	**Mean**	**Median**	**SD**
Typicality	3.2	3	0.86
Sincerity	3.09	3	1.13
Intensity	3.27	3	1.12

Table 5. Comparison of typicality, sincerity, and intensity rates for congruent and incongruent channels - angry facial expression

Angry/Happy	Mean	Median	SD
Typicality	3.05	3	0.98
Sincerity	3.28	3	1.14
Intensity	3.43	3	1.21
Angry/Angry	**Mean**	**Median**	**SD**
Typicality	3.43	3	0.68
Sincerity	3.62	4	0.87
Intensity	3.35	3	1.01
Angry/Neutral	**Mean**	**Median**	**SD**
Typicality	3.5	3	0.74
Sincerity	3.92	4	0.93
Intensity	3.7	4	0.92

Table 6. Comparison of typicality, sincerity, and intensity rates for congruent and incongruent neutral stimuli (neutral facial expression)

Neutral/Happy	Mean	Median	SD
Typicality	2.89	3	0.9
Sincerity	2.64	3	1.19
Intensity	2.31	3	1.21
Neutral/Angry	**Mean**	**Median**	**SD**
Typicality	2.85	3	0.95
Sincerity	2.66	3	1.14
Intensity	2.34	3	1.25
Neutral/Neutral	**Mean**	**Median**	**SD**
Typicality	2.97	3	0.92
Sincerity	2.78	3	1.11
Intensity	2.6	3	1.2

each of the demographic values. The regression was created in SAS and conducted using a MIXED procedure, which allows the random variables to be compared holistically with all fixed variables. The equation used to calculate the data for the mixed effect regression model was as follows:

$$typicality = \alpha + \beta_{angry} * I(Angry) + \beta_{happy} * I(Happy) + \epsilon + \tau_{id},$$
$$\epsilon \sim N(0, \sigma^2), \quad \tau_{id} \sim N(0, \sigma^2_{id}), \quad I(\cdot) \text{ indicator function}$$

The typicality value can be replaced with either intensity or sincerity de- pending on the response being calculated within the function. We treat the participants within the study as a random effect to account for the correlation for each individual subject.

Results of the analysis showed that participants' age and animation experience had no effect on intensity, typicality and sincerity ratings across all emotions and conditions (p-values > 0.05). Participants' gender did not have significance for intensity and typicality ratings but had a significant effect on sincerity ratings. Female participants gave significantly higher sincerity ratings than the other participants across all emotions and across all conditions (p-values < 0.05).

5 Discussion and Conclusion

The study reported in the paper examined the roles of facial expressions and tone of voice in the perception of animated agents' emotions. Findings from the study support the first and second hypotheses: emotion recognition rate and ratings of emotion intensity, typicality and sincerity are highest when the agent's face and voice are congruent. However, when the channels are incongruent, subjects tend to identify the emotion more accurately from the agent's facial expression than the tone of voice. Results also show an effect of participants' gender on emotion sincerity ratings, thus supporting in part the third hypothesis. Female participants perceived the emotions displayed by the agents as significantly more sincere than the other participants across all emotions and conditions.

The study had several limitations that could be overcome in future research. The sample size was small (37 subjects) and participants' genders were not represented equally. Future studies should use a larger number of subjects with a more even distribution of genders.

The study comprised only two stylized characters and three voice lines spoken in three different tones. Part of the results could be due to the intrinsic design characteristics of the characters and to the intrinsic linguistic and paralinguistic cues of the voice lines. Future experiments should include a higher variety of voice lines and characters with different degrees of stylization. For instance, it would be interesting to examine whether participants' perception of the agents' emotions is different for stylized versus realistic characters. It could be possible that the face is the strongest emotion expression modality for cartoon characters while the voice is the strongest emotion expression channel for realistic gents.

The study focused on only two of Ekman's six basic emotions. Future experiments should consider the other four emotions. The short duration of the stimuli animations may have affected the participants ability to perceive the characters' emotions in all conditions. Future research should use animation sequences of longer duration and with two or more characters interacting with each other.

A substantial body of research has examined the role of voice for recognizing people's emotions, however, to our knowledge, no studies have attempted to examine the role of vocal versus facial cues for identifying the affective states of animated agents. To advance knowledge in this area, there is a need for experimental research studies that systematically investigate the extent to which specific affective channels contribute to enhance the perception of animated characters' emotions. The study reported in the paper is a small step in this direction. Studies like this not only have important implications for research, but also for practice. They can provide useful guidelines for animators and instructional designers for enhancing the appeal and emotional impact of animated characters and, possibly, the educational effectiveness of animated pedagogical agents.

Acknowledgements. This work is supported in part by NSF- RETTL Collaborative Research: Using Artificial Intelligence to Transform Online Video Lectures into Effective and Inclusive Agent-Based Presentations; Award # 2201019. The authors would like to thank Purdue Statistical Consulting Service for their help with the data analysis.

References

Schroeder, N., Adesope, O.O., Barouch Gilbert, R.: How effective are pedagogical agents for learning? a meta-analytic review. J. Educ. Comput. Res. **49**(1) (2013). https://doi.org/10.2190/EC.49

Adamo, N., et al.: Multimodal affective pedagogical agents for different types of learners. In: Russo, D., Ahram, T., Karwowski, W., DiBucchianico, G., Taiar, R. (eds.) Intelligent Human Systems Integration 2021. AISC, vol. 1322, pp. 218–224. Springer, Cham (2021). https://doi.org/10.1007/978-3-030-68017-6_33

Kim, Y., Baylor, A.L.: Pedagogical agents as social models to influence learner attitudes. Educ. Technol. **47**(01), 23–28 (2007)

Noroozi, F., Kaminska, D., Corneanu, C., Sapinski, T., Escalera, S., Anbarjafari, G.: Survey on EMOTIONAL BODY GESTURE RECOGNITION. IEEE Trans. Affect. Comput. 1–20 (2018)

Buchanan, A.: Facial expressions for empathic communication of emotion in animated characters. Animation studies (2009). https://journal.animationstudies.org/andrew-buchanan-facial-expressions-for-empathic-communication-of-emotion-in-animated-characters/

Kraus, M.W.: Voice-only communication enhances empathic accuracy. Am. Psychol. **72**(7), 644–654 (2017)

Ekman, P., Friesen, E.: Facial Action Coding System: A Technique for the Measurement of Facial Movement. Consulting Psychologists Press, Palo Alto (1978)

Kerlow, I.: Creative Human Character Animation: The Incredibles vs. The Polar Express. vfxworld.com (2014)

Pelachaud, C.: Modelling multimodal expression of emotion in a virtual agent. Phil. Trans. R. Soc. B **2009**(364), 3539–3548 (2009). https://doi.org/10.1098/rstb.2009.0186

Ekman, P., Friesen, W.: Unmasking the Face: A Guide to Recognizing Emotions from Facial Clues. Prentice-Hall Inc., Eaglewood Cliffs (1975)

Ekman, P.: Emotions revealed. Times Books (US)/Weidenfeld & Nicolson, New York/London (2003)

Becker, C., Wachsmuth, I.: Modeling primary and secondary emotions for a believable communication agent. In: Proceedings of International Workshop on Emotion and Computing, in conj. with the 29th Annual German Conference on Artificial Intelligence (KI2006), Bremen, Germany, pp. 31–34 (2006)

Pandzic, I.S., Forcheimer, R. (eds) MPEG4 Facial Animation – The Standard, Implementations and Applications. John Wiley and Sons, Chichester, UK (2002)

Garcia-Rojas, A., et al.: Emotional face expression profiles supported by virtual human ontology. Comp. Anim. Virtual Worlds **17**, 259–269 (2006). https://doi.org/10.1002/cav.130

Meyer, Z., Adamo, N., Benes, B.: Bodily expression of emotions in animated agents. In: Bebis, G., et al. (eds.) Advances in Visual Computing, vol. 13018, pp. 475–487. Springer, Cham (2021). https://doi.org/10.1007/978-3-030-90436-4_38

Bui, D., Heylen, D., Poel, M., Nijholt, A.: Combination of facial movements on a 3D talking head. In: Computer Graphics International, pp. 284–290 (2004)

Scherer, K.R.: Appraisal considered as a process of multilevel sequential checking. In: Scherer, K., Schorr, A., Johnstone, T. (eds.) Appraisal Processes in Emotion: Theory, Methods, Research, pp. 92–119. Oxford University Press, New York (2001)

Paleari, M., Lisetti, C.L.: Psychologically grounded avatars expressions. In: Proceedings of First Workshop on Emotion and Computing at KI 2006, 29th Annual Conference on Artificial Intelligence, Bremen, Germany (2006)

Anasingaraju, S., Adamo-Villani, N., Dib, H.N.: The contribution of different body channels to the expression of emotion in animated pedagogical agents. Int. J. Technol. Human Interact. (IJTHI), 16(4) (2020). https://doi.org/10.4018/IJTHI.202010010

Ekman, P., Friesen, W.: Detecting deception from the body or face. J. Pers. Soc. Psychol. 29, 288–298 (1974)

Avezier, H., Trope, Y., Todorov, A.: Body cues, not facial expressions, discriminate between intense positive and negative emotions. Science 338(6111), 1225–1229 (2012)

Cheng, J., Zhou, W., Lei, X., Adamo, N., Benes, B.: The effects of body gestures and gender on viewer's perception of animated pedagogical agent's emotions. In: Kurosu, M. (ed.) Human-Computer Interaction. Multimodal and Natural Interaction. LNCS, vol. 12182, pp. 169–186. Springer, Cham (2020). https://doi.org/10.1007/978-3-030-49062-1_11

Karg, M., Samadani, A. -A., Gorbet, R., Kühnlenz, K., Hoey Kulić, D.: Body movements for affective expression: a survey of automatic recognition and generation. IEEE Trans. Affect. Comput. 4(4), 341–359 (2013). https://doi.org/10.1109/T-AFFC.2013.29

Gunes, H., Shan, C., Chen, S., Tian, Y.: Bodily expression for automatic affectrecognition. In: Emotion Recognition, pp. 343–377. Wiley (2015)

SimonThomas, E.R., Keltner, D.J., Sauter, D., SinicropiYao, L., Abramson, A.: The voice conveys specific emotions: evidence from vocal burst displays. Emotion 9, 838–846 (2009). https://doi.org/10.1037/a0017810

Zaki, J., Bolger, N., Ochsner, K.: Unpacking the informational bases of empathic accuracy. Emotion 9, 478–487 (2009). https://doi.org/10.1037/a0016551

Gesn, P.R., Ickes, W.: The development of meaning contexts for empathic accuracy: channel and sequence effects. J. Pers. Soc. Psychol. 77, 746–761 (1999). https://doi.org/10.1037/0022-3514.77.4.746

Williams, R.: The Animator's Survival Kit: A Manual of Methods, Principles and Formulas for Classical, Computer, Games, Stop Motion and Internet Animators. Farrar, Straus and Giroux. 4th Edn. (2012)

Expected Human Performance Behavior in Chess Using Centipawn Loss Analysis

Rafael V. Leite[1] and Anderson V. C. de Oliveira[2]($^{(\boxtimes)}$) (iD)

[1] Academia Xadrez Brasil, São Paulo , Brazil
rafaelvleite@xadrezbrasil.com.br
[2] Sidia Instituto de Ciência e Tecnologia - Sidia Amazon Innovation - SW Solutions
Av. Torquato Tapajós, 6770 Novo Israel, 69039-125 Manaus, Brazil
anderson.oliveira@sidia.com
http://www.xadrezbrasil.com.br, http://www.sidia.com

Abstract. In this work, we establish a ratio between a range of Elo ratings of chess players and their ability to find the best moves according to the chess engine. To do this, we collect over 7,800 games in the classical modality of ten grandmasters, from when these players had Elo rating about 2200 until they reached about 2700. We compare each move of all these games with the best move suggested by the chess engine in order to determine the expected human performance in chess according to the player rating. We found values for two metrics: average centipawn loss (AVCPL) and standard deviation centipawn loss (STDCPL) with more than 0.98% correlation with the Elo rating. Experimental results with other chess players not used to build the model show that the behavior of these metrics follows the expected behavior. The established model can be used as an auxiliary tool to help detect cheating in the game.

Keywords: chess · centipawn · AVCPL · STDCPL · cheat detection

1 Introduction

Chess is one of the most ancient and popular strategy games in the world. After only four moves of both players, there are almost 1 billion options to consider [6]. The huge number of possibilities requires many studies to become a strong player. Together with other activities such as math and music, chess is one of the few modalities able to identify a prodigious genius. As a strategy game to find the best moves, computers can solve chess problems very well and determine the best move from a position. Since IBM supercomputer Deep Blue defeated the then-world chess champion Garry Kasparov in 1997, computers ushered in a new era of chess engines where humans were no longer able to win a machine. This was confirmed in 2006 when Deep Fritz defeated the then-world champion Vladimir Kramnik. Nowadays, any mobile chess engine is able to beat a human chess grandmaster easily. Therefore, the use of chess engine leads to many cases of cheating in the game.

Supported by Sidia Instituto de Ciência e Tecnologia.

In online competitions, once the players are at home, a cheater can reproduce the moves of his game on another computer or browser tab and play the moves suggested by the engine. The biggest chess site in the world chess.com has very efficient cheat detection systems by using technical features such as screen changes during the game, time usage on critical moves and others. They closed over 550,000 accounts until 2020, including professional chess players [4].

In face-to-face tournaments, cheating can occur in other ways. For example, a player can obtain the strategies, openings and variations planned by his opponent from a member of his staff before the game. Other types of cheating are similar to cheating in school tests: the player asks to go to the toilet, and there he sets the game setup on the mobile and see the engine suggestion. In July 2019, the 58-year-old grandmaster Igors Rausis was caught cheating on the toilet during tournament [2]. The player was banned from chess official tournaments for six-year and his GM title was stripped. Steps to prevent these types of cheating include metal detection before the games and delay in game broadcasting.

However, although it is well known that a computer plays chess differently than a human [8], in face-to-face games the detection of cheating is very difficult to be detected and proved. In this work, we use the concept of it centipawn loss (a metric used by chess engines) to determine the level of good moves that a player can perform during a game. So we start with two assumptions. First, as the player gets stronger in the game, his average centipawn loss tends to decrease. Second, as the player gets stronger, the variance of each move in a game relative to the average centipawn loss in all the games also tends to decrease. And these quantities are strongly related to the Elo rating. Therefore, we can find a well-defined ratio between these quantities and the Elo rating. The results can be used to determine with high confidence a player's strength and also aid in cheat detection.

In Sect. 2, we define the concept of centipawn loss, used to design the model, which is presented in Sect. 3. We present experimental results to validate the model in Sect. 4 and show the conclusions of this work in Sect. 5.

2 Centipawn Loss Metric

Before computers played chess, evaluating a chess position was a very complex task. Of course, a strong player knows if his position at a given moment in the game is better or worse than his opponent, but it is not possible for a human to quantify how much a position is better or worse.

In chess, it is common to associate a value to each of the pieces, such that the value depends on its ability to move around on the board. These values are shown in Fig. 1. Therefore, the *Queen* is the strongest piece on the board with 9 points, followed by *Rook* which has 5 points, *knight* and *Bishop* with 3 and *Pawn* with 1. It is not defined a value for the *King*, as it cannot be captured.

Also, it is common to associate a piece with a combination of other pieces according to the values shown in Fig. 1. For example, after a sequence of captures, a player can exchange a knight for three opponent's pawns, or a rook and a pawn

Pawn = 1 point

Bishop = 3 points

Knight = 3 points

Rook = 5 points

Queen = 9 points

Fig. 1. Chess pieces values.

by a knight and a bishop. Although these values give an idea about which player has any advantage, the position of each piece on the board is a fundamental issue to determine an advantage. And it is here that chess engines have the best judgment.

Figure 2 a) shows the initial setup of the game. We can see a left bar showing an evaluation of zero for both payers. However, Fig. 2 b) shows an advantage of 3 for back pieces although white pieces have one pawn of advantage. But the position can be interpreted as if the black has three pawns of advantage.

(a) Initial position   (b) Black advantage example

Fig. 2. Engine evaluation.

In Fig. 2, it is black to move, and the engine suggests c5 as the best move for black to keep the advantage of 3. If the player with the black pieces plays c5 then his centipawn loss is zero in that move, and he keeps the advantage of 3. Any other move gives a lower advantage or even an advantage for white pieces. For example, if black plays a move that results in an advantage of 2.5 then his centipawn loss is 50, which means half a pawn. Therefore, a centipawn is the hundredth part of a pawn, and it is used by engines to evaluate the position during the game, and it measures how distant the evaluation of the move a player made in a game is from the suggested computer's best move. Of course, it is very difficult for humans to determine those values, and even different engines provide a different evaluation. Also, it is normal that the very same engine provides different evaluations when it is used with different hardware and setup.

Throughout the game, the centipawn loss is added up, and in the end, we have the average of centipawn loss (AVCPL) for each payer. It is reasonable to think that as a chess player gets better and more professional, the lower will be the AVCPL. Also, it is reasonable to think that amateur players tend to play moves that vary a lot around the AVCPL, with some good moves and then bad moves. But professional players tend to play more consistently because they will hit the best moves more often, so the variance will be lower. Thus, we use the standard deviation centipawn loss (STDCPL) to measure how consistent the moves are.

3   Designing a Model

In chess, a player's strength is measured by his ELO rating. In general, a grand-master (GM) has Elo rating of over 2,500. Some players with Elo rating over 2,700 are unofficially called "super grandmasters". The best chess engine currently (Stockfish 15 [3]) is estimated to have about 3,620. So we use that engine as a reference to get values for centipawn loss. And it is reasonable to think that there is some correlation between Elo rating with AVCPL and STDCPL[1].

In order to build a model, we get almost 8,000 games from ten chess grand-masters that are listed on Table 1. We selected games in the time period when each of these players had the Elo rating growing from about 2200 to about 2700, as indicated in the column "Period". All the games are in the classical modality of chess (long time to think), and they are public games.

Table 1. Chess players selected to build the model.

Player	Age[*]	Games	Period	Elo range
GM Andrey Esipenko	20	870	June 2013 to September 2022	2191 to 2723
GM Vincent Keymer	18	583	April 2015 to September 2022	2235 to 2693
GM Magnus Carlsen	32	899	July 2002 to September 2010	2073 to 2826
GM Fabiano Caruana	30	906	November 2004 to November 2012	2196 to 2786
GM Jan-Krzysztof Duda	24	663	January 2010 to September 2018	2086 to 2739
GM Ian Nepomniachtchi	32	640	September 2001 to March 2011	2243 to 2733
GM Vidit Gujrathi	28	772	October 2006 to February 2018	2192 to 2723
GM Wesley So	29	918	July 2005 to March 2017	2165 to 2822
GM Ding Liren	30	361	November 2004 to October 2013	1978 to 2718
GM Maxime Vachier-Lagrave	23	1200	May 2012 to January 2017	2172 to 2615
	Total Games	7812	*(*) in the end of 2022*	

The games indicated in Table 1 totalize 358,170 moves. Each move was evaluated by Stockfish 15 with depth 20. After this step, we organized the resulting data into seven ranges of Elo rating, from 2200 to 2800, and we got the results shown in Figs. 3 a) and b). As expected, the AVCPL and the STDCPL decrease as the Elo rating increases. Figure 3 a) shows that a chess player with Elo rating of about 2200 tends to have AVCPL around 30 and STDCPL around 55 on average for a lot of games while a 2700 player tends to have AVCPL around 19 and STDCPL around 35. Some of the players selected to build the model have achieved Elo rating of 2800, which provides the lowest values: AVCPL of 16 and STDCPL of 28, as shown in the figure.

---

[1] These results were first disclosed in reference [7].

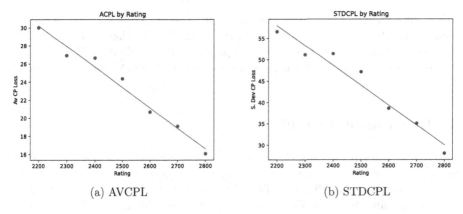

(a) AVCPL   (b) STDCPL

Fig. 3. Expected AVCPL and STDCPL by Elo rating range for a human chess player.

The red lines shown in Figs. 3 a) and b) show a perfect correlation of the obtained points for both AVCPL and STDCPL. The correlation between these two entities with the Elo rating is shown in Table 2, with 99.1134% for AVCPL and 98.0297% for STDCP. Negative signal means that it has inverse relation: the higher the elo rating is, the lower the AVCPL and STDCP are.

Table 2. Correlation matrix between AVCPL, STDCPL and ELO rating.

	ELO Rating	Av CP Loss	Dev. CP Loss
ELO Rating	1.000000	-0.991134	-0.980297
Av CP Loss	-0.991134	1.000000	0.997384
Dev. CP Loss	-0.980297	0.997384	1.000000

The results in Figs. 3 are summarized in Table 3. Note that these values are expected as average for a lot of games, such that some isolated games can provide different values and it does not mean a case of cheat was detected.

Table 3. Model obtained for AVCPL and STDCPL.

Tier	Av. ELO	Av CP Loss	Dev. CP Loss	Games
2200	2256.13	30.09	56.68	384
2300	2353.01	27.37	51.59	491
2400	2451.75	26.70	51.39	1014
2500	2549.52	24.06	46.18	1727
2600	2653.61	20.73	38.95	2355
2700	2738.03	19.03	34.93	2183
2800	2824.13	16.00	27.94	215

Note that the total games in the Tables 1 and 3 are different due to the following: when a player in Table 1 plays a game against a not selected player, it is counted as one game (only the moves of the selected player will be considered). But when two selected players play against each other, it is counted as two games because the moves from both players will be evaluated. Then the sum of the games in Table 3 is greater than the number of "PGN" files, indicated in Table 1.

4 Experimental Results

In order to validate the model set out in Sect. 3, we selected other games from another chess grandmasters that are not present in the dataset of Table 1, and we searched for their AVCPL and STDCP to compare with those found at Fig. 3. The results are shown in Figs. from 4 to 10, also indicating information on number of games, period, rating range and correlation.

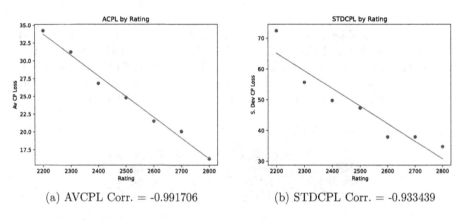

(a) AVCPL Corr. = -0.991706   (b) STDCPL Corr. = -0.933439

Fig. 4. GM Alireza Firouzja (19 years old): 622 games from November 2014 to September 2022. Elo rating ranging from 2277 to 2804.

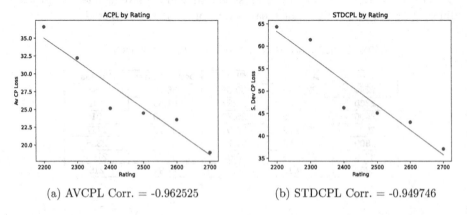

(a) AVCPL Corr. = -0.962525   (b) STDCPL Corr. = -0.949746

Fig. 5. GM Daniil Dubov (26 years old): 584 games from August 2008 to March 2018. Elo rating ranging from 2125 to 2701.

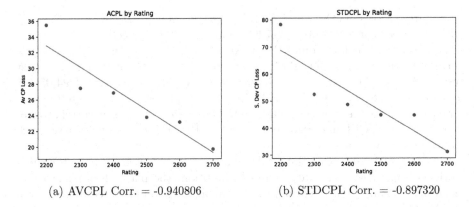

(a) AVCPL Corr. = -0.940806   (b) STDCPL Corr. = -0.897320

Fig. 6. GM Dommaraju Gukesh (16 years old): 702 games from December 2016 to September 2022. Elo rating ranging from 2236 to 2726.

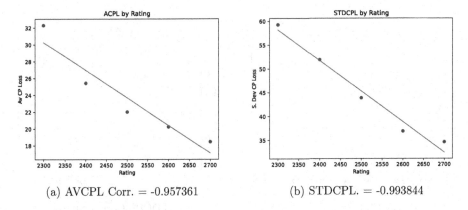

(a) AVCPL Corr. = -0.957361   (b) STDCPL. = -0.993844

Fig. 7. GM Anish Giri (28 years old): 718 games from October 2006 to May 2014. Elo rating ranging from 2155 to 2749.

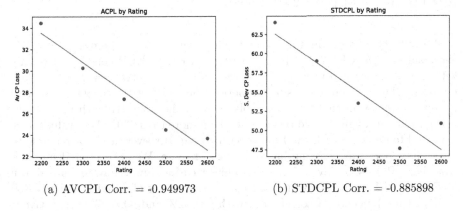

(a) AVCPL Corr. = -0.949973   (b) STDCPL Corr. = -0.885898

Fig. 8. GM Hans Niemann (19 years old): 697 games from October 2014 to September 2022. Elo rating ranging from 1867 to 2688.

Figure 4 shows AVCPL and STDCP for the young GM Alireza Firouzja with a perfect correlation of 99.1706% and 93.3439% respectively, and points in accordance with those found Fig. 3. Also, results for GM Daniil Dubov show correlation of 96.2525% for AVCPL and 94.9746% for STDCP. The youngest tested player, GM Dommaraju Gukesh, has AVCPL correlation of 94.0806% and STDCP of 89.7320%. GM Anish Giri has also presented an expected behavior according to the defined model. GM Hans Niemann has a correlation of 94.9973% for AVCPL and 88.5898% for STDCP, which does not differ so much from the expected values.

In September 2022, GM Hans Niemann was accused of cheating by the then-world champion Magnus Carlsen [5]. In addition, the player has a history of cheating in online games, reaching up to having his account closed in chess.com [1]. As the cheat accusations against GM Hans Niemann began in 2018, we have made a study in his games from this period until September 2022. The results are presented in Fig. 9

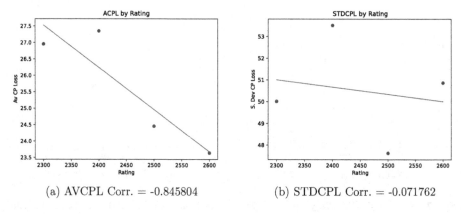

(a) AVCPL Corr. = -0.845804   (b) STDCPL Corr. = -0.071762

Fig. 9. GM Hans Niemann (19 years old): 511 games from January 2018 to September 2022. Elo rating ranging from 2302 to 2688.

We can clearly see in Figs. 9 that when we select his games from 2018, the results for AVCPL and STDCP decrease a lot. STDCP correlation is only 7.1762% as shown in Fig. 9 b). These results were not observed in other players even when we limited a smaller period, but with a significant number of games. It can mean that we have a player with the same strength throughout this period, although the Elo rating has grown more than 200. These values were expected to decrease with the Elo rating increase. However, it is not possible to state that there was cheating based on these results. We also selected matches from Igors Rausis, a player that was caught cheating, and the results are shown in Fig. 10. Although he is a proven cheater, the results of AVCPL and STDCP show normal behavior of correlation, with 90.232% and 99.8086% respectively. Even so, a strange fact to observe is the value of about 17 for AVCPL for Elo rating of 2600 in Fig. 10 a) when top GMs with Elo ranging of 2800 get 16 and the ones with 2700 get 19. Likewise, Rausis shows STDCP of 31 for Elo rating 2600 when is expected 34 for Elo rating of 2700, according to Table 3.

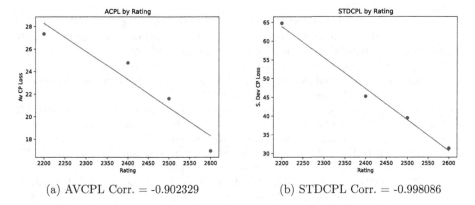

(a) AVCPL Corr. = -0.902329   (b) STDCPL Corr. = -0.998086

Fig. 10. IM Igors Rausis (61 years old): 707 games from February 2008 to May 2019. Elo rating ranging from 2215 to 2657.

5   Conclusions

Cheat detection in chess games is a complex task. We have successfully found expected values for average centipawn loss (AVCPL) and standard deviation centipawn loss (STDPL). The built model is consistent with the Elo rating range and it is shown to be proven for many players tested. Of course, it does not mean that every time a 2600 player plays he will get an AVCPL of 20 and an STDPL of 39, but in a set of games it will be the expected behavior. The study means that only having a precision of a certain level that a player gets to achieve a certain Elo rating range. The model is limited to this, it cannot go beyond. So, it is not possible to use it to state if a player is a cheater or not, but it can be used together with other tools to collect evidence since the numbers cannot be so much different from that.

In a face-to-face game, a cheater that also is a strong player needs only two move tips in critical moments to win the game, and it is impossible to be detected by any statistical model. Igors Rausis games show points with a strong correlation but AVCPL and STDCP are lower than expected for his Elo rating. Hans Niemann games provide uncorrelated points to STDCP for the controversial period of cheating accusations, but even if there was cheating, it is not possible to determine with certainty in which games they happened. The proof of expected behavior exists but it is possible that there are outlier players with AVCPL and STDCP below the expected and also players with high AVCPL and STDCP but get Elo rating increase.

Furthermore, the designed model for expected human performance in chess also can be used for other purposes such as for a coach to assess the level of evolution of students, assemble a team for a tournament, measure the strength of ancient players and others.

References

1. Doggers, P.: Niemann has likely cheated in more than 100 online chess games. Accessed 6 Oct 2022
2. Dorn, S.: Chess grandmaster allegedly caught cheating on toilet during tournament, https://nypost.com/2019/07/13/chess-grandmaster-allegedly-caught-cheating-on-toilet-during-tournament/. Accessed 7 Feb 2022
3. Engine, O.S.C.: https://stockfishchess.org/. Accessed 21 Sep 2022
4. International, C.: About online chess cheating. https://www.chess.com/article/view/online-chess-cheating. Accessed 7 Dec 2023
5. Keener, G.: Magnus carlsen accuses hans niemann of cheating. Accessed 3 Oct 2022
6. Labelle, F.: Chess problems by computer - Statistics on chess positions, http://wismuth.com/chess/statistics-positions.html. Accessed 17 Jan 2023
7. Leite, R.V.: How I found perfect correlation between chess player rating and ACPL and STDCPL. https://bit.ly/3CWO2j6, Accessed 03 Oct 2022
8. Levy, D., Newborn, M.: How Computers Play Chess, pp. 24–39. Springer, Heidelberg (1982). https://doi.org/10.1007/978-3-642-85538-2_2

Prediction of Quality of Experience (QoE) of Cloud-Gaming Through an Approach to Extracting the Indicators from User Generated Content (UGC)

Siqi Li[1] , Tao Wen[2] (✉), Hongyan Yan[2], and Xiangang Qin[1]

[1] Beijing University of Posts and Telecommunications, Beijing 100876, China
qinxiangang@aliyun.com
[2] Department of User and Market, China Mobile Research Institute, Beijing 100053, China
wentao@chinamobile.com

Abstract. The existing approaches (e.g., questionnaire survey, interview survey) to investigating the factors causing positive and negative quality of experience (QoE) in cloud gaming rely mainly on user responses to a pre-designed questionnaire generated by researchers or guided to some extent by researchers. Despite its merits, this traditional approach costs time and money and also has the problem of low ecological validity. However, user-generated content created voluntarily by users on the internet has the advantages of high ecological validity and easy data collection, and the sample size can be much larger at low loss. This study proposes an approach to predicting the quality of experience of cloud gaming (CGQoE) by using user-generated content (UGC). 14 feature words related to QoE extracted from UGC texts can, to some extent, characterize the emotional information in UGC. The result shows that this approach has some use for analyzing the factors that affect the CGQoE and predicting its QoE. It also leaves room for future studies to compare its validity and reliability to other ways of measuring the QoE of cloud gaming.

Keywords: Cloud gaming · Quality of Experience (QoE) · User generated content (UGC)

1 Introduction

The development and pervasiveness of 5G networks have reduced the obstacles in terms of bandwidth and network latency for cloud-based mobile services. Cloud gaming technology can theoretically provide users with a high-quality gaming experience on any terminal [1]. In the context of cloud gaming, the QoE is affected by the interaction of many man-machine-environment factors, such as the personal characteristics of game players, the quality of the telecommunications network, game terminals, and the environment. It is a challenge to deploy network and computing power according to the dynamic network environment where cloud gaming players are located to provide reliable and stable QoE [2]. Reliable measurement is the premise for evaluating the CGQoE

© The Author(s), under exclusive license to Springer Nature Switzerland AG 2023
X. Fang (Ed.): HCII 2023, LNCS 14047, pp. 253–262, 2023.
https://doi.org/10.1007/978-3-031-35979-8_20

[3]. Therefore, a lot of efforts have been made to evaluate and improve the CGQoE in recent decades.

The evaluation approaches of CGQoE can be divided into two types: with and without intervention, depending on whether the evaluators interfere with the user's evaluation. The intervention approach is the current mainstream CGQoE evaluation approach. For example, the data obtained by the commonly used QoE evaluation approaches such as the experiment survey, questionnaire survey, and interview survey are to a certain extent framed by the evaluation questionnaires and dimensions set by the evaluators before the evaluation [4, 5], which affects the ecological validity of the evaluation data. Among the intervention approaches, the subjective questionnaire survey combined with experimental tasks is a commonly used game QoE evaluation approach. For example, in the subjective evaluation approaches for game quality recommended by ITU-T P.809 [6], 33 questions are used to evaluate the game experience. The structural quantitative approach represented by the questionnaire measurement approach has the advantage that it cannot only understand the overall experience level of the product but also obtain the components of the overall experience level, as well as the weight of these components and the degree of correlation among them. That is, it provides high-quality data for further statistical analysis due to its high reliability and validity. However, the questionnaire survey approach also has problems such as high implementation costs, high financial costs (user compensation), low ecological validity, high sampling error, etc. In most cases, the sample size obtained in one survey is way smaller than that obtained through big data. Subsequently, it needs to rely on complex inferential statistical approaches to answer questions such as the relationship between different measurement dimensions and the difference in QoE of different products [7].

In recent years, with the emergence of mobile application stores in the specific field of cloud gaming and the open-resource evaluation platforms of operators (such as MiguPlay, NetEase cloud gaming, etc.), users of cloud gaming have generated a large amount of user-generated content (UGC) without or with little interference from cloud gaming evaluators. The text in the comments contains rich emotional information, which reflects the QoE of the product or service to a certain extent. As a result, researchers have done a lot of valuable research on how UGC is used to analyze the experience of products and services. Some studies draw on the concept of the psychometrics measurement to establish a structured evaluation indicators system and model by analyzing the emotional dimension of UGC, thereby providing the possibility of exploring a QoE evaluation approach that is non-intervention, structured, low-cost, has high ecological validity, and can even replace or supplement the traditional questionnaire survey approach.

To achieve the goal of extracting indicators from UGC containing abundant emotional information and predicting the CGQoE, this study, explores the approach of structured and quantitative evaluation of CGQoE using the emotional information in UGC text and analyzes the reliability and validity of the approach. The main technical routes are as follows:

1. Use CountVectorizer and transfer.fit_transform in sklearn.feature_extraction.text in Python to extract feature words and statistics frequency, and vectorize each comment text using the feature words and frequencies.
2. Select feature words related to QoE based on the expertise of CGQoE;

3. Using the approach of Emotion Distribution Learning (EDL), map the emotion information contained in the cloud gaming-related text UGC into the emotion distribution represented by multiple emotion feature words to form structured and quantitative QoE evaluation data composed of S (number of UGC texts) * Di (number of feature words).
4. Analyze the reliability and validity of structured and quantitative data and analyze the possibility and problems of replacing the traditional questionnaire survey approach.

The contributions of this paper include:

5. Using the emotional information in the UGC texts of cloud gaming and the existing expertise in the field of CGQoE to create an exclusive emotional dictionary of CGQoE and extract the indicators for evaluating the QoE of cloud gaming.
6. Using the CGQoE dictionary to map the UGC texts in the cloud gaming into the emotion distribution, structured quantitative measurement data of cloud gaming QoE can be obtained without relying on a sampling survey.
7. Based on the results of the reliability and validity analysis, the value and problems to be solved in the structured and quantitative measurement of CGQoE using UGC text are discussed.

2 Related Work

2.1 Structured and Quantitative QoE Evaluation Approach Based on Questionnaires

A questionnaire survey is a common and established way of assessing the CGQoE. The typical questionnaire survey approach employs sampling surveys, which allow users of a specified sample size to score the quality of their experiences with products or services using a pre-designed questionnaire or scale containing several items. To ensure quality, a questionnaire survey typically adopts the idea of psychometric measurement to assess the reliability and validity of many QoE-related items.

For instance, the Mean Opinion Score (MOS) is one of the most often used surveys for evaluating QoE. It consists of seven items: (1) Global Impression; (2) Listening Effort; (3) Comprehension Problems; (4) Speech Sound Articulation; (5) Pronunciation; (6) Speaking Rate; (7) Voice Pleasantness. Six of the seven items can be described by two MOS factors: intelligibility of voice communication (items 2–5) and naturalness (items 1–7), however, item 6 is unrelated to the two principal components. Due to its high reliability and validity, MOS has been frequently used to measure the QoE of different service types, despite being created to assess the QoE of voice services.

The measurement approaches and tools in the field of CGQoE also adopt the idea of psychometrics measurement to ensure validity and reliability. For example, the 19 measurement items of the Game Engagement Questionnaire (GEngQ) constitute 4 factors (immersion, presence, flow, and Tension) [8], and the 21 items of the Player Experience of Need Satisfaction (PENS) constitute 5 factors such as competitiveness, autonomy, presence, relevance, and intuitive control.

Internal consistency reliability (alpha) and split-half reliability can be used to evaluate the reliability of measurement items. Internal consistency reliability reflects whether numerous feature words can be explained by a single hidden QoE. Internal consistency is also an important premise for testing the construct validity of emotional labeling. The split-half reliability indicates the correlation between all feature words that represent the emotional distribution of CGQoE. It is difficult to measure the CGQoE as a whole because of the low correlation between these feature words and their emotional content.

Exploratory Factor Analysis (EFA) can be used to evaluate the construct validity of measurement items. Whether the feature words are suitable for EFA needs to be tested by Kaiser-Meyer-Olkin (KMO) and Bartlett's test of Sphericity. KMO reflects the extent to which each item may be predicted by other items in the topic set. It is believed that EFA can be utilized to investigate the structural relationship between feature keywords only when KMO is more than 0.5, and 0.8 is optimum [9]. The spherical test is also used to determine whether the correlation between items satisfies the requirements of EFA. The basis for the judgment is the difference between the correlation matrix made of items and the identity matrix composed of items with zero correlation. If the result is smaller than the selected significance level (such as 0.05 or 0.1), the correlation between items is deemed to satisfy the standards of EFA.

2.2 Emotion Distribution Learning Approach Based on an Emotion Dictionary

The purpose of this study is to obtain indicators from UGC texts, use those indicators to predict the CGQoE, and test whether the CGQoE can be measured in structure and quantity based on sparse and unstructured UGC texts.

Inspired by the concept of a questionnaire survey approach with psychometric measurement, each feature word is capable of being mapped to a single item or scale of the questionnaire. To achieve the purpose of this study, it is crucial to extract several feature words from UGC and then utilize them to structurally evaluate the QoE included in each UGC text.

In the traditional single-label text emotion distribution approach, each piece of text information can only be represented by a single emotion tag [10], which cannot meet the purpose of assessing the CGQoE through multiple structured items in this study. The Emotion Distribution Learning (EDL) approach can map UGC text in the form of one or more sentences or paragraphs to a distribution of multiple emotion tags or feature words. In this work, the EDL approach was chosen to characterize the CGQoE in UGC.

In addition to the necessity to characterize the emotional distribution of UGC, this study investigated the data structure of multiple feature keywords utilized to characterize UGC. However, the approach of emotional distribution representation by neural networks is a black box in the process of determining the relationship between emotional feature words; therefore, it cannot satisfy the requirements of this study.

Some studies have shown that the emotional information in a sentence can be characterized by the emotional words contained therein [11], which provides the possibility of label emotion distribution based on the emotional feature words. The idea is to map the text's emotional information into a vector space characterized by several emotional feature words, with each distribution labeling also containing information about emotional intensity. Some scholars have found that the EDL approach based on six emotion feature words (joy, fear, anger, surprise, happiness, and disgust) is superior to other approaches in the prediction performance of emotion and the prediction effect of single emotion feature words in the Sem Val training set [12]. Other scholars introduced the idea of an emotion wheel to strengthen the emotion distribution marking since the separate emotion lexicon does not consider the relevance between emotion words. The results show that the performance of this approach in an emotion recognition task on seven Chinese and English text emotion datasets is better than that of other emotion distribution marking approaches [10].

3 Method for EDL

The goal of EDL in this study is to use the feature words related to CGQoE in UGC text to evaluate the CGQoE quantitatively with structural validity and reliability. To reach the goal, it is important to find a way to map the information about emotions in the UGC texts to the distribution of emotions shown by several emotional feature words [10].

$$d_i = \{d_i^j\}_{j-1}^C \tag{1}$$

d_i^j refers to the extent to which that text t_i in UGC can be represented by the emotional feature word j. This study examines two approaches of EDL: 1) Based on the frequency of feature words in UGC texts; 2) Based on the semantic similarity between feature words and UGC texts.

The EDL approaches proposed in this study include the following steps:

1. Use jieba.cut in Python to cut UGC text in Chinese and extract feature words.
2. Use the CountVectorizer in sklearn.feature_extraction.text counts the frequency of feature words after word segmentation
3. Use transfer fit_ Transform converts each text into a vector represented by a plurality of feature words (the number is 2 or more to meet the requirements of structural degree)
4. Based on the expertise of CGQoE, simplify the feature word base to make a word base that only contains QoE-related feature words
5. Use the sentiments in snowNLP to rate the emotion of each comment text
6. Use the sentiments in snowNLP to rate the emotion of each feature word extracted from the UGC
7. Characterization of emotion distribution:
   – When the frequency approach is used, d_i^j is represented by the product of the frequency of the feature word j appearing in the text t_i and the emotion score of the feature word j, and finally all d_i^j forms an emotion distribution d_f of frequency approach.
   – In the similarity approach, use the similarity in simtext to calculate the semantic similarity between the feature word j and the UGC text s_f, that is, use the sentiments in snowNLP to rate the emotion of each comment text. s_i^j is represented by the product of the semantic similarity between the feature word j and the text t_i, and finally, all s_i^j form an emotion distribution d_s of frequency approach. The results of two EDL approaches are tested in the experimental part.

4 Experiment

4.1 Dataset

Due to the lack of an available dataset in the field of cloud gaming UGC text, the first part of this study is to establish a dataset:

1. In the first step, 23147 text comments and corresponding Likert 5-point quantitative scores of the four cloud gaming platforms were collected. The Likert 5-point quantitative scores given by the user are also collected as the criterion for evaluating the reliability of the emotion analysis results.
2. The second step, the dataset was cleaned by removing the content with non-Chinese characters, fewer than 5 Chinese characters, and inconsistent emotion classification (by snowNLP) with the quantitative score.

Finally, the dataset contains UGC text of 803 cloud gaming users. The correlation between the text emotion score based on snowNLP and the user's quantitative score is increased from 0.61 to 0.93, indicating that the distribution characteristics of the text emotion information in the text dataset fully reflect the user's score.

4.2 Extraction of Feature Words Based on the UGC Dataset

First, the Jieba.cut tool was used to segment the UGC text and generate 1944 feature words. Based on the expertise of CGQoE, the feature words unrelated to CGQoE are removed, and a dictionary of CGQoE including 60 feature words is formed. Among them, 24 were positive and 36 were negative (based on the emotion score). (Table 1).

4.3 Text EDL Approaches

In the frequency approach, the EDL score of each UGC on each feature word is calculated by the emotion score of the feature word. Before weighting with frequency data, the average snowNLP emotion score of all texts was 0.59, and the average emotion score of 60 feature words was 0.49. After recalculating each word in the QoE dictionary based on the occurrence frequency of the feature word and the emotion score of the feature word itself, the average emotion score of the 60 feature words is 0.60, which is very close to the average emotion score of all UGC and higher than the result of using only the original emotion information of the 60 feature words. Therefore, the final EDL is the product of the frequency of the feature word and the emotion score of the feature word itself.

In the similarity approach, calculate the sematic similarity between each feature word and the comment text based on the package of similarity in the simtext, so that the EDL score of each comment text can be labeled by the product of the sematic similarity with 60 feature words and the emotion score of comment text. After that, the overall correlation was 0.60. The results of the frequency approach and the text similarity approach for labeling the emotional distribution are generally highly correlated with the emotion score of the UGC comment text as a group.

Table 1. The dictionary of CGQoE

Negative feature words				Positive feature words	
Word	Score	Word	Score	Word	Score
会卡顿 (will freeze)	0.47	卡爆 (stuck explode)	0.09	流畅 (fluent)	0.94
迟钝 (retarded)	0.43	花屏 (blurred screen)	0.08	能流畅(be fluent)	0.94
变慢 (become slow)	0.43	网差 (poor network)	0.08	不卡 (not stuck))	0.91
模糊 (vague)	0.40	卡差评 (bad review about stuck)	0.03	不卡顿 (no stuck)	0.90
模糊不清 (unclear)	0.36	很糊 (very confused)	0.30	很快 (soon)	0.88
断开(disconnection)	0.35	好糊 (so pasty)	0.30	挺快 (quite fast)	0.87
崩溃 (collapse)	0.31	迷糊 (confused)	0.38	精致 (refined)	0.85
延时 (time delay)	0.30	挺糊 (quite vague)	0.30	网不卡 (network isn't stuck)	0.84
不动 (no movement)	0.30	看不清 (can't see clearly)	038	畅快 (unblocked)	0.83
卡得 (stuck to)	0.30	会断(will disconnect)	0.35	断断续(intermittent)	0.81
清晰度 (clarity)	0.28	卡屏(freeze)	0.25	顺畅 (smooth)	0.81
网卡 (stuck network)	0.27	卡顿 (stopped)	0.47	清晰 (clarity)	0.80
白屏 (white screen)	0.25			轻快 (clipping)	0.80
卡成 (stuck into)	0.22			高清 (hd)	0.75
退出 (quit)	0.22			精美 (exquisite)	0.75
延迟 (delay)	0.21			清晰可见 (clear and distinct)	0.75
太慢 (very slow)	0.21			通畅 (unobstructed)	0.75
卡住 (it is stuck)	0.20			连续 (continuous)	0.74
卡无语 (stuck speechless)	0.18			好快 (so fast)	0.67
好慢 (so slow)	0.18			掉线(disconnected)	0.55
卡死 (stuck)	0.15			清楚(clear)	0.53
闪退 (flashback)	0.13			网好(good network)	0.50
马赛克 (mosaic)	0.13			飞快(fast)	0.81
断开(disconnection)	0.11			没断(not broken)	0.84

5 Results

5.1 Reliability and Validity

The results of reliability analysis (alpha and split half in Table 2) show that the EDL results of both approaches using 60 QoE feature words are relatively inconsistent and thus not reliable as measurements of the CGQoE. Neither KMO nor sphericity meet the standard of factor analysis, which indicates that the EDL results using 60 QoE feature words are not valid as measurements of the CGQoE.

To improve the reliability and validity of EDL, based on the hypothesis that some feature words cannot explain the variance of emotional information in UGC texts, the 60 QoE feature words are reduced using regression analysis. The results show that neither the reliability nor the KMO of the EDL results meet the requirements of a high-quality questionnaire survey. However, sphericity is smaller than .01 and indicates that the remained feature words in both approaches have correlations and can to some extent be structured into a valid psychometric scale.

Finally, the feature words are cleaned again by deleting the ones without significant correlation with any other ones. Although the low values of alpha and split half indicate that the EDL results based on the remaining feature words are not reliable enough, KMO and sphericity are improved and meet the threshold for conducting factor analysis.

Table 2. The reliability analysis of EDL approaches

	Similarity approach			Frequency approach		
	All	Regression	Manual reduction	All	Regression	Manual reduction
Feature Words	60	20	11	60	22	12
Variance Explained[a]	49.3	49.3	37.9	48.1	48.1	36.2
Alpha	0.29	0.064	0.106	0.22	0.157	0.17
Split-half	0.285	0.279	0.259	0.22	0.027	0.259
KMO	NA	0.41	0.51	NA	0.44	0.52
Bartley	NA	< .01	< .01	NA	< .01	< .01
No. of factors	15	10	5	41	13	5
Variance Explained[b]	41.2	62.1	54	80.1	68.6	59.5

5.2 Structure of EDL

According to the factor analysis results (Table 3 and Table 4), both the final feature words used to label emotion distribution in the two EDL approaches can be explained by five potential factors, with eigen value greater than 1 as the criterion for the number of extracted factors. However, some feature words with similar semantics are explained by different latent factors. For instance, "卡顿" (stuttering), "卡住" and "卡死" have similar semantics but are explained by different factors in the similarity approach. Besides, the extracted latent factors explained a larger variance of the feature words in the frequency approach (54% versus 59.5%). Consequently, the frequency approach provides more valid data for structuring and quantifying the feature words.

Table 3. The structure of feature words in Factor Analysis based on similarity approach

Factors	Feature words in Chinese	1	2	3	4	5
卡顿/清晰度 (Stuck/Clarity)	不动	.96				
	清晰度	.96				
延迟 (Latency)	延迟		.68			
	卡成		.61			
	卡死		.55			
流畅性/退出 (Fluency/drop-out)	闪退			.75		
	流畅			.71		
卡顿 (Stuttering)	卡顿				.67	
	卡住				.66	
画面质量 (Interface Quality)	清晰					.70
	精美					.64

Table 4. The structure of feature words in Factor Analysis based on frequency approach

Factors	Feature words	1	2	3	4	5
流畅性 (Fluency)	流畅	.83				
	挺快	.66				
连续性 (Continuity)	不动		.79			
	断断续续		.75			
	没断		.69			
退出 (Drop-out)	闪退			.770		
	卡死			.591		
速度 (Speed)	太慢				.786	
	延迟				.614	
画面质量 (Interface quality)	清楚					.814
	精美					-.578

6 Discussion and Future Work

This study proposes two EDL approach to predict the CGQoE based on UGC texts and quantitative scores in the cloud gaming platform. The research results show that the feature words related to QoE extracted from UGC texts can, to some extent, represent the emotional information in UGC texts. It indicates that the EDL method proposed in this study has the potential to supplement or replace the traditional questionnaire survey method while maintaining a certain level of validity. However, the method proposed in this study has low internal consistency and split-half reliability among different feature words. This study leaves room for subsequent studies to explore methods for improving the reliability of EDL by cleaning UGC texts with a higher frequency and higher distribution density of feature words among all UGC texts.

Acknowledgements. This paper is funded by Beijing University of Posts and Telecommunications-China Mobile Research Institute Joint Innovation Center.

References

1. Slivar, I., Skorin-Kapov, L., Suznjevic, M.: Cloud gaming QoE models for deriving video encoding adaptation strategies. In: Proceedings of the 7th International Conference on Multimedia Systems, New York, NY, USA, May 2016, pp. 1–12 (2016). https://doi.org/10.1145/2910017.2910602
2. Abar, T., Ben Letaifa, A., El Asmi, S.: Chapter five - user behavior-ensemble learning based improving QoE fairness in HTTP adaptive streaming over SDN approach. In: Hurson, A.R. (Ed.) Advances in Computers, vol. 123, pp. 245–269. Elsevier (2021). https://doi.org/10.1016/bs.adcom.2021.01.004
3. Krasula, L., Le Callet, P.: Chapter 4 - Emerging science of QoE in multimedia applications: concepts, experimental guidelines, and validation of models. In: Chellappa, R., Theodoridis, S. (Eds.) Academic Press Library in Signal Processing, vol. 6, pp. 163–209. Academic Press (2018). https://doi.org/10.1016/B978-0-12-811889-4.00004-X
4. Aciar, S., Aciar, G.: Analyzing user experience through web opinion mining. In: Meiselwitz, G. (ed.) Social Computing and Social Media. Applications and Analytics. LNCS, vol. 10283, pp. 203–214. Springer, Cham (2017). https://doi.org/10.1007/978-3-319-58562-8_16
5. Olson, J.S., Kellogg, W.A. (eds.): Ways of Knowing in HCI. Springer, New York (2014). https://doi.org/10.1007/978-1-4939-0378-8
6. "ITU-T. 2018. P.809: Subjective evaluation methods for gaming quality. Recommendation ITU-T P.809. https://www.itu.int/ITU-T/recommendations/rec.aspx?rec=13626&lang=en. Accessed 02 Feb 2023
7. Lin, C., Hu, J., Kong, X.: Survey on models and evaluation of quality of experience: survey on models and evaluation of quality of experience. Chinese J. Comput. **35**(1), 1–15 (2012). https://doi.org/10.3724/SP.J.1016.2012.00001
8. Brockmyer, J.H., Fox, C.M., Curtiss, K.A., McBroom, E., Burkhart, K.M., Pidruzny, J.N.: The development of the game engagement questionnaire: a measure of engagement in video game-playing. J. Exp. Soc. Psychol. **45**(4), 624–634 (2009). https://doi.org/10.1016/j.jesp.2009.02.016
9. Kaiser, H.F., Rice, J.: Little Jiffy, Mark Iv. Educ. Psychol. Measur. **34**(1), 111–117 (1974). https://doi.org/10.1177/001316447403400115
10. Zeng, X., Hua, X., Liu, P., Zuo, J., Wang, M.: Emotion Wheel and Lexicon based emotion distribution Label Enhancemen (in Chinese). Chinese J. Comput. **44**(06), 1080–1094 (2021)
11. Teng, Z., Vo, D.-T., Zhang, Y.: Context-sensitive lexicon features for neural sentiment analysis. In: Proceedings of the 2016 Conference on Empirical Methods in Natural Language Processing, Austin, Texas, pp. 1629–1638, November 2016. https://doi.org/10.18653/v1/D16-1169
12. Zhang, J. Fu, Y., She, D., Zhang, Y., Wang, S., Yang J.: Text emotion distribution learning via multi-task convolutional neural network. In: Proceedings of the Twenty-Seventh International Joint Conference on Artificial Intelligence, Stockholm, Sweden, July 2018, pp. 4595–4601 (2018). https://doi.org/10.24963/ijcai.2018/639

Fiat Lux! Does the Lighting Design Affect Viewers' Perception of an Animated Character Personality?

Abdelrahman Mehrez⦿, Nicoletta Adamo$^{(\boxtimes)}$ ⦿, Nandhini Giri⦿, and Derek Larson⦿

Purdue University, West Lafayette, IN 47907, USA
{amehrez,nadamovi,girin,dglarson}@purdue.edu

Abstract. The personality of an animated character can be expressed not only thorough facial expressions and body gestures, but also through external elements such as the lighting design, the style of camera editing, the soundtrack, and more. The objective of the research work reported in the paper was to examine the role that the lighting scheme plays in the perception of the personality of animated characters performing a variety of actions. In particular, the study examined the extent to which the color, temperature, and brightness of the lights in the scene affect the viewer's perception of a character's degree of extraversion. Twenty-one subjects participated in the study; the stimuli were two sets of 10 animation clips, one set featuring an introvert character (Nora), and one set featuring an extrovert character (Lisa). Five clips for each set had a basic lighting setup and 5 clips included a carefully designed lighting scheme. The evaluation instrument was an online survey which included a few demographics questions, the stimuli videos presented in random order, and two questions related to the perception of the character's personality presented to the participant after each video. The first question asked the participant to rate the degree of extraversion of the character using a 5-point Likert scale; the second question asked the participant to explain what affected their decision when rating the personality of the character. Findings revealed an effect of lighting design on the perception of the introverted character's personality when the participant was female or non-binary / third gender; results showed no significant effects of lighting design on the perception of the extroverted character's personality.

Keywords: Animated Agents · Perception · Personality · Lighting Design · Extraversion

1 Introduction

Many studies on the perception of animated agents' personality have been conducted at the intersection of the animation and psychology fields, with research studying the effects of factors such as characters' facial cues [1], body gestures [3], gait parameters [2], gaze [4], shading style [11], brightness and shadow [12]. These studies have provided

© The Author(s), under exclusive license to Springer Nature Switzerland AG 2023
X. Fang (Ed.): HCII 2023, LNCS 14047, pp. 263–272, 2023.
https://doi.org/10.1007/978-3-031-35979-8_21

preliminary evidence that there is a relationship between the perception of a character's personality and elements that are internal and also external to the character. However, most of the past research has focused primarily on the effect of characters' body motions and facial expressions on the perception of their personality, leaving out important factors such as the lighting design of the scene in which the character is placed. The study reported in the paper aimed to fill this research gap.

Drawing from prior research on the psychology of lighting and best practices in digital lighting and rendering, the main hypothesis of the study is that a carefully designed lighting scheme will enhance significantly the perception of a character's personality. More specifically, the scene lighting color, temperature and brightness will emphasize the personality of a character and help viewers perceive it more accurately. The study focused on one of the basic five dimensions of the big-five model of personality, namely extraversion.

2 Related Work

2.1 The Five-Factor Model of Personality

Personality has been, and still is, a subject of active debate. However, for several years, the five-factor model, or the big five model, has been accepted by many as the most fundamental and comprehensive model of personality. McCrae and John describe the five-factor model of personality as a hierarchical organization of personality traits in terms of five basic dimensions: Extraversion, Agreeableness, Conscientiousness, Neuroticism, and Openness to Experience (p. 1) [5]. In their article, McCrae & John summarize various studies on the categorization of personality types and their appropriate taxonomies and classify the five-factor model as a break-through in psychology, and a fundamental stepping-stone on which future studies of personality may be based. They describe each personality type with the following adjectives: Extraversion-active, assertive, energetic, enthusiastic, outgoing; Agreeableness-appreciative, forgiving, generous, kind, sympathetic, trusting; Conscientiousness-efficient, organized, reliable, responsible, thorough; Neuroticism-anxious, self-pitying, tense, touchy, unstable, worrying; Openness to Experience-artistic, curious, imaginative, insightful, original, wide interests. Of the five types of personalities mentioned in the big five model, extraversion has been correlated most to positive emotions and leadership.

The terms 'extraversion' and 'introversion' were coined by Carl Jung. As the founder of analytical psychology, Jung made many breakthroughs about personality and its significance. Jung believed that every person has an extroverted and an introverted side. But one side is more dominant than the other, thus classifying a person as an extrovert or an introvert [7]. Eysenck's model describes the extrovert personality as sociable, lively, active, assertive, sensation seeking, carefree, dominant, venturesome (p. 22) [8]. Neff et al. following the big five model suggest that extroverts talk more, at a faster pace, more loudly and more repetitively than introverts [9].

2.2 Lighting and Animated Characters

Lighting is a powerful design element in photography, film and animation. An effective lighting set up can highlight important characters or objects within the frame; it can help convey certain psychological traits of the characters, for example, by shading sections of the face and body the character could look mysterious; it can also reflect a character's mood and hidden emotions. [10] used the well-known DreamWorks Animation franchise 'How to Train Your Dragon' to demonstrate how to construct an effective lighting design that supports the story, conveys the intended atmosphere and allows the character's personality to shine.

Wisessing et al. [12] investigated the effects of brightness and shadow on the perception of character emotion, emotion intensity, and appeal. Results from a series of experiments with stylized characters showed a contrasting effect of brightness on the intensity of happy and sad emotions; brightness intensified happiness, while darkness intensified sadness. Brightness also appeared to increase character appeal, whereas the ratio of the intensity of the key and fill lights did not appear to have an effect on appeal or emotion intensity.

Wisessing, Dingliana, & McDonell [11] examined the effects of different lighting directions, intensities, and shading techniques on recognition of character emotion, perception of emotion intensity and character appeal. The researchers used two shading techniques, CG and toon shading and different lighting directions. The experiment included 100 trials with 5 emotions for the participants to rate, 2 shading styles, 5 lighting conditions, and 2 repetitions. Results revealed that shading style does not have a significant effect on recognition of emotion but does influence the perception of that emotion's intensity. The toon-shaded renders were rated as displaying less intense emotions than the CG-shaded ones. Other factors such as shadow or lighting had little to no effect on the perception of emotion intensity. Further, CG-shading was rated as the more appealing option.

3 Methods

The objective of this study was to examine the effect of lighting color, temperature and brightness on viewers' perception of an animated character's degree of extraversion. The study used a within-subject design and collected both quantitative and qualitative data. The independent variables were the presence/absence of the lighting design and the gender of the participants; the dependent variable was the participant's rating of the animated character's degree of extraversion on a 5-point Likert scale (1=low extraversion; 5=high extraversion). The study considered two conditions: condition 1, which referred to the character animation without the lighting design, and condition 2 which referred to the addition of the lighting design to the animation. The main hypothesis was that there would be differences in the participants' perception of the character's personality between condition 1 and condition 2. The viewers' perception of the character's personality would be more accurate in condition 2. The study also hypothesized that there would be significant differences in perception based on the participants' gender.

3.1 Participants

Twenty-one participants were recruited through email announcements and through personal connections. Nine were males, 9 females, 2 non-binary/third gender, and 1 participant who preferred not to say.

3.2 Materials

Evaluation instrument. The evaluation instrument was an online Qualtrics survey which included a set of demographic questions, 20 stimuli videos, and 2 questions related to the perception of the character's personality, which were presented to the participant after each video. The first question asked the participants to rate the character's degree of extraversion on a 5-point Likert scale, the second question asked the participants to explain what affected their rating. The participant had 3 options to select from: Character's Body Poses, Lighting, and Other (open ended question with text box to write comments).

Stimuli. The stimuli were 2 sets of 10 animation clips (20 clips in total): one set featured an introvert character (Nora), and one set featured an extrovert character (Lisa). Five clips for each set featured no lighting design and 5 clips included a lighting scheme that was designed based on research by [13–16], and best practices in 3D lighting and rendering [17].

The animations were created by an experienced game character animator; the character models/rigs and the environment assets were purchased online, and the lighting scheme was implemented by the animator using the free lighting script AwesomeLights [18]. One of the characters (Nora) was animated to convey an introverted personality, while the second character (Lisa) was animated to convey an extraverted personality. Each character performed 5 types of action (one per clip), namely idle, walk, emote, attack, die. Figure 1 shows 8 frames extracted from the animation stimuli clips.

The aspects of lighting that were manipulated between conditions were the lighting color, temperature, and brightness. The goal, in condition 2, was to craft a lighting scheme that would complement and accentuate the animated character's personality. A three-point lighting setup with the addition of a few secondary lights was used in both conditions for both animated characters.

The introverted character (Nora). In condition 1 the lights' temperature was set to medium warm (simulating about 3500K), the colors to white, and the brightness was set to simulate about 600 lx. In condition 2, the brightness of the main lights was lowered and the colors were changed to various shades of purple and black (lack of lighting), with the shades of purple being low on saturation. Purple suggests mystery [14], and low sociability, which is a correlated trait adjective of Extraversion/Introversion [19]. Purple is also used to convey a feeling of seclusion and a sense of magic. Black, or lack of light, was utilized in condition 2 to generate moments in which only part of the character was lit, with the character itself being in various degrees of shade (depending on the animation) and the rest of the environment being in shadow or very low lighting. Black suggests intimacy when it is used to "light" areas around the main activity space, while the main space has the main lighting with a soft perimeter lighting [15]. This is a lighting setup that introverts tend to prefer [20].

In condition 2, Nora also has two high-brightness, high-temperature, low-saturation, purple point lights coming from the orb she carries with her left hand. The color of the orb is purple mixed with white. White conveys a feeling of safety [13, 15], and the character's orb is a source of comfort and protection for her.

The extraverted character (Lisa). In condition 1 the lights' temperature was set to medium warm (simulating about 3500K), the colors to a low saturated yellow, and the

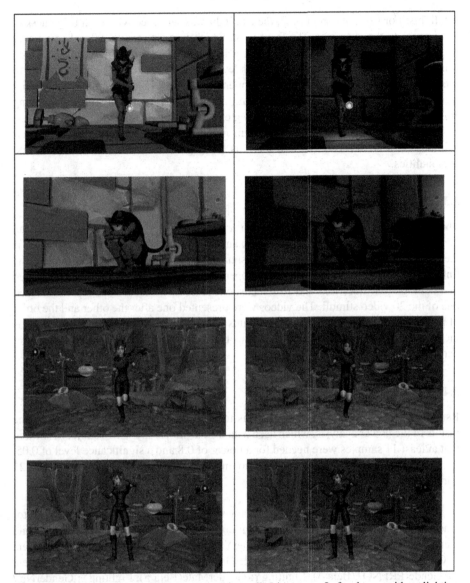

Fig. 1. From the top: Nora walk, Nora emote, Lisa walk, Lisa emote. Left column: without lighting design; right column: with lighting design.

brightness was set to simulate about 800 lx. In condition 2, the colors of the lights were changed to shades of red and white. Red colored lights exude energy, excitement, and friendship [14], which relate to the sociable, energetic, and adventurous aspects of extraversion [19]. White was used sparingly to emphasize a sense of outdoor space [15] and to tone down the shades of red. As previously mentioned, the lighting setup in both conditions involved 3 main lights for both characters, namely the front, rim, and key lights. For Lisa, in condition 2, the rim light was set to red with high brightness to add impact to the character. The front light, which was also red in color, had a lower brightness to emphasize the three dimensionality of the character. The key light, which was set to white, had a medium brightness level to simulate outdoor lighting and not to drown the scene in pure red light. The temperature levels of Lisa's lights in condition 2 were higher than in condition 1 due to saturated hues having the effect of intensifying emotions [17], and in this case, intensifying emotions that are related to extroversion.

For both characters, the lighting designs in conditions 2 were validated by 5 expert animators/CG artists who assessed them as being good reflections of the characters' personalities.

3.3 Procedure

The participants were sent an email with a brief summary of the research study, an invitation to participate in the experiment, and a consent form to sign electronically. If they agreed to participate in the study and signed the consent form, they could access the link to the online survey, which remained open for two weeks. The web survey consisted of 2 demographic questions and 20 screens, one screen per video. Each screen included one of the 20 video stimuli. The videos were presented one after the other and the order of presentation was randomized. Participants could watch each video as many times as they wanted before answering the questions related to their perception of the character personality.

3.4 Findings

Rstudio was used to run a power analysis to determine the needed sample size. The results of the power analysis, which used data from a pilot study with 6 subjects, showed that at least 11 samples were needed for a power of 0.8 and a significance level of 0.05.

A Linear Mixed Model was used to interpret the data collected from the 21 participants for each character:

Score = Lighting * Gender + Subject.

where lighting is a within-subject factor while gender is a between subject factor where the subject is treated as the random effect. LightingN (No lighting design) and GenderFemale are the baseline, and LightingY (Yes lighting design) is equivalent to Beta 1. Gender also has variables which include GenderMale(Beta 2), GenderNb / TG(Beta 3), GenderPRFNOT(Beta 4), LightingY: GenderMale(Beta 5), LightingY: GenderNb / TG(Beta 6), and LightingY: GenderPRFTNOT(Beta 7). The intercept's variable is Beta 0; Rstudio was used to run the model once per character. Figure 2 shows all the fixed effects for Nora's character.

For Nora, LightingY had a slightly significant standard error of the estimate at 1.3333, where Pr(>|t|) is 0.008633, LightingY: GenderNb / TG had a significant standard error of estimate at -2.3333 where Pr(>|t|) is 0.040759, and LightingY: GenderPRFNOT had a significant standard error of estimate at -3.3333 where Pr(>|t|) is 0.031363. Gender-Male, GenderNb/TG, GenderPRFNOT, and LightingY: gendermale were not significant enough to be considered. To calculate the effects of the variables, the significant variables were substituted into the formula mentioned above and then compared to the baseline.

```
Fixed effects:
                      Estimate Std. Error      df t value Pr(>|t|)
(Intercept)            10.5556     2.3027 17.3267   4.584 0.000252 ***
LightingY               1.3333     0.4493 17.0000   2.967 0.008633 **
GenderMale             -0.3333     3.2565 17.3267  -0.102 0.919647
GenderNb / TG          -4.0556     5.4003 17.3267  -0.751 0.462741
GenderPRFNOT           -3.5556     7.2818 17.3267  -0.488 0.631474
LightingY:GenderMale   -0.4444     0.6354 17.0000  -0.699 0.493741
LightingY:GenderNb / TG -2.3333    1.0537 17.0000  -2.214 0.040759 *
LightingY:GenderPRFNOT -3.3333     1.4209 17.0000  -2.346 0.031363 *
---
Signif. codes:  0 '***' 0.001 '**' 0.01 '*' 0.05 '.' 0.1 ' ' 1
```

Fig. 2. Fixed effects for Nora (the introverted character)

LightingY (GenderF) = Beta0 + Beta1 = 10.5556 + 1.3333 = 11.8889.
Compared to baseline: 10.5556 < 11.8889.

If lighting design is present (LightingY) and the gender of the participant is female, the perception of Nora as an extrovert is slightly increased when compared to the baseline of No Light & Female.

LightingY: GenderNb / TG = Beta0 + Beta1 + Beta3 + Beta6 = 10.5556 + 1.3333 + (-4.0556) + (-2.3333) = 5.5

Compared to baseline: 10.5556 > 5.5

When comparing the Lighting Y and the participant's gender being Non-Binary or Third Gender, Nora appears significantly less extroverted.

LightingY: GenderPRFNOT = Beta0 + Beta1 + Beta4 + Beta7 = 10.5556 + 1.3333 + (-4.0556) + (-3.3333) = 4.5

Compared to baseline: 10.5556 > 4.5

When compared to baseline, having LightingY and the gender of the participant being Prefer Not to Say, Nora appears significantly less extroverted.

The same variables were used for Lisa, but the results did not show any significant change in Extraversion ratings regardless of change in lighting and participant's gender. Only the intercept, which is the mean score for the baseline, is significant. Figure 3 shows all the fixed effects for Lisa (the extroverted character).

Qualitative data was also collected to find out what affected the subject's decision when rating the personality of the characters. For Nora, "Body Poses" was the most selected answer (18 out of 21), Lighting coming behind it at 1, and Other at 1 response. One of the responses was also a tie between Lighting and Body. For Lisa, "Body Poses" was the most selected answer (17 out of 21), "Lighting" after it at 2, and "Other" at 1. One of the responses was a tie between Lighting and Body Poses.

```
Fixed effects:
                        Estimate Std. Error      df t value Pr(>|t|)
(Intercept)              20.4444     1.0538 19.5088  19.400 3.23e-14 ***
LightingY                -0.5556     0.5539 17.0000  -1.003    0.330
GenderMale               -1.4444     1.4903 19.5088  -0.969    0.344
GenderNb / TG            -0.9444     2.4715 19.5088  -0.382    0.706
GenderPRFNOT             -1.4444     3.3325 19.5088  -0.433    0.669
LightingY:GenderMale      0.1111     0.7834 17.0000   0.142    0.889
LightingY:GenderNb / TG   2.0556     1.2991 17.0000   1.582    0.132
LightingY:GenderPRFNOT    0.5556     1.7516 17.0000   0.317    0.755
---
Signif. codes:  0 '***' 0.001 '**' 0.01 '*' 0.05 '.' 0.1 ' ' 1
```

Fig. 3. Fixed effects for Lisa (the extroverted character)

4 Discussion and Conclusion

The study reported in the paper examined how different lighting conditions affected participants' recognition of animated characters' personalities. Findings showed an effect of lighting design on the perception of the introverted character personality for subjects of certain genders. The lighting design did not appear to affect personality perception for the extraverted character, regardless of the participant's gender. In the case of the introverted character, the lighting design did not increase personality perception accuracy for female participants, while it did improve it for non-binary and third gender subjects.

The results from the study in part support the main hypothesis that a carefully designed lighting scheme may enhance the perception of an animated character's personality. Findings support the secondary hypothesis that there are differences in perception between the two conditions based on the participants' gender.

The study had several limitations that could be overcome in future research. The sample size was small (21 subjects) and participants' genders were not represented equally. Future studies should use a larger number of subjects with a more even distribution of genders.

The study comprised only two female stylized characters and two environment designs. Part of the results could be due to the intrinsic design characteristics of the characters and environments. Future experiments should include a higher variety of background scene elements and characters of different genders and different degrees of stylization. For instance, it would be interesting to examine whether certain lighting elements have the same effect on the viewers' perception of cartoony characters versus realistic characters.

The study focused on only one of the big five personality traits, e.g., extraversion. Future experiments should examine the effects of lighting design on audience perception of all five personality traits.

The short duration of the stimuli animations and the limited variety of actions could have affected the participants ability to perceive the characters' personality in all conditions. This could explain the lack of lighting effect in the case of the extraverted character and the small effect for the introverted character. Future research should use more complex animation sequences of longer duration.

Finally, the study assumed that the participants were familiar with the concepts of extraversion and introversion. However, if some of the participants were unfamiliar with these concepts, this might have influenced the outcome of the study.

In conclusion, lighting is a powerful element that can be used in live action films and animation to convey the mood of a scene, to form a cohesive narrative which supports the story, and to intensify the personality, emotions and appeal of the characters. Currently, except for a few studies, the relationship between lighting and audience perception of the characters is mostly drawn from best practices in film and animation and from observations. To advance knowledge in this area, there is a need for experimental research studies that systematically investigate the extent to which certain elements of lighting contribute to enhance perception of specific traits of the character. The study reported in the paper is a small step in this direction. Studies like this not only have important implications for research, but also for practice. They can provide useful guidelines for animators and visual artists for enhancing the appeal and emotional impact of their characters.

Acknowledgements. This work is supported in part by NSF- RETTL Collaborative Research: Using Artificial Intelligence to Transform Online Video Lectures into Effective and Inclusive Agent-Based Presentations; Award # 2201019. The authors would like to thank Purdue Statistical Consulting Service for their help with the data analysis.

References

1. Arya, A., Jefferies, L.N., Enns, J.T., DiPaola, S.: Facial actions as visual cues for personality. Comput. Anim. Virtual Worlds **17**(5), 371–382 (2006). https://doi.org/10.1002/cav.140
2. Badathala, S.P., Adamo, N., Villani, N.J., Dib, H.N.: The effect of gait parameters on the perception of animated agents' personality. In: DePaolis, L.T., Bourdot, P. (eds.) Augmented Reality, Virtual Reality, and Computer Graphics. LNCS, vol. 10850, pp. 464–479. Springer, Cham (2018). https://doi.org/10.1007/978-3-319-95270-3_39
3. Cheng, J., Zhou, W., Lei, X., Adamo, N., Benes, B.: The effects of body gestures and gender on viewer's perception of animated pedagogical agent's emotions. In: Kurosu, M. (ed.) Human-Computer Interaction. Multimodal and Natural Interaction. LNCS, vol. 12182, pp. 169–186. Springer, Cham (2020). https://doi.org/10.1007/978-3-030-49062-1_11
4. Ait Challal, T., Grynszpan, O.: What gaze tells us about personality. In: Proceedings of the 6th International Conference on Human-Agent Interaction, pp. 129–137 (2018). https://doi.org/10.1145/3284432.3284455
5. McCrae, R.R., John, O.P.: An introduction to the five-factor model and its applications. J. Personal. **60**(2), 175–215 (1992). https://doi.org/10.1111/j.1467-6494.1992.tb00970.x
6. Jung, C.G.: Memories, Dreams. Reflections. Vintage, New York (1989)
7. Eysenck, H.J.: The Biological Basis of Personality. Transaction Publishers, New Brunswick (1967)
8. Neff, M., Wang, Y., Abbott, R., Walker, M.: Evaluating the effect of gesture and language on personality perception in conversational agents. In: Allbeck, J., Badler, N., Bickmore, T., Pelachaud, C., Safonova, A. (eds.) Intelligent Virtual Agents. LNCS (LNAI), vol. 6356, pp. 222–235. Springer, Heidelberg (2010). https://doi.org/10.1007/978-3-642-15892-6_24
9. Walvoord, D.: Lighting design for stylized animation. In: ACM SIGGRAPH 2019 Courses, pp. 1–42 (2019). https://doi.org/10.1145/3305366.3328063

10. Wisessing, P., Dingliana, J., McDonell, R.: Perception of lighting and shading for animated virtual characters. In: ACM Symposium on Applied Perception (2016). https://doi.org/10.1145/2931002.2931015

11. Wisessing, P., Zibrek, K., Cunningham, D.W., Dingliana, J., McDonnell, R.: enlighten me: importance of brightness and shadow for character emotion and appeal. ACM Transa. Graph. **39**(3), 1–12 (2020). https://doi.org/10.1145/3383195

12. Kaplan, R., Kaplan, S.: The experience of nature: A psychological perspective. Cambridge University Press (1989)

13. Sharpe, D.T.: The psychology of color and design. Nelson-Hall (1974)

14. TCP Lighting: The Psychological impact of Light and Color, 12 December 2017. https://www.tcpi.com/psychological-impact-light-color/

15. Küller, R., Ballal, S., Laike, T., Mikellides, B., Tonello, G.: The impact of light and colour on psychological mood: a cross-cultural study of indoor work environments. Ergonomics **49**(14), 1496–1507 (2006). https://doi.org/10.1080/00140130600858142

16. Birn, J.: Digital Lighting & Rendering (Voices That Matter) 3rd Edition. New Riders Publishers (2013)

17. MayaTools. AwsomeLights script (2022). https://animationmethods.com/tools.html

18. John, O.P., Srivastava, S.: The big-five trait taxonomy: history, measurement, and theoretical perspectives. In: Pervin, L.A., John, O.P. (eds.) Handbook of personality: Theory and research, vol. 2, pp. 102–138. Guilford Press, New York (1999)

19. Oishi, S., Choi, H.: Personality and space: introversion and seclusion. J. Res. Personal. **85**, 103933 (2020). https://doi.org/10.1016/j.jrp.2020.103933

From Stone Age to New Age Statistics: How Neural Networks Overcome the Irreproducibility Problems in Choice Based Profile Creation

Hermann Prossinger[1,2](✉) ⓘ, Silvia Boschetti[3] ⓘ, Daniel Říha[2] ⓘ, Libor Pacovský[2], and Jakub Binter[2](✉) ⓘ

[1] Department of Evolutionary Anthropology, Faculty of Life Sciences, University of Vienna, Vienna, Austria
hermann.prossinger@univie.a.at

[2] Faculty of Social and Economic Studies, University of Jan Evangelista Purkyně, Ústí Nad Labem, Czech Republic
jakub.binter@fhs.cuni.cz

[3] Faculty of Science, Charles University, Prague, Czech Republic

Abstract. In the gaming world, as well as in assistive technologies, profile creation and further characterizations of humans are basic. Oftentimes, Likert-type scales are needed to collect responses in questionnaires. A subsequent mistake by the analyst occurs when he/she computes the composition score derived from these response categories. Because: such a score can only be computed if these categorical responses are converted into computable numbers. An AI method, namely the application of artificial neural networks, can extract information and overcome various erroneous statistical methods (such as: linearizing responses of Likert scales, computing scores and correlations, and disregarding the 'curse of dimensionality').

We collected data from 480 respondents who were asked to specify boundaries between the colors of the blackbody spectrum ('rainbow'). We first used an auto-encoder for dimension reduction, then searched for categories by implementing clustering algorithms, computed likelihood plots, and calculated confusion matrices based on Dirichlet distributions.

We found that every respondent was a member of one of only three clusters. Each cluster is characterized by a different distribution of the color boundaries between purple-blue, blue-green, and so on. Surprisingly, the boundaries between some colors in one cluster where within the color interval for members of another cluster. Conclusion: where people see a color boundary is far from obvious even within a shared range.

There are implications for several fields that have been using 'Stone Age statistics' involving scores, etc. as listed above, among them psychology, sociology, behavioral economy, and human-computer interaction. The modern approach, based on AI, should be adopted by researchers in these fields to ensure reproducibility and provide insight into participant/user/citizen profiles.

© The Author(s), under exclusive license to Springer Nature Switzerland AG 2023
X. Fang (Ed.): HCII 2023, LNCS 14047, pp. 273–284, 2023.
https://doi.org/10.1007/978-3-031-35979-8_22

Keywords: One-hot Encoding · Artificial Neural Network · Confusion Matrix · Visible Spectrum · Color Boundaries · Kernel Density Estimation · Profile Creation · Cold Start Problem

1   Introduction

Currently, profile creation is a big topic in many fields involving technology. In an ideal case, there exists both a large data set and prolonged development of the field that has already been supplied with 'natural' layperson terminology for distinguishing features defined by the layperson's limited choices. Thus, while this may not be the case in many fields such as technology users and online gamers, for citizens responding to nudges, etc. that are uninitiated, such approaches cannot be applied from scratch. This brings the *cold start problem* into play (Eke et al. 2019). The system that is used for recommendation, profiling and divergence is unable to provide any meaningful inferences since too much information is lacking (Eke et al. 2019).

There are two main approaches to deal with this described problem. One involves extended, long-term data collection, including updates and adjustments, and a bean-counting summary description; the second one bases the distinctions on the data gathered from the prospective users via a questionnaire-type set of queries (Eke et al. 2019).

Questionnaires, the major tool in political polls, communication research, customer satisfaction research, and psychometrics, consist of a list of queries. Participants are requested to respond by making a choice for each of the categorical variables offered. For some queries, the options can be ranked; then the response option list is called a Likert scale (for review see Jebb et al. 2021). The length of the list of response options need not be the same for every query, nor need all queries be Likert scales. Indeed, in the study we present here, we specifically cannot ensure the same number of response options for every query.

The conventional approach to analyzing a questionnaire with these response distributions is to map the categorical responses into cardinal numbers. Doing so in the conventional manner leads to individuals who answered differently (for example, 1, 5, 3 by one individual and 3, 4, 2 by another to 3 questionnaire queries with 5 response options per query) to be assigned the same profile (9 and 9)—a statistical bias that will be included in—and render meaningless—the subsequent analyses. Even if the response options are offered to the participant as numbers, these numbers are by no means cardinal numbers (they are ordinal numbers; Blalock 1960), so it is impossible to calculate variances, averages or other statistical point estimators. The response options (categorical variable registrations) must be converted into cardinal numbers. This mapping of ordinal numbers into cardinal numbers is by no means unique. Table 1 shows a selection of the infinitely many maps that are possible.

The conventional mapping (Conv in Table 1) is the most ubiquitous. This choice of mapping has been criticized (Prossinger et al., 2022). Nonetheless, researchers in the aforementioned fields still use it almost exclusively. To summarize: the variances and means of the responses in a questionnaire will vary, depending on the mapping chosen.

Table 1. A selection of possible conversions (maps) of categorical variables that are responses to queries.

Label	Map	A	B	C	D	E	F
Conv	Conventional	1	2	3	4	5	6
Form	Formula I	8	10	12	15	18	25
MGP	MotoGP	10	11	13	16	20	25
Alp	FIS Alpine	47	51	55	60	80	100
Pri	Odd prime numbers	3	5	7	11	13	17
Lo1	Lottery 1	6	10	12	13	15	41
Lo2	Lottery 2	2	9	11	26	39	42
RConv	Reciprocal Conv	$\frac{1}{6}$	$\frac{1}{5}$	$\frac{1}{4}$	$\frac{1}{3}$	$\frac{1}{2}$	1
RPri	Reciprocal Odd Primes	$\frac{1}{17}$	$\frac{1}{13}$	$\frac{1}{11}$	$\frac{1}{7}$	$\frac{1}{5}$	$\frac{1}{3}$

To avoid specific, case-study implications and maintain the linear nature of the presented phenomenon, we decided to present our participants with the blackbody spectrum ('rainbow') of an object at 6000 K surface temperature and asked them to choose the boundaries separating two neighboring colors. The human eye is very perceptive to these wavelengths (as these are the ones present in large amplitudes in sunlight). These colors have been previously investigated in the classical work about human visual perception *Wavelength discrimination at detection threshold* by Mullen and Kulikowski (1990). More recently, Vlad et al. (2021) adopted a similar approach but used digitized color production to ensure the mechanism is applicable to digital media (the ubiquitous current devices). Our aim was to map how many clusters (profiles that share commonalities) will form in such a straightforward task as color boundary perception. Another one was to identify the existence of overlaps between the clusters based on participant's visual perceptions. This paper should be mainly understood as a methodological study of *hot start profiling*.

2 Materials

2.1 Questionnaire

A spectrum of visible light (the blackbody spectrum of light emitted by a black body at 6000 K surface temperature) was presented. At certain positions along the spectrum, letters of the Latin alphabet (hence ordered categorical variables) were supplied (Fig. 1). Each participant was asked to choose the letter he/she considered closest to the boundary queried (such as blue-green). In total, a total of five boundaries were queried: purple-blue, blue-green, green-yellow, yellow-orange, and orange-red. Each participant therefore entered a total of five responses (as letters) into the data set. Query responses were collected with Qualtrix®.

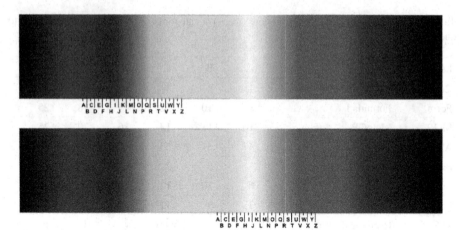

Fig. 1. The visible spectrum together with the two category markings presented to the participants. The participants were to choose the letter (category) that they considered closest to their
perception of the boundary between the colors queried in the questionnaire. Although the marked
rulings appear with constant intervals, it is not clear (to the participant) whether the wavelengths
corresponding to these markings are also equidistant. Above: The spectrum presented for the
queried boundaries purple-blue and blue-green. Below: The spectrum presented for the queried
boundaries green-yellow, yellow-orange and orange-red. (Color figure online)

2.2 Participants

A total of 480 participants were involved in this study; each participant supplied age
and biological sex. Their ages ranged from 18–50 years for both the 170 males and
310 females. We estimated the age distributions and their descriptive parameters using
a KDE (Kernel Density Estimation) with a Gaussian kernel.

3 Methods

3.1 Age Distributions, Male Versus Female

We used KDE to find the distribution of ages of the female and the male raters, separately.
We then determined the estimators, in particular the $HDI_{95\%}$ (the Highest Density Interval
at 95% significance; Kruschke 2015). A large overlap of this interval documents no
significant difference in the age distributions.

3.2 Feature vector construction: One-hot encoding

Each score by each participant for each queried color boundary is an ordinal variable.
Contrary to the fallacious method of mapping these scores into cardinal integers, we
convert the sequence of scores by a participant into a (concatenated) feature vector. For
example, assume the score for a participant (in this example, we use the choices from
participant #13) for the purple-blue boundary is E (from the range of all registered scores
$A–P$ (Fig. 1) □16 options), the score for the blue-green boundary is S (from the range

of all registered scores $K-W$ (Fig. 1) □ 13 options), the score for the green-yellow boundary is H (from the range of all registered scores $C-K$ (Fig. 1)□ 9 options), the score for the yellow-orange boundary is L (from the range of all registered scores $H-T$ (Fig. 1)□13 options), and, the score for the orange-red boundary is S (from the range of all registered scores $M-Z$ (Fig. 1)□14 options). Then the one-hot encoded feature vectors are.

for purple-blue: $(0000100000000000)^T$
for blue-green: $(0000000010000)^T$
for green-yellow: $(100000000)^T$
for yellow-orange: $(0000100000000)^T$
for orange-red: $(00000010000000)^T$.

The one-hot encoded feature vector for this participant is then

$$(0000100000000000000100000000000 \cdots 00000010000000)^T.$$

The feature vector for every participant's five scores has $16+13+9+13+14 = 65$ components, and the norm of this feature vector is $\sqrt{5}$. In the case of participant #13, the nonzero entries are the components $5, 16+9 = 25, 16+13+1 = 30, 16+13+9+5 = 43$, and $16+13+9+13+7 = 58$.

3.3 Dimension Reduction and Clustering

Each participant's feature vector is therefore a point in 65-dimensional space. There are three reasons why a dimension reduction algorithm is needed: (a) not all possible feature vectors occur, (b) due to the 'curse of dimensionality' (Bellmann, 1961), the variance grows (it is additive and always positive) with the squares of the realizations of the random variable(s)—therefore much faster than the signal, and (c) the feature vectors of the participants have interdependencies (which we are looking for). There are two modern methods that can be used for dimension reduction: SVD (singular value decomposition) and a ANN (artificial neural network). In SVD, we look for a linear interdependence of the feature vectors, while for ANN, nonlinear interdependencies can also be included. We choose a special ANN, namely an autoencoder, in order to reduce each participant's feature vector to a 2D one (Fig. 4a).

The dimension-reduced feature vectors are not uniformly distributed in the plane. We use the DBSCAN clustering algorithm (Ester et al. 1996) to detect clusters. In order to determine how well the clusters are separated, we use a KDE distribution with a triweight kernel.

We construct the confusion matrix to estimate the significance of the overlap. For each pair of clusters (cluster$_A$ and cluster$_B$, say), we compute the confusion matrix

$$\begin{pmatrix} \dfrac{pdf(KDE_{\text{cluster}_A}) > pdf(KDE_{\text{cluster}_B})}{n_{\text{cluster}_A}} & \dfrac{pdf(KDE_{\text{cluster}_A}) \leq pdf(KDE_{\text{cluster}_B})}{n_{\text{cluster}_A}} \\ \dfrac{pdf(KDE_{\text{cluster}_B}) \leq pdf(KDE_{\text{cluster}_A})}{n_{\text{cluster}_B}} & \dfrac{pdf(KDE_{\text{cluster}_B}) > pdf(KDE_{\text{cluster}_A})}{n_{\text{cluster}_B}} \end{pmatrix}$$

We 'backtrack' from the dimension-reduced feature vectors to the scores for all participants in a cluster.

In order to determine the significance of the differences in the five boundaries for the different clusters, we again use the machinery of confusion matrices. We determine the union of entries, for a given boundary and a given pair of clusters, and tally the frequencies. The *pdf*s of these frequencies are the concentration parameters of two Dirichlet distributions, one for each cluster of the clusters being compared.

4   Results

Figure 2 and Table 2 show that the distributions of the male and female raters have different modes. We use KDE (kernel density estimation) with a Gaussian kernel because, as Fig. 1 shows, it is not to be expected that raters of either sex have a parametric distribution or even a superposition of one or two such parametric distributions. We also note that modes and expectation values differ between the sexes and also for the same sex. The $HDI_{95\%}$ uncertainty interval is very broad, so we can consider the distributions for both sexes to be comparable to a uniform distribution of respective ages. The confusion matrix shows that the two distributions are not significantly different. There is, therefore, no age-effect for the boundary sets we find.

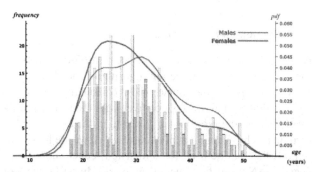

Fig. 2. The distribution of male and female ages of the participants. The histogram shows the ages entered by the participants. The curves are the *pdf*s (probability density functions) of the KDE (kernel density estimation) distributions of the ages, by biological sex, using a Gaussian kernel. The graphed *pdf* curves have been scaled (in this figure) so as to be comparable with the histogram rectangles. The numerical values of the *pdf*s are shown as a (gray) scale on the right. The age distributions of the males and females are not significantly different (*significance* = 55%).

Figure 3 shows the heat map of the boundary choices. We observe that the distribution of boundary choices varies considerably for some color boundaries. We note that: (a) Only one boundary query has no gaps, while the others have one, three, and five. (b) The 'length' (number of scores/responses) varies from query to query. It is therefore impossible to use Cronbach's Alpha or some other coefficient of reliability. We also note that the largest tally numbers for each boundary do not match a central tendency for the boundary query.

Table 2. The descriptors of the ages of the participants, separated by (biological) sex. Only the mean is a point estimator. All other descriptors are derived from the KDE (using a Gaussian kernel). N is the sample size and E; is the expectation value. Because the KDE is neither a symmetric nor a parametric distribution, calculating a standard deviation is not meaningful. We note that the uncertainty $HDI_{95\%}$ is neither symmetric about the mode, nor about the expectation value. We also note that the modes cannot be calculated from the raw data, but must be estimated from the KDEs. The distributions (KDEs), which have been estimated from the data, are not significantly different (see text). Consequently, none of the descriptors (except for the sample sizes) are significantly different.

Age Descriptor	Male	Female
N	170	310
Mean (years)	31.4	30.2
(years)	30.2	29.1
$HDI_{95\%}$ (years)	16.2–49.8	16.8–48.8
Mode (years)	31.0	24.6

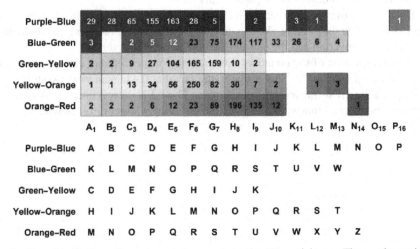

Fig. 3. The grid of tallies of boundary choices made by the 480 participants. The numbers within the squares are the number of participants that chose the (displayed) color as the boundary. Each horizontal row of tallies sums to 480. The colors of the squares are the colors of the boundary chosen by the participants. The letters chosen by the participants differed from boundary query to boundary query. These letters have been replaced by indexed symbols in the first row. Below this row of indexed symbols are the actual labels (Fig. 1) of the participant's scores. There is no encoding in the choice of black or white numbers of the tallies displayed; rather, the choice of black or white was made to enhance the contrast between the displayed numbers and the background color.

Table 3. The confusion matrices of significant overlap between the likelihood functions estimated via KDE using a triweight kernel (Fig. 4b-c). All the overlaps are significantly different. The top row in each confusion matrix is for the cluster with the smaller ordinal number (index).

Cluster No.1 Cluster No. 2	$\begin{pmatrix} 98.64 & 1.36 \\ 0 & 100 \end{pmatrix}\%$
Cluster No.1 Cluster No. 3	$\begin{pmatrix} 98.87 & 1.13 \\ 0 & 100 \end{pmatrix}\%$
Cluster No.2 Cluster No. 3	$\begin{pmatrix} 100 & 0 \\ 0 & 100 \end{pmatrix}\%$

We obtain three clusters of boundary sets (Fig. 4). The clusters were found using the DBSCAN algorithm (Ester et al. 1996). One cluster is by far the largest, with 441 participants (91.9%), the second largest cluster consists of 25 participants (5.2%), and the smallest cluster consists of 14 participants (2.9%).

The pairwise overlap between the likelihood functions is so small that the confusion matrices are either diagonal or close to diagonal (Table 3). We therefore conclude there is no significant overlap and the clusters are significantly different.

Visual inspection of the boundary distributions for the different clusters reveals no evident differences (Fig. 5). This is due to the fact that the human visual system is not good at detecting non-linear interdependencies. The ANN detects interdependencies of the chosen boundaries that we are surprised at observing when confronted with the graph (Table 4).

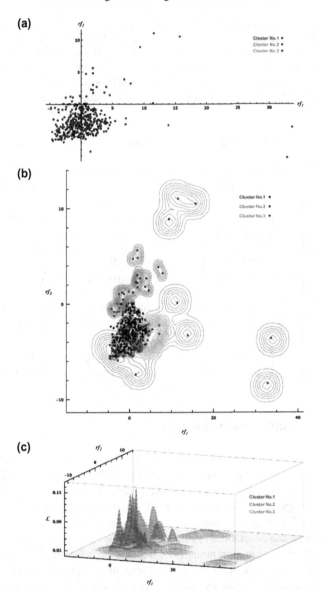

Fig. 4. The distributions of clusters of the dimension-reduced feature vectors of the color boundaries chosen by the participants. **(a)** The distributions of each cluster in the dimension-reduced feature vector space (here: a plane). The separation of clusters seems not to be very large in some regions of the 2-D feature space. **(b)** The projection of the contour plots of the likelihood surfaces obtained by the KDEs (each of the three with a triweight kernel of the functional form $\frac{35}{32}\left(1 - u^2\right)^3$). Contours for each likelihood surface are in steps of $\frac{1}{15}$max of the cluster (Λ is the likelihood). Some contours overlap. **(c)** A 3D graph of the likelihood surfaces obtained by the KDEs. The likelihood surfaces are very broad for Cluster No.3 and very peaked for Cluster No.1. As a consequence, the separation between clusters is highly significant (Table 3).

Table 4. The confusion matrices of significant differences between the boundaries in the different clusters. The entries in these confusion matrices are in %. These confusion matrices have been calculated by generating 15000 random numbers from each of the Dirichlet distributions, boundary by boundary. The top row in each confusion matrix is for the cluster with the smaller ordinal number (index). We observe that only for Cluster 2 versus Cluster 3 are the off-diagonal elements of the confusion matrices nonzero. However, even for this cluster comparison, the difference is significant.

Boundary	Clusters 12	Clusters 13	Clusters 23
Purple blue	$\begin{pmatrix} 100.0 & 0.0 \\ 0.0 & 100.0 \end{pmatrix}$	$\begin{pmatrix} 100.0 & 0.0 \\ 0.0 & 100.0 \end{pmatrix}$	$\begin{pmatrix} 99.90 & 0.10 \\ 0.10 & 99.90 \end{pmatrix}$
Blue green	$\begin{pmatrix} 100.0 & 0.0 \\ 0.0 & 100.0 \end{pmatrix}$	$\begin{pmatrix} 100.0 & 0.0 \\ 0.0 & 100.0 \end{pmatrix}$	$\begin{pmatrix} 99.59 & 0.41 \\ 0.35 & 99.65 \end{pmatrix}$
Green yellow	$\begin{pmatrix} 100.0 & 0.0 \\ 0.0 & 100.0 \end{pmatrix}$	$\begin{pmatrix} 100.0 & 0.0 \\ 0.0 & 100.0 \end{pmatrix}$	$\begin{pmatrix} 97.75 & 2.25 \\ 1.89 & 98.11 \end{pmatrix}$
Yellow orange	$\begin{pmatrix} 100.0 & 0.0 \\ 0.0 & 100.0 \end{pmatrix}$	$\begin{pmatrix} 100.0 & 0.0 \\ 0.0 & 100.0 \end{pmatrix}$	$\begin{pmatrix} 99.98 & 0.02 \\ 0.03 & 99.97 \end{pmatrix}$
Orange red	$\begin{pmatrix} 100.0 & 0.0 \\ 0.0 & 100.0 \end{pmatrix}$	$\begin{pmatrix} 100.0 & 0.0 \\ 0.0 & 100.0 \end{pmatrix}$	$\begin{pmatrix} 99.53 & 0.47 \\ 0.41 & 99.59 \end{pmatrix}$

5   Discussion and Conclusions

Profile creation is becoming more and more important as the method availability is quasi-exponentially growing because of technological advancements. The *cold start problem* can be resolved by obtaining the data from the prospective users beforehand and creating groups (clusters) based on their responses using questionnaire queries. Many 'antiquated' techniques have been implemented to deal with this problem: from Cronbach´s Alpha and MacDonald's Omega to various versions of FA (factor analysis), and to SEM (structural equation modeling). Because both FA and SEM lack a rigorous mathematical foundation (when using ordinal responses), rules of thumb are employed to achieve a 'presentable' result and satisfy peer reviewers. Unfortunately, FA and SEM of ordinal responses are still in widespread use in the psychological and behavioral sciences (thereby producing non-repeatable and biased outcomes).

AI (artificial intelligence) has become a buzzword. However, in an actual study such as this one, which focuses on the (seemingly simple) task of finding color boundaries by applying a novel methodology on previously tested outcomes, we were able to identify three independent clusters—an unanticipated new finding. To our knowledge, no previously tested outcomes have found any clustering. One cluster constitutes over 90% of the participants and other methods would have failed to identify the remaining two clusters that are decisively different (and small). Since optical perception mechanisms, like color

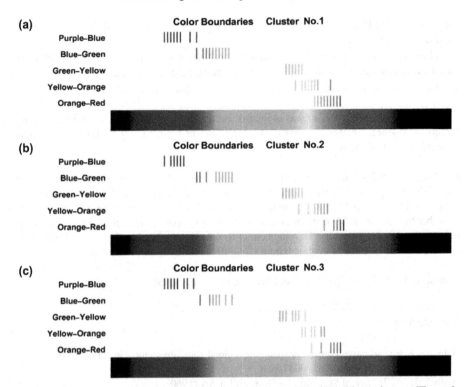

Fig. 5. The distributions of boundaries chosen by the participants in the three clusters. The multiplicity of the chosen boundaries is not shown. **(a)** Cluster No. 1 (441 participants; 92%), **(b)** Cluster No. 2 (25 participants; 5,2%), and **(c)** Cluster No. 3 (14 participants; 2.9%).

perception, are thought to be non-uniformly distributed in the human population, this finding of the existence of three clusters is an important insight because, among other implications, it signals a warning to avoid FA and SEM.

We show how the tools of AI can be implemented, how they can be applied to categorical variables (here: ordinal ones), and how dimension reduction methods can overcome the 'curse of dimensionality' (Bellman 1961). We show how AI algorithm outputs can then be analyzed by using clustering algorithms, then computing likelihood plots, and finally calculating confusion matrices; all these allow for finding and defining categories of the participants as profiles. Many of these methods are implementable in both supervised AI and unsupervised AI.

It should be pointed out that the task was intentionally chosen to be straightforward and would avoid distractors such as emotional involvement, political preferences or socio-historical components. We were still able to identify decisively different groups (clusters, in statistical parlance) in a population. If we take into account the above mentioned possibilities, the proportions in the clusters can be expected to exhibit the different clusters in a population. Bearing in mind that governments (nudging) or corporate companies (human-computer interaction) may involve millions of individuals being affected by their decisions and their profiling, these new methods should be adopted as soon as possible to properly address the complexity within the population and provide meaningful solutions.

These approaches should by all means be combined with the prospective adaptations based on user/citizen profiles to achieve best results (Eke et al. 2019; Farnandi et al., 2018).

Ethics Statement. The project was evaluated and approved by the Ethical Committee of the Faculty of Science, Charles University, as part of broader project (7/2018). GDPR regulations were followed at all times.

Funding and Acknowledgement. This article was authored with the support of the Doctoral School: Applied and Behavioral Studies project (Grant Number: CZ.02.2.69/0.0/0.0/16 _018/000272), University of Jan Evangelista Purkyně, Ústí nad Labem, Czech Republic. D.Ř. is further funded by the Ministry of Education, Youth and Sports, Czech Republic and the Institutional Support for Long-term Development of Research Organizations, Faculty of Humanities, Charles University, Czech Republic (Grant COOPERATIO "Arts and Culture").

Conflicts of Interest.. The authors declare no conflict of interest.

References

Bellman, R.E.: Adaptive control processes: a guided tour. Princeton University Press (1961). https://doi.org/10.1515/9781400874668

Blalock, H.M., Jr.: Social Statistics. McGraw Hill, USA (1960)

Eke, C.I., Norman, A.A., Shuib, L., Nweke, H.F.: A survey of user profiling: state-of-the-art, challenges, and solutions. IEEE Access **7**, 144907–144924 (2019)

Ester, M., Kriegel, H-P., Sander, J, Xu, X.: In: Simoudis, E., Han, J., Fayyad, U.M. (eds.). A density-based algorithm for discovering clusters in large spatial databases with noise. Proceedings of the Second International Conference on Knowledge Discovery and Data Mining (KDD-1996), pp. 226–231. AAAI Press. CiteSeerX 10.1.1.121.9220 (1996). ISBN 1-57735-004-9

Farnadi, G., Tang, J., De Cock, M., Moens, M.F.: User profiling through deep multimodal fusion. In: Proceedings of the Eleventh ACM International Conference on Web Search and Data Mining, pp. 171–179 (2018)

Jebb, A.T., Ng, V., Tay, L.: A review of key Likert scale development advances: 1995–2019. Front. Psychol. **12**, 637547 (2021)

Kruschke, J.K. (2015) Doing Bayesian Data Analysis. A Tutorial with R, JAGS, and STAN. Elsevier, Waltham, MA, USA

Mullen, K.T., Kulikowski, J.J.: Wavelength discrimination at detection threshold. JOSA A **7**(4), 733–742 (1990)

Prossinger, H., Binter, J., Machova, K., Riha, D., Boschetti, S.: Machine learning detects pairwise associations between SOI and BIS/BAS subscales, making correlation analyses obsolete. In: Human Interaction and Emerging Technologies (IHIET-AI 2022). Artificial Intelligence & Future Applications, Vol 23. AHFE International, USA (2022). https://doi.org/10.54941/ahf e100903

Vlad, V., Toti, M., Dumitru, S., Simota, C., Dumitru, M.: Developing reliably distinguishable color schemes for legends of natural resource taxonomy-based maps. Cartogr. Geogr. Inf. Sci. **48**(5), 393–416 (2021)

Playable Characters in Digital Games: Aesthetics and Gender Identity in Digital Game Player's Preferences

Tânia Ribeiro(✉) [ID], Rebeca Mendes [ID], and Ana Isabel Veloso

DigiMedia, University of Aveiro, Aveiro, Portugal
rebecamendes@ua.pt

Abstract. Characters are the interface throughout most of the players' experience many digital games. In digital games, the Playable Character faces a problem that generates conflict lived by the player who is willing to spend time and energy to experience a breach of the character's life as if it were their own. The present research paper aims to describe some aesthetical features of the favorite playable characters of a group of players. A survey was conducted to assess the favorite playable character of the players, collecting 301 valid responses (236 from male players, 55 from female players, and 10 from non-binary players) from 48 countries, nominating 147 different playable characters, pointed as their favorite ones. The characters enumerated were categorized regarding the following dimensions of playable character: visualization or perspective (first person or third person); type of figure (human or non-human); character gender identity (male, female, or non-binary); and character type of face (babyface or mature male face). The results show that players tend to have more meaningful gaming experiences with fictional characters with the body presented on the screen (third-person view). Those bodies tend to be human and male, with a bias for female babyface features and mature male faces in the most cited favorite playable characters.

Keywords: Playable Character · Digital Games · Character Design · and Character Aesthetic

1 Introduction

Even though a game character is a virtual representation on a screen that requires the practice of a specific conceptual model through the manipulation of the controller's artificial interaction mediators (mice, keyboard, joystick, or controller), players, being social creatures, can quickly put themselves in the role of this fictional "other" and are able, from a psychological and physical point of view, to feel the emotions of sadness, pain, or distress in the precisely same way as they would if it had happened to them [1]. Fictional characters impact players; the feeling of identification of a player with a character is a phenomenon identified and discussed in the literature as a factor contributing to the players' satisfaction during the digital game [2] and, sometimes, goes beyond the game's magic circle [3] resulting into social communities of fans or in endless series

© The Author(s), under exclusive license to Springer Nature Switzerland AG 2023
X. Fang (Ed.): HCII 2023, LNCS 14047, pp. 285–300, 2023.
https://doi.org/10.1007/978-3-031-35979-8_23

of multiple games (typically referred as a franchise) where the characters' narrative is explored.

This research aims to understand the favorite playable character of a group of players (collected via a survey in an open-ended question) and to analyze third-person characters' aesthetical features. With this, it is intended to identify the aesthetical features that may attract the players throughout the analysis of the dimensions of playable character visualization, the type of figure, the gender identity, and the facial features.

The presented paper is divided into the related work, methodology, results, and discussion and finishes with the conclusion to achieve the proposed aim. In the first section, state-of-the-art, the concepts linked to the analysis are framed through three parts: i) "Playability and visualization of digital game characters" – attending to the different aspects of the playable characters' in-game from a technical approach; ii) "Aesthetic liking and pleasure" – which briefly describes aesthetic and its relation with the visual attributes; and iii) "Playable characters' design" – attending to the characters' design techniques and visual attributes, explaining how they impact in the player. In the second section, the paper presents the research method in detail, supported in a linear mixed methodology, through a survey technique followed by the favorite playable character analyses. Results are explained in the third section with the sample characterization and the presentation of players' favorite characters, followed by a mixed linear analysis – qualitative and quantitative – of the visual attributes of the sample to determine the aesthetic features and gender identity of playable characters between players, in line with the literature review presented. The paper ends with a discussion and conclusion, intending to understand better the impact of playable characters in third-person digital games, aiming to contribute to digital game design and development.

2 Related Work

Characters are the primary engagement point of the audience with digital games [4]. Generally, they represent the audience's fears and desires, whether symbolic, representative, or historical [5]. In digital games, the protagonist – the main character in the story – faces a problem that generates a conflict. In most digital games, the digital game protagonist is the playable character, and from their perspective, the game world is experienced [6]. The character's impact level and the gameplay are fundamental elements of players' engagement, enabling the game experience provided [7].

Attending to the gap in the literature regarding playable characters' aesthetics and gender identity, and given the cultural relevance of digital games in modern society – constantly intending to achieve greater immersion and engagement – this paper focuses on digital games' playable characters in a third-person perspective. It is intended to explore the players' preferences regarding the characters' aesthetics and gender identity.

2.1 Playability and Visualization of Digital Game Characters

The playable character is the primary mediator between the player and the digital game world. The character is the one through which the player can discover what the game world offers, progressively uncovering the game narrative [1].

Characters can be absent or represented by a figure, appealing to different game perspectives (1st and 3rd person points of view or perspectives) [7]. This way, characters can assume two significant types of visualization regarding the different points of view (PoV) enabled by the digital games [8]: first-person PoV, where the player sees the environment of the game from the playable characters' perspective, with the screen presenting the view from the character's eyes, with no aesthetical representation of the character's physical body; and third-person PoV, where the player can see the complete visualization of the character on the screen, interacting with the game-world by manipulating the character's body movements. In third-person PoV, the digital game camera is placed at a distance, providing an upper view of the character and the environment [7], enabling the player to perceive the character's body and actions, and providing a broader perspective of the surroundings, that facilitates the navigation in the digital game, easing the playability [9].

Given the playability, characters can be cathegorized into a five type taxonomy [10]: avatar – the character's aesthetics is personalized by the player (for instance, their genre, facial features, and clothes); class characters – specific characters provided by the digital game system that enable the player to choose one character for the game or level between a specific set of characters, each one of a different class, having a particular role in terms of playability, were the player can (sometimes) personalize their aesthetics, mainly regarding the character's clothes or accessories; group characters – collective fictional playable characters, where the player has to play with more than one character during the digital game (for instance, digital football games); real-life character – characters that represent real-life personalities, enabling the player to role-play their known skills (for example, famous soccer players, golf players, or skaters); fictional characters – characters that do not exist anywhere besides the digital game system, and that the player has usually no or only minor control over their aesthetical personalization.

Although third-person PoV provides a less immersive experience to players [11], this perspective increases the attention on the playable character, enabling the player to observe their visual attributes and behavioral responses represented in the game world. By attending to the aesthetics and gender identity of playable characters, this paper focuses exclusively on third-person PoV digital games.

2.2 Aesthetic Liking and Pleasure.

Humans can tell whether they like all the artifacts in everyday visual perception in an almost permanent judgment action [12, 13]. This internal process includes objects and domains typically associated with aesthetics, for instance, photos, artworks, landscapes, buildings, the body, and the face of others [14].

Aesthetics is a complex construct, explained by the Pleasure-Interest Model of Aesthetic Liking (PIA Model; [15]). This model distinguishes between aesthetic liking and attractiveness – the first triggers pleasure, and the second develops interest [13].

Aesthetic pleasure, driving from liking, is the positive response to figures, considered the pleasurable subjective experience elicited by an object (stimulus) and not moderated by reasoning [13]. Graf & Landwehr (2015) explain that an encountered stimulus triggers an immediate response that requires mini-mum cognitive processing, occurring without the perceiver's intention, and activates pleasurable sensations. Aesthetic pleasure is, in this way, unintentional and mandatory.

By opposition, aesthetic interest drives from controlled processing, starting when a stimulus receives increased attention from a perceiver, overwriting the previous automatic response [13]. Controlled processing encompasses perceiver-driven attention toward the object, reducing the fluency of stimulus-driven automated processing. Thus, aesthetic interest occurs from the interpretative and meaningful analysis of the stimulus, requiring a high-order cognitive processing response [13].

The MDA (mechanic, dynamic, and aesthetic) model [16] describes aesthetics as the player's desirable emotional responses evoked when interacting with the game system. Characters, as primary elements of players' engagement with the digital game, can significantly impact the player's response [6, 16].

The physical appearance of playable characters impacts how the player sees the character and interprets the digital game. How a playable character is presented in the game world may tell the player about its behavioral characteristics, providing clues about its personality traits [17].

Although aesthetic features may not be reasonable and impartial cues to determine the character's role in the game narrative or mechanics, its visual attributes influence the player, triggering aesthetic liking or pleasure [18, 19].

2.3 Playable Characters' Design.

The character's physical appearance impacts how they are seen by the player [50]. The way a particular character is presented in the game world may tell the player about the physical aspects and behavioral characteristics, providing clues about their personality traits [6]. Although aesthetic features are not reasonable and impartial cues to communicate personality traits in the real world – due to the reduced inferential potential of those clues regarding individual diversity – in the game world, the role of a character in the game narrative or mechanics is supported by its visual attributes, intending to influence the players' interpretation on psychological and social characteristics [17, 20].

The characters' influence over the players' perceptions can have an impact on judgment and is related to the physical characteristics, mainly supported by the attractiveness of the character's design – relying on specific body images and facial details that can trigger players' attention and increase engagement with the digital game – appealing to visual attributes of the represented figures [17, 20].

Concerning physical appearance, playable characters can have different types of body anatomies and are categorized by several dimensions. Humans, or humanoids, are characterized by their resemblance to a human body shape, and non-humanoids do not attempt to resemble the human form. Characters whose body shapes resemble known objects, for instance, vehicles, machines, or animals, are found with that corresponding body type. Monsters are typically characters with asymmetrical body shapes and facial features that can be laid out differently, usually designed by appealing to repulsive visual aspects or absurd proportions. There are also characters with hybrid bodies, combining two types of body shapes: animalistic humans or machine humans [6, 8].

The face and facial expressions are also significant elements in communicating with the player and promoting engagement with the character [20]. Babyfaces refer to aesthetic and behavioral qualities typically attributed to children or infants, such as the need for protection or their ability to manipulate others [17, 20]. From the aesthetic point of view, they may fashion large eyes or pupils, a small chin and nose, a forehead and eyebrows positioned higher on the face, and lips and cheeks, which are more inflated than average [21]. Characters with these characteristics tend to be submissive, reliable, and cordial but also manipulative. In fact, according to an experimental study [22], female babyface and mature male faces may capture selective visual attention faster and gain more attentional focus. Mature male faces are aesthetically more robust, with long and symmetrical face and body features, a straight profile, often associated with a strong chin, related with attractiveness in men [20].

"One motivation for social interaction is sexual interest, whether for men or women" [20]. Non-human figures (for instance, cartoons or machines) can remove the physical attraction and explain the broader cross-gender appeal of digital games that present these characteristics. The characters' gender acknowledgment and their respective behavior might facilitate the immersive experience provided and increase the interest between males and females [20].

Although several demographic variables can distinguish players' preferences, gender is the most relevant and frequent in the literature, not only because gaming – the frequent play of digital games – has been related to males, with social stereotypes tending to be more appealing to this gender, but also because the gender concept is culturally different across the globe and time.

Gender is the learned and adopted path after birth regarding the identity of the self with none, one, or more sexes [20]. Although some evidence support that gender differences might influence game preferences among players, that seems to have a reduced impact on a character's choice [20]. As females increasingly play digital games, it becomes essential that the characters' design not only appeals to the male gender [20]. Besides, whether men, women, or non-binary, players have different preferences regarding digital games, and games with various characters' choices have allowed both sexes to try different gender roles [23].

3   Material and Methods

Attending the research aims to understand the aesthetical features that may attract players through the analysis of the characteristics of their favorite playable character; this exploratory research is supported by a linear mixed methodology divided into the following two phases:

Phase 1 – Survey: an online questionnaire was applicated to collect qualitative data regarding the favorite playable character of frequent players, appealing to the survey technique to achieve the sample of the present study;

Phase 2 – Character analysis: a visual exploration (qualitative analysis) followed by a descriptive and exploratory (quantitative) analysis was developed on favorite playable characters in a third-person point of view focusing on the aesthetic features – the type of character (humanoid or non-humanoid) and facial expression (babyface and mature male face) – and gender identity (male, female, non-binary) of the playable characters, to assess the standard features on the sample.

3.1 Phase 1 – Survey

The population of the survey consists of frequent digital game players. The qualitative data was collected by survey technique through an online questionnaire with five questions divided into two parts regarding the favorite playable character in digital games (Table 1). Inclusion criteria at this phase encompassed the agreement with the study's informed consent and being a frequent player – subjects who have played (at least) three complete digital games to ensure they had enough familiarity with the medium.

The data was collected between June and November 2021 on several social media platforms – Reddit, Discord, and Facebook – appealing to private players' communities.

The qualitative data collected intends further to identify the favorite playable characters of frequent players. The parameters under analysis and the survey sections are presented in Table 1:

Table 1. Survey sections and parameters in the analysis.

Survey section	Questions	Answer type and options
1. Sample Characterization	Gender	Female Male Non-binary
	Age group	10–15 16–20 21–25 26–30 31–35 36–40 41–45 46–50 51–55 56–60
	Country	Open-ended question
	Played (at least) three complete digital games	Yes No
2. Favorite Playable Character	Character Name	Open-ended question
	Character Digital Game	Open-ended question

3.2 Phase 2 – Character Analysis

To better understand the playable character and their characteristics, results were supported by the character image analysis and playing the respective digital games. The population in this phase regards the favorite playable characters previously identified by survey respondents.

Visual and quantitative analyses were developed in the character analysis phase, focusing exclusively on third-person digital games. The analyses attended on favorite playable characters' aesthetics and gender identity (Table 2). For this categorization, two researchers classified all the characters, and then the two classifications were evaluated, checking for unconformities between the two analyses. Minor unconformities were detected and debated with a frequent player, an external research member.

Table 2. Playable Characters' analysis parameters.

Dimensions	Indicators
(A) Type of visualization	First-person Third-person
(B) Type of figure	Humanoid Non-humanoid
(C) Character Gender Identity	Masculine Feminine Non-binary
(D) Type of face	Babyface Mature male face Other

4 Results

Results are presented in this section through: study phase 1 – the sample characterization of the survey; and study phase 2 – the sample characterization of favorite playable characters and the mixed linear analysis (qualitative and quantitative) of playable characters presented in a third-person point of view, regarding the parameters previously determined (Table 2).

4.1 Survey Sample Characterization

Examining the gender identity of the survey respondents (N = 301), N = 236 are male, N = 55 female and N = 10 identify as non-binary. Of the non-binary respondents, N = 1 identifies as agender (an umbrella term encompassing people who commonly do not have a gender and, or have a gender that they describe as neutral [24]), N = 1 identifies as AFAB (an acronym meaning "assigned female at birth" [24]), N = 1 identify as genderqueer (an identity commonly used by people who do not identify or express their gender within the gender binary [24], and the rest (N = 7, 0.7%) didn't respond to the optional question.

Regarding the age group, most of the respondents have 21–25 years (N = 95, 31.6%), followed by the group of 26–30 years (N = 69, 22.9%) respondents, then the group of 16–20 years with N = 57 (18.9%); with less representation of respondents from the age groups of 31–35 years (N = 32, 10.6%), 36–40 years (N = 20, 6.6%), 41–45 years (N = 9, 3.0%), 46–50 years (N = 7, 2.3%), 10–15 years (N = 6, 2.0%), 51–55 years (N = 4, 1.3%), and with only two respondents (N = 2, 0.7%) having the age group of 56–60 (Table 3).

Regarding the educational background, most player respondents have a Bachelor's Degree (N = 110, 36,5%) or completed High School (N = 109, 36.2%), followed by less represented subjects with a Master's Degree (N = 47, 15.6%), a Doctoral Degree (N = 15, 5.0%), Middle School conclusion (N = 10, 3.3%), Associate Degree (N = 5, 1.7%), "Other" (N = 4, 1.3%), and one (N = 1, 0.3%) respondent answered that his higher level of education was an elementary school (Table 3).

Table 3. Survey sample Characterization.

Survey sample			
Gender identity	Male	N = 236	77.9%
Age group	Female	N = 57	18.8%
	Non-binary	N = 10	3.3%
	10–15	N = 6	2.0%
	16–20	N = 57	18.9%
	21–25	N = 95	31.6%
	26–30	N = 69	22.9%
	31–35	N = 32	10.6%
	36–40	N = 20	6.6%
	41–45	N = 9	3.0%
	46–50	N = 7	2.3%
	51–55	N = 4	1.3%
	56–60	N = 2	0.7%
Education	Bachelor's Degree	N = 110	36.5%
	High School	N = 109	36.2%
	Master's Degree	N = 47	15.6%
	Doctoral Degree (Ph.D.)	N = 15	5.0%
	Middle School	N = 10	3.3%
	Associate degree	N = 5	1.7%
	Other	N = 4	1.3%
	Elementary School	N = 1	0.3%

Participants are players from 48 different countries, Portugal being the most represented country (N = 95, 31.4%), followed by respondents from the United States of America (USA) (N = 74, 24.4%), United Kingdom (N = 18, 5.9%) and Germany (N = 9, 3.0%). Australia, France, India, and Poland appear with a total of N = 7, representing each 2.3% of the sample. The countries Canada, the Philippines, and Sweden emerged with N = 5 respondents, representing each 1.7% of the sample. From Brazil, Chile, Costa Rica, Italy, Mexico, and South Africa, present N = 4 (1.3%) respondents were from each country. Belgium and Greece are countries with 3 respondents each (1%). With N = 2 each (0.7%) are Argentina, Austria, Malaysia, and the Netherlands. N = 25 countries had one respondent only (0.3%), and another singular respondent (0.3%) replied to have double nationality, both USA and Japanese (Fig. 1).

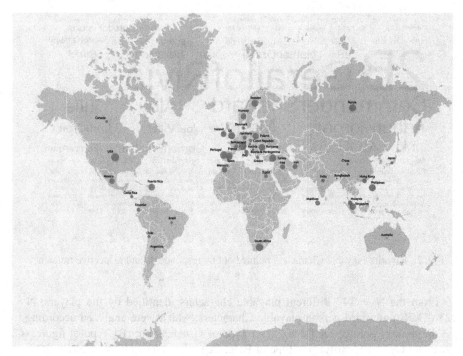

Fig. 1. Survey sample geographic distribution: the size of the circles is proportional to the number of responses from the corresponding location (Mercator Projection).

4.2 Favorite Playable Characters

From the N = 301 valid answers, N = 147 different playable characters were nominated. Some characters were impossible to identify (N = 12, 3.9%), being unclear in their name or respective game.

The most pointed character is "2B" (with N = 23 references) from the digital game "Nier Automata" followed by "Geralt of Rivia" (N = 16) from the "The Witcher" digital game series. The other relevant characters are "Commander Shepard" (N = 9) from "Mass Effect" and "Mario" (N = 8) from "Super Mario". "Aloy" from "Horizon Zero Dawn", "Arthur Morgan" from "Red Dead Redemption" [25], and "Ellie" from "The Last of Us" [26] are all N = 7. With a total of N = 5 references for each character, there is "Link" from "The Legend of Zelda" [27], "A2" a secondary playable character from "Nier Automata", "Kratos" from "God of War", and "Gordon Freeman" from "Half-Life". The other characters cited and their respective frequency is systematized in Fig. 2.

Fig. 2. Favorite Playable Characters pointed out by respondents and respective frequency.

From the N = 147 different playable characters identified by the players, N = 123 (83.7%) are third-person playable Characters, which were analyzed according to the dimensions pointed on Table 2: (A) Type of visualization; (B) Type of figure; (C) Character Gender Identity; (D) Type of Face. Regarding (A), only N = 24 (16.3%) are played through the character's eyes, being first-person characters.

Isolating the third-person playable characters (N = 123, 83.7%), N = 111 (91.0%) are characters with a human-like form, and N = 12 (9%) don't have animal-like or doll-like aesthetics (B). "Amaterasu" from the digital game "Okami" and "Riolu" from "Pokemon Mystery Dungeon Explorers of Sky" are examples of characters not considered human-like in this paper.

4.3   Aesthetic Features and Gender Identity of the Favorite Playable Characters

Regarding the (C) Character Gender Identity N = 70 (57.5%) are male, N = 44 (36.7%) female, and N = 9 (7.3%) the player can personalize de character's gender (avatar and classes type), or the character gender identity is not preserved in their name or aesthetics, and the game narrative doesn't give any clues about it. For instance, the "Traveller" from the digital game "Journey" doesn't provide clues about the character's gender. The playable character "Hawke" from the digital game "Dragon Age 2" is an example of an avatar playable character where the player can choose the character's gender identity.

Regarding (D) Type of Face, N = 48 (39.0%) are characters with a babyface, and 61% not presenting these features. N = 37 (30.1%) have a mature male face, and 69.9% do not present these features. Regarding other types of faces, with no stereotypes attributed (N = 29, 24%), in N = 9 (0.07%), the player can personalize the characters' facial features.

Most of the characters identified by the respondents are fictional characters N = 115 (93.5%), N = 6 (4.2%) are avatars, and there are N = 1 (0.8%) of class, from the digital game "Dota 2", and collective, corresponding to the digital game "The Sims".

The results from the analysis are synthesized in the following image (Fig. 3).

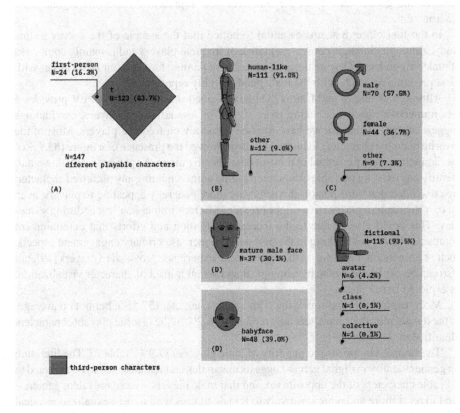

Fig. 3. Playable Characters attributes summary and frequency.

5 Discussion

Digital games have become modern communication vehicles in the interconnected era, not only because of their underlying message, intending to communicate with the player through the game environment and characters, but also by frequently enabling direct communication with other players. As vehicles of communication to and between generations, digital games have an essential role in societies. The messages they convey can impact players, from the clear to the unconscious clues provided. For instance, it is frequently evident that the development of specific skills of the player during the gameplay, such as eye-hand coordination or automated control, but it is not so clear how the underlying messages driven by the visual attributes of the digital game are received and interpreted as intended by the designer.

This paper has focused on the visual attributes of playable characters in a third-person perspective to understand better the players' perspective regarding the aesthetic features and gender identity of the characters that represent them in the digital game environment.

In the first place, it seems essential to notice that the sample of the survey in this study, although global, is not representative of frequent players and is mainly composed of male respondents. Despite the growing trend of gaming females, our study aligns with most previous research, with the male gender highly represented.

Although Denisova and Cairns [11] have argued that third-person PoV provides a less immersive experience, being more suited for less advanced players, our findings suggest otherwise because we have focused our study on frequent players. Most of the favorite playable characters identified by them showed the presence of a figure (83.7% of the characters were presented in third-person visualization). As players were allowed to identify any existing playable character in digital games, naming any preferred character, we concluded that third-person characters are more generally appealing to players, even though the camera perspective might provide different immersion levels during gameplay. This could also be due to the increased attention and efforts that entertainment companies have been making in the past years to increase primary engagement aspects, such as immersion, focusing on the digital game experience provided to players [19], but also can be explained by the psychological and social impact of character visualization, as explored in our paper.

Most respondents prefer playing with a male character (57.5%), but not on average, as the female playable characters only represent 36.7% of the favorite playable characters identified in this study.

The sample comprises the majority of male players (77.9%, Table 3). The literature on gender identity in digital games suggests that males and females tend to be attracted to playable characters of the opposite sex and that male players – more prevalent gamers – tend to react more and more positively to female figures with hyper-sexualized physical attributes [20], it is not surprising to have an increased preference for this type of characters. However, the favorite playable character in our sample shows a preference for male characters and no representativity regarding the non-binary characters. Besides, between the favorite playable characters enabling gender customization (7.3%), the variation is restricted to the female and male genders.

The most cited favorite playable character is "2B", from the digital game "Nier Automata", with 23 references in this study. The fictional character 2B – that stands for YoRHa No. 2 Type B – is the main playable character and the protagonist of the game narrative. Regarding 2B's aesthetical appearance, the character is a female, presented in a sexualized outfit with high heels and leather high-knee boots with a short dress that exposes her underwear. Their face presents babyface features: she has a small chin and nose, and her lips and cheeks are more inflated than average. The facial feature doesn't apply to babyface characteristics (in the first sign) as her eyes are covered with a blindfold. The character's behavior aligns with the stereotyped design presented by Isbister [19]; in the game narrative, she is an android soldier who is reliable, submissive, and cordial. The Japanese artist Akihiko Yoshida, a well-known Manga artist, designed this character. In the manga design, characters typically have babyface features, although the elected character of our participants does not present one [28].

"Geralt of Rivia" is the second-most favorite playable character (N = 16). "Geralt" is a fictional male human Character from the digital game saga "The Witcher". The character's face corresponds to a mature male man who is a witcher with gray hair and a beard. The face doesn't present any babyface features but has prominent scars and a big nose, also responding to current design techniques – mature male faces [20]. His body figure has a considerable size, and strong muscular arms, with his figure being aligned with "the bad guy" [20].

These two favorite playable characters correspond to the literature [22], suggesting that humans tend to have an attentional priority on the opposite gender, babyface features, and mature male faces with aesthetic features playing an essential role in traducing the personality traits and social characteristics of the playable characters. Indeed, if we carefully analyze the respondents' favorite playable characters, they tend to prefer characters with mature male faces in their top ten favorite playable characters. The exceptions to this tendency are the following: "Link" from "The Legend of Zelda", "Mario" in "Super Mario", and "Aloy" from the game series "Horizon".

"Link" and "Mario" are male characters with babyface features that may be explained by the fact that they were characters initially created for the Japanese market. "Aloy" differs from these characters, as a female character presenting more features corresponding to babyface in the first game, "Horizon Zero Dawn". Still, in the recent game, "Horizon Forbidden West", she lost that feature, mainly because the character has aged according to the game narrative. The character aged aesthetically by the loss of the babyface features, generating a wave of hate speech around social media [29, 30], accusing the character of being "chunkier", "ugly", and "masculine" [31].

As enlightened in the related work section, several demographic variables can distinguish players' preferences, and the respondents in our sample came from 48 different countries. This research supports the literature referring to the gender identity of the characters as being a relevant and frequent aspect that interferes with medium consumption [5]. This factor may occur because gaming has been related to males and social stereotypes, as the literature suggests [8].

6 Conclusion

According to the results based on a sample of 301 frequent players, this research concludes that players enjoy playing digital games with a Character whose body they can see – third person's perspective. Male gender is still the most prevalent regarding digital games consumption worldwide, and playable Characters' design features play an essential role in engaging the players and responding to their interests.

From our results is concluded that frequent players tend to select the character based on gender identity and aesthetic features, with an increased preference for characters from the same gender as the player, presenting physical shapes and facial expressions that can trigger specific stereotypes that players enjoy to see represented in the digital games. It is evident the lack of preference for avatars once only 4.2% of the favorite playable characters are integrated into this category (Fig. 2), despite the possibility of role-playing fictional characters with no gender identity known.

The results show a lack of representation of female and non-binary players, which may reflect the selection of the favorite characters (Fig. 1). In the favorite character selection, there are no transgender characters or explicit non-binary characters. Regarding the characters' aesthetics, digital games still perpetuate social stereotypes, with gender bias seeming deeply rooted in players' communities, suggesting that male players have preferences over mature male figures or fragile and obedient female figures.

This research can support digital game designers and developers by intending to explore and better understand the primary engagement element between digital games and their target population – playable characters.

7 Research Limitations and Future Work

This paper does not have a representative sample of the universe of frequent players of digital games. Still, we have outlined some relevant clues to understanding better the players' perspective on playable characters of digital games. Despite the geographical extent of our sample, useful to a multicultural perspective on the theme, it was not representative of all countries and regions, with Europe being the most represented continent, with the rest of the continents less represented (Fig. 1).

Besides the results and the favorite playable character dimensions analyzed (Table 2): (A) Type of visualization; (B) Type of figure; (C) Character Gender Identity, and (D) Type of face, this study does not analyze the character narrative arch, a topic that may impact the player's attachment to the character and their attraction.

The results show a lack of representation of female and non-binary frequent players, suggesting that further analysis should attend to these populations, providing evidence that can be further compared between studies.

Acknowledgments. The study reported in this publication was supported by FCT – Foundation for Science and Technology (Fundação para a Ciência e Tecnologia), I.P. nr. SFRH/BD/143863/2019 and DigiMedia Research Center, under the project UIDB/05460/2020.

References

1. Morrison, I., Ziemke, T.: Empathy with computer game characters : a cognitive neuroscience perspective. In: AISB'05 Convention Social Intelligence and Interaction in Animals, Robots and Agents: 12–15 April 2005 University of Hertfordshire, Hatfield, UK : Proceedings of the Joint Symposium on Virtual Social Agents: Social Presence Cues for Virtual Humanoids Empa. The Society for the Study of Artificial, United Kingdom (2005)
2. Salen, K., Zimmerman, E.: Salen, Zimmerman_Rules of Play: Game Design Fundamentals. MIT Press (2004)
3. Huizinga J.: Homo Ludens: A Study of the Play-element in Culture (1955)
4. Evans, E.J.: Character, audience agency and transmedia drama. Media Cult. Soc. **30**, 197–213 (2008). https://doi.org/10.1177/0163443707086861
5. Simons, J.: Game studies - narrative, games, and theory. Int. J. Comput. Game Res. **7** (2007):
6. Fullerton, T.: Game Design Workshop: A Playcentric Approach to Creating Innovative Games, 2nd edn. CRC Press, New York (2008)
7. Lemarchand, R.: A Playful Production Process: For Game Designers (and Everyone). The MIT Press (2021)
8. Adams, E.: Fundamentals of Game Design, 2nd edn. New Riders (2003)
9. Denisova, A., Cairns, P.: First person vs. third person perspective in digital games. In: Proceedings of the 33rd Annual ACM Conference on Human Factors in Computing Systems. ACM, New York, NY, USA, pp. 145–148 (2015)
10. Ribeiro, T., Veloso, A.I.: Playable characters in digital games: a genre taxonomy proposal. In: H. B, P. G (eds.) 23rd International Conference on Intelligent Games and Simulation, GAME-ON 2022. EUROSIS, pp. 32–37 (2022)
11. Denisova, A., Cairns, P.: First person vs. Third person perspective in digital games: do player preferences affect immersion? In: Conference on Human Factors in Computing Systems - Proceedings 2015-April, pp. 145–148 (2015). https://doi.org/10.1145/2702123.2702256
12. Forster, M., Fabi, W., Leder. H.: Do I really feel it? The contributions of subjective fluency and compatibility in low-level effects on aesthetic appreciation. Front. Hum. Neurosci. **9** (2015). https://doi.org/10.3389/fnhum.2015.00373
13. Graf, L.K.M., Landwehr, J.R.: aesthetic pleasure versus aesthetic interest: the two routes to aesthetic liking. Front. Psychol. **8** (2017). https://doi.org/10.3389/fpsyg.2017.00015
14. Blijlevens, J., Carbon, C.-C., Mugge, R., Schoormans, J.P.L.: Aesthetic appraisal of product designs: Independent effects of typicality and arousal. Br. J. Psychol. **103**, 44–57 (2012). https://doi.org/10.1111/j.2044-8295.2011.02038.x
15. Graf, L.K.M., Landwehr, J.R.: A dual-process perspective on fluency-based aesthetics. Pers. Soc. Psychol. Rev. **19**, 395–410 (2015). https://doi.org/10.1177/1088868315574978
16. Game Research. In; AAAI Workshop - Technical Report 1.
17. Ribeiro, T., Ribeiro, G., Veloso, A.I.: Playable Characters Attributes: An Empirical Analysis Based on the Theoretical Proposal from Katherine Isbister and Ernest Adams, pp. 84–100 (2022)
18. Bakan, U., Bakan, U.: Gender and Racial Stereotypes of Video Game Characters in (MMO) RPGs (MMO)RPG Video Oyun Karakterlerinin Cinsiyet ve Etnik Stereotipleri. Türkiye İletişim Araştırmaları Dergisi 34:100–114 (2019). https://doi.org/10.17829/turcom.514500
19. Isbister, K.: Better game characters by design : a psychological approach. In: Better Game Characters by Design. CRC Press (2006). https://doi.org/10.1201/9780367807641
20. Isbister, K.: Better Game Characters by Design: A Psychological Approach. Elsevier/Morgan Kaufmann (2006)
21. Berry, D.S., McArthur, L.Z.: Some components and consequences of a babyface. J. Pers. Soc. Psychol. **48**, 312–323 (1985). https://doi.org/10.1037/0022-3514.48.2.312

22. Zheng, W., Luo, T., Hu, P., Peng, K.: Glued to Which Face? Attentional priority effect of female babyface and male mature face. Front. Psychol. **9** (2018). https://doi.org/10.3389/fpsyg.2018.00286
23. ESA (2021) 2020 Essential Facts About the Video Game Industry
24. TSER (2022) Trans Student Educational Resourses. https://transstudent.org/about/defini tions/. Accessed 13 Jan 2022
25. Rockstar North;, Rockstar San Diego (2010) Red Dead Redemption
26. Minkoff J, Naughty Dog (2013) The Last of Us
27. Aonuma, E.: Nintendo entertainment planning & development. The Legend of Zelda: Breath of the Wild (2017)
28. (2023) YoRHa No.2 Type B. In: https://nier.fandom.com/wiki/YoRHa_No.2_Type_B
29. GameFAQS users. This game is wonderful but Aloy is awful - Topic Archived (2021). https://gamefaqs.gamespot.com/boards/168644-horizon-zero-dawn/75045459
30. Zophixious. Aloy's looking quite different in Forbidden West (2021). https://www.reddit.com/r/horizon/comments/nn10qb/aloys_looking_quite_different_in_forbidden_west/
31. Henley, S.: The Complaints About Aloy's Look Highlight the Hypocrisy around Realism (2021). https://www.thegamer.com/aloy-snapchat-filter-realism-horizon-forbidden-west/

Be a Gamer: A Psycho-Social Characterization
of the Player

Tânia Ribeiro[1]([✉]) [iD], Ana Isabel Veloso[1] [iD], and Peter Brinson[2] [iD]

[1] DigiMedia, University of Aveiro, Aveiro, Portugal
ribeirotania@ua.pt
[2] USC Games, University of Southern California, Los Angeles, USA

Abstract. Over the past few decades, digital game audiences have increased, gaining relevance and weight in popular culture, and with this, the stereotype of the person who plays digital games as if these persons belong to a separate social world. In popular slang, a Player is sometimes called a "gamer".

In this paper, the systematization of the data collected in a survey spread in closed Gamer's internet social networks forums is made. The reality of N = 301 respondents is analyzed, showing descriptive statistics of the group.

The results show a lack of representation of marginalized groups, with most gamers being white, male, young, and from the middle class. Their political inclination is toward Left-wing ideologies; on average, they tend to be Atheists.

They like to explore the game world instead of enrolling in violent activities, which matches their agreeableness score (a construct related to prosocial behavior). Regarding their personality, they tend to be introverted but open-minded. The majority spent between 5 to 24 h playing per week.

Keywords: Gamer · Game Players · Digital games · Big-five

1 Introduction

Over the past few decades, Digital Game audiences have increased, gaining their own relevance and weight in popular culture [1, 2]. Today, Digital Games are no longer considered a niche medium for entertainment, rather, they are seen as a popular form of entertainment with a positive impact identified at many levels of society, such as health and education [3, 4].

Before Player Profiles can be identified, it is first necessary to define the concept of Player by assessing their profile and social and behavioral traits. This can help to differentiate a common, casual consumer of videogames [5] from a more invested kind of Player whose favorite medium of entertainment is videogames [1].

In this section the concept of human personality is explained in the first section – "Be a human: the personality" – then the digital game audience, followed by the description in – "Be a gamer: a historical background" regarding the historical and cultural background and the audience behavior in their favorite medium.

In the second section of the paper – "Method: Survey Design and structure" – the collect data instrument is described regarding their structure, validation method, and dissemination. In next section "Data Collection and Analysis" – a description of the collected data is reported.

In the third section, the data are discussed, putting into dialogue the findings relating to the aspects of the survey questions. The paper ends with a section dedicated to the research conclusion in Sect. 4, and Sect. 5 points to the research limitations and suggestions for future work.

1.1 Be a Human: The Personality

Despite what each of us does in our leisure time, each of us holds an identity: a personality and a sense of self that makes us unique and inimitable, which presents us to society through a persona – a character that projects the self socially and reflects our own social identity [6, 7]. Even though there is no consensus on the definition of identity, it can be stated it is a concept related to the individual sphere of any person. It reflects every physical, psychological, and interpersonal trait that makes them a singular being. Identity involves cultural traits, such as ethnicity. Still, it also involves physical appearance, emotions, memories, personal goals, ethics and morals, expectations, dreams, and beliefs [6]. In cognitive psychology, personal identity is the notion that an individual object is itself, even if it changes over time [8–10].

The one "self" is individual and private from the personal sphere. However, it projects itself onto the social sphere through a public "self": a series of attributes that individuals choose to communicate to their social sphere. Consequently, the individual's social perception is built on their social identity [11].

Human Personality can be defined by the configuration of characteristics and behaviors that comprises an individual's unique adjustment to life. These configurations include major traits, interests, drives, values, self-concept, abilities, and emotional patterns. Personality is generally viewed as a complex, dynamic integration or totality shaped by many factors, including hereditary and constitutional tendencies; physical maturation; early training; identification with some individuals and groups; culturally or socially conditioned values and roles, or even critical experiences and relationships [12].

Psychology-related disciplines have proposed various theories trying to explain the structure and development of personality differently. Still, all agree that personality helps determine behavior. Despite a considerable variety of methods and proposals for categorizing an individual's personality traits, the model utilized the most by the scientific and medical community is the Five-Factor Model (FFM). Its popularity can be attributed to its compromise between its extensiveness, simplicity, and robustness in its description of human personality [9].

The FFM is a hierarchical taxonomy of personality traits described by the lexical methodology, i.e., it is based on linguistic analyses and attempts to describe and categorize each individual's personality aspects, grading them in five dimensions: openness to experimentation or intellect, conscientiousness, extraversion, neuroticism or negative emotion, and agreeableness [13]. Several scales to access personality based on FFM structure have been published [14], some very comprehensive with more than a hundred items and some short forms [15, 16].

1.2 Be a Gamer: A Historical Background

In popular slang and conversations on certain social media dedicated to sharing content about Digital Games, a Player is often referred as a "gamer". From a historical point of view, the development of this identity dates to the 1980s when the so-called "game crash". During this time, when the global network Internet had not yet been conceived, the number of available games was large, but their quality was lacking, and it was challenging for the consumer to assess the quality of a product, be it a game or a console, and whether it fits their personal preferences. Back then, a "gamer" was a Player with a deep pool of knowledge about the gaming industry and was seen by the community as an expert who was aware of the higher quality games, consoles, the most exciting magazines, and which products fit which tastes.

According to data from 2018, digital game consumers are male (54%), on average in their 30s, who play after work (54%) on a mobile device (60%), and prefer to play with other people in the same place as themselves and who sleep about 7 h a night [17].

Despite the data detailing average consumer habits, not all Digital Game consumers consider themselves "gamers" [1, 18, 19]. According to scientific research, a "gamer" is seen as a person who spends large amounts of time playing Digital Games where a commitment linked to the activity's periodicity is needed. A "gamer" often possesses certain types of hardware, such as game consoles and accessories, marketed to play Digital Games and have a social identity linked to this nomenclature. According to studies based on network analyses, identifying someone with the term "gamer" is directly related to their cybernetic identity. If their network considers a Player to be a "gamer", it is highly likely that they identify as such.

A "gamer" is a consumer of Digital Games who is deeply immersed in "gamer" culture, which discusses games and game world experiences in social contexts beyond the gaming context, who spends significant periods of time playing or dedicating the entirety of their free time to this end. According to De Grove [1] and colleagues, a "gamer" is particularly fond of action games and RPGs and is typically a young male teenager.

It is essential to know which types of Players there are in terms of behavior and routines during the game experience. Among other approaches [20], one of the first authors to mention the interaction of a Player in a game and categorize the players' profiles was Bartle [21].

Bartle (1996), [21] identifies four Player profiles, Achievers, Killers, Socializers, and Explorers. Practically speaking, Achievers are Players typically interested in performing actions in the game world, "acting with" the environment. They are Players who act with foresight and strategize to dominate the game. Killers interact with other players to demonstrate their "superiority" and typically use the game to perform actions that may be considered illegal or deplorable outside of the game world. They feel proud of their reputation and skill. Socializers are Players interested in interacting with other Players more positively and consider that meeting new people is more advantageous than trying to dominate them or interact with them through conflict. They are proud of their friendships, contacts, and influence. Explorers are interested in interacting with the game world, and the surprise element they are doing so will bring. They do not influence on a large scale the game's dynamics but are essential to "know where to go" and find new areas of the game map to visit [1, 22]. To maintain a balanced game, Players interact with each other and the game world, creating dynamics that promote the system's balance and sustainability [21].

2   Method: Survey Design and Structure

A survey was designed and validated through focus group sessions (a total of three): two sessions of specialists from human-computer interaction and social sciences-related fields and the last focus group with gamers.

After the validation, the survey was online between June and November 2021. It was spread on the social platforms Reddit, Discord, and Facebook in private gamers' communities and forums dedicated to discussing Digital Games-related subjects, collecting 301 valid responses, a method inspired by De Grove and colleagues that studies gamers by network analyses [1, 22].

Thus, this paper attempts to answer the following research question – Which psychosocial characteristics can define a gamer? – and attempt to answer it in its five sections were the survey data is discussed: in the first section – 1. Sample personal characterization – we ask about the respondent's gender, age group, education, and country; in the second section – 2. Context and beliefs – we questioned their Ethnic group (based on [23]); in the third section – 3. Gaming Habits characterization aims to know how many hours the respondents played for the week and the life period more active in gaming; in the next section – 4. Typology of Player – we asked about the typology of their most preferable gaming activities based on [15], and in the last section, an FFM personality test was implemented, namely, the BFI-2-S [14], a short form of 30 items aimed at accessing the tendencies of gamers regarding their personal sphere. In Table 1, the survey structure is systematized.

2.1   Data Collection and Analysis

Examining respondents' social characterization, N = 236 are male, N = 57 Female, and N = 10 identify as non-binary. Of the non-binary respondents, N = 1 identify themselves as agender (an umbrella term encompassing people who commonly do not have a gender and, or have a gender that they describe as neutral [24]); N = 1 identify as Afab (Acronym means "assigned female at birth" [24]); N = 1 identify as genderqueer (an identity commonly used by people who do not identify or express their gender within the gender binary [24].

Looking at the sample age group, most of the respondents are from the age range of 21–25 years (N = 95, 31.6%), followed by the group of 26–30 with N = 69 (22.9%) respondents, then the group of 16–20 with N = 57 (18.9%); with less representation of respondents, the age group of 36–40 (N = 20, 6.6%); 41–45 (N = 9; 3.0%); 46–45 (N =,); 10–15 (N =,); 51–55 (N =,) and with only two respondents (0,7%) having the age group of 56–60 (Table 2).

Table 1. Survey structure:

Survey section:	Questions:	Typology:
1. Sample personal Characterization	Gender	Multiple choice
	Age group	Multiple choice
	Education	Multiple choice
	Country	Open question
2. Context and beliefs	Ethnic Group	Multiple choice
	Income	Multiple choice
	Political spectrum	Multiple choice
	Religion	Multiple choice
3. Gaming Habits Characterization	Hours played for the week	Bachelor's Degree
	Life period more active in the gaming	High School
4. Typology of Player	Typology player-playable character [21]	Ranking
5. Personality traits of the Player	BFI-2 [16]	Likert-scale (30 items)

Regarding the educational background, most of the gamer respondents have a Bachelor's Degree (N = 110; 36,5%) or completed High School (N = 109; 36.2%), with less representation Master's Degree (N = 47 15.6%), with a Doctoral Degree (Ph.D.) N = 15, representing 5.0%; with the Middle School complete N = 10; 3.3)%; with an Associate degree N = 5 respondents (1.7%). N = 4 answer "Other" (open-ended question). Only one respondent answered elementary school as his level of education (Table 2).

The survey collected answers from gamers from 48 countries, Portugal being the most represented country with N = 95, corresponding to 31.4% of the total respondents, followed by respondents N = 74 from the United States of America (USA) (24.4%), United Kingdom (N = 18; 5.9%); Germany (N = 9; 3.0%). Australia, France, India, and Poland appear with a total of N = 7, representing each 2.3% of the total sample.

Canada, the Philippines, and Sweden emerge with a total of N = 5 respondents, representing each 1.7% of the total sample. From Brazil, Chile, Costa Rica, Italy, Mexico, and South Africa, N = 4 (1.3%) respondents were from each country. Belgium and Greece are countries with N = 3 respondents each. With N = 2 each, there is Argentina, Austria, Malaysia, and the Netherlands. N = 25 countries had one respondent only, and N = 1 respondent replying had double nationality, both American and Japanese (Fig. 1).

Regarding the Ethnic group in which the gamers respondents identify themselves, N = 260 identify with one ethnic group, N = 31 with two ethnic groups, and N = 6 with three ethnic groups. Of the ones who identify with only one ethnic group, most of them identify as White Caucasian N = 191, while the remaining identify as Latino N = 31, Indian N = 12, Chinese N = 5, Nordic N = 3, Filipino N = 3, Arab N = 2, Korean N =

Table 2. Sample personal characterization: gender, age group, and education:

Section:	Topic:	Response options:	Occurrences:	Percentage:
1. Sample personal characterization	Gender	Male	N = 236	77.9%
		Female	N = 57	18.8%
		Non-binary	N = 10	3.3%
	Age group	10–15	N = 6	2.0%
		16–20	N = 57	18.9%
		21–25	N = 95	31.6%
		26–30	N = 69	22.9%
		31–35	N = 32	10.6%
		36–40	N = 20	6.6%
		41–45	N = 9	3.0%
		46–50	N = 7	2.3%
		51–55	N = 4	1.3%
		56–60	N = 2	0.7%
	Education	Bachelor's Degree	N = 110	36.5%
		High School	N = 109	36.2%
		Master's Degree	N = 47	15.6%
		Doctoral Degree (Ph.D.)	N = 15	5.0%
		Middle School	N = 10	3.3%
		Associate degree	N = 5	1.7%
		Other	N = 4	1.3%
		Elementary School	N = 1	0.3%

2, Japanese N = 2 and other ethnic groups with less representation as it can be checked on Fig. 2.

Most gamer respondents identified themselves on the political spectrum with Left-wing parties (N = 110), and N = 95 didn't care about politics (Table 3).

Concerning their context and beliefs, most respondents identify as white Caucasian, followed by Latino, Indian, and other ethnic groups with less representation. Several respondents identify themselves with more than one ethnic group. In specific,

The Gamer's income is more than their country's average (N = 130) or their country's minimum wage, representing 81.4% of the sample. With less representation, some responders do not have any income: and struggle to have money for basic needs N = 25 representing 8.3% of the sample. N = 17 declared to be parent-dependent (5.6%). N = 10 (3.3%) pointed to the "other" economic reality without specifying it (Table 3).

Regarding political tendency, most gamer respondents N = 111 (36.9%) identify with left-wing ideologies, N = 95 do not care about politics (31.6%); From the center, N = 63, 20.6%; right-wing is the less representative group with N = 22, representing 7.3%

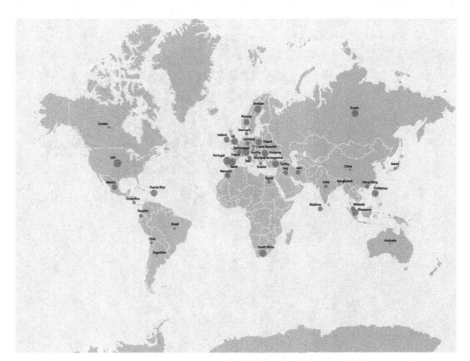

Fig. 1. Survey sample geographic distribution: the size of the circles is proportional to the number of responses from the corresponding location (Mercator Projection)

of the respondents. N = 11 report has "other" political tendencies such as American independent (N = 1); Anarchist (N = 1); Center Right (N = 1); Independent (N = 1); Liberal (N = 1); Progressive (N = 1); Quite left, but also not involved too much in politics (N = 1) and Situational (N = 1), (Table 3).

Almost half of the respondents declare to not believe in any god (N = 143, 47.3%), N = 77 declare to have a religion (N = 77, 25.6%), and N = 63 declare to have some good. Still, they aren't affiliated with any religion. N = 18, 6.2% pointed "other" beliefs such as N = 1 Agnostic, N = 1 Apatheist; N = 1 believe we're all gods; N = 1 don't know, N = 1 have a religion by culture, but won't necessarily practice it; N = 1 is very spiritual, but their beliefs do not fit inside the bounds of a single religion; N = 1 Neither and N = 1 not sure (Table 4).

Concerning their behavior, as gamers, most of the respondents (N = 102) spent five up to 14 h per week playing digital games, representing 33.9% of the sample; the time of their life in which they spent the most time playing digital games was in their teenage and young adult years (Table 3).

About gamers' in-game world preferences, they prefer to explore the Game World preferences N = 139, representing almost half of the respondents 46.2%, followed by Conquer objectives or achievements N = 75, 24.9%; then Socialize with in-game N = 49 (16.3%), and the least preferable activity is Fight and Kill others in-game N = 3, 12.6%.

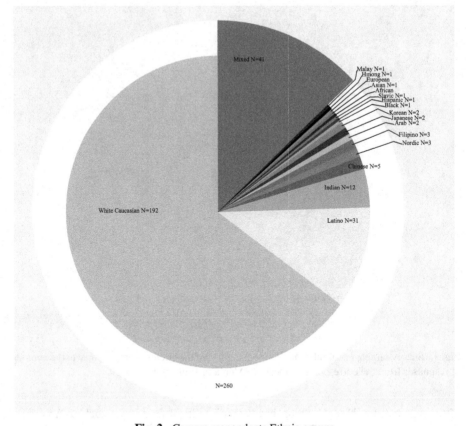

Fig. 2. Gamers respondents Ethnic groups

About their Personality traits [9], on a scale of 1–5, the Extraversion mean of 2.6, and Std. Deviation (ST) is 0.9; Agreeableness mean of 3.5 with an ST = 0.7; Conscientiousness mean of 3.0, ST = 0.7; Open-mind means of 3.8 with an ST = 0.7; Negative Emotionality Score or neuroticism of 3.1, ST = 0.9 (Fig. 1). The median equals the standard on every factor (Fig. 3).

3 Discussion

This paper reports the data collected in a survey aimed at picturing what a gamer is regarding their social and psychological categorization. The survey described this audience in five dimensions: 1. Personal Characterization, 2. Context and Beliefs; 3. Gaming Habits 4. Typology of Player, and 5. Personality traits of the Player (Table 1).

According to the 301 responses collected from June and November 2021 in social media gaming related, gamers are in their majority white males 77.9% (N = 236), who play more in their teenage and young adulthood 16–30 years (N = 221, 73.4%), which matches in part with the research carried on by DeGrove and colleagues in 2005 which found that a gamer is typically a young male teenager. Most of them spend five to 24

Table 3. Sample social context and beliefs: average income, political spectrum, and religion:

Section:	Topic:	Response options:	Occurrences:	Percentage:
2. Context and beliefs	Income	More than the average of their country	N = 130	43.2%
		On average, the minimum wage in their country	N = 115	38.2%
		Any income: struggle to have money for basic needs	N = 25	8.3%
		Parents dependent	N = 17	5.6%
		Other	N = 10	3.3%
		I have way more money than I need to live; I don't need to work	N = 4	1.3%
	Political spectrum	Don't care about politics	N = 95	31.6%
		Left-wing	N = 111	36.9%
		Center	N = 63	20.6%
		Right-wing	N = 22	7.3%
		Other (open question)	N = 11	3.7%
	Religion	Atheist	N = 142	47.2%
		Agnostic	N = 63	20.9%
		Have a religion	N = 77	25.6%
		Other	N = 19	6.3%

h per week playing, which contradicts the 2018 ESA report that consumers are male (54%), on average, in their 30s (*c.f.* Table 2).

Regarding their educational background, the Gamer has a Bachelor's Degree or High School on average N = 219 representing 72.7%. On average, their basic needs are fulfilled once they live on more than the minimum wage of their respective county. Most of them are Left-wing N = 111 (36.9%) or out of politics N = 95 (31.6%). Most of the respondents are Atheists N = 142 (47.2%) (Table 3).

For most gamers respondents, the most exciting activity to do in the game is to Explore the Game World N = 139 (46.2%). This could mean they are interested in finding and interacting with what the game world offers and tend to take advantage of the surprise element that their world knowledge can bring. This kind of Player tends not to influence the game's dynamics but is essential to make other players "know where to go" and find new areas of the game map to explore and visit.

Table 4. Sample social context and beliefs: average income, political spectrum, and religion:

Section:	Topic:	Response options:	Occurrences:	Percentage:
3. Gaming Habits Characterization	Hours played for the week	5 up to 14 h per week	N = 102	33.9%
		15 up to 24 h per week	N = 71	23.6%
		1 up to 4 h per week	N = 49	16.3%
		25 up to 40 h per week	N = 42	14.0%
		up to 1h per week	N = 12	4.0%
		I don't spend any time playing video games right now	N = 9	3.0%
		More than 50 h per week	N = 9	3.0%
		40 up to 50 h per week	N = 7	2.3%
	Life period more active in gaming	Teen (14–17)	N = 128	42.5%
		Young Adult (18–24)	N = 104	34.6%
		Twenties & Thirties (25–35)	N = 29	9.6%
		Preteen (10–13)	27	9.0%
		Thirties & Forties (35–50)	N = 7	2.3%
		Kid (7–9)	N = 5	1.7%
		Infant/Toddler (0–3)	N = 1	.3%

As pointed out in the paper's first section, personality helps determine behavior, and in the case of the data collected, this exploration preference seems to match the average FFM score regarding their personal sphere, specifically regarding the open mind and the extroversion score (Fig. 3).

Their agreeableness, on average, is 3.5 (on a scale of 1 to 5). Agreeableness is synonymous with good nature. Individuals with a high score in this factor are usually modest, gentle, and cooperative. Agreeable people differ from their peers in their responsiveness to emotional stimuli – namely in empathic responses [25, 26]– and in reports where they feel connected and similar to others at the same level [11]. Lower levels of agreeableness are usually signs of a generally negative opinion of others.

Besides, this score was not too high the respondent's score did not seem to match the social perception of gamers often portrayed as violent individuals [27, 28].

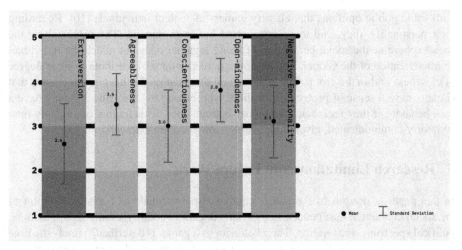

Fig. 3. Gamers respondents' FFM score: mean and SD

On the other hand, their Extraversion score is less than the neutrality on an average of 2.6 (Fig. 3). Extraversion is characterized by a person's greater orientation of interests and a drive toward the outside world – the social experience. In the case of the gamers in the sample, the value indicates that maybe they prefer the inside world or subjective experience. They tend to be introverts.

The gamers respondents also score a little high on Open-mindedness, 3.8 in five. Openness to experimentation is related to intellect. Individuals with high scores in this dimension are usually people who can be considered open to novelty and may be creative, sensitive, practical, and unconventional. A low score in this dimension means the individual is insensitive and conventional – or conservative, which identifies the sampling case if we consider the political and religious tendencies pointed out at the beginning of the chapter and in Table 2. Open-mindedness is the most controversial of the big five due to its ample nature. Some scholars state that openness to experimentation has a more expansive meaning than other FFM factors [11]. Yet, being open to experimentation is one of the main predictors of creativity.

4 Conclusion

On average, according to the results based on a sample of 301 respondents answering the research question – Which psycho-social characteristics can define a gamer? – a Gamer is a young middle-class white male. If he chooses to go to vote, he probably votes for a left-wing party; he does not have many religious beliefs. He does not tend to play more than 40 h per week, and the preferred activity in-game is to explore the game world. He may be introverted but open-minded and agreeable.

The results show a lack of representation of marginalized groups and female gamers, which seems to match other scientific studies on this topic [1, 18, 19]. They like to explore the game world instead of enrolling in violent activities, which seems to match their agreeableness score (a construct related to prosocial behavior). These findings collide with some public opinions that classify gamers as violent individuals [10]. Regarding their personality, they tend to be introverted but open-minded. The results show the social sphere or the social perception of being a gamer does not match the individual characterization of the Gamer. This different perception may contribute to some degree of closeness within the group. The hypothetical justification for this phenomenon is that Gamers have a sense of protection for those who belong to their tribe and may have a rush behavior if they feel their community is threatened. This feeling of empathy may be poorly communicated, given their average low score on extraversion [29].

5   Research Limitations and Future Work

In this paper, a portrait of the gamer characteristics is made as a systematization of the social characteristics: gender, age group, education, country, ethnic group, income, political spectrum, and religion. Their behavior as a gamer is described, namely the time they spend playing, the life period more active in gaming, and their preferred typology of playing [21]. A summary of their personality (BFI-2-S) [9, 16] is also enframed. This paper explains a data set by generating summaries about 301 gamers respondents and descriptive statistics. While these descriptives help understand data attributes showing an overview of what being a gamer is, they cannot be used to make inferences or predictions. The results also have to be analyzed with precaution, considering that 301 gamers respondents do not necessarily represent all the gamers in the world, as it is possible to check in Fig. 1.

In future work, correlation tests should be conducted to evaluate the strength of the association between the several variables described in this paper. The authors also recommend a test of the data distribution, testing the reliability and validity tests.

Ethical Concerns. As mentioned in this paper, the questionnaire was spread in closed internet social network forums. The leading researcher used her personal account for the questionnaire spreading, always informing the other community members about their intentions. The present research follows the European Union General Data Protection Regulation (GDPR) of May 25, 2018. No personal data that can personally identify the participants were recorded in the process

Acknowledgments. The study reported in this publication was supported by FCT – Foundation for Science and Technology (Fundação para a Ciência e Tecnologia), I.P. nr. SFRH/BD/143863/2019 and DigiMedia Research Center, under the project UIDB/05460/2020.

References

1. de Grove, F., Courtois, C., van Looy, J.: How to be a gamer! Exploring personal and social indicators of gamer identity. J. Comput.-Mediat. Commun. **20**, 346–361 (2015). https://doi.org/10.1111/jcc4.12114
2. ESA. 2020 Essential Facts About the Video Game Industry (2021)
3. Griffiths, M.: The therapeutic value of video games. In: Handbook of Computer Game Studies, pp. 161–171 (2005)

4. Griffiths, M., Kuss, D.J., Ortiz de Gortari, A.B.: Videogames as therapy: a review of the medical and psychological literature. In: Cruz-Cunha, M.M., Miranda, I.M, Gonçalves, P. (eds.) Handbook of Research on ICTs and Management Systems for Improving Efficiency in Healthcare and Social Care. IGI Global (2013)

5. Juul, J.: A Casual Revolution: Video Games and Their Players (2020)

6. Erikson, E.H.: Identity and the Life Cycle. W. W. Norton & Company (1980)

7. VandenBos, G.R., American Psychological Association. APA Dictionary of Psychology. American Psychological Association (2015)

8. VandenBos, G.R.: APA Dictionary of Psychology. American Psychological Association (2016)

9. Soto, C.J., Kronauer, A., Liang, J.K.: Five-factor model of personality. In: The Encyclopedia of Adulthood and Aging, pp. 1–5. Wiley, Hoboken (2015)

10. Oliveira, J.P.: Psychometric properties of the Portuguese version of the mini-IPIP five-factor model personality scale. Curr. Psychol. **38**(2), 432–439 (2017). https://doi.org/10.1007/s12 144-017-9625-5

11. Matsumoto, D.: The Cambridge Dictionary of Psychology. Cambridge University Press, San Francisco (2009)

12. American Psychological Association. APA Dictionary of Psychology (2015)

13. McCrae, R.R., John, O.P.: An introduction to the five-factor model and its applications. J. Pers. **60**, 175–215 (1992). https://doi.org/10.1111/j.1467-6494.1992.tb00970.x

14. McCrae, R.R., Allik, J.: The Five-Factor Model of Personality Across Cultures. Springer, New York (2002). https://doi.org/10.1007/978-1-4615-0763-5

15. Goldberg, L.R.: An alternative "description of personality": the big-five factor structure. J. Pers. Soc. Psychol. **59**, 1216–1229 (1990). https://doi.org/10.1037/0022-3514.59.6.1216

16. Soto, C.J., John, O.P.: Short and extra-short forms of the Big Five Inventory–2: the BFI-2-S and BFI-2-XS. J. Res. Pers. **68**, 69–81 (2017). https://doi.org/10.1016/J.JRP.2017.02.004

17. ESA. Essential facts about the Computer and Video Game Industry (2019)

18. Shaw, A.: On not becoming gamers: moving beyond the constructed audience. ADA J. Gender New Media Technol. **1**, 1–25 (2013). https://doi.org/10.7264/N33N21B3

19. Shaw, A.: Do you identify as a gamer? Gender, race, sexuality, and gamer identity. New Media Soc. **14**, 28–44 (2012). https://doi.org/10.1177/1461444811410394

20. Vahlo, J., Kaakinen, J.K., Holm, S.K., Koponen, A.: Digital game dynamics preferences and player types. J. Comput.-Mediat. Commun. **22**, 88–103 (2017). https://doi.org/10.1111/jcc4. 12181

21. Bartle, R., Muse, L.: Hearts, Clubs, diamonds, spades: players who suit MUDs. J. MUD Res. **6**, 39 (1996). https://doi.org/10.1007/s00256-004-0875-6

22. de Grove, F., Cauberghe, V., van Looy, J.: In Pursuit of play: toward a social cognitive understanding of determinants of digital play. Commun. Theory **24**, 205–223 (2014). https:// doi.org/10.1111/comt.12030

23. Office of Public Affairs (OPA). Ethnic groups. In: The World Facebook (2022)

24. TSER (2022) Trans Student Educational Resources. https://transstudent.org/about/defini tions/. Accessed 13 Jan 2022

25. Hong, H., Han, A.: A systematic review on empathy measurement tools for care professionals. Educ. Gerontol. **46**, 72–83 (2020). https://doi.org/10.1080/03601277.2020.1712058

26. Ratka, A.: Empathy and the development of affective skills. Am. J. Pharm. Educ. **82**, 7192 (2018). https://doi.org/10.5688/ajpe7192

27. Markey, P.M., Ivory, J.D., Slotter, E.B., et al.: He does not look like video games made him do it: racial stereotypes and school shootings. Psychol. Popul. Media **9**, 493–498 (2020). https:// doi.org/10.1037/PPM0000255

28. Tänzler, D.: Time. In: Kühnhardt, L., Mayer, T. (eds.) The Bonn Handbook of Globality, pp. 1387–1396. Springer, Cham (2019). https://doi.org/10.1007/978-3-319-90382-8_58
29. Trå, H.V., Volden, F., Watten, R.G.: High Sensitivity: factor structure of the highly sensitive person scale and personality traits in a high and low sensitivity group. Two gender—matched studies. Nord Psychol. 1–23 (2022). https://doi.org/10.1080/19012276.2022.2093778

A Metamodel for Immersive Gaming Experiences in Virtual Reality

Fabiola Rivera and Francisco J. Gutierrez[✉]

Department of Computer Science, University of Chile,
Beauchef 851, West Building, Third Floor, Santiago, Chile
fabiolarivera@ug.uchile.cl, frgutier@dcc.uchile.cl

Abstract. Due to the increasing adoption of specialized hardware, the development of novel gaming experiences in virtual reality (VR) has gained traction. Despite the popularity that VR has achieved so far, it is still not clear how to address the design of immersion, which is critical for providing meaningful, enjoyable, and engaging experiences in VR video games. Aiming to bridge this gap, in this paper we reviewed the recent literature in this domain and formalized it as a conceptual metamodel for analyzing and designing meaningful gaming experiences in VR. The main dimensions addressed in this metamodel interrelate user, software, and hardware components, explicitly addressing immersion and player involvement. We argue that the proposed metamodel can be useful to both researchers and designers interested in conceiving immersive, innovative, and engaging VR gaming experiences.

Keywords: Immersion · Involvement · Virtual Reality · Video Games

1 Introduction

The video game industry has been embracing over the years a variety of hardware to conceive different kinds of interactive experiences. These range from casual—quick bite—games running on smartphones, to AAA titles with state-of-the-art graphics running on specialized consoles and gaming PCs. Therefore, as in any tech business, this industry has being pushing its limits hand-on-hand with the advances in hardware development.

These advances have allowed video game designers and developers to explore novel ways to provide playful experiences [5]. Among these, one of the most relevant criteria to address in a successful video game is to ensure a certain level of engagement [18], i.e., the capability to generate in players a sense of emotional connection, which could ease them to return to the game. Following this same line of reasoning, video game designers usually imply that ensuring a certain degree of immersion is critical for achieving a state of engagement.

However, the current body of literature in video game design has not reached yet a full agreement on the very notion of immersion. In 1980, Minsky [15] gave one of its first definitions, relating it to the concept of "telepresence", which is the way in which a remote machine can shift the sense of local existence to a distant place. In 1992, Sheridan [22] then specialized this notion, referring to

© The Author(s), under exclusive license to Springer Nature Switzerland AG 2023
X. Fang (Ed.): HCII 2023, LNCS 14047, pp. 315–326, 2023.
https://doi.org/10.1007/978-3-031-35979-8_25

the concept of "virtual presence" to name the specific experience of presence in virtual environments. Later on, Lombard et al. [14] in 1997 explicitly linked the concepts of presence and immersion, defining these notions as a perceptual illusion that is not necessarily mediated by a particular agent. Finally, Stokols et al. [23] in 2003 showed how this definition can be applied to the domain of video games, but fail to provide an analysis on how it can be put into practice.

Trying to conceptualize the notion of immersion, Brown and Cairns [1] described it as one of the three levels in which a player can feel "absorbed" by a video game. According to these authors, immersion is understood as the deepest level of engagement in an interactive experience, where the emotions of a player are directly affected by the video game, ultimately feeling present, more like as a single entity with the virtual experience. Then, in 2005, Ermi and Mäyrä [4] formalized a model covering three dimensions of gameplay experience: sensorial, challenge-based, and imaginative. Finally, Calleja [2] proposed the *Player Involvement Model* in 2011, which sought to consolidate the multidimensional features of immersion, highlighting the gaps existing in the previous research efforts reported at the time in the literature. Such a model interrelates six dimensions of involvement: (1) kinesthetic (i.e., how the player controls the physical elements of the virtual environment); (2) spatial (i.e., how the player explores and navigates within the virtual environment); (3) shared (i.e., how the player becomes aware of the other components involved in the virtual environment); (4) narrative (i.e., how the player engages with the overall game story and their interaction with the video game components in the virtual environment); (5) affective (i.e., how the player relates emotionally to the virtual environment); and (6) ludic (i.e., how the player makes decisions and overcomes the proposed challenges in the virtual environment).

Despite that the model proposed by Calleja addresses the most significant ideas around the notion of immersion and player involvement, it was developed at a time where virtual reality (VR) was not widely adopted. In fact, advances in the design of interactive computing systems are slowly but surely evolving toward a new generation, where interpersonal encounters and user experiences are shifting to be conducted virtually in the so-called *metaverse*. This new space holds on to the promise to seamlessly allow people to connect, collaborate, learn, conduct financial transactions, and entertain themselves in a virtual ecosystem that effectively blurs—if not, make disappear—temporal and spatial barriers [10].

Responding to the massification of VR technology, the increasing interest in the video game industry to develop new experiences in this domain, and building upon the Player Experience Model proposed by Calleja [2], we seek to extend its applicability to video games controlled in a VR environment. In this paper we review the most recent body of literature on immersion and gaming experiences as a way to formalize a metamodel to assist video game designers and developers on conceiving engaging, playful, and immersive experiences in VR.

The proposed literature analysis and metamodel can be used to inform the analysis and design of interactive computing applications, and more specifically, video games in VR environments. In other words, the proposed components, interactions, and structural dimensions can be useful for assisting designers in formalizing the application domain, i.e., identifying the underlying concepts, variables, relations, and constraints that need to be addressed during development. As a result, the main contribution of this work becomes relevant when considering the current state of practice in which VR technology—colloquially speaking, the *metaverse*—is increasingly impacting society with novel ways for interacting, collaborating, and playing.

The rest of this paper is structured as follows. Section 2 presents and discusses the literature that sustains the definition of the metamodel. Section 3 formalizes the main components and their dimensions, for analyzing and designing immersive gaming experiences in VR. Section 4 proposes a set of implications for design, derived from the metamodel. Finally, Sect. 5 concludes and provides perspectives on future work.

2   Literature Review

Following an approach inspired on systematic literature reviews [11], we examined the recent published research on immersive gaming experiences in VR. To do so, we conducted a manual search on the proceedings of the most prestigious research conferences in the domain: CHI, CHI PLAY, VRST, and IEEE VR. We reviewed titles, abstracts, and index terms according to the following set of keywords: *immersion, virtual reality, video games, presence, engagement,* and *involvement.* We structured the analyzed corpus in two main categories: (1) immersion as a factor of player experience and (2) the relation between hardware and software components in immersive experiences.

2.1   Immersion as a Factor of Player Experience

Measuring player experience is not an easy task to accomplish, given the integrated nature of variables that are encompassed by the phenomenon [8]. More so, research in player-computer interaction tends to lack coherence when following theoretical frameworks, as well as consistency in its analysis [12].

Several authors have proposed assessment frameworks that aim to measure player experience addressing immersion among its components [25]. For instance, Jennett et al. [9] concluded that immersion can be measured both subjectively (i.e., through a questionnaire addressing cognitive, emotional, affective, and social components) and objectively (i.e., through computing performance metrics, such as task completion and eyetracking). Likewise, Qin et al. [20] explored how core elements, such as the game narrative and proposed challenges influence player curiosity, empathy, and game control.

Other models address the relationship between immersion and presence. For instance, Witmer and Singer [26] proposed that presence can be measured in virtual environments through measuring the levels of control, distraction, and realism. Likewise, O'Brien and Toms [17] proposed a scale to measure engagement in software applications as a combination of aesthetics, challenges, attention, affect, control, motivation, and interest.

Literature also reports a set of instruments that are focused in explicitly measuring player experience, incorporating immersion as one of the studied dimensions. For instance, Sweetser and Wyeth [24] proposed *Gameflow*, which measures the enjoyment related to the sensation of flow within a video game. Likewise, Högberg et al. [6] developed *GamefulQuest*, an instrument to measure the perceived playability of an application or system. Finally, IJsselsteijn et al. proposed the *Game Experience Questionnaire* [7], which is a valid and reliable instrument for measuring player experience in gaming, widely used in academic research and in the video game industry [13].

2.2 Hardware and Software as Immersion Components

Porter and Robb [19] analyzed consumer trends in VR. They found that the specific hardware used to interact in VR should act as an enabler to amplify immersion. In particular, the technical capabilities of the head-mounted display (i.e., the device typically used to interact in VR environments) should be robust enough to offer smooth experiences, with a reasonable refresh rate and ergonomic controls. Likewise, other kinds of sensors and actuators (such as gestural inputs and haptic feedback) are essential for providing immersive gaming experiences.

Following a similar line of reasoning, the authors also identified factors that prevented users to perceive immersion and flow. Among these, the technical malfunctioning of the display (e.g., dead pixels or lagging) is a critical disruptor of the overall experience. In terms of ergonomics, a lack of intuitive affordances that do not match the player's mental model is also criticized.

3   Formalizing the Metamodel

After analyzing the most recent body of knowledge in immersive gaming experiences in VR, we structure a metamodel for supporting researchers and video game designers when conceiving and studying novel mechanisms that favor player engagement, involvement, and flow.

Our model—depicted in Fig. 1—is composed of three main dimensions: user, hardware, and software. Just as Calleja [2] proposed that the dimensions of his model are not isolate components, our metamodel considers that its three core dimensions are interrelated and should be addressed jointly in analysis, design, development, and evaluation.

For instance, ergonomic controls favor a positive experience, whereas motion sickness (caused by a bad control of the user, bad quality of the display, or subpar rendering) is an enabler for a negative experience [3]. In the latter case, we see that motion sickness can be a consequence of a multidimensional degradation in user experience originated by, the user, hardware, and software component, respectively (*cf.* Fig. 2). Therefore, in addition to the described dependency among model dimensions, we also need to account for the interaction between

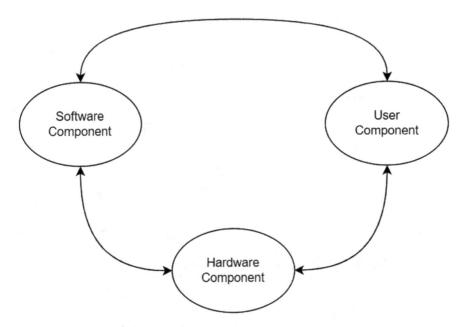

Fig. 1. Main Components of the Metamodel for Immersive Gaming Experiences in VR

these components, which could positively or negatively affect player experience with regard to immersion.

The following subsections present more in detail the main components of the proposed metamodel: (1) user component, (2) hardware component, (3) software component, and (4) the interaction between metamodel components.

3.1 User Component

In this component we address the factors that are related to the user, which could be subclassified in attitudinal, behavioral, cognitive, and social. More in particular, we identify that these considerations can be grouped in two subdimensions: (1) user preferences and (2) user capabilities. Just as the metamodel as a macrostructure, these subdimensions are also interrelated, so should be considered jointly when analyzing or designing a particular experience (*cf.* Fig. 3).

On the one hand, the user preference dimension addresses elements such as player personality and how it influences the overall experience. One of the most relevant models currently accepted by the community is BrainHex [16], which maps player personality traits to gaming preferences and motivational triggers. Following this line of reasoning, different player profiles (for example, those characterized by BrainHex) can be affected—positively or negatively— by specific game mechanics when analyzing their overall play experience. In other words, some players might enjoy specific features of a game (e.g., collectathons), whereas other players could react indifferently, or even reject, those

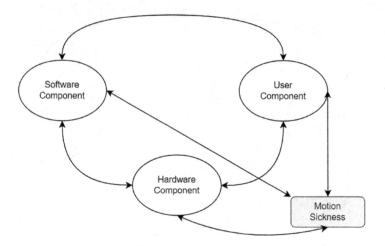

Fig. 2. Interaction between components: Motion Sickness

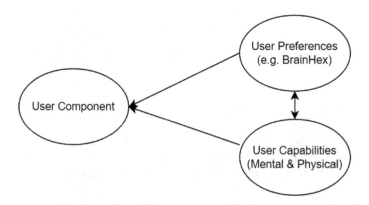

Fig. 3. User Component Dimensions

same features. Therefore, understanding the underlying drives and preferences of the different classes of players, can influence in how presence, immersion, and involvement are experienced in the video game. This can be reached by tailoring aesthetics, environment features, narrative, and game mechanics.

On the other hand, the user capability dimension addresses both physical and psychological drives that push the player to interact with the video game. This can be explained as VR games build up a sense of reality, which enables the interactivity between the player and the proposed immersive experience. In particular, as with any interactive system, it is critical to address the anthropological, behavioral, cognitive, and social factors that sustain the design of presence, immersion, and involvement, given that they set up the boundaries of what the user would be capable of doing [21].

3.2   Hardware Component

This components considers the physical materials that the player uses to interact with the video game (*cf.* Fig. 4). Therefore, it encompasses the hardware features that are in charge of ensuring interactivity, immersion, and flow: (1) the head-mounted display and (2) game controls.

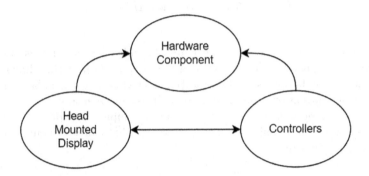

Fig. 4. Hardware Component Dimensions

These dimensions—in the same vein as the metamodel itself—are interrelated. In other words, they should not be analyzed independently from each other. For instance, ergonomic controllers could map specific navigation and control mechanisms, which should enact acceptable rendering and flow in the head mounted display. If these devices are not properly in sync, the user might suffer from motion sickness, which leads to a negative player experience [3]. Likewise, given that VR headsets are still fairly novel technology in the mass market, ergonomic features in both display and controllers, user onboarding, and smooth learning curves through clear affordances should be favored.

3.3   Software Component

This component considers the gaming aspects of the experience. This is, the design elements that control the running software. In particular, this component is sustained in the dimensions defined by Calleja [2] in his Player Involvement Model (*cf.* Fig. 5).

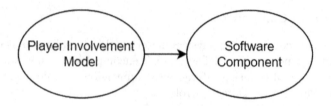

Fig. 5. Software Component Dimensions

Such a model considers the key features of a video games in terms of immersion and player involvement. However, a major limitation of this dimension is that Calleja built his proposal for traditional video games (i.e., those that are controlled by conventional navigation and control mechanisms). To the best of our knowledge, there is currently no substantial empirical evidence to support what game mechanics could enhance immersion, player involvement, and sense of presence in VR games.

3.4   Interaction Between Metamodel Components

Finally, the proposed metamodel considers that the different dimensions are all interrelated and should be considered jointly when analyzing or designing immersive gaming experiences in VR. These interactions are depicted with dashed lines (– – –) in Fig. 6.

One of these interactions is between the hardware component and the Kinetic Involvement subdimension of the software component, as well as with the user capability subdimension of the user component. Both of these consider the interaction with the physical environment, which encompass those elements that the user has to their disposition for enabling, mediating, and consequently, enacting the interaction. On the one hand, regarding the kinetic involvement, this is related to the sense of control that is perceived by the player. For instance, by improving the hardware capabilities for controlling and navegating within the virtual world, then the player would interact more smoothly with the physical controls and/or the head-mounted display, which benefits player experience, their sense of presence, immersion, and involvement. On the other hand, regarding the user capabilities, they are related to the physical and cognitive loads that the player face for sustaining their interaction.

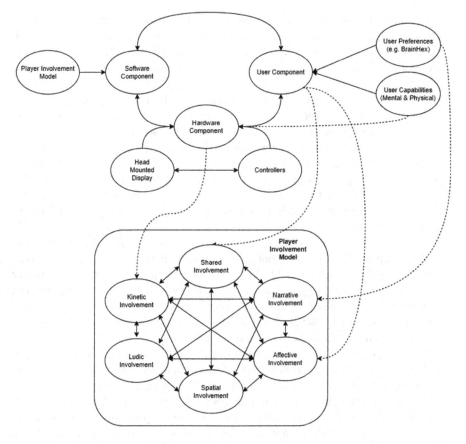

Fig. 6. Metamodel for Immersive Gaming Experiences in VR

Likewise, we note the interactions between the user component and both Shared and Affective Involvement subdimensions of the software component. These consider the interaction between the player and other social agents, as well as their emmotional relatedness and affection toward the gaming experience. For instance, if the design of the video game does not consider social agents for sustaining the interaction with the player, then the shared involvement dimension would be compromised.

4   Implications for Design

Building on the formalization of the metamodel described in the previous section, we now present a set of guidelines that can be useful for VR video game designers, researchers, and practitioners working in this application domain. In particular, we stress the importance of presence, involvement, and immersion or achieving successful interactive player experiences.

- Consider not only player preferences, but also their capabilities and limitations. Building upon the user component dimensions of the metamodel, different types of players have different approaches when interacting with VR technology. This directly impacts on their expectations toward different game mechanics and environment features, such as narrative, sound involvement, and aesthetics. Therefore, VR games may benefit from targeting players in a broad spectrum of technology access, previous experiences, expectations, and consequently adapt and/or personalize the interactive elements of the software. For instance, if a player is skilled, then the game may allow free movements or propose a complex navigation. Conversely, for a more novice player, then the game can provide explicit affordances and restrictions to limit movement or rely on teletransportation as a way to control their exposure to the 3D environment by trying to mitigate the potential negative effects of motion sickness.
- Provide meaningful experiences for different types of players. Once again, building upon the user component dimensions of the metamodel, the ludic elements and/or mechanics of the video game can be perceived differently in the broader taxonomy of player types. Likewise, the software component of the metamodel may tackle how these different stimuli can be arranged and presented to the player, in a way that the different dimensions articulate themselves to provide a positive play experience.
- VR video games are more than pieces of software. They are controlled by specialized hardware, which is not always broadly adopted by players. Therefore, video game designers should acknowledge the potential novelty effect that is introduced by the affordances and access to this rather novel kind of technology, in a way to ease player interaction and reduce potential negative effects of their (mis)use, such as motion sickness. This is reflected in the hardware and software components of the metamodel, which also interact with the user component during analysis and design of the immersive elements of the video game. In particular, the kinetic dimension of the metamodel explains how the avatar should be controlled and how the game provides affordable mechanisms of navigation and control. In other words, both software and hardware should be tightly coupled for providing meaningful and positive player experiences.

5 Conclusion and Future Work

Despite the rapid development of affordable mass-market VR hardware in the gaming industry, we still face a challenge in properly understanding how to design—and analyze—immersive gaming experiences in this domain. While the promise of the metaverse relies on ensuring a seamless interaction between people and the virtual environment, this is critical for video games. In this paper, we reviewed recent literature in this domain and we structured such a body of knowledge in the form of a metamodel for assisting researchers and practitioners interested in designing novel interaction mechanisms in VR games, which favor immersion, engagement, and flow.

The next steps in this research consist in evaluating the appropriateness of the proposed metamodel for: (1) designing and evaluating a prototype video game and (2) evaluate its fit with already published titles (e.g., in Steam and PlayStation Store) as a way to confirm the correctness and completeness of the model components and subdimensions.

References

1. Brown, E., Cairns, P.: A grounded investigation of game immersion. In: CHI'04 Extended Abstracts on Human Factors in Computing Systems, pp. 1297–1300 (2004)
2. Calleja, G.: In-Game: From Immersion to Incorporation. MIT Press, Cambridge (2011)
3. Chattha, U.A., Janjua, U.I., Anwar, F., Madni, T.M., Cheema, M.F., Janjua, S.I.: Motion sickness in virtual reality: an empirical evaluation. IEEE Access 8, 130486–130499 (2020)
4. Ermi, L., Mäyrä, F.: Player-centred game design: experiences in using scenario study to inform mobile game design. Game Studies 5(1), 1–10 (2005)
5. Freeman, D.: Creating emotion in games: The craft and art of emotioneering^{TM}. Comput. Entertain. 2(3), 15 (2004)
6. Högberg, J., Hamari, J., Wästlund, E.: Gameful experience questionnaire (gamefulquest): an instrument for measuring the perceived gamefulness of system use. User Model. User-Adap. Inter. 29(3), 619–660 (2019)
7. IJsselsteijn, W.A., de Kort, Y.A.W., Poels, K.: The Game Experience Questionnaire. Technische Universiteit Eindhoven (2013)
8. IJsselsteijn, W., De Kort, Y., Poels, K., Jurgelionis, A., Bellotti, F.: Characterising and measuring user experiences in digital games. In: International Conference on Advances in Computer Entertainment Technology, vol. 2, p. 27 (2007)
9. Jennett, C., Cox, A.L., Cairns, P., Dhoparee, S., Epps, A., Tijs, T., Walton, A.: Measuring and defining the experience of immersion in games. Int. J. Hum Comput Stud. 66(9), 641–661 (2008)
10. Jian, S., Chen, X., Yan, J.: From online games to "metaverse": the expanding impact of virtual reality in daily life. In: Rauterberg, M. (ed.) Culture and Computing, HCII 2022. LNCS, vol. 13324, pp. 34–43. Springer, Cham (2022).https://doi.org/10.1007/978-3-031-05434-1_3
11. Kitchenham, B., Pearl Brereton, O., Budgen, D., Turner, M., Bailey, J., Linkman, S.: Systematic literature reviews in software engineering - a systematic literature review. Inf. Softw. Technol. 51(1), 7–15 (2009)
12. Koivisto, J., Hamari, J.: The rise of motivational information systems: a review of gamification research. Int. J. Inf. Manag. 45, 191–210 (2019)
13. Law, E.L.C., Brühlmann, F., Mekler, E.D.: Systematic review and validation of the game experience questionnaire (GEQ) - implications for citation and reporting practice. In: Proceedings of the 2018 Annual Symposium on Computer-Human Interaction in Play, pp. 257–270. CHI PLAY 2018 (2018)
14. Lombard, M., Ditton, T.: At the heart of it all: The concept of presence. J. Comput.-Mediat. Commun. 3(2), JCMC321 (1997)
15. Minsky, M.: Telepresence. OMNI Mag. 44–52 .(1980)
16. Nacke, L.E., Bateman, C., Mandryk, R.L.: Brainhex: a neurobiological gamer typology survey. Entertain. Comput. 5(1), 55–62 (2014)

17. O'Brien, H.L., Toms, E.G.: The development and evaluation of a survey to measure user engagement. J. Am. Soc. Inform. Sci. Technol. **61**(1), 50–69 (2010)
18. Oliver, M.B., Bowman, N.D., Woolley, J.K., Rogers, R., Sherrick, B.I., Chung, M.Y.: Video games as meaningful entertainment experiences. Psychol. Pop. Media Cult. **5**(4), 390 (2016)
19. Porter III, J., Robb, A.: An analysis of longitudinal trends in consumer thoughts on presence and simulator sickness in VR games. In: Proceedings of the Annual Symposium on Computer-Human Interaction in Play, pp. 277–285 (2019)
20. Qin, H., Patrick Rau, P.L., Salvendy, G.: Measuring player immersion in the computer game narrative. Intl. J. Human-Comp. Interact. **25**(2), 107–133 (2009)
21. Ritter, F.E., Baxter, G.D., Churchill, E.F.: Foundations for Designing User-Centered Systems. Springer-Verlag, London (2014). https://doi.org/10.1007/978-1-4471-5134-0
22. Sheridan, T.B.: Musings on telepresence and virtual presence. Presence Teleoperat. Virtual Environ. **1**(1), 120–126 (1992)
23. Stokols, D., Grzywacz, J.G., McMahan, S., Phillips, K.: Increasing the health promotive capacity of human environments. Am. J. Health Promot. **18**(1), 4–13 (2003)
24. Sweetser, P., Wyeth, P.: Gameflow: a model for evaluating player enjoyment in games. Comput. Entertain. **3**(3), 3–3 (2005)
25. Wang, X., Goh, D.H.L.: Components of game experience: an automatic text analysis of online reviews. Entertain. Comput. **33**, 100338 (2020)
26. Witmer, B.G., Singer, M.J.: Measuring presence in virtual environments: a presence questionnaire. Presence **7**(3), 225–240 (1998)

Task Significance in Digital Games: Controlled Experiment Shows Impact of Narrative Framing and Upgrades on Player Experience

Owen Schaffer[✉]

Computer Science and Information Systems, Bradley University, 1501 W Bradley Ave, Peoria, IL 61625, USA
OSchaffer@Bradley.edu

Abstract. A between-subjects controlled experiment with a 4×4 factorial design was conducted with 391 participants to test the impact of narrative framing and upgrades on player experience. Participants played one of 16 versions of a custom research game online, and then completed an online survey. Two ways to facilitate Task Significance in games were tested: narrative framing and character upgrading mechanisms. The Enjoyment Questionnaire (EQ) and Sources of Enjoyment Questionnaire (SoEQ) were used as measures to assess player experience. A Prosocial Narrative Framing focused on helping people in need had a significant positive effect on task significance, social responsibility, clear task purpose, and honor, but did not have a significant effect on enjoyment. Upgrade mechanisms had a significant but smaller effect on task significance, and a significant effect on enjoyment. Narrative framing was a more effective way to design for task significance or meaning, while upgrade mechanisms were a more effective way to design for enjoyment. This results of this experiment advance the study of meaning and enjoyment in digital games.

Keywords: Enjoyment · Meaning · Task Significance · Narrative Framing · Character Upgrades · Eudemonia · Controlled Experiment · Flow · Task Engagement · Intrinsic Motivation · Digital Games · Computer Games · Video Games

1 Introduction

We define task significance as the extent to which people perceive what they are doing as important or meaningful. How can practitioners and researchers design systems to provide task significance? Does task significance increase enjoyment? The present research uses controlled experiments with different versions of a custom research game to explore these questions.

Understanding how to design for task significance is not only important for game design, but for gamification and serious games as well. Gamification is "the use of game design elements in non-game contexts" [1], such as to make non-game systems more

© The Author(s), under exclusive license to Springer Nature Switzerland AG 2023
X. Fang (Ed.): HCII 2023, LNCS 14047, pp. 327–340, 2023.
https://doi.org/10.1007/978-3-031-35979-8_26

game-like and enjoyable. Serious games are "full-fledged games for non-entertainment purposes" [1], such as education, research, exercise, or persuasion.

There is extensive literature on meaning in life, from Aristotle's eudemonia [2] to Viktor Frankl's logotherapy [3]. Meaning, as we define it here, is the sense that what you are doing contributes to a life well lived, or a life that you will perceive more positively in retrospect at the end of your life. To use a more specific term, we define task significance as the extent to which you perceive what you are doing as important or meaningful. However, there has been little to no empirical research exploring how to design for meaning or task significance in digital games. The present research aims to fill that gap in the literature.

The research questions guiding this study are:

1. Do games designed for task significance lead to more digital game enjoyment compared to control conditions?
2. Between narrative framing and upgrade mechanisms, which is the most effective way to design digital games for task significance?

This study contributes both to the theory and practice of designing interactive systems for meaning and enjoyment.

2 Related Work

For those interested in designing games and other interactive systems for enjoyment, Positive Psychology is a useful field from which to draw ideas. Positive Psychology is not just the study of what leads to happiness, but can be thought of more broadly as the empirical study of what makes life worth living, or what will lead to a positive evaluation of one's life. While happiness and enjoyment are both the extent of positive evaluation, the unit of analysis or focus of evaluation is one's life in the case of happiness and an experience in the vase of enjoyment. The sources of that positive evaluation that makes up happiness and enjoyment may be the same or heavily overlap. Peterson, Park, and Seligman [4] identified three paths to happiness, which they called orientations to happiness: pleasure, engagement and meaning. Meaning is perhaps the least well understood of these three, especially in terms of how to design meaningful interactive experiences to increase enjoyment.

Nakamura and Csikszentmihalyi proposed a concept called vital engagement, which they defined as "a relationship to the world that is characterized both by experiences of flow (enjoyed absorption) and by meaning (subjective significance)" [5]. Through interviews with artists and scientists, Nakamura and Csikszentmihalyi suggested that subjective meaning can grow out of sustained interest in an activity that provides flow and enjoyment, an experience they called emergent meaning. Vital engagement involves a strong connection between the self and the object being engaged with, regardless of what or who the object is [5].

One path to a life of meaning explored in Positive Psychology has its roots in the virtue ethics of Aristotle [2]. Aristotle suggested that voluntarily taking virtuous actions until virtuous actions become a habit leads to virtuous character, which in turn leads to *eudaimonia*, or a life well lived. *Eudaimonia* or a life of meaning we define as a life that is evaluated positively in retrospect at the end of life. Peterson and Seligman [6] developed the Values in Action Classification of Character Strengths and Virtues (CSV) as Positive Psychology's response to Clinical Psychology's *Diagnostic and Statistical Manual of Mental Disorders* (DSM) [7]. The CSV presents 24 character strengths categorized into 6 virtues: Wisdom and Knowledge, Courage, Humanity, Justice, Temperance, and Transcendence [6]. While each kind of virtuous action may be a fulfilling source of enjoyment, character strengths focus on the traits of the individual rather than on qualities of an experience or a task.

Wong [8] developed the PURE model of meaning for meaning therapy, consisting of Purpose, Understanding, Responsible Action, and Evaluation. McDonald et al. [9] developed a Personal Meaning Profile consisting of seven sources of meaning: Achievement, Relationship, Religion, Self-transcendence, Self-acceptance, Intimacy, and Fair treatment. Edwards [10] combined several existing measures of meaning in life and used exploratory factor analysis to identify 10 factors: Achievement, Framework/Purpose, Religion, Death Acceptance, Interpersonal Satisfaction, Fulfillment/Excitement, Giving to the World, Existential Vacuum, Intimacy, and Control.

Much of the Psychological research has focused on individuals assessing themselves and their life as a whole. In contrast, the Human-Computer Interaction (HCI) field focuses on evaluation of experiences, which could mean evaluating an experience using an interactive system after using that system or evaluating one's moment-to-moment experience using an Experience Sampling Method approach [11]. Mekler and Hornbæk [12] made this distinction between meaning in life and the experience of meaning as well, and presented a framework for the experience of meaning in HCI. Their framework consisted of five components of meaning: Connectedness, Purpose, Coherence, Resonance, and Significance. They defined significance as "the sense that our experiences and actions at a given moment feel important and worthwhile, yet also consequential and enduring" [12]. As Mekler and Hornbæk pointed out, significance has also been called value, mattering, and the affective or evaluative component of meaning. For example, George and Park [13, 14] created a model and measure of existential meaning in life with three dimensions: Comprehension, Purpose, and Mattering, and the Mattering subscale would be a measure of significance in life.

Schaffer and Fang conducted a card sorting study to develop a new model of the sources of computer game enjoyment [15, 16]. Sixty participants sorted 167 sources of digital game enjoyment drawn from the literature into categories, and the cards and categories refined after every ten participants. Through this process, 34 categories of enjoyment sources were identified. One of those categories was "Significance, Meaning, Purpose, and Legacy", which was described in part as "Knowing why your actions are important, significant, or meaningful" [16].

One of the classic works of existential psychology is Frankl's [3] book *Man's Search for Meaning*, in which he developed a psychotherapy approach focused on helping people find meaning in their lives that he called logotherapy. Frankl described his experience surviving Nazi concentration camps, and what he learned about finding meaning in life from that experience. Frankl quoted Nietzsche [17], "He who has a *why* to live for can bear almost any *how*," and adds that "in the Nazi concentration camps...those who knew that there was a task waiting for them to fulfill were most apt to survive" [3]. This aspect of meaning is reflected in the Purpose component of meaning.

Frankl wrote that "the categorical imperative of logotherapy" is to "Live as if you were living already for the second time and as if you had acted the first time as wrongly as you are about to act now!" [3]. This imperative serves a similar function to focusing on living a life that will be evaluated positively in retrospect at the end of life except that it focuses more on the present moment. Frankl wrote that this imperative confronts people with life's finiteness and the finality of what one makes out of life and themselves [3]. This seems to be one route to giving people a sense that their actions are significant or important.

Frankl continues that the aim of logotherapy is to make people "fully aware of their own responsibleness; therefore, it must leave to [them] the option for what, to what, or to whom [they] understand [themselves] to be responsible" [3] For Frankl, responsible action is the path to meaning in life, regardless of what, to what, or to whom one decide to be responsible. Frankl emphasized that this responsibility must be directed to something or someone other than oneself, that self-actualization is only possible "as a side-effect of self-transcendence" [3]. Frankl describes self-transcendence as forgetting oneself or giving oneself to a cause or another person [3]. So, one way to understand meaning in life is as self-transcendence, deciding what or whom one will be responsible for, and taking responsible action. Shifting from the more global assessment of meaning in life to the more specific assessment of moment-to-moment experience, the experience of taking actions perceived as responsible may lead to more meaning and enjoyment than actions not perceived as responsible actions.

The meaning path to happiness is about what makes life worth living. To use a more specific term, we define Task Significance as the extent to which you perceive what you are doing as important or meaningful. While there has been extensive research on sensory pleasure and flow in digital games, there has been little to no research on task significance in digital games. The present research aims to fill that gap in the literature.

3   Method

3.1   Participants

Three-hundred and ninety-one participants were recruited with Amazon Mechanical Turk. Participants were between 18 and 76 years old, US-only, and had an approval rate of at least 95% on at least 1000 HITs. Participants were screened to ensure they were accessing the survey with a laptop or desktop computer to be sure they could play the research game. Participants were excluded from analysis if they responded incorrectly to attention-checking questions using the Conscientious Responders Scale [18], if they spent less than 15 min on the survey, or if their responses to the open-ended qualitative questions were incomplete or did not answer the questions that were asked. The minimum time to complete the survey was determined from pilot testing. Participant demographics and gameplay habits are summarized in Table 1 below.

Table 1. Participant Demographics

Total N	391 participants
Females	222 (56.6%)
Males	167 (42.6%)
Self-described as non-binary or gender-fluid	2
Mean average age	40.51 years
Age range	18–76 years
Mean average years playing digital games	18.85 years
Range of years played digital games	0–46 years
Mean average hours played per week	8.973 h
Range of hours played per week	0–72 h
Mean average hours played per day	2.004 h
Range of hours played per day	0–16 h

3.2 Procedure

An online, between-subjects controlled experiment was conducted with 391 participants. Participants were randomly assigned to play one of sixteen versions of the same custom research game. Participants were recruited using Amazon Mechanical Turk (MTurk). MTurk has been found to be a reliable tool for recruiting participants for Human-Computer Interaction Research [19] as long as sufficient precautions are taken to ensure data quality, such as using attention checks and excluding respondents who are not paying attention [18, 20]. Participants were given information about informed consent played a custom research game for 30 min and then responded to a survey questionnaire about their experience playing the game. The study took approximately one hour to complete. Participants were given $4.53 USD as an incentive to participate. The study was approved by the Bradley University Internal Review Board, the Committee on the Use of Human Subjects in Research.

3.3 Measures

Participants responded to the long versions of the *Enjoyment Questionnaire* (EQ) and the *Sources of Enjoyment Questionnaire* (SoEQ) [21] about their experience playing the research game to assess how much they experienced enjoyment and 39 sources of enjoyment, positive experience including task significance, using 7-point Likert scales of agreement with each scale point labeled.

3.4 Study Design and Experimental Conditions

A between-subjects controlled experiment was conducted with sixteen experimental conditions. Each version of the custom research game was developed for this study with

Unity and C#. The games were built to WebGL and embedded in a Qualtrics survey. The randomizer branching logic feature of Qualtrics was used to randomly assign participants to play one version of the game.

The research game was a 2D top-down pickup-and-delivery game, where players picked up and delivered as many boxes as they could from one type of location to another before a timer ran out while avoiding enemies and obstacles. The sixteen versions of the game make up a 4 × 4 factorial experimental design as shown in Fig. 1 below.

		Independent Variable A: Upgrade Mechanisms			
		Upgrade Mechanisms	Cosmetic Upgrades	Free Upgrades	No Upgrade Mechanisms
	Helping People in Need (Prosocial)	Upgrade Mechanisms & Helping People Framing	Cosmetic Upgrades & Helping People Framing	Free Upgrades & Helping People Framing	No Upgrade Mechanisms & Helping People Framing
	Working for Money	Upgrade Mechanisms & Working for Money Framing	Cosmetic Upgrades & Working for Money Framing	Free Upgrades & Working for Money Framing	No Upgrade Mechanisms & Working for Money Framing
IV B: Narrative Framing	No Reason	Upgrade Mechanisms & No Reason Framing	Cosmetic Upgrades & No Reason Framing	Free Upgrades & No Reason Framing	No Upgrade Mechanisms & No Reason Framing
	Undone Reason	Upgrade Mechanisms & Undone Reason Framing	Cosmetic Upgrades & Undone Reason Framing	Free Upgrades & Undone Reason Framing	No Upgrade Mechanisms & Undone Reason Framing

Fig. 1. 4 × 4 factorial design of experiment testing the impact of narrative framing and upgrade mechanisms on enjoyment and the sources of enjoyment in digital games

Two different ways to facilitate task significance in games were tested: narrative framing and character upgrading mechanisms.

There were four Narrative Framing conditions. In each of these conditions, the text and images on screen at the beginning and end of each round of the game were different. In the Helping People in Need narrative framing condition, the text described the player's task in the game as delivering boxes of free food to elderly poor people self-quarantining at home during the COVID-19 pandemic. This was designed to give players a meaningful and important reason for their actions within the fictional world of the game to increase task significance.

In the Working for Money condition, the images showed impatient customers waiting for their delivery and money being given, and the text framed the task as being motivated by making money. In the No Reason narrative framing condition, the text did not describe a purpose for the player's task in the game – instead the images and text focused on the setting of the game, showing images of the snowy town where the game is taking place.

In the Undone Reason narrative framing conditions, the player was delivering flyers rather than boxes. The player's task was described at the beginning of the game as posting flyers for an upcoming auction. At the end of each round, on screen text informed players that their efforts were wasted, such as because the date on the flyer was wrong, the wind swept all the flyers away, or the event was rescheduled. Then at the start of each round after the first players were told their task is to repost the flyers. This narrative framing was intended to be more devoid of meaning than the No Reason condition. This condition was inspired by the Sisyphus condition from Ariely et al.'s [22] experiment, where a Lego model building task was made more meaningless by having the experimenter take apart the Lego models participants built after each model was built, while in their more meaningful condition the Lego models were not taken apart and were allowed to accumulate. Participants seeing their work undone were demotivated by seeing their effort go to waste as the Lego models they just built were taken apart in front of them as they finished building each one.

In the Upgrade Mechanisms condition, the player was able to spend points collected during the game on upgrades to their player character's movement speed and a variety of abilities between each round of the game. In the Free Upgrades condition, the player could select one upgrade after each of the ten rounds of the game without needing to use points earned in the game to purchase the upgrades. In the No Upgrade Mechanisms condition, points were still accumulated, but the points could not be spent or used for any purpose. In the Cosmetic Upgrades condition, the player could purchase upgrades with the points, but the upgrades had no effect on the player's actual abilities and power to be effective in the game. The cosmetic upgrades may change the appearance of the player character, but they do not make players more powerful or effective at increasing their score. Having all four of these upgrade conditions allows us to test if just being able to purchase upgrades with points is sufficient to increase enjoyment compared to having no upgrades (Cosmetic vs No Upgrades), if the upgrades must provide functional abilities that make the player more effective in the game (Upgrades vs. No Upgrades), and if the player needs to spend points they accumulate in the game based on their performance or if unlocking one upgrade for free after each round of the game provides the same positive experience (Upgrades vs. Free Upgrades).

The idea behind these upgrade conditions is that when the player is able to spend the points collected for a purpose, then this game mechanism may make the player feel that what they are doing in the game is for a specific purpose within the game. In other words, having upgrades may make players feel that what they are doing is important (increase Task Significance) because their actions have an impact on the gameplay mechanisms of the game and their actual abilities within the game rather than because of the fictional narrative framing of their actions.

4 Results

A 4×4 factorial MANOVA was conducted to test the effect of narrative framing and upgrade mechanisms on enjoyment and each of the 39 sources of enjoyment of the long version of the *Sources of Enjoyment Questionnaire* (SoEQ) [21] including task significance.

The main effect results for narrative version are shown in Table 2 below and the main effect results for upgrade version are shown in Table 3 below. In both tables, all statistically significant ($p < 0.05$) main effects are shown, and in addition some variables of interest in this study are shown in the tables regardless of whether they were statistically significant. Task Significance, Clear Task Purpose, Social Responsibility, and Honor were included because they were related to Task Significance, which was the intended independent variable of interest. Task significance is how much participants feel that what they are doing is important or meaningful [21]. Social Responsibility is how much they feel that what they are doing is benefiting society or making the world a better place. Clear task purpose is how much participants know the reason that their actions were important or significant in the game. Honor is how much participants feel that their actions were in accordance with their personal code of conduct or moral standards. So, each of those subscales of the *Sources of Enjoyment Questionnaire* (SoEQ) were conceptually related or similar even though they were separate factors each with their own meaning. Enjoyment was included in the tables because it was one of the main dependent variables. Enjoyment is how positively participants evaluated their experience playing the game. Each of the following flow indicators, or factors that indicate how much a person is in a flow state [23], were included as dependent variables to assess the impact of that main effect on how much players were in flow: Sense of Control, Focusing of Full Attention, Merging of Action and Awareness, Loss of Self-Consciousness, and Altered Perception of Time.

Main effects analysis showed that narrative framing had a statistically significant effect on Social Responsibility ($p < 0.001$, $\eta^2_p = 0.268$), Clear Task Purpose ($p < 0.001$, $\eta^2_p = 0.161$), Task Significance ($p < 0.001$, $\eta^2_p = 0.141$), and Honor ($p < 0.001$, $\eta^2_p = 0.084$). Poc-hoc Tukey HSD tests showed participants in the Helping People in Need (Prosocial) narrative framing condition rated their experience significantly higher on Social Responsibility ($p < 0.001$), Task Significance ($p < 0.001$), Clear Task Purpose ($p < 0.001$), and Honor ($p < 0.001$) compared to participants in the other three narrative framing conditions.

This shows that the prosocial narrative condition successfully provided participants with more task significance, which was the intended aim of this experimental manipulation. This can be considered a successful manipulation check, and shows the design difference between the versions had the intended impact on how much participants experienced task significance.

However, the narrative framing did not have a statistically significant effect on enjoyment ($p = 0.127$, $\eta^2_p = 0.015$). The prosocial narrative framing was effective at increasing task significance, making the player feel that what they were doing was meaningful and important, but that task significance did not significantly increase how much players enjoyed the game.

Table 2. MANOVA Results for Main Effect of Narrative Framing

Subscale	Partial		
	F	p	η2
Social Responsibility	45.688	<0.001	0.268
Clear Task Purpose	23.951	<0.001	0.161
Task Significance	20.502	<0.001	0.141
Honor	11.433	<0.001	0.084
Theme	9.650	<0.001	0.072
Story	6.453	<0.001	0.049
Creating	5.393	0.001	0.041
Cooperation	4.760	0.003	0.037
Achievement	4.991	0.002	0.038
Goal Attainability	4.845	0.003	0.037
Leading-Directing	4.284	0.005	0.033
Competition	3.113	0.026	0.024
Suspense-Surprise	2.932	0.033	0.023
Autonomy	2.918	0.034	0.023
Learning	2.869	0.036	0.022
Collecting	2.684	0.047	0.021
Enjoyment	1.914	0.127	0.015
Sense Of Control	0.866	0.459	0.007
Merging Of Action and Awareness	0.843	0.471	0.007
Focusing Of Full Attention	0.546	0.651	0.004
Loss Of Self-Consciousness	0.334	0.800	0.003
Altered Perception of Time	0.166	0.919	0.001

There were several other main effects of narrative framing found, though their effect sizes were smaller than the effect on task significance and the three factors that were conceptually similar to it. Each of these effects are shown in Table 2 above. Tukey HSD tests showed participants in the Helping People in Need (Prosocial) narrative framing condition rated the Theme of the game ($p < 0.005$) and the Story of the game ($p < 0.05$) significantly higher than those in the other three narrative framing conditions.

Main effects analysis showed that upgrade mechanisms had a statistically significant effect on task significance ($p < 0.005$, $\eta^2_p = 0.035$) and on enjoyment ($p < 0.001$, $\eta^2_p = 0.057$). However, the size of the effect of upgrade mechanisms on task significance ($\eta^2_p = 0.035$) was much smaller than the effect of narrative framing on task significance ($\eta^2_p = 0.141$). Examining the post-hoc Tukey's HSD tests showed participants in the Upgrade and Free Upgrades conditions experienced significantly more enjoyment than

Table 3. MANOVA Results for Main Effect of Upgrade Mechanisms

Subscale	Partial		
	F	p	η2
Optimal Variety	10.058	< 0.001	0.074
Organizing	8.544	< 0.001	0.064
Sense of Control	7.657	< 0.001	0.058
Enjoyment	7.593	< 0.001	0.057
Improving Skills	6.964	< 0.001	0.053
Savoring	6.187	< 0.001	0.047
Achievement	5.844	0.001	0.045
Relaxation	5.117	0.002	0.039
Optimal Challenge	5.100	0.002	0.039
Autonomy	4.862	0.002	0.037
Creating	4.764	0.003	0.037
Strategizing	4.527	0.004	0.035
Task Significance	4.510	0.004	0.035
Presence	4.009	0.008	0.031
Optimal Pacing	3.978	0.008	0.031
Competition	3.962	0.008	0.031
Honor	3.675	0.012	0.029
Altered Perception of Time	3.364	0.019	0.026
Learning	3.373	0.019	0.026
Sensory Pleasure and Beauty	3.181	0.024	0.025
Vitality	3.114	0.026	0.024
Clear Goals and Clear Navigation	3.008	0.030	0.023
Clear Task Purpose	2.859	0.037	0.022
Loss of Self-Consciousness	2.829	0.038	0.022
Cooperation	2.784	0.041	0.022
Merging of Action and Awareness	2.386	0.069	0.019
Focusing of Full Attention	2.075	0.103	0.016
Social Responsibility	1.637	0.180	0.013

those in the Cosmetic condition ($p < 0.005$) and those in the No Upgrades condition ($p < 0.05$). The Tukey tests showed those in the Upgrade and Free Upgrades conditions experienced significantly more task significance than those in the Cosmetic upgrades condition ($p < 0.05$), but no significant difference in task significance was found between the No Upgrades condition and the other three conditions.

The lack of a statistically significant difference between the Upgrade and Free Upgrade conditions on enjoyment and task significance means that it did not matter whether players earned the upgrades by accumulating points in the game and spending them to buy the upgrades after each round of the game (Upgrade) or players choose one upgrade after each round and the points in the game are not used for anything (Free Upgrades). In both the Upgrade and Free Upgrades conditions the player chose their upgrades and the upgrades had beneficial effects in the game. This is in contrast to the Cosmetic and No Upgrades conditions, where there were not upgrades that actually impacted gameplay. The Cosmetic Upgrades let the player see the upgrade menu and purchase upgrades with points, but the upgrade had no impact on gameplay. Because those in the Upgrade and Free Upgrade conditions reported significantly higher enjoyment and task significance than in the Cosmetic Upgrades condition, that means those differences were a result of the beneficial impact those upgrades had on gameplay and not a result of seeing the upgrade menu or choosing upgrades from the menu.

Upgrade mechanisms had many other main effects, many of which had larger effect sizes than the effect on task significance. Each of these main effects are shown in Table 3. The three effects of upgrades with the largest effect sizes were those on optimal variety ($p < 0.001$, $\eta^2_p = 0.074$), organizing ($p < 0.001$, $\eta^2_p = 0.064$) and sense of control ($p < 0.001$, $\eta^2_p = 0.056$). Tukey HSD tests showed that those in the Upgrade and Free Upgrades conditions experienced significantly more optimal variety ($p < 0.005$), improving skills ($p < 0.05$), and savoring ($p < 0.05$) than those in the Cosmetic Upgrades and No Upgrades conditions. Those in the Free Upgrades condition – but not those in the Upgrades condition – experienced significantly more organizing ($p < 0.001$) and sense of control ($p < 0.001$) than those in the Cosmetic Upgrades and No Upgrades conditions.

Our first research question asked if games designed for task significance lead to more enjoyment compared to control conditions. The results on this question were mixed in this study: upgrade mechanisms significantly increased enjoyment while narrative framing did not. Our second research question asked whether narrative framing or upgrade mechanisms are more effective ways to design digital games for task significance. While both had a significant impact on task significance, narrative framing was more effective than upgrades at providing task significance.

5 Discussion

Prosocial narrative framing led to significantly more task significance but not more enjoyment, while upgrade mechanisms led to more task significance and more enjoyment. Comparing the effect sizes, prosocial narrative framing had a much larger impact on task significance than upgrades did, and yet narrative framing did not significantly increase enjoyment, while upgrades did.

The reason upgrades were chosen as a way to design for task significance was so the upgrades would make players feel that their actions in the game were important, and thereby increase task significance, because their actions could have an impact on the gameplay mechanisms of the game and their actual abilities within the game rather than because of the fictional narrative framing of their actions. Perhaps the reason the upgrades positively impacted enjoyment while the narrative framing did not is because the upgrades had an impact on the gameplay mechanisms and players' actual abilities within the game while the narrative framing did not affect the gameplay.

Another possible interpretation is that task significance and meaning may not lead to more enjoyment. Because the prosocial narrative framing led to more task significance than the upgrades but did not significantly increase enjoyment, it is possible that designing for more task significance and meaning may not lead to more enjoyment. Task significance may be an intrinsically positive experience players could desire and developers can design for to make the experience more meaningful. However, in this study prosocial narrative framing had a large and significantly positive impact on task significance and it did not significantly increase enjoyment.

If task significance does not increase enjoyment, it is possible that the other effects of upgrade mechanisms other than task significance caused the increase in player enjoyment. While upgrades did have a significant impact on task significance, they also had significant impacts on each of these other sources of enjoyment which had larger effect sizes than the impact on task significance: optimal variety, organizing, sense of control, improving skills, savoring, achievement, relaxation, optimal challenge, autonomy, creating. So, the upgrades increased player enjoyment, and that may have been because the upgrades increased these other sources of enjoyment such as by providing more variety in the content of the game, giving players a sense of achievement when they unlocked new upgrades, choosing upgrades could have made players feel more in control, or any combination of these factors.

If task significance is a positive experience that people value for its own sake rather than as a means to the end of enjoyment, then perhaps it would be better to treat all of the positive experiences in the Sources of Enjoyment Questionnaire (SoEQ) in the same way as intrinsically valued dependent variables rather than means to another end. Perhaps it would be better to evaluate design differences across experimental conditions using the SoEQ and Enjoyment Questionnaire (EQ) without trying to use those differences to evaluate how well the sources of enjoyment contribute to enjoyment. Or maybe instead additional criteria or factors need to be identified so the sources of enjoyment can be evaluated by other criteria in addition to how well they contribute to enjoyment. For example, maybe task significance does not increase enjoyment, but maybe it contributes to meaning, or maybe players could rate task significance as important to them or as an experience they desire. These are possibilities worth exploring further in future research.

6   Conclusion

A between-subjects controlled experiment was conducted to test the impact of narrative framing and upgrades on player experience using multiple versions of a custom-built research game with specific design differences between the versions. The Enjoyment Questionnaire and Sources of Enjoyment Questionnaire (SoEQ) [21] were used as measures to assess player experience across the different versions.

Prosocial narrative framing with text and images framing the actions of the player in the game as delivering food to help hungry people in need led to significantly more task significance but not more enjoyment, while upgrade mechanisms led to more task significance and more enjoyment. Narrative framing was a more effective way to design for task significance or meaning, while upgrade mechanisms were a more effective way to design for enjoyment. The hope is that these findings will be useful for practitioners and researchers who wish to design for enjoyment or meaning.

Acknowledgements. This work was supported by a grant from the Caterpillar Fellowship Award. We thank Matthew Kirchoff for assistance with game development.

References

1. Deterding, S., Dixon, D., Khaled, R., Nacke, L.: From game design elements to gamefulness: defining gamification. In: Proceedings of the 15th international academic MindTrek Conference: Envisioning Future Media Environments, pp. 9–15. ACM (2011)
2. Aristotle: Nicomachean Ethics. Hackett Publishing Company, Inc., Indianapolis (2019)
3. Frankl, V.E.: Man's Search for Meaning. Simon and Schuster (1985)
4. Peterson, C., Park, N., Seligman, M.E.: Orientations to happiness and life satisfaction: the full life versus the empty life. J. Happiness Stud. **6**, 25–41 (2005)
5. Nakamura, J., Csikzentmihalyi, M.: The construction of meaning through vital engagement. In: Flourishing: Positive Psychology and the Life Well-Lived. pp. 83–104. American Psychological Association, Washington, DC (2003). https://doi.org/10.1037/10594-004
6. Peterson, C., Seligman, M.E.: Character strengths and Virtues: A Handbook and Classification. Oxford University Press, Oxford (2004)
7. Association, A.P.: Diagnostic and Statistical Manual of Mental Disorders (DSM-5®). American Psychiatric Publishing (2013)
8. Wong, P.T.P.: Meaning therapy: an integrative and positive existential psychotherapy. J Contemp. Psychother. **40**, 85–93 (2010). https://doi.org/10.1007/s10879-009-9132-6
9. McDonald, M.J., Wong, P.T., Gingras, D.T.: Meaning-in-life measures and development of a brief version of the personal meaning profile. Hum. Quest Meaning Theories Res. Appl. **2** (2012)
10. Edwards, M.J.: The Dimensionality and Construct Valid Measurement of Life Meaning, (2007)
11. Hektner, J.M., Schmidt, J.A., Csikszentmihalyi, M.: Experience Sampling Method: Measuring the Quality of Everyday Life. Sage (2007)
12. Mekler, E.D., Hornbæk, K.: a framework for the experience of meaning in human-computer interaction. In: Proceedings of the 2019 CHI Conference on Human Factors in Computing Systems. pp. 1–15. Association for Computing Machinery, New York, NY, USA (2019). https://doi.org/10.1145/3290605.3300455
13. George, L., Park, C.: Meaning in life as comprehension, purpose, and mattering: toward integration and new research questions. Rev. Gen. Psychol. **20** (2016). https://doi.org/10.1037/gpr0000077
14. George, L.S., Park, C.L.: The multidimensional existential meaning scale: a tripartite approach to measuring meaning in life. J. Posit. Psychol. **12**, 613–627 (2017)
15. Schaffer, O., Fang, X.: Sources of Computer game enjoyment: card sorting to develop a new model. In: Kurosu, M. (ed.) HCI 2017. LNCS, vol. 10272, pp. 99–108. Springer, Cham (2017). https://doi.org/10.1007/978-3-319-58077-7_9
16. Schaffer, O., Fang, X.: What makes games fun? card sort reveals 34 sources of computer game enjoyment. Presented at the Americas Conference on Information Systems (AMCIS) 2018, New Orleans (2018)

17. Nietzsche, F.: Twilight of the Idols. CreateSpace Independent Publishing Platform (2012)
18. Marjanovic, Z., Struthers, C.W., Cribbie, R., Greenglass, E.R.: The conscientious responders scale: a new tool for discriminating between conscientious and random responders. SAGE Open (2014). https://doi.org/10.1177/2158244014545964
19. Mason, W., Suri, S.: Conducting behavioral research on Amazon's Mechanical Turk. Behav. Res. **44**, 1–23 (2012). https://doi.org/10.3758/s13428-011-0124-6
20. Thomas, K.A., Clifford, S.: Validity and Mechanical Turk: An assessment of exclusion methods and interactive experiments. Comput. Hum. Behav. **77**, 184–197 (2017). https://doi.org/10.1016/j.chb.2017.08.038
21. Schaffer, O.: Development and preliminary validation of the enjoyment questionnaire and the sources of enjoyment questionnaire. In: Extended Abstracts of the 2022 CHI Conference on Human Factors in Computing Systems. pp. 1–7. Association for Computing Machinery, New York, NY, USA (2022). https://doi.org/10.1145/3491101.3519819
22. Ariely, D., Kamenica, E., Prelec, D.: Man's search for meaning: the case of Legos. J. Econ. Behav. Organ. **67**, 671–677 (2008)
23. Schaffer, O., Fang, X.: The feedback loop of flow: controlled experiment shows task-relevant feedback increases flow. AIS Trans. Hum.-Comput. Interact. **14**, 356–389 (2022). https://doi.org/10.17705/1thci.00172

Author Index

Printed in the United States
by Baker & Taylor Publisher Services